# MONUMENTAL CONFLICTS

*Monumental Conflicts* examines twentieth-century wars from World War I to the First Gulf War, each chapter analyzing how public memory has evolved over time. The chapters raise fascinating questions about war and memory:

- Why are wars remembered as they are?
- What factors drive changes in public perception?
- What implications arise from remembering and commemorating a war or particular aspects of a war?
- What does public memory of a war say about us as a society?

The volume is divided into three sections focusing on political evolution, negotiated memories of war, and national pride and covers international wars from Afghanistan to Vietnam and matters ranging from German deserter monuments to Vietnamese war tourism.

**Derek R. Mallett** is Assistant Professor of History at the US Army Command and General Staff College, Fort Gordon, USA. His publications include *Hitler's Generals in America: Nazi POWs and Allied Military Intelligence* (2013).

# MONUMENTAL CONFLICTS

Twentieth-Century Wars and the Evolution of Public Memory

Edited by Derek R. Mallett

LONDON AND NEW YORK

First published 2018
by Routledge
2 Park Square, Milton Park, Abingdon, Oxon OX14 4RN

and by Routledge
711 Third Avenue, New York, NY 10017

*Routledge is an imprint of the Taylor & Francis Group, an informa business*

© 2018 Derek R. Mallett

The right of Derek R. Mallett to be identified as the author of the editorial material, and of the authors for their individual chapters, has been asserted in accordance with sections 77 and 78 of the Copyright, Designs and Patents Act 1988.

All rights reserved. No part of this book may be reprinted or reproduced or utilised in any form or by any electronic, mechanical, or other means, now known or hereafter invented, including photocopying and recording, or in any information storage or retrieval system, without permission in writing from the publishers.

*Trademark notice*: Product or corporate names may be trademarks or registered trademarks, and are used only for identification and explanation without intent to infringe.

*British Library Cataloguing-in-Publication Data*
A catalogue record for this book is available from the British Library

*Library of Congress Cataloging-in-Publication Data*
A catalog record for this book has been requested

ISBN: 978-1-138-28227-8 (hbk)
ISBN: 978-1-138-28228-5 (pbk)
ISBN: 978-1-315-12254-0 (ebk)

Typeset in Bembo
by Sunrise Setting Ltd, Brixham, UK

# CONTENTS

List of figures     vii
List of maps     ix
List of tables     x
Acknowledgements     xi

    Introduction     1
    *Derek R. Mallett*

### PART I
### Monumental conflicts: The sacred and the political     11

1  "There is absolutely nothing like the carving of names": Imperial War Graves Commission sites and World War I memory     13
   *Hanna Smyth*

2  War Mall: Civic art, memory, and war on America's national public space     38
   *William Thomas Allison*

3  Re-carving the stone: Reinterpreting World War II monuments in Brazil     56
   *Uri Rosenheck*

4  Memorializing the "unknown heroes" of World War II: German deserter monuments     69
   *Steven R. Welch*

## PART II
## Negotiated memories of war 89

5 Emperors, bones, and dissonant memories: Japanese commemoration of the battle for Peleliu Island 91
*Stephen C. Murray*

6 Divided nation, divided memories 111
*Brendan Wright*

7 War tourism and geographies of memory in Vietnam 130
*Christina Schwenkel*

## PART III
## Expeditionary wars and national pride 147

8 "Curse you Red Baron!": World War I aviation's impact on popular visions of flight 149
*Guillaume de Syon*

9 The British public and the Falklands War 165
*Davide Borsani*

10 Remembering the Soviet–Afghan War in Russia 179
*Roger R. Reese*

11 The Persian Gulf War in American popular memory 201
*Robert T. Jones*

Conclusion 217
*Derek R. Mallett*

*Index* 226

# FIGURES

1.1  Cross of Sacrifice, Redan Ridge Cemetery No. 2, 2016. Photo by the author — 16
1.2  Stone of Remembrance, Serre Road Cemetery No. 2, 2016. Photo by the author — 17
1.3  Preserved landscape, Beaumont-Hamel, 2016. Photo by the author — 18
1.4  Vimy Memorial, 2016. Photo by the author — 20
1.5  Example of IWGC headstone, Hooge Crater Cemetery, 2016. Photo by the author — 22
1.6  Beaumont-Hamel Memorial, 2016. Photo by the author — 25
1.7  Neuve Chapelle Memorial, 2016. Photo by the author — 27
1.8  Mother Canada and the empty tomb, Vimy Memorial, 2016. Photo by the author — 29
1.9  The Female Mourner sculpture, Vimy Memorial, 2016. Photo by the author — 30
1.10 Thiepval Memorial, 2016. Photo by the author — 31
3.1  Homenagem às Forças Armadas: Monumento, Marinha, Exército, Aeronautica, December 28, 1972. Photo by the author — 61
4.1  Kassel memorial plaque. From the author's personal collection — 71
4.2  Bremen memorial to the unknown deserter. From the Archiv der Bundesarbeitsgemeinschaft der Deserteure-Initiativen (BAG DI). Published with permission of Rudi Seibt on behalf of the BAG DI — 72
4.3  *Stein des Anstoßes* in Ulm. From the Archiv der Bundesarbeitsgemeinschaft der Deserteure-Initiativen. Published with permission of Rudi Seibt on behalf of the BAG DI — 74
4.4  Monument to the Unknown Deserter, Potsdam. From the author's personal collection — 76

| | | |
|---|---|---|
| 4.5 | Chalk inscription in front of Potsdam monument in 1995. From the author's personal collection | 77 |
| 4.6 | Deserter monument in Stuttgart (photo by Wolfgang Krauß; used with permission) | 78 |
| 4.7 | Deserter monument in Göttingen. From the author's personal collection | 79 |
| 4.8 | Deserter monument in Erfurt. From the author's personal collection | 80 |
| 4.9 | Hamburg deserter monument. Photo credit Johannes Arlt/laif | 81 |
| 5.1 | The Shinto shrine erected on Peleliu's Bloody Nose Ridge by the right-wing group Seiryusha in 2002. Photo by the author | 98 |
| 5.2 | Tour guide Nakagawa Tsukane explains the battle of Peleliu to Japanese visitors, 2003. Photo by Siegfried Nakamura | 102 |
| 5.3 | Photos displayed in the lodge of tour guide Nakagawa Tsukane on Peleliu, 2003. Photo by the author | 104 |
| 7.1 | Guide posing in "original" tunnel, 2004. Photo by the author | 134 |
| 7.2 | Khe Sanh Museum, 2011. Photo by the author | 138 |
| 7.3 | Descent into the bunker, 2015. Photo by the author | 140 |
| 7.4 | Bomb shelter overview, 2015. Photo by the author | 141 |
| 7.5 | Joan Baez's return to the shelter. Photo by the author | 142 |

# MAPS

5.1  Micronesia in the Central Pacific region                          92
5.2  The Palau Islands. Map by S.C. Murray                              94

# TABLES

3.1  FEB monuments, 1945–1984 57
3.2  Comparative abundance of war monuments per fallen soldiers 58
3.3  Distribution of monuments and soldiers by region and state 63
3.4  Distribution of monuments and soldiers in the states of
     Rio de Janeiro and São Paulo and their capitals 64

# ACKNOWLEDGEMENTS

In assembling a collection of essays such as this one, an editor/author accrues many debts. I would be remiss if I did not acknowledge at least some of the most important contributions to this volume. I hope this small token will serve as an appropriate display of my sincere appreciation.

First and foremost, I wish to thank the eleven authors who wrote individual essays for this volume. Hanna, Bill, Uri, Steven, Stephen, Brendan, Christina, Guillaume, Davide, Roger, and Robert all proved to be not only excellent scholars but a pleasure to work with as well. Thanks to each of you for your willingness to join me in this endeavor and, of course, for continuing to respond to my many e-mail messages. My thanks also go to Jeffrey K. Johnson for our early collaboration that started this journey years ago, and to Kimberly Guinta for her encouragement to stay with this project.

I also wish to thank my editor at Routledge, Eve Setch. Eve patiently responded to each of my many queries and provided solid guidance all along the way. Thanks for all of your contributions to this work. Thanks as well to Amy Welmers, Zoe Meyer, Kristy Barker, and Colin Read who worked to move this volume toward publication.

I offer special thanks to Michael R. Dolski and Bradley Keefer. Michael read an early draft of the introduction. His thorough review and critical analysis corrected several errors and shaped my understanding in important ways. What sound perspective the introduction may display is in part due to Michael's assistance. Brad read and commented on the entire manuscript twice, as well as reviewing the conclusion a third time. He went above and beyond what any reviewer could reasonably be asked to do and provided excellent comments and suggestions. Thank you both for helping make this volume what it is.

Finally, I am ever grateful for the love and support of my wife, Tasha, and my two wonderful daughters, Aviaq and Annika. The three of you will always be the brightest stars in my universe.

# INTRODUCTION

*Derek R. Mallett*

In the 1986 Warner Brothers film *Heartbreak Ridge*, a US Marine Corps force recon platoon led by Gunnery Sergeant Tom Highway—played by Clint Eastwood—rescues American medical students trapped on the island of Grenada. Following the rescue, "Gunny" Highway reports to his superior officer, Major Malcolm Powers, that his unit met heavy resistance along the way to the school. When Powers suggests that it was probably just "local fanatics," Highway emphatically states that these were "Cuban regulars with Russian rifles."[1]

This portrayal of Operation Urgent Fury, the name assigned to the 1983 American occupation of the Caribbean island of Grenada, is fictional. First, US Army Rangers—not Marines—evacuated the American students stranded at St. George's University Medical School on Grenada. More importantly, Grenadians comprised a sizable number of the soldiers who opposed American forces during the campaign. In addition, the overwhelming majority of the Cuban soldiers who fought on Grenada consisted of construction workers with basic militia training, not regular army soldiers.

This might seem like quibbling, except that this motion picture represents the most popular portrayal of Operation Urgent Fury. In addition to emphasizing the role of the US Marines at the expense of the US Army, Clint Eastwood's film reinforces the idea initially put forth by the Reagan Administration that Cuban forces on the island were a formidable opponent. The film also supports the notion that American military personnel landed in Grenada primarily to protect American citizens enrolled in the medical school. Consequently, as one might expect, the US government produced the first public narrative of the causes and conduct of the American military campaign in Grenada. This narrative was then corroborated by what the scholar Viet Thanh Nguyen characterizes as the "industry of memory."[2]

Why does it matter? First, as previously noted, *Heartbreak Ridge* is the most popular portrayal of this campaign. Among all of the depictions of Urgent

Fury—film or print—produced to date, Eastwood's film reached by far the largest audience. The film sold more than 11 million tickets in theaters in the United States and earned another $21 million in rentals.[3] It was even nominated for an Academy Award for sound at the 59th Academy Awards in 1987.[4] Yet box-office success does not necessarily equate to any kind of substantial impact on popular memory.

So, how does the public remember a war? Popular memory of important events, wars in particular, evolves over time. New information emerges. Present events force us to re-evaluate the past. Political currents that shape public perspectives ebb and flow. Distance from the events in question, measured in decades, can facilitate a different perspective. And often the national pride—or shame—engendered by a particular war shapes a society's "memory" of the reasons the war was fought or the manner in which the war was waged.

Film depictions of historical events—like that of *Heartbreak Ridge*—fall into what Marita Sturken labels "cultural memory," the type of memory "that is shared outside the avenues of formal historical discourse yet is entangled with cultural products and imbued with cultural meaning."[5] These cultural memories are only one of the means through which the public "remembers" war. Where personal memories are recollections about our own individual experiences, public memories are the things a society believes about its past, obtained from any number and variety of sources.

Jay Winter has been understandably critical of the use of vague terms in memory studies. For example, he encourages use of the term "remembrance" rather than "memory" in order

> to insist on specifying agency, on answering the question who remembers, when, where, and how? And, on being aware of the transience of remembrance, so dependent on the frailties and commitments of the men and women who take the time and effort to engage in it.[6]

In other words, collective memory is a process. Societies actively remember past wars in ways that suit present needs. This process can be highly contentious and continually evolves alongside the varied and often disparate needs and perspectives of a given society.

Nigel Hunt offers a compelling explanation of how this process works. Hunt argues that narrative is essential to human existence. All of us tell stories in some form or another in order to make an impression, to help us cope with various life experiences, and ultimately to explain our place in the world. Composing narratives is as important for societies as it is for individuals. Public memory is, in essence, our collective narrative; what we think we know or what we tell ourselves about our society's existence and purpose. Hunt's developmental process goes a long way toward explaining why public memory evolves over time. Memories change with the demands of each generation, from those who lived the events, to the generations who grew up hearing about them, and ultimately to those who only inherited some version of the narrative.[7] And each generation wrestles with its own needs, political perspectives, and cultural views that shape its memory of the past.

As Hunt points out, this process may be a bit more complicated in regard to twentieth-century wars. The twentieth century witnessed significant memorialization and commemoration of its wars, perhaps because warfare grew to an unprecedented scale—at least in the first half of the century.[8] With massive numbers of soldiers and civilians dying in World Wars I and II and society now placing a renewed emphasis on the value of individual life, the need to remember these lost lives arose.

There may be another factor at play as well, at least in the United States. Erika Doss describes the final few decades of the twentieth century as the beginning of a "memorial mania" in America. She chronicles an "obsession with issues of memory and history and an urgent desire to express and claim those issues in visibly public contexts."[9] Doss further describes the modern American memorial as "often equivocal, unresolved, and ambivalent." The meanings of these memorials fluctuate with time and contemporary passions, and they are more likely to commemorate victims than heroes.[10] Thus, the twentieth century represents the birth of widespread memorialization. And the process and manner of memorialization and commemoration itself appears to have evolved significantly by the end of the century. For these reasons alone, an examination of many of the past century's wars and the changing ways in which they are remembered is a worthy endeavor.

One final consideration may also be in order. The twentieth century also witnessed the immense growth of an "industry of memory," of which Clint Eastwood's films exemplify one of the prominent aspects. A variety of smaller "memory industries" comprise the larger "industry of memory," according to Viet Thanh Nguyen, like producers of smaller commodities that make up a larger economy. Nguyen writes that "an industry of memory includes the material and ideological forces that determine how and why memories are produced and circulated, and who has access to, and control of, the memory industries." Consequently, "the memories of the wealthy and the powerful exert more influence because they own the means of production."[11]

Nguyen asserts that no other nation's or society's industry of memory compares to that of the United States. In the same manner that the US military can project power around the globe, so too can the American industry of memory project American popular memory into the global consciousness. "And just as many countries let themselves become territories where American soldiers can operate," Nguyen explains,

> even more countries have let down their defenses against the intrusion of American memory, the soft power exports of cinema, literature, language, ideas, values, commodities, and lifestyles, the whole Hollywood–Coca Cola–McDonald's network found in many big cities and not a few small ones, including in Vietnam, from its metropolitan centers to its suburbs with their smooth sidewalks, fast food outlets, and detached single family homes.[12]

This does not mean the United States alone dictates collective memory to the world. Rather, it means the powerful who control the industry of memory have far greater influence in how public memory of the past is constructed than do the weaker and poorer. Some of the chapters in this volume demonstrate the impact of this industry of memory, largely, but not exclusively, American.

This volume is not intended to be comprehensive. It serves as a basic introduction to the field of war and memory studies and a sampling of some of the most recent scholarship on the memory of twentieth-century wars. Even within the twentieth century, the list of wars considered is not exhaustive. Had the number of topics not been constrained by space, examinations of the memory of the Balkans War, the Spanish Civil War, and the Franco-Algerian War, to name just a few, would have further enriched this collection of essays. Moreover, the volume explores only a limited number of themes about the wars under consideration. And, by electing to use the term "public memory," the volume risks committing the sin of using overly broad terminology about which Jay Winter warned. Ultimately, however, since the volume is intended as only an introduction to war and memory studies, this editor elected to use "public memory" as an inclusive umbrella term that encompasses a variety of other, similar terms such as popular memory, collective memory, and collective remembrance. This decision notwithstanding, the volume acknowledges Winter's point about the centrality of agency in the formation of "public" memory.[13]

The volume relies on a handful of other common terms that would benefit from some clarification. Significantly, the memory scholar Michael R. Dolski distinguishes the term "monument"—defined as "a single structure intended to celebrate, honor, educate, or aid memory recall"—from the term "memorial"—meaning either an area of remembrance featuring a single or multiple monuments or "an honorific designation bestowed upon something extant."[14] This volume often uses the terms interchangeably to mean a single structure, or multiple structures, intended for the purpose of remembrance. Dolski's differentiation of "remembrance"—"the process of constructing the past for present/future purposes"—from "commemoration"—"an open, public, and often celebratory approach to remembering the past"—is also elucidating.[15]

The thirteen chapters in this collection examine twentieth-century wars from World War I through the Persian Gulf War. The collection includes eleven historical essays dealing with twentieth-century wars or aspects of these wars. The essays each analyze how public memory of their respective war has evolved over time. The collection's essays raise fascinating questions about war and memory. Why are wars remembered as they are? What factors drive changes in public perception? What implications arise from remembering or commemorating a war or particular aspects of a war? What does public memory of a war say about a society?

Viet Thanh Nguyen contends that "The tendency is to remember any given war, to the extent it is remembered at all, for a detail or two." For Americans, for example, "World War II is the 'Good War' ... while the tragedy in Vietnam is the bad war." Nguyen calls for

> a just memory that strives both to remember one's own and others, while at the same time drawing attention to the life cycle of memories and their industrial production, how they are fashioned and forgotten, how they evolve and change.[16]

To that end, this volume examines fresh, less considered perspectives of many of the wars under discussion.

The eleven chapters comprising the main body of this collection are divided into three sections. The four essays in the first section, entitled "Monumental conflicts: The sacred and the political," examine tangible memorials such as monuments, statues, and cemeteries, and their relationship to public memory. These four chapters question what qualifies as a "monumental conflict"—i.e., a war or facet of a war that is worthy of physical commemoration.

During most wars, desertion is punishable by death. Yet some late twentieth-century Germans came to see desertion as "monumental." War monuments also demonstrate how physical commemoration can serve disparate political ends, sometimes even concurrently, and how a free society often constructs them only after a tortuous political process. Indeed, the concept of present political and cultural influences on the construction of monuments to the past emerges as the dominant theme in this first section. The conception and construction of a war monument requires compromise and negotiation regarding how the past will be remembered. The public then continually reinterprets these physical objects of remembrance. The American struggle to reach a consensus on how best to commemorate its past wars resembles the ways in which Brazilians of different political persuasions use the very same monuments to further different political agendas. A similar political negotiation appears in German attempts to re-conceptualize and thereby come to terms with their past, as well as the ways in which British attempts to remember those individuals who lost their lives in World War I speak volumes about how they remember the war itself.

Hanna Smyth is a doctoral student in the Globalising and Localising the Great War Research Network at the University of Oxford. She examines British empire commemoration of World War I. Specifically, she looks at the role that Imperial War Graves Commission cemeteries and memorials play in the commemoration process. Smyth demonstrates that these IWGC sites play incredibly significant, and active, roles not just as "sites of memory" but as sites of identity. The IWGC sites commemorate loss, serve as places for personal and collective remembrance, and offer "specific messages about who fought, what they died for, and which aspects of their identities were most worth remembering."

William Thomas Allison, a professor of history at Georgia Southern University, has published widely on American military history and twentieth-century wars.[17] He addresses the struggle of a free society to arrive at a common "truth" about the past and examines modern controversies surrounding American monuments and the "battleground" of American public memory. His chapter chronicles the struggle to shape the major war memorials on the National Mall and demonstrates how the construction of these monuments in turn helped shape American national identity, but only after an arduous process of negotiation and compromise. Allison chronicles the evolution of the style of physical commemoration on the National Mall in Washington, DC. Well situated in Constitution Gardens between the Lincoln and Washington Monuments, Maya Lin's Vietnam Veterans Memorial set the stage for all the war monuments that followed. First, it features a strongly modernist design, simple and featuring individual names but no overt political message. The monument quickly became a very personal site and succeeded, according to Allison, in ways that no one—including its creator—could have imagined. This "veterans" memorial contrasts with the National World War II Memorial, which is in actuality a "national" war memorial, not a veterans' one. Its lavish and all-encompassing design contrasts with Lin's simple and personal one. Moreover, the World War II Memorial contributes to the American national narrative—it furthers the "greatest generation" myth, as Allison notes—as opposed to simply honoring the dead.

Uri Rosenheck, a research fellow at the Sverdlin Institute for Latin American History and Culture at Tel Aviv University, analyzes the manner in which war commemoration often reflects contemporary politics. Rosenheck looks at hundreds of Brazilian World War II monuments and traces the evolution of public interaction with these memorials. He contends that the design and construction of an actual monument is only the first step in a long process of public remembrance. Rosenheck illustrates how different segments of Brazilian society reinterpreted World War II monuments to both support and contest the same political leadership, revealing the very subjective nature of public commemoration. Yet Rosenheck also highlights the local context of the agents of memory. The monuments' locations reveal that communities' collective memories of World War II are not uniform. In particular, the World War II monuments in smaller communities in rural areas assumed a much more personal connotation than did those in larger, urban centers. While not quite "sacred," these monuments at least continue to be compelling places of commemoration, where many of the monuments in larger areas are now largely ignored.

Steven R. Welch is a senior lecturer in Modern European History at the University of Melbourne. He looks at the deserter monument movement in Germany beginning in the 1980s, a topic he is currently developing for a forthcoming book. Additionally, Welch previously examined some aspects of this movement in an article published in the *Journal of Contemporary History* in 2012.[18] Some of the monuments that Welch analyzes honor deserters from the *Wehrmacht* in particular, while others honor the act of desertion in general. The former reflect political currents that view the Nazi-controlled *Wehrmacht* as having been an evil regime, and thus one from which desertion would seem to have been honorable. The latter places desertion on a level commensurate with conscientious objection. Both have fascinating implications for how Germans and non-Germans alike might view deserters from other past and future wars.

The next two sections deal largely with cultural remembrance, or the less tangible aspects of public memory, including but not limited to photographs, television programs, films, fiction, and the arts. The three chapters in the second section, entitled "Negotiated memories of war," examine one battle and two wars that have received a great deal of past attention. A significant number of publications have examined public memory of these events, though usually from the American perspective. These essays, by contrast, look at these wars from the "other side," so to speak.

The three chapters in this section demonstrate the prevalence of negotiation in shaping popular memory of wars among the populations in the local areas where the war was waged. Former Japanese colonizers' commemorations of an iconic battle feature divergent attempts—some exculpatory and some apologetic—to explain their role in World War II. In similar ways, the nation of South Korea must balance its interest in acknowledging the damage from a twentieth-century war and the realities of the postwar American involvement in their nation's affairs with their continuing need for American financial and military support. And Vietnam's public memory emerges from the confluence of recovery from the war's destruction and the lucrative influx of tourists who commemorate it. Negotiations of these financial, political, diplomatic, and military concerns seem to shape how all of these populations remember their respective wars.

Stephen C. Murray, an independent scholar and anthropologist, traces the building of monuments to Japanese war dead from the World War II battle of Peleliu. This research emerges from his book *The Battle over Peleliu: Islander, Japanese, and American Memories of War*, published in 2016.[19] He argues that the construction and interpretation of these monuments serves as a surrogate forum for Japanese political groups to express their views about the war in ways they are unable to use in Japan. Peleliu Island had been a Japanese-controlled territory since the end of World War I and, by the time of World War II, consisted of a mixed population of Palauans and Japanese settlers. Murray demonstrates the extent to which contemporary Japanese commemoration of the battle ignores the indigenous Palauan inhabitants of Peleliu, who remember the battle in very distinct ways of their own.

Murray's may be a bit of an exception among this section's essays, as the Japanese largely ceased to be part of the "local society" of Peleliu after 1945. Indeed, some of their political struggles and negotiations are as akin to the processes discussed by the chapters in the third section as they are to those in this one. Yet Japanese settlers comprised a significant portion of the Palauan population at the time of the battle and enjoyed disproportionate political control. Consequently, their role resembles that of the United States in both the Korean and Vietnam Wars in interesting ways and, thus, offers more in regard to the themes of this section.

Brendan Wright and Christina Schwenkel examine public memory of two highly contested American Cold War conflicts: the Korean War and the Vietnam War, respectively. Scholars and popular writers have written a great deal about how Americans view these wars, the Vietnam War in particular. Yet, like Murray before them, these two scholars trace the memory of these wars from the perspective of the local populace. Brendan Wright, a lecturer at Carleton University in Ottawa, Canada, looks at South Korean popular culture, media, and textbooks, to discern how the South Korean public's views of the Korean War, the United States, and American involvement in their nation's "civil war" has significantly evolved since the armistice in 1953.

Christina Schwenkel, an associate professor of anthropology at the University of California-Riverside, has published extensively on collective memory in Vietnam.[20] Here she analyzes Vietnamese public memory of the United States' war in Vietnam and dissects the fascinating relationship between the promotion of war tourism in Vietnam and the shaping of public memory of the event. Both essays suggest interesting contemporary implications: a South Korean public still dependent to some degree upon American support and protection and a Vietnamese popular memory shaped in some measure by the need to continue to promote a thriving tourist industry.

The four chapters in the third section of the volume, entitled "Expeditionary wars and national pride," examine a thematic element of World War I, a postcolonial conflict, and two conflicts that mark the end of the Cold War and the beginning of the post-Cold War era. Pride emerges as the dominant theme of these final four historical essays. Pride in the heroes of the air offered nations something and someone to celebrate in an otherwise dismal war. Later in the century, pride undergirded British public memory of the Falklands War as well. Curiously, popular Russian memory of their experience in Afghanistan and American memory of their first war in Iraq appear to have evolved in opposite directions, sparked from the same catalyst. The Russian public long viewed their war in Afghanistan as a failure and, hence, a loss of national pride, until the American military effort in Afghanistan met a similar fate. By contrast, Americans initially took great pride in their quick, overwhelming victory in the Persian Gulf War. Yet the return of the American military to Iraq a little over a decade later seemed to take its toll on American memory of the first war and, ultimately, American pride.

Guillaume de Syon is Chair of the Department of History at Albright College in Reading, Pennsylvania. His publications include more than 30 articles and book chapters and two books on the history of technology, aviation in particular.[21] He examines public memory of World War I aviation. He contends that a number of national populations during the war inflated the importance of aviators as an alternative to the mass death and stalemate of the ground forces on the Western Front. While aviation's role was in its infancy during the war, it was celebrated and remembered afterward in an outsized manner. Hence, de Syon illustrates public memory's significant divergence from the actual nature of aviation during World War I, mostly for reasons of pride.

Davide Borsani is currently a postdoctoral research fellow in the History of International Relations at Catholic University of the Sacred Heart in Milan, Italy. He studies the Falklands War of the 1980s.[22] Borsani suggests that, despite its brevity, the war emboldened the British public and political leadership and provided a renewed self-respect. British memory of the war tends toward positive reflection, owing to the sense of pride they gained from their experience and, ultimately, from their victory in the war. This renewed pride resulted in greater British willingness to engage in military endeavors overseas as well as a prevalent British belief that they should continue to defend the Falkland Islands in the future.

Roger R. Reese and Robert T. Jones trace public memory of the Soviet–Afghan War and America's First Gulf War, respectively. Roger Reese is a professor of history at Texas A&M University and has published extensively on the Soviet Red Army.[23] His essay illustrates the influence of very practical matters such as veterans' benefits on the construction and evolution of public memory. Moreover, he also traces the effect of the American involvement in Afghanistan, which began in 2001, on Russian memory of their own decade-long war in that country in the 1980s. The ongoing US and NATO effort against the Taliban and Al-Qaeda in Afghanistan rehabilitated the Russian view of the Soviet–Afghan War, initially popularly seen as a failure. Now, public memory of the war has transformed it into a heroic early defense against Islamic extremism. In this sense, the later American struggles in Afghanistan have made the earlier aborted Russian effort look better by comparison.

Conversely, Robert T. Jones, an assistant professor in the Department of Army Tactics at the US Army Command and General Staff College, demonstrates how the twenty-first-century American war in Iraq, what he calls the "Second Gulf War," transformed American public memory of the Persian Gulf War. The quick, overwhelming—almost easy—victory in the Persian Gulf War sparked tremendous American pride. Indeed, Jones demonstrates that the original images of a bloodless techno-war endured for years following the American triumph. The second American war in Iraq in 2003, however, compelled Americans to question the relative success of the First Gulf War. Ironically, the same American war—the Global War on Terror that included both Operation Enduring Freedom in Afghanistan beginning in 2001 and Operation Iraqi Freedom in 2003—inspired both Russian reconsideration of the Soviet–Afghan War and American reconsideration of the Persian Gulf War, albeit with very different consequences.

These eleven essays demonstrate the important part that present and future concerns and negotiation play in the public memory of past wars. Whether those present concerns involve commemorating the dead, constructing a past in which a society can take pride, or shaping a society's way forward, they all involve negotiation. The voices of the many diverse elements in modern society compete to be heard and remembered. Whether the remembrance arises from small communities or national public spaces, from authoritarian state propaganda or the most prominent industry of memory in the world, how the public remembers war says more about those who remember than it does about who or what they are remembering.

The views expressed in this volume are solely those of the authors and do not represent the views of the US Army or the US Department of Defense.

## Notes

1 *Heartbreak Ridge*, 130 minutes, Warner Brothers, 1986.
2 Viet Thanh Nguyen, *Nothing Ever Dies: Vietnam and the Memory of War* (Cambridge, MA: Harvard University Press, 2016), 103–128.
3 "Heartbreak Ridge," Box Office Mojo (Internet Movie Database), http://boxofficemojo. com/movies/?id=heartbreakridge.htm&adjust_yr=1&p=.htm (accessed 23 March 2016).
4 Academy of Motion Picture Arts and Sciences, "The 59th Academy Awards, 1987" (*Oscars.org*), https://www.oscars.org/oscars/ceremonies/1987/H?qt-honorees=1#block-quicktabs-honorees (accessed 28 March 2016).
5 Marita Sturken, *Tangled Memories: the Vietnam War, the AIDS Epidemic, and the Politics of Remembering* (Berkeley: University of California Press, 1997), 3.

6 Jay Winter, *Remembering War: The Great War Between Memory and History in the Twentieth Century* (New Haven: Yale University Press, 2006), 3.
7 Nigel C. Hunt, *Memory, War and Trauma* (Cambridge, UK: Cambridge University Press, 2010), 197–198.
8 Ibid.
9 Erika Doss, *Memorial Mania: Public Feeling in America* (Chicago: University of Chicago Press, 2010), 2.
10 Ibid., 44–46.
11 Nguyen, *Nothing Ever Dies*, 107.
12 Ibid., 115–116.
13 Michael R. Dolski's comments and questions were instrumental in clarifying for the author the importance of agency in memory studies and for correcting numerous other errors of interpretation in an early draft of this introductory chapter.
14 Michael R. Dolski, *D-Day Remembered: The Normandy Landings in American Collective Memory* (Knoxville, TN: The University of Tennessee Press, 2016), xxii–xxiii.
15 Ibid.
16 Nguyen, *Nothing Ever Dies*, 5, 12.
17 Most recently, see William Thomas Allison, *My Lai: An American Atrocity in the Vietnam War* (Baltimore: Johns Hopkins University Press, 2012); *The Gulf War, 1990–1991* (New York: Palgrave Macmillan, 2012); *The Tet Offensive: A Brief History with Documents* (New York: Routledge, 2008); and *Military Justice in Vietnam: The Rule of Law in an American War* (Lawrence: University Press of Kansas, 2007).
18 Steven R. Welch, "Commemorating 'Heroes of a Special Kind': Deserter Monuments in Germany," *Journal of Contemporary History* 47:2 (2016), 370–401.
19 Stephen C. Murray, *The Battle over Peleliu: Islander, Japanese, and American Memories of War* (Tuscaloosa, AL: University of Alabama Press, 2016).
20 Christina Schwenkel has published numerous articles in academic journals including *American Ethnologist, South East Asia Research, International Journal for History, Culture and Modernity, Critical Asian Studies, Cultural Anthropology*, and numerous others. For her most recent book, see Christina Schwenkel, *The American War in Contemporary Vietnam: Transnational Remembrance and Representation* (Bloomington: Indiana University Press, 2009).
21 See Guillaume de Syon, *Science and Technology in Modern European Life* (Westport, CT: Greenwood, 2008); and *Zeppelin! Germany and the Airship, 1900–1939* (Baltimore: Johns Hopkins University Press, 2002).
22 Davide Borsani has published numerous journal articles and book chapters on post-World War II international history, the Falklands War in particular. Most recently, see Davide Borsani, *La special relationship anglo-americana e la Guerra delle Falkland* [The Anglo-American "Special Relationship" and the Falklands War] (Florence: Le Lettere, 2016).
23 Most recently, see Roger R. Reese, *Why Stalin's Soldiers Fought: The Red Army's Military Effectiveness in World War II* (Lawrence: University Press of Kansas, 2011); *Red Commanders: A Social History of the Soviet Officer Corps, 1918–1991* (Lawrence: University Press of Kansas, 2005); and *The Soviet Military Experience: A History of the Soviet Army, 1917–1941* (London: Routledge, 2000). He has also published more than a dozen academic journal articles and book chapters in venues including *Journal of Slavic Military Studies, War & Society, Global War Studies: The Journal for the Study of Warfare and Weapons, 1919–1945*, and *Journal of Military History*.

# PART I
# Monumental conflicts: The sacred and the political

# 1

# "THERE IS ABSOLUTELY NOTHING LIKE THE CARVING OF NAMES": IMPERIAL WAR GRAVES COMMISSION SITES AND WORLD WAR I MEMORY

*Hanna Smyth*

It is 1917. World War I is still more than a year from being over, and men are dying and being wounded in the millions. Britain has instituted a repatriation ban, dictating that no bodies of its fallen soldiers will be returned home. These circumstances present a massive logistical challenge: how to find, bury, organize, and commemorate the war dead. For Britain and her empire, a new organization was formed to undertake this: the Imperial War Graves Commission (IWGC), founded by Fabian Ware.

The war presented many new logistical challenges, but this one—the care and commemoration of the dead—was uniquely emotional and wide-ranging, encompassing and manifesting both the individual and the collective sorrow of those left behind. "Those left behind" were in countries often hundreds if not thousands of miles from the battlefields, as the dominions and colonies of Britain had been compelled to fight as well. Although by law they did not have a choice, loyalty to Britain and high numbers of British-born people among their citizens meant that, at the outbreak of war, the dominions embraced their involvement with a substantial amount of zeal.[1] Sentiments such as those expressed in this 1914 poem were widespread:

> We are coming, Mother, coming—we are coming Home to fight. To defend the Empire's honour, to uphold the Empire's might. From the Plains of Manitoba, from the diggings of the Rand, we are coming, Mother Britain—coming home to lend a hand ... From the islands and the highlands, from the outposts of the earth, from a hundred ships we hasten to your side to prove our worth. We've come to stick through thin and thick and woe betide the ones who dare to smite the Mother-might, forgetting of the sons ... From the jungles of Rhodesia, from the snows of Saskatoon, we are coming, Mother Britain, and we hope to see you soon.[2]

The distance between the dominions and the Western Front made it extremely difficult for most people to make the journey. Deep ties were created between these countries and the foreign fields where their lost were buried or named. Canadian Prime Minister Arthur Meighen eloquently stated in 1921, speaking about a specific IWGC cemetery with a high concentration of Canadians, "Across the leagues of the Atlantic the heartstrings of our Canadian nation will reach through all time to these graves in France."[3]

The results of the IWGC's efforts were thousands of cemeteries and memorials, mainly located along the fighting fronts. Cemeteries and memorials are an example of "material culture" (they are tangible *things*), and the term "the material culture of remembrance" is an important one that will be used throughout this chapter to refer to them. The Western Front (modern France and Belgium) is the focus of this chapter, but it is worth noting that IWGC sites also exist in 152 other countries, including World War I commemoration sites in Iraq, Turkey, and Egypt.[4]

These memorials and cemeteries are an important lens through which to understand the evolution of both individual and collective relationships with World War I. What roles have these locations played as sites of memory, and how has this changed over time? Far from merely being a backdrop against which these relationships have been negotiated and performed, from the time of their construction stretching to the present, these sites have played active roles in representing, shaping, and reinforcing public memory(ies) and identity(ies) in relationship to the war. World War I was not only a "monumental conflict," but also a conflict characterized by its monuments: The number, importance, and scale of World War I monuments established them to an unprecedented degree as authoritative loci for the interpretation and perpetuation of memory and identity. This role continues today. By the time of World War I's centenary in the period 2014–18, living memory of the war had been effectively extinguished, meaning that even more weight is being given to the tangible expressions of that memory which have been left behind: memorials and cemeteries, artifacts, and the written word (namely memoirs and letters). As yet another generation grapples with defining, exploring, and performing how it "should" remember the war, these expressions are treated as signposts pointing the way to a past which can be imagined but never re-inhabited.

## IWGC past and present

The Imperial War Graves Commission still exists today, albeit under a different name. It is now called the *Commonwealth* War Graves Commission (CWGC), having been updated in 1960 to reflect the changing nature of the British Empire. Its remit, as outlined in its Royal Charter of Incorporation in 1917, is

> to make fit provision for the burial of officers and men of Our said forces and the care of all graves in such cemeteries, to erect buildings and permanent memorials therein, and generally to provide for the maintenance and upkeep of such cemeteries, buildings, and memorials.

It currently cares for the material culture of remembrance for more than one million dead of World War I.[5]

The term "war dead" is not as strictly defined as one might think. The conflict created new aspects of identity for many people, and also exacerbated existing ones; these were frequently overlapping and sometimes contradictory. This extended even to death, and affected whether a person was eligible for commemoration by the IWGC. If someone is killed in a battle this is clearly a war death, but other cases are not so clear-cut. Soldiers who died of disease or succumbed to their war injuries after the war was over, civilians killed by enemy action, and non-combatant deaths such as medical services and Labour Corps members all present more challenging decisions regarding classification as a war death.

The fundamental principles of the IWGC's commemoration of the dead were equality and uniformity.[6] The son of Herbert Asquith, the United Kingdom's Prime Minister from 1908 to 1916, is buried in France with the same-sized headstone as untold scores of privates whose families may not have been able to afford a headstone at all.[7] No matter how much money or influence a family had, they could not pay for special graves or have their dead soldier sons sent back home to them for burial. Each body would be buried as near as possible to where it fell, and if the body was never found then the person's name would be inscribed on a "memorial to the missing." Occasionally the principles of equality and uniformity contradicted each other, and religion is a prime example of this. To treat all of its fallen equally, the IWGC allowed for breaks in uniformity to accommodate various religious symbols, and in some cases even different burial practices, particularly regarding Muslim, Sikh, and Hindu soldiers.

Any overview of the IWGC must include introductions to its principal figures. In addition to founder Fabian Ware, among the crucial figures who helped to bring these "silent cities" of the dead to life were three architects and a poet.[8] Edwin Lutyens left his mark on the material culture of World War I remembrance by creating several of its best-known iterations. He designed the IWGC Thiepval memorial to the missing of the Somme, the national Australian memorial at Villers-Bretonneux, and the Stone of Remembrance, an architectural feature repeated across the larger IWGC cemeteries (more on all of these below).[9] He also created more than 60 war memorials in Britain and abroad and was responsible for designing 140 IWGC cemeteries on the Western Front.[10] Before the war, he had been a leading country-house architect in Britain and also an architect of imperial Britain, namely in India.[11]

His colleague and rival Herbert Baker, whose notable designs include the national memorials at Neuve Chapelle and Delville Wood, was also an imperially minded architect.[12] As early as 1916, he had a vision for the memorials that would be created in the war's aftermath. He argued that "the outcome of this war will be an uplifting of the ideals of our Nation and of our Empire,"[13] and the memorials he designed "promote[d] his vision of a harmonious imperial system across space and time and to represent the grandeur of the British Empire."[14] The third principal architect was Reginald Blomfield, former president of the Royal Institute of British Architects. Among other contributions, he came up with the final design for the

Cross of Sacrifice that adorns most IWGC cemeteries, designed the Menin Gate Memorial, and was responsible for the first three "experimental" IWGC cemeteries on the Western Front.[15]

The last name on this list is not an architect but a poet. Rudyard Kipling was well known in Britain at the time of the war, and his son John ("Jack") went missing in 1915. Jack's body was finally identified in the 1990s, and his grave's headstone in St Mary's ADS Cemetery now bears his name.[16] Kipling was asked to craft many of the inscriptions for IWGC memorials, and also contributed stock phrases—often drawn from the Bible—that are repeated in hundreds of IWGC cemeteries.

An element of "great man history" is inevitable with such instrumental figures.[17] However, there are thousands more IWGC workers who should also not be forgotten: the myriad junior architects of the IWGC[18] and, despite the comparative dearth of information about them, the stonemasons, gardeners, soldier employees, and administrative staff who labored to bury the dead and transform the landscapes into the pristinely beautiful sites of memory we see today. This work continues: The CWGC is a major horticultural employer worldwide.[19]

To understand an IWGC site, it is imperative to become familiar with the key features that are repeated throughout its locations. Its memorials are usually unique, but its cemeteries have a homogeneous consistency of identifiable characteristics, while allowing for variations. The Cross of Sacrifice is found in almost every IWGC cemetery that holds more than 40 graves (see Figure 1.1).[20]

**FIGURE 1.1** Cross of Sacrifice, Redan Ridge Cemetery No. 2, 2016. Photo by the author

**FIGURE 1.2** Stone of Remembrance, Serre Road Cemetery No. 2, 2016. Photo by the author

Designed to represent "the faith of the majority," its size varies in proportion to the size of the cemetery it overlooks.[21] Larger cemeteries also have a "Stone of Remembrance," a low oblong structure intended to echo an altar or a tomb (see Figure 1.2). The Stone of Remembrance does not contain a body; rather, it often acts as a focal point for commemorative rituals and deposited items (such as poppies). It bears the words "Their name liveth for evermore," marshalling a collective identity for the dead interred in its cemetery, who are commemorated individually by their headstones.

"Their name liveth for evermore," taken from *Ecclesiasticus* 44:14 of the King James Bible, is well known today. Lesser known is that the full line from the Bible is "Their bodies are buried in peace; but their name liveth for evermore." Kipling specifically omitted the first half when he selected the Stone's inscription.[22] This may have been due to the fact that many of the war's bodies were *not* "buried in peace"—particularly those dead categorized as "missing," which included Kipling's son Jack. However, John Keegan and Philip Longworth plausibly argue an additional factor for this decision: respect for fallen Hindu soldiers.[23] Due to the importance of cremation in Hinduism, any suggestion of the presence of a body—"here lies" rather than "here fell," references to a "grave" instead of a "resting place," or, in this inscription, "bodies buried in peace"—would be anathema. Since the Stone was planned to appear at multiple sites with a Hindu presence, including the Indian national memorial at Neuve Chapelle, the reference to the physical presence of bodies would have been deemed unacceptable for the inscription. Stones of Remembrance at IWGC sites all over the world carry this hidden reminder that the war was fought by those of many faiths. Lastly, every cemetery contains a "Cemetery Register," a book that lists the grave plot locations for every soldier in the cemetery. It is usually set into a wall niche near the entrance to assist mourners and visitors.

The landscape and fauna of IWGC sites are a fundamental element which both represents IWGC principles and continues to shape perceptions and memories today. IWGC cemeteries and memorials are impeccably landscaped, with the cemeteries designed to evoke the sense of an English garden.[24] At several—the Beaumont-Hamel and Vimy sites are particularly notable examples—the battlefield landscape has been preserved to a substantial degree (see Figure 1.3).[25]

While most IWGC sites do not explicitly state a behavioral code to conform with the reverence these locations provoke, a notable exception is the monumental Thiepval memorial which, until 2017, bore a sign to visitors as they passed through a low stone wall delineating its boundaries which read: "Please help to maintain the beauty and tranquillity of this sacred place by befitting conduct." The location of these sites on and within the battlefield landscapes, regardless of the extent to which these landscapes are visibly extant, magnifies the perception of these sites as sacred spaces. This was evinced by Canadian Prime Minister Meighen in his speech at the unveiling of the Cross of Sacrifice at the IWGC cemetery Thélus in 1921:

**FIGURE 1.3** Preserved landscape, Beaumont-Hamel, 2016. Photo by the author

We live among the ruins and the echoes of Armageddon. Its shadow is receding slowly backward into history. At this time the proper occupation of the living is, first, to honour our heroic dead; next, to repair the havoc, human and material, that surrounds us; and lastly, to learn aright and apply with courage the lessons of the war ... in earth which has resounded to the drums and tramplings of many contests, they rest in the quiet of God's acre with the brave of all the world.[26]

Jeremy Foster argues that this connection between the dead and their landscapes is a triangulation, positing "a significant part of a memorial's imaginative charge stems from the triangulation it sets up between the living, the dead and geographical place."[27] These are secular sacred spaces.[28] They are outdoor shrines for a secular cult of the war dead: a form of collective mourning that shared parallels with religious practices, which did not replace traditional religion but was a social phenomenon uniting the living in reverence for those who fell.[29] These sites were and are instinctively treated as sacred places, and the war dead were non-contentious symbols, guaranteed respect and admiration by virtually all segments of society.[30]

## Representing and reinforcing identity

The title of this chapter comes from *The Stone Carvers* by Jane Urquhart, which explores the creation of the Vimy Memorial. Vimy is an IWGC monument in France, and is Canada's national World War I memorial on the Western Front (see Figure 1.4).

"There is absolutely nothing ... like the carving of names. Nothing like committing to stone this record of someone who is utterly lost."[31] The "carving of names" was a fundamental act through which the IWGC upheld its commitment to honoring individual identity, and their tactility—names carved in stone—is an integral link facilitating the imagined relationship between the dead and the living. Even today, 100 years after these deaths occurred, the role that carved names play in remembrance is striking. Watch a group of students in a cemetery or at a memorial; almost unfailingly, they will instinctively, inexorably reach out to touch the headstone or the wall of names in front of them.

Urquhart's quote also emphasizes *commitment*. IWGC sites were designed to serve as perpetual fixtures in their landscapes. What did they (or do they) promise, and to whom? One answer can be found within the same phrase by Urquhart: They are records—of individual and collective achievement, sacrifice, and grief. By doing this, one can argue that the people they commemorate are not "utterly lost" at all. At the opening of the IWGC Menin Gate Memorial in 1927, General Plumer famously opined of each missing soldier it commemorated, "He is not missing. He is here."[32]

A distinction that is often missed or under-discussed when examining British Empire World War I memorials is that "World War I memorials" consist of several different categories of monuments. Most of the following categories are not necessarily mutually exclusive, but distinguishing between them provides important

FIGURE 1.4  Vimy Memorial, 2016. Photo by the author

context for understanding their roles in shaping memory and identity. On the battle fronts, there are "battle exploit memorials" and memorials to the dead and missing. The former are erected at places of significant successes, usually for specific units, and glorify the achievements of the victors. Originally, there were intended to be national exploit memorials, with the UK government appointing the "Midleton Committee" (National Battlefields Memorial Committee) in May 1920 to put forth proposals.[33] However, by 1922 this had dissolved due to practical concerns, with national focus shifting instead to memorials for the missing and concomitant emphasis directed at individual army units to erect their own exploit memorials, 135 of which were erected or under construction by 1922.[34]

The latter may be erected at places of success (e.g., the Canadian memorial at Vimy), but are also frequently erected at places whose dominating narrative in the commemorator's memory was one of loss rather than success (e.g., the Newfoundland memorial at Beaumont-Hamel, where, after the July 1, 1916 attack, only 68 of the Newfoundland Regiment's more than 800 soldiers were able to report to roll call the following day. Note, however, that even "victorious" places were won at a high cost; consider, e.g., the loss of 3,598 Canadians capturing Vimy Ridge). The battlefield landscapes also contain regimental and unit memorials (e.g., the

Accrington Pals memorial in the Somme). Domestically, combatant countries erected both national memorials and spates of community monuments, the latter honoring the fallen (or occasionally all who served) from communities, universities, workplaces, and religious groups. With only 53 "thankful villages"—those where every World War I soldier returned home—in all of England, one can extrapolate the very high number of memorials that were created.[35] By focusing solely on IWGC sites in France and Belgium, this chapter restricts itself to battlefront memorials to the dead and missing, but all memorials and their histories are important sources providing insights into who needed them and why.

No examination of World War I memorials is complete without also discussing cemeteries, because the two are deeply intertwined conceptually and, often, spatially. Many memorials on the Western Front share a site with a cemetery, whose burials are a visible reminder of the sacrifices made for the sentiments expressed on the memorial. The dates of death on the headstones often make this link explicit. Less visible are the interconnections between memorial and cemetery that the dead themselves provide. The distinctions between types of tangible remembrance points are artificial—or perhaps practical—in that they are based entirely on date of death, location of death, and presence or absence of a body, rather than the emotional and experiential connections between those being commemorated. A poignant letter from a bereaved parent illustrates this point:

> [October 1919] Thanking you for your letter of 4th inst. in reference to a memorial to be placed in some British cemetery to my son D.H. Christie 2nd Lieut. 16th Royal Sussex Regt. Killed in action 21/9/18 and whose body was never recovered. I wish to inform you that it would be a satisfaction to his parents to have it placed in Corbie cemetery near Amiens near the grave of his brother, R.F. Christie, Lieut. R.E., died of wounds 16/12/15.[36]

This request was not granted. The 22-year-old Richard Christie's body is in grave I.B.2 at Corbie Communal Cemetery; his brother, the missing Denis, is listed alongside 9,836 other names on the Vis-en-Artois memorial, 54 kilometers away.

The identifying facts about these brothers offered by their father in the above letter demonstrate the key pieces of information that the IWGC used to keep track of the dead, and which thus became key elements of each headstone. IWGC headstones on the Western Front are generally rectangular in shape (not a cross, as French, American, and many German World War I Western Front headstones were), with a curved top. For identified casualties, the soldier's regimental (or, for the dominions, national—e.g., a maple leaf for Canada, a fern for New Zealand) symbol occupies the top portion of the headstone face, followed by his service number and rank, name, unit, date of death, and age at death. Below this is usually a religious symbol, with the cross as standard, followed, in most cases, by an epitaph chosen by next of kin at the bottom of the headstone (see Figure 1.5).

The identities and locations of the dead and their commemoration were also not stable. Exhumations, name changes, varying religious burial practices, and shifts in

**FIGURE 1.5** Example of IWGC headstone, Hooge Crater Cemetery, 2016. Photo by the author

and out of the "missing" designation, for example, all contributed to the blurring of many lines in categorizing the dead and fixing individual points of remembrance for them. The category of "missing" continues to evolve even today. World War I bodies are still found in the landscape, usually by farmers.[37] In many cases, they can be identified by components of their uniform, their personal effects, and/or DNA testing.[38] Once a name can be associated with the body, technically that name should no longer be recorded on a memorial to the missing. While today such adjustments occur in a trickle, they were occurring in a flood during the immediate postwar period of the 1920s and 1930s, when the national memorials to the missing were being built.[39] Precise calculations were required to accurately space the names on to the memorials' panels—without the use of computers!

The emphasis on individual commemoration, whether on memorials or headstones, combined with the unprecedented mechanization of methods of death during World War I and the obliteration they caused, meant that the term "missing" was a relatively new means of distinguishing the dead. In early IWGC documents, it is constantly referred to in quotation marks, as a newly introduced rather than established and accepted term.[40] The "missing" designation also came with religious complications. When the Hindu religion of Indian soldiers was certain and cremations took place, a problem was posed for the IWGC in multiple cases. The IWGC largely operated on a dual-option framework of conceptualizing the dead: It either had a soldier's body, or he was missing. Therefore, the prior cremation of Hindu soldiers posed a significant quandary. In some cases this was resolved by erecting dedicated memorial plaques near the cremation spots (which were predominantly within existing IWGC cemeteries).

However, in at least two instances, the IWGC made an alternative decision, with disturbing repercussions: Despite knowing the ultimate fates of these Hindu bodies (cremation), it designated these men as "missing." At first glance, the documentary evidence for this seems damning: "I agree that the 197 Indians cremated at Rouen must be recorded as 'Missing'";[41] "a few men who died [in France] in 1919 are 'Missing,' which are presumably cremation cases";[42] and, in a non-Western Front example, "It has been agreed by the Commission that the Indians buried at Ahwaz should go 'Missing.'"[43] Despite the wording of these statements, which is rather chilling, in reality the "missing" designation given to cremated Hindus does not seem to have had malicious intent. Rather, it was usually due to confusion about location: where they had died, where the cremation had taken place, and/or the location of the cremated remains.[44]

Whether missing or found, the presence of *names* was of paramount importance in the World War I material culture of remembrance. Combined with Britain's privilege in having both the resources and the victorious outcome that allowed individual commemoration, the primacy given to individual identity by the British Empire in this conflict's remembrance is one of the most striking features of IWGC sites. Care was taken not to duplicate names. Each could only be listed once, so that the single name carved in stone could act as a clear touchstone for the memory of this lost individual.[45]

The prominence of names in commemoration posed an interesting challenge during the creation of the IWGC South African national memorial at Delville Wood. This memorial bears no names. However, in 2016 the Delville Wood Memorial Wall was unveiled, stretching between the original memorial and the nearby museum, listing the names of all South Africans, black and white, who died during World War I. The South African missing are listed alongside British names, rather than on their separate national monument. This raised an important question: is a memorial still a "memorial to the missing" if it does not have any names? The decision to have no names on the Delville Wood memorial, and instead list them alongside British names on other memorials, was made by South African representatives rather than the IWGC.[46] This raised a consideration that distinguished Delville Wood from the Vimy, Villers-Bretonneux, and Neuve Chapelle memorials: It meant that now, unlike the others, this was not a memorial to the missing. The IWGC warned the Delville Wood Memorial Committee that:

> It must be understood that if the names of the missing are not engraved on the Delville Wood Memorial, then that memorial ceases to fulfill, from the Commission's point of view, the purpose of a Memorial to the Missing, and the Commission's contribution to the cost of the Delville Wood Memorial can consequently not be made.[47]

The decision-making process regarding names was also a storied affair for Australia's Villers-Bretonneux memorial. In 1922, it was suggested that if Australia was not willing to divide its missing among multiple memorials and list them alongside British names, Amiens would be the best place to collect them in commemoration should a single "Australian" site be needed.[48] However, it was acknowledged that "of all the Australian operations on the Western Front," it was Villers-Bretonneux that had "most impressed the public imagination."[49]

The debate over dividing Australian names did not reach a quick resolution. Further complications arose during the planning for the Menin Gate memorial, when Australia threatened to withdraw permission to have Australian names on the monument.[50] Along with Tyne Cot, the Gate was intended to be an "Empire Memorial," including dominion and Indian names (divided chronologically between the two memorials).[51] However, Australia wanted to list all of its Western Front missing by name on one memorial at Villers-Bretonneux, so its proposed solution to the Menin Gate conundrum was to have some names repeated on both memorials.[52] This proposal did not become reality because it violated the IWGC's policy of having only a single site of individual named commemoration for each fallen soldier.[53]

By 1930, it was agreed that Australia's Belgian missing would be listed on Menin Gate and Tyne Cot, leaving only its missing in France to be listed at Villers-Bretonneux. At the time, this total was estimated to be 18,557 names,[54] but the number of names of Australians missing in France was finally discerned to be 10,982, all of which were inscribed on the memorial.[55] In the ensuing 79 years since its unveiling, dozens of Australian "missing" have since been identified and buried, reducing the number of people officially commemorated on the Villers-Bretonneux Memorial to 10,738 as of January 2017.[56]

Questions of representing and reinforcing identity at IWGC sites on the Western Front become particularly complicated when the imperial monuments are considered. Britain's five dominions and India all have separate monuments in France and Belgium over which they exerted a significant degree of influence, and which continue to serve as significant representations of these countries' national identities today. The British dominions and undivided India were in a unique position regarding autonomy and commemorative agency during the construction of these memorials in the 1920s and 1930s. All six had participated in the war in relatively significant proportions. They all had their independence and imperial relationship affected by the war. Moreover, they were connected by the shared institution of the IWGC for commemoration, rather than having full control over their own remembrance. Unity of empire and unity of sacrifice were concepts bound up in unity of remembrance for these countries. The duality of the situation of the dominions and India is intriguing: They were distinct entities, yet enmeshed within the IWGC regarding the material culture of their battlefront memorialization. A survey of how this manifested for each country will illustrate these principles.

The first "national" dominion memorial to be erected on the Western Front was Newfoundland's memorial at Beaumont-Hamel in the Somme, which

FIGURE 1.6  Beaumont-Hamel Memorial, 2016. Photo by the author

was completed in 1925.[57] Its iconic bronze caribou, a massive sculpture of the Royal Newfoundland Regiment's emblematic animal, dominates the preserved battlefield landscape in which it stands (Figure 1.6). Newfoundland was a separate dominion within the British Empire until 1949, when it became the tenth province of Canada. Accordingly, in tandem with Canada's national memorial at Vimy, Beaumont-Hamel is managed by the Canadian government as a national historic site.

The Newfoundland narrative of loss at the site, embodied and concretized in public memory by the monument, overshadows the fact that other units fought at Beaumont-Hamel on that terrible July 1 as well.[58] The large scale of the site—a memorial, preserved landscape, and three IWGC cemeteries—allows for more flexibility in diluting the cohesive "national" narrative, by having two other memorials onsite. These secondary memorials, located near each other at the far end of the site, commemorate the 51st (Highland) and 29th Divisions of the British army.

This question of which narrative to privilege in the spatial interpretation and "preservation" of the landscape for visitors highlights the complex layers of experience and memory which have to be navigated during the somewhat inevitable creation of the semblance of a more cohesive narrative. Paul Gough aptly synthesizes this by arguing:

> [Beaumont-Hamel Memorial Park] has three primary modes of discourse: one that projects it as a sacred and reverential domain dedicated to recording a very particular act of war; another that identifies the site with distant, regional memory; thirdly, the site has become a dramaturgical space where terrain has been rearranged to create a sequence of spatial and timed narratives. In common with the many romantic and pastoral mythologies associated with the trench war on the Western Front, the Park has also been presented as an 'enchanted place' where hundreds of soldiers became 'lost' in the void of no man's land.[59]

After Beaumont-Hamel, the next major memorial to be unveiled was South Africa's, at Delville Wood in 1926. Its remit was broad, as it was a memorial not just to the missing, nor just to the fallen, nor just to South Africans on the Western Front;[60] it was in fact designated as a memorial to all South Africans who served in all theaters of the war.[61] The memorial consists of an arch flanked by a semicircular stone wall, capped by identical buildings imitating a famous house of the Cape Colony's first governor.[62] The arch has a bilingual inscription in English and Afrikaans to the dead who "at the call of duty made the Great Sacrifice." The dual languages reflect the complicated political situation and history of British and Dutch colonialism in South Africa.

Topping the arch is a sculpture by British artist Alfred Turner, depicting Castor and Pollux "clasping hands in friendship," intended as a "symbol of all the peoples of South Africa who are united in their determination to defend their common ideals."[63] Castor and Pollux are twins from Greek mythology, and their twinship here represents parity between the two "white races" of the South African Union.[64] Aside from the egregious omission of Black South Africans from this symbolism, it is also worth noting that in Greek mythology Castor and Pollux had different fathers, meaning that Pollux was half-divine whereas Castor was only mortal. Considered in this context, the sculpture seems to privilege one of the South African white "races" over the other, and, based on the circumstances, it may be read as an assertion of British superiority. The demarcation between dominion and British identity is less distinct here, since Britishness is being portrayed as an integral part of South African identity, instead of a foil against which the emergent South Africa should position itself.

India's national memorial at Neuve Chapelle was completed almost exactly a year after Delville Wood's unveiling, in October 1927 (see Figure 1.7).

Initial plans for monumental structures at cemeteries in France which housed large numbers of Indian soldiers included the construction of a Hindu temple and a Muslim mosque at each.[65] This is an unusual decision considering that, despite the overwhelmingly Christian burials that comprised the majority of IWGC sites on the Western Front, it was not common practice to consider building a Christian

**FIGURE 1.7**  Neuve Chapelle Memorial, 2016. Photo by the author

church on their grounds. The Sikh Deputation in England raised a voice of dissent to the plan. If Hindus and Muslims were each given a religious building at Indian-centric sites, why would Sikhs not receive a gurdwara in the same space?[66] The government of India also echoed this criticism and added that further complications were incurred by the Gurkhas, who, "although they were Hindus, desired to have a memorial which would separate them from their co-religionists."[67]

This debate was nullified by a letter from the India Office to the IWGC in 1920, which resulted in the IWGC issuing several resolutions, including "that the mosque and temple originally proposed should be dropped on the score of expense."[68] Another resolution was "that instead there should be separate stones of remembrance with certain inscriptions." This was passed over in favor of a singular stone identical to those featured in other IWGC cemeteries, whose inscription is discussed below. The construction of religious buildings would have been a provocative sacralization of a secularly sacred space. Despite differences of religion, it is clear that all actors involved in this debate shared a common sentiment: these sites were sacred ground.

Commemoration of pre-partition India on the Western Front eventually came to be concentrated in one memorial at Neuve Chapelle. This decision was reached despite the protests of the Indian government, who stated that "Indian opinion, except among Mahommedans, appeared to favor separate memorials rather than collective ones."[69] The designer of the memorial, British IWGC architect Herbert Baker, had the very challenging remit of creating a structure that commemorated Hindu, Muslim, and other Indian soldiers in a way that allowed for differentiation of names by religion yet united them on a single memorial, with symbolism that would satisfy all religions without privileging any one of them. The final design was a stone-walled enclosure encircling a nine-meter stone column flanked by tigers and capped by a lotus and crown. The walls bear the names of Indian missing. A central component of the memorial is the inscription on the column, stating "God is one, His is the Victory" in four languages.

Unlike India and the other dominions, New Zealand did not concentrate the material culture of its Western Front remembrance at a single site. Instead, it has seven memorials throughout France and Belgium, with the names of its missing distributed among them based on geographic proximity to the soldiers' last known locations. The case for this unusual decision was neatly summarized by a letter from the IWGC Vice-Chairman to the High Commissioner for New Zealand in 1922, although it should be noted that the decision lay ultimately with New Zealand rather than the IWGC:

> The Commission realise that the practical conditions which make the commemoration of the Missing in the cemeteries nearest to which they fell impossible do not apply in the case of New Zealand which had a comparatively small and compact force in the field and may consequently be able, as Great Britain and the larger dominions are not, to determine with approximate accuracy the locality where each of the Missing fell, and that New Zealand may, therefore, decide to take advantage of these more favourable circumstances and not join in the policy of centralised memorials to the Missing.[70]

After this spate of memorial unveilings in the mid- to late 1920s, it took almost ten years for Canada and Australia to add their presence to the landscape via national memorials, in 1936 and 1938 respectively. Canada's Vimy memorial was unveiled to a crowd of 50,000 that included 8,000 Canadian veterans and their families.[71] The largest individual sculpture on the monument highlights Canada's sorrow specifically: the 30-ton Mother Canada mourning her fallen sons stands in perpetual grief overlooking the empty tomb at the base of the monument, a "young nation mourning her dead" (see Figure 1.8).[72]

However, alongside this representation of an embodied, unified Canada, there are allegorical sculptures on the monument depicting Canada's shared identity with Britain and France based on common values and experiences. These demonstrate the degree to which Canada's newly asserted national identity was still proudly founded on its ties to Britain. The memorial's pylons are topped by anthropomorphized Peace and Justice, and other stone figures built into the monument personify Hope, Sacrifice, Charity, Faith, Honor, Knowledge, Truth, and "Bearing the Torch."[73] The triumphant idealism of these figures provides a counterpoint to a

IWGC sites and World War I memory  29

FIGURE 1.8   Mother Canada and the empty tomb, Vimy Memorial, 2016. Photo by the author

second type of figural sculpture in the memorial, one that instead focuses on a shared experience of loss. Groups of sculptures depict "Sympathy for the Helpless," "Mourning," and "The Breaking of the Sword" (see Figure 1.9).

Several twenty-first-century initiatives relating to the Vimy memorial illustrate the continuation of this site's prominence as a locus for the interpretation and perpetuation of memory and identity. The monument underwent an extensive 30-million-dollar restoration timed to coincide with the 90th anniversary of the battle for Vimy in 2007.[74] It also gave its name to the Vimy Charter for the Conservation of Battlefield Terrain, written in 2000, in which the Vimy site (along with Beaumont-Hamel) was treated as a "living laboratory" for participants in a Veterans Affairs Canada workshop entitled "Preserving Meaning and Emotion Through Battlefield Terrain."[75]

The verticality that characterizes the Vimy Memorial, with its twin pylons, is also a fundamental characteristic of Australia's national memorial at Villers-Bretonneux. Flanked by stone walls listing the missing, the monument's most striking feature is its 30-meter tower. In 1925, a competition was held to find an architect for the "Great Overseas Memorial" at Villers-Bretonneux.[76] Only Australian architects who had either served "with the sea or land forces of the British Empire" or had children who had done so were eligible.[77] The original winner was Australian

**FIGURE 1.9** The Female Mourner sculpture, Vimy Memorial, 2016. Photo by the author

architect William Lucas, but, under very contentious circumstances, the commission was later given to British IWGC architect Edwin Lutyens.[78] Unveiled on the brink of a second worldwide war, the late date of the Villers-Bretonneux memorial's creation epitomizes the close and interlinked timeline of these two global conflicts. Although intended to be unchanging in form, they were located in a war zone during World War II, resulting in extensive structural damage most notably to Villers-Bretonneux.[79]

In addition to these national memorials, two massive IWGC monuments were also erected on the Western Front during the 1920s and 1930s that were more distinctly "British" sites of memory, although imperial identities remained deeply intertwined. The Menin Gate and Thiepval memorials immediately dominated their surrounding landscapes and continue to occupy a proportionally dominant role in representing, shaping, and reinforcing British memory of the war. The Menin Gate memorial spans one of the main road entrances into the city center of Ypres. Hosting more than 54,000 names, it commemorates men from the United Kingdom, Australia, Canada, India, and South Africa who went missing in Belgium.

Lastly, the largest IWGC memorial in the world, Thiepval, starkly proclaims its status as the Memorial to the Missing of the Somme (see Figure 1.10). This battle, which arguably had the most indelible impact upon British memory of the war, also created an absence of 72,000 men, which this memorial attempts to fill with stone.[80] Presiding over a joint Anglo-French cemetery with 300 graves of each nationality, and flying both flags from its pinnacle, the memorial acts as a bastion both for shared loss and for the ideal of cooperation. As mentioned above, quietly among the names on the memorial are also those of many of South Africa's missing, but none of other dominions.

World War I is characterized by its monuments not just through their forms, but also through the rituals and behaviors they elicit and partake in. When viewing a memorial, one must always ask oneself, "who is this *for*?" The concept of the "gaze" is one borrowed from other historiographies, but is equally important for all facets of material culture. Who is looking at this, and what are they intended to see?

Most of the memorials introduced above are sites of substantial commemorative events, but one of the latter, Menin Gate, is particularly apt as an example when examining the performance of identity. Every night at Menin Gate, a Last Post ceremony halts traffic for nearly an hour as crowds gather. Now frequently numbering in the hundreds, the people wanting to remember have congregated underneath the Menin Gate arch for this 8pm ritual every single night since 1929, in all weathers, except in the four years of German occupation during World War II.

A letter from the IWGC's deputy controller to Fabian Ware in September 1927, two months after its opening, repeatedly references various measures being taken to control the memorial space. He confirmed that "No part of the Menin Gate is closed to the public, or ever has been," but a man was employed to keep the area continuously clean and litter-free and a by-law was hurriedly passed preventing "hawkers" who negatively altered the tone of the site.[81] As early as August 1927, the town of Ypres was writing to the IWGC inquiring about installing a permanent security presence at the monument.[82] Additionally, around the time the bylaw was being passed in September, an op-ed in *The Times* ran:

> The interior of this gate is at least as sacred to us as any church. Yet, while inside it scanning the columns for well-loved names, we were constantly pestered by local vendors of post-cards, photographs, and "souvenirs"—the

**FIGURE 1.10** Thiepval Memorial, 2016. Photo by the author

latter surely unnecessary to those who go there to honour our dead. Cannot our gallant Allies turn these mendicants out of the temple of the fallen who have no known grave?[83]

This letter also touches on the central concept of "pilgrim versus tourist" that characterized Western Front tourism, a phenomenon that emerged in the 1920s and 1930s and is enjoying a resurgence in today's society.[84] Tourism to the battlefields boomed during the interwar period, but those with connections to these sites through service or the loss of loved ones there (or both) often delineated themselves as "pilgrims" rather than "tourists," the latter with its connotations of relative moral inferiority. Formal and informal pilgrimages have occurred at IWGC sites since their unveilings, particularly at the memorials. Whether travelling a few miles or thousands, these journeys act as important bridges to span the "distant grief" of families whose men are buried or missing far from home.[85]

Rituals are not just limited to Western Front IWGC sites. The centenary has provoked an increased engagement with IWGC sites in the UK itself, most notably the CWGC's *Living Memory* initiative launched in 2016. This project encourages local communities to remember and engage with the 300,000 World War I graves in 12,000 locations throughout the UK. Most of these men died in hospitals or from the influenza outbreak that came on the heels of the war.[86]

## Conclusions

Imperial War Graves Commission sites played incredibly significant, and active, roles not just as "sites of memory" but as sites of identity. They not only serve as tangible representations of loss and fixed points for personal and collective remembrance; they also embody specific messages about who fought, what they died for, and which aspects of their identities were most worth remembering. The carving of names, whether on a memorial to the missing or on one headstone among many in the "silent cities" of the dead, was a characteristic of British imperial World War I remembrance remarkable in both its prioritization and the extent of its manifestation. In a war for which the state handled commemoration and burial logistics to an unprecedented degree, names served as lodestones for individuality and personal mourning among the collective homogeneity of this war's material culture of remembrance.

As the war's centenary continues, it becomes increasingly clear that the conflict was characterized by its monuments not just in the postwar commemorative era of the 1920s and 1930s but also in contemporary Britain and in its now independent dominions. As living memory has faded, these memorials and cemeteries have remained. Intended as perennial testaments to those who were lost, they now also serve as perennial testaments to those who missed them: the ones left behind, who created these monuments, carved these headstones, and buried these bodies. As the museum curator of an award-winning World War I centenary exhibit in England remarked in 2015, "We're not only commemorating those who were killed in the war; the fact is, *all* of them are dead now."[87] With the loss of those living witnesses, the material culture of remembrance gains ever more importance as a tangible anchor to *all* the people of 1914–1918 and what they experienced.

## Notes

1 For more on the British Empire's rationales and justifications for the war, see Piers Brendon, *The Decline and Fall of the British Empire 1781–1997* (London: Jonathan Cape, 2007), 253; Ashley Jackson, *Distant Drums: The Role of Colonies in British Imperial Warfare* (Brighton: Sussex Academic Press, 2010), 8; W. F. Mandle, *Going It Alone: Australia's National Identity in the Twentieth Century* (Ringwood, Australia: A. Lane, 1978), 15; Mark David Sheftall, *Altered Memories of the Great War: Divergent Narratives of Britain, Australia, New Zealand and Canada* (London: I.B. Tauris, 2010), 45.
2 Herbert Kaufman, "Mother Britain and Her Sons," in *Reynolds Newspaper*; printed in New Zealand's *Wanganui Chronicle*, issue 20219, 11 November 1914, https://paperspast.natlib.govt.nz/newspapers/WC19141111.2.33.
3 CWGC Historic Archive Add 1/1/93, "The Maples of Canada Planted on Vimy Ridge," *Bristol Evening News*, 4 July 1921. All subsequent archival references in this chapter are from the CWGC Historic Archive unless otherwise indicated.
4 The CWGC now cares for 23,000 memorials and cemeteries commemorating people who died in both World Wars I and II; see http://www.cwgc.org/about-us.aspx for further information.
5 For the text of its remit, see the scan of the 1917 Royal Charter at http://media.cwgc.org/media/394524/royal_charter_of_incorporation.pdf. For the figure of World War I dead, see the CWGC website *Find War Dead* and its searchable database: http://www.cwgc.org/find-war-dead.aspx.
6 Matthew Stuart Smith, "The Relationship between Australians and the Overseas Graves of the First World War" (MA thesis, Queensland University of Technology, 2010), 18; David Crane, *Empires of the Dead: How One Man's Vision Led to the Creation of WWI's War Graves* (London: Collins, 2013), 201.
7 Lieutenant Raymond Asquith, 3rd Bn. Grenadier Guards, died 15 September 1916 aged 37; grave reference I.B.3, buried Guillemont Road Cemetery, France.
8 A fourth architect, Charles Holden, was also important in the IWGC: see Tim Godden, "Refining a Style: Charles Holden, the Imperial War Graves Commission and the Birth of British Modern" (PG Cert History of Architecture dissertation, Birkbeck, 2012). See also Crane, *Empires*, 169.
9 For more detail on Lutyens and the Stone, see Kingsley Baird, "The Material of Remembrance: Their Name Liveth for Evermore?" in *Endurance and the First World War: Experiences and Legacies in New Zealand and Australia*, David Monger, Sarah Murray, and Katie Pickles, eds. (Newcastle-upon-Tyne: Cambridge Scholars, 2014), 263–283.
10 Tim Skelton, *Lutyens and the Great War* (London: Frances Lincoln, 2008), 15; for an itemization and analysis of "his" 140 cemeteries, see Jeroen Geurst, *Cemeteries of the Great War by Sir Edwin Lutyens*, trans. George Hall and Gerard van den Hooff (Rotterdam: 010 Publishers, 2010).
11 Crane, *Empires*, 106–107. Lutyens has been the subject of extensive writing, including Skelton, *Lutyens*, and Christopher Hussey, *The Life of Sir Edwin Lutyens* (London: Country Life, 1950).
12 Crane, *Empires*, 105.
13 Quoted in Andrew Prescott Keating, "The Empire of the Dead: British Burial Abroad and the Formation of National Identity" (PhD dissertation, University of California Berkeley, 2011), 113.
14 Keating, "Empire of the Dead," 114.

15 Crane, *Empires*, 116, 168–169; see also Philip Longworth, *The Unending Vigil: A History of the Commonwealth War Graves Commission, 1817–1984* (London: Leo Cooper, 1985), 36.
16 Grave reference VII.D.2.
17 The "Great Man Theory" of history, originating in the 1840s with Thomas Carlyle, argues that historical processes are driven by the actions of significant individuals: "The History of the World, I said already, was the Biography of Great Men." Thomas Carlyle, *On Heroes, Hero-Worship, and the Heroic in History* (London: Chapman & Hall, 1840), 17.
18 For more information on the architects (especially juniors) of the IWGC, see Tim Godden's research, e.g., "Khakitects: Experience, Memory and Design in the War Cemeteries of the Old Western Front" (unpublished lecture, Ypres, October 2015), and his forthcoming PhD thesis from the University of Kent.
19 CWGC, "Horticulture," http://www.cwgc.org/about-us/what-we-do/horticulture.aspx.
20 CWGC, "Our Cemetery Design and Features," http://www.cwgc.org/about-us/what-we-do/architecture/our-cemetery-design-and-features.aspx.
21 Ibid.
22 John Keegan, "There's Rosemary for Remembrance," *The American Scholar* 66:3 (1997), 342.
23 Ibid.; Longworth, *Unending Vigil*, 37.
24 Skelton, *Lutyens*, 123.
25 Jeremy Foster, "Creating a Temenos, Positing 'South Africanism': Material Memory, Landscape Practice and the Circulation of Identity at Delville Wood," *Cultural Geography* 11 (2004), 269, 274; Jacqueline Hucker, "'Battle and Burial': Recapturing the Cultural Meaning of Canada's National Memorial on Vimy Ridge," *The Public Historian* 31:1 (Winter 2009), 101–103; David W. Lloyd, *Battlefield Tourism: Pilgrimage and the Commemoration of the Great War in Britain, Australia, and Canada 1919–1939* (Oxford: Berg, 1998), 1; John Schofield, *Combat Archaeology: Material Culture and Modern Conflict* (London: Duckworth, 2005), 45; Jonathan Vance, *Death So Noble: Memory, Meaning, and the First World War* (Vancouver: UBC Press, 1997), 60. For greater detail on this topic in relation to the Vimy Memorial, see Natalie Bull and David Panton, "Drafting the Vimy Charter for Conservation of Battlefield Terrain," *Association for Preservation Technology International Bulletin*, "Managing Cultural Landscapes" 31:4 (2000), 5–11.
26 Add 1/1/93, "Canada's Heroes," *Daily Telegraph*, 4 July 1921.
27 Foster, "Creating a Temenos," 260.
28 For further reading on battlefields as secular sacred spaces, see Thomas Chambers, *Memories of War: Visiting Battlegrounds and Bonefields in the Early American Republic* (Ithaca: Cornell University Press, 2012); Keir Reeves et al., eds, *Battlefield Events: Landscape, Commemoration and Heritage* (New York: Routledge, 2016); Bruce Scates, *Return to Gallipoli: Walking the Battlefields of the Great War* (Cambridge, UK: Cambridge University Press, 2006); Jonathan Spielvogel, *Interpreting Sacred Ground: The Rhetoric of National Civil War Parks and Battlefields* (Tuscaloosa: University of Alabama Press, 2013); Ahenk Yilmaz, "Memorialization on War-Broken Ground: Gallipoli War Cemeteries and Memorials Designed by Sir John James Burnet," *Journal of the Society of Architectural Historians* 73:3 (2014), 328–346.
29 Lloyd, *Battlefield Tourism*, 6; Tanja Luckins, *The Gates of Memory: Australian People's Experiences and Memories of Loss and the Great War* (Freemantle: Curtin University Books, 2004), 91; Jay Winter, *Remembering War: The Great War between Memory and History in the Twentieth Century* (New Haven: Yale University Press, 2006), 26; Bart Ziino, *A Distant Grief: Australians, War Graves, and the Great War* (Crawley: University of Western Australia Press, 2007), 2, 21. For greater detail, see "Chapter 2: Christ in Flanders," in Vance, *Death So Noble*, 35–71.
30 Foster, "Creating a Temenos," 268; Hucker, "Battle and Burial," 100; Janet L. Lermitte, "Returning to Vimy Ridge: Canada's Narrative of Battle and Remembrance" (MA thesis, University of British Columbia, 2010), 13; Lloyd, *Battlefield Tourism*, 5; Bill Nasson, "Delville Wood and South African Great War Commemoration," *English Historical Review* 119:480 (February 2004), 67; Sheftall, *Altered Memories*, 147, 171–172; Vance, *Death So Noble*, 60, 67; Ziino, *Distant Grief*, 131.

31 Jane Urquhart, *The Stone Carvers* (Toronto: McClelland & Stewart, 2001), 347.
32 This is widely and variously quoted; I have trusted Jay Winter's archivally attributed version in his *Sites of Memory, Sites of Mourning: The Great War in European Cultural History* (Cambridge, UK: Cambridge University Press, 1995), 53n.110.
33 WG 219 Pt 2, "1st February 1922" (letter from IWGC Vice-Chairman to High Commissioner for New Zealand).
34 Ibid.; see also Gavin Stamp, *Memorial to the Missing of the Somme* (London: Profile, 2006), 101–102. Other examples epitomizing this shift in focus from exploit to missing include George MacDonogh's statement that "the memorial at Ypres [Menin Gate] should be a memorial to the missing and not a battle exploit memorial" (WG 219/1, "Proceedings of the Third Meeting of the Committee on Memorials to the Missing, Tuesday the 6th July 1921", 2), and the High Commissioner for New Zealand's remarks that "[a] policy of joint commemoration of the missing and the military effort should not, in my opinion, be agreed to by New Zealand, for I feel that the sentiment of our people is against [it]" (WG 219 Pt 2, "Draft Letter to the Rt. Hon. the Prime Minister" [1922 or 1923], 4).
35 As an indication of this high number of memorials, note that Denise Coss, in her PhD thesis "First World War Memorials, Commemoration and Community in North East England, 1918–1939" (Durham University, 2012), counted 2,227 memorials in England's North East alone. Arthur Mee coined the term "thankful villages" in the 1930s: see Alice Spawls, "Thankful Villages," *London Review of Books*, 10 June, 2016, http://www.lrb.co.uk/blog/2016/06/10/alice-spawls/thankful-villages/.
36 WG 219 Pt 1, "11th October 1919." The "memorial" in question refers to the IWGC's early plan to distribute names of the missing on panels among 85 Western Front cemeteries (WG 219/1, "Proceedings from the Third Meeting of the Committee on Memorials to the Missing," 6 July 1921, 4).
37 For a very recent example at the time of writing, see "British First World War Soldiers Identified through DNA Testing," *La Boisselle Study Group*, 8 September 2016, http://www.laboisselleproject.com/2016/09/08/british-first-world-war-soldiers-identified-through-dna-testing/.
38 In an excellent example of interdisciplinary research, forensic archaeologist Layla Renshaw specializes in human identification, genetic testing, and contemporary public understanding and participation in the recovery process of British and Australian World War I soldiers on the Western Front: see for example Layla Renshaw, "Anzac Anxieties: Overcoming Geographical and Temporal Distance in the Recovery and Reburial of Australian War Dead at Fromelles," unpublished conference paper, Foreign Fields: The Recovery and Commemoration of War Dead in Post-Colonial Contexts conference, September 2015, Kingston University.
39 Adjustments due to discovering errors in name spellings or assumed names were also prevalent. See WG 219/10/1 "6 August 1930," "24 May 1930," "30 April 1930," "19 May 1930," "14 February 1930," "9 September 1929," "18 August 1930," "22 April 1930."
40 For one of many examples, see WG 219/8, "17 March 1924."
41 WG 909/7, "9 May 1925."
42 WG 861/2/4, "8 January 1925."
43 WG 219/16/1, "29 October 1925."
44 WG 219/16/1, "9 November 1925," WG 909/7 "8 May 1925."
45 WG 219/2/1 Pt 2, "8 May 1924."
46 WG 1049/1 Pt 2, "16 May 1924" and "17 May 1924."
47 WG 1049/1 Pt 2, "29 April 1924."
48 WG 857/3/2 Pt 1, "30 August 1922."
49 WG 857/3/2 Pt 1, "30 August 1922."
50 WG 219/2/1 Pt 2, "8 May 1924."
51 WG 219/2/1 Pt 2, "29 July 1927" and "17 November 1926."
52 WG 219/2/1 Pt 2, "3 May 1924."
53 WG 219/2/1 Pt 2, "8 May 1924."
54 WG 857/3/2 Pt 1, "December 1930."

55 "Cemetery Details: Villers-Bretonneux Memorial," *CWGC*, http://www.cwgc.org/find-a-cemetery/cemetery/93000/VILLERS-BRETONNEUX%20MEMORIAL.
56 Ibid.
57 Robert J. Harding, "Glorious Tragedy: Newfoundland's Cultural Memory of the Attack at Beaumont Hamel, 1916–1925," *Newfoundland and Labrador Studies* 21:1 (2006), no pagination https://journals.lib.unb.ca/index.php/nflds/article/view/5884/6891.
58 Paul Gough, "Sites in the Imagination: The Beaumont Hamel Newfoundland Memorial on the Somme," *Cultural Geographies* 11 (2004), 251.
59 Gough, "Sites," 248.
60 "Cemetery Details: The South Africa (Delville Wood) National Memorial," *CWGC*, http://www.cwgc.org/find-a-cemetery/cemetery/4007351/THE%20SOUTH%20AFRICA%20(DELVILLE%20WOOD)%20NATIONAL%20MEMORIAL.
61 Ibid.
62 "Delville Wood: The Memorial," *South African Commemorative Museum Trust*, http://www.delvillewood.com/Memorial2.htm.
63 Ibid.
64 "Cemetery Details: The South Africa (Delville Wood) National Memorial," *CWGC*.
65 WG 861, "31 January 1920," WG 909/7 "Undated memo."
66 WG 909/7, "13 August 1920."
67 WG 909/7, "Undated memo."
68 WG 909/7, "20 May 1921," "29 July 1920."
69 WG 909/7, "Undated memo."
70 WG 219 Pt 2, "1 February 1922," 3.
71 SDC 45, "King Pays Homage to Canada's Dead: Tribute to 'Splendour of Their Sacrifice'," *Daily Telegraph*, 27 July 1936. Other sources estimate the crowd at 100,000–200,000 and the number of Canadians at 6,000.
72 "Canadian National Vimy Memorial: Self-Guided Tour Map," Government of Canada, 2016.
73 Laura Brandon, "History As Monument: The Sculptures on the Vimy Memorial," *Canadian War Museum*, http://www.warmuseum.ca/cwm/exhibitions/vimy/sculptures_e.shtml.
74 See Andrea Picard, "Restoring Loss At Vimy," *The Canadian Architect* 51:5 (2006), 74–77.
75 Bull and Panton, "Drafting the Vimy Charter."
76 WG 857/3/2 Pt 1, "Great Overseas Memorial."
77 WG 857/3/2 Pt 1, "National War Memorial," 1.
78 For a more detailed treatment of the circumstances surrounding Lucas' failed memorial, see Katti Williams, "Sublime Ruins: William Lucas' Project for the Australian WWI War Memorial at Villers-Bretonneux, France," *Melbourne Art Journal* 11:12 (2008–9), 65–85, and her 2017 PhD thesis from the University of Melbourne.
79 Department of Veterans' Affairs and the Office of Australian War Graves, "Australian National Memorial: Villers-Bretonneux," Brochure P1096 (October 2004), 4–5; G. Kingsley Ward and Edwin Gibson, *Courage Remembered: The Story Behind the Construction and Maintenance of the Commonwealth's Military Cemeteries and Memorials of the Wars of 1914–1918 and 1939–1945* (London: HMSO, 1995), 161.
80 The historiography on the battle of the Somme, its memory, and its lessons is much too extensive to address here. For a sense of the scale and depth of its continuing presence in British public memory, look at news articles from July 1, 2016, when 10,000 people, including royals and heads of state, gathered at Thiepval to mark the 100th anniversary of the beginning of the battle.
81 WG 219/2/1 Pt 2, "20 September 1927."
82 WG 219/2/1 Pt 2, "2 août 1927."
83 WG 219/2/1 Pt 2, "Points from Letters: The Menin Gate" (20 September 1927).
84 Lloyd's *Battlefield Tourism* is invaluable on this topic, as is Jennifer Iles' work (particularly her "Recalling the Ghosts of War: Performing Tourism on the Battlefields of the Western Front," *Text and Performance Quarterly* 26:2 (2006), 162–180). Promising new work is

also being done in this field by PhD student Simon Gregor at Wolverhampton, e.g., "Changing Spaces, Fading Landscapes: Battlefield Pilgrimage 1914–1929," unpublished conference paper, Oxford, Globalising and Localising the Great War graduate conference, March 2016.
85 Bart Ziino pioneered the term and concept "distant grief" in his book by the same name. Tanja Luckins' *Gates of Memory* also deals with this concept through specific case studies of how personal and public memory-making and bereavement manifested for Australians.
86 See the Living Memory project website at http://www.cwgc.org/about-us/cwgc-projects/living-memory.aspx.
87 Angela Clare, curator of *For King and Country: Calderdale's First World War Centenary 2014–18* (Bankfield Museum, winning exhibit 2015 Royal Historical Society Public History Prize), recorded interview by the author for MA thesis, May 2015.

# 2
# WAR MALL: CIVIC ART, MEMORY, AND WAR ON AMERICA'S NATIONAL PUBLIC SPACE

*William Thomas Allison*

Like many peoples, Americans remember wars and those who served and sacrificed in those conflicts in diverse ways. War memorials run the gamut of what Americans will place a name on, attach a plaque to, or erect a statue to. From highways to football stadiums, from buildings to parks—and even fountains within parks—Americans proudly make permanent remembrance of this or that war, a local regiment, or an individual who did a town proud through conspicuous action above and beyond the call of duty. Across the United States, organizations both public and private raise funds, design monuments, build them, then bask in emotional contentment that they have done right by those who fought and those who died for the nation, regardless of the righteousness of the cause or the outcome.

The National Mall in Washington, DC, America's "National Space," once catered solely to a narrative of great men and the ideals of the Republic for which they stood. Since the early 1980s, however, that narrative has changed. Americans decided, in part because of the nightmare of Vietnam, to build a national narrative through the creation of war memorials. Reconciling the ideals of the Republic with war and the service and deaths of hundreds of thousands of its citizens over 200 years of national existence is, to say the least, difficult. Considering the mental and emotional gymnastics required to bring divergent publics, entities, and other stakeholders together to weave a cohesive, effective national narrative through civic art, the transformation of the National Mall to a War Mall is astonishing.

Millions of Americans and people from around the world visit the memorials on the National Mall in Washington, DC. People of all ages take selfies at the Lincoln and Jefferson Memorials and some wait in long lines to see the view of the capital city from atop the Washington Monument. But why does their behavior change when walking through the National World War II Memorial or pondering the faces of the haunting figures of the Korean War Veterans Memorial? Why do they touch the names of the dead on the Vietnam Veterans Memorial, then allow their children to climb about the Three Servicemen? For a nation that did little to memorialize its wars for more than 200 years, why did the United States wait until after its worst defeat and build a memorial to honor the dead of that defeat before embarking on a war memorial-building frenzy?

Since the dedication of the Vietnam Veterans Memorial in 1982, the once war memorial-free National Mall now hosts the Korean War Memorial, the National World War II Memorial, the Women in Military Service for America Memorial (at Arlington National Cemetery), and the National Japanese American Memorial to Patriotism during World War II, as well as the yet-to-be built Black Revolutionary War Patriots Memorial and National World War I Memorial (at Pershing Park in Washington, DC). This impressive list of war memorials does not, of course, include the recent Franklin D. Roosevelt Memorial, the Martin Luther King, Jr. Memorial, the National Holocaust Memorial and Museum, or the planned Eisenhower Memorial, among other proposed monuments. What do these war memorials mean and how did they come about? What do they commemorate? What narratives do they impart to the public of a free society? Do they make good "our enormous responsibility" to the hundreds of thousands of dead from these wars?[1]

Public memorials primarily arise from the initiative of a few and serve a public end for many, be it national, state, or local; but such monuments also must answer to the many "publics" throughout the design and building process. These are without exception political. The process of war memorialization and commemoration is itself a battlefield of identity politics and competing voices, as "conflicting social groups assert conflicting memories" in the hope of establishing and then preserving a dominant memory. Commemorating war and establishing memory of war, for good or ill, is still a principal attribute of national identity, providing people as a collective and as individuals with national symbols to memorialize wars and the people who fought them. These memorials also promote a narrative of what we want, or what someone wants us, to remember about why we fought these wars.[2] In the case of the United States, memory of war is indeed a complex construct. As a nation and society that has been so much shaped by war, the memory and commemoration of conflict has likewise shaped American national identity and national myths.[3]

The study of war memory and commemoration in the past twenty years or so has attracted the attention of a wide range of scholars—historians of all flavors, geographers, artists, sociologists, among others. It is a rich field of inquiry and will continue to be so. These scholars are asking useful questions: What makes up the "texture of memory" and what is the purpose of "civic art"?[4] At their best, war memorials, or any memorial or monument for that matter, give a sense of a particular present, one that future generations of visitors should understand even if that particular present is divorced from the memorialized event. As members of that culture or society, visitors at any moment in time should be able to relate to what stands before them to enhance that emotional sense of belonging. Otherwise, memorials become objects of poorly understood curiosity, artifacts of a bygone time.

Permanent memorials are, well, permanent. Physically they do not change, but their meaning can change, evolve, or, though less likely, disappear altogether. "Grand plans," argues art historian Kirk Savage, "are transformed into actual places, and those places are in turn transformed by the people who occupy and use them."[5] As Erika Doss, from the perspective of American studies, notes further, "contemporary American memorials embody the feelings of particular publics at particular historical moments, and frame cultural narratives about self-identity and national purpose." "Memorials," Doss continues, "embody the histories and feelings that respective Americans choose to remember at particular moments." Our war memorials, like other national places of commemoration, shape an understanding of our past, of how we think of ourselves as citizens and identify as Americans.[6]

That identity is what makes American nationalism, the foundation of which is the willingness of citizens to kill and die for the nation. Most Americans do not consider this concept in their day-to-day lives, but the occasional visit to a war memorial elicits collective grief for and remembrance of those who sacrificed and who served, thus reinforcing the values of the nation. To paraphrase sociologist Jeffrey Olick, memories make a nation, but a nation must have memories.[7]

War memorials play a tremendous role in this process and can be manipulated to suit the political or social needs of the moment (think of Abraham Lincoln's address at the dedication of the national cemetery at Gettysburg). Such manipulation need not be overt; subtle messaging can invent a past for a nation. The trick is how those memories are formed in relation to war. War memorials must to some degree hide the trauma of war, lest citizens be unintentionally convinced that fighting and dying for the nation is not worth the sacrifice. Thus, according to political scientist Jenny Edkins, the nation rewrites the trauma for which it was responsible into a "linear narrative of national heroism."[8] Minimize the trauma, maximize heroism and sacrifice; thus is born a national story that can best be told by a memorial. Occasionally, however, focusing on the trauma spotlights the victims—the dead—to obscure the event. The relationship between trauma and national memory can work both ways.[9] As cultural historian Kristin Ann Hass noted, because of the important role played by war memorials, "the stakes in the memorial process could, in fact, hardly be higher."[10]

The war memorials on the National Mall in Washington, DC, then, play a central role in this story of nation and memory, trauma and heroism. Is it not intriguing, if not telling, that more than 60 years removed from arguably America's greatest triumphal moment, the zenith of the mythological Greatest Generation, the United States as a nation finally formally commemorated World War II? A memorial for veterans of the Korean War, a very non-triumphal moment, was dedicated 42 years after the fact in 1995, and, irony of ironies, the Vietnam Veterans Memorial opened in 1982, less than a decade after the end of what arguably was the most disastrous war ever undertaken by the United States. And only the hundredth anniversary of World War I spurred public and private action to perhaps finally convert Washington's Pershing Square into a national World War I memorial.

Washington, DC, was designed to have monuments, lots of them. Over the course of the late nineteenth and early twentieth centuries, the American capital became home to one of the more remarkable neoclassical architecture gardens in the world. Beginning with his appointment in 1791 to design a "federal city" to serve as the seat of the new national government, engineer Pierre Charles L'Enfant envisioned the national capital as a classical city, true to antiquity, complete with a forum or national public space—what is now the National Mall and its surrounding buildings—to commemorate "great American leaders and their triumphal ideals about democracy."[11] L'Enfant's plan, however, actually called for an eighteenth-century-styled park, complete with trees, gardens, paths, fountains, and, yes, monuments in the European tradition. This plan fell by the wayside. Part of the problem was practical—the young nation had neither the money nor the time to invest in such a grand scheme. Part of the problem, too, was that the site chosen for the new capital was dismal, mosquito-ridden swampland butting against the flood plain of the Potomac River.

L'Enfant's vision of a statue-laden park also violated the republican ideals of the new nation. Statues fit the needs of kings, not the virtuous leaders of a free republic. The European traditions of commemoration, especially monuments and other pageantry, brought skepticism among Americans as "mere gestures of a powerful few rather than spontaneous outpourings of popular feeling."[12] After all, had not the patriots toppled statues of King George III?[13] The young republic celebrated the present rather than glorifying its past, in keeping with Enlightenment ideas that so greatly influenced the founding of the nation. Great Americans could be celebrated with words rather than ostentatious statuary. As Savage put it, "True memory lay not in a head of dead stones but in the hearts and minds of the people; no monument could substitute for living social memory, nourished by liberty and education." Having rejected monarchy, steeped in Puritanism's rejection of idolatry and in the throes of Enlightenment prose rather than the physical ruins of ancient Greece and Rome, the American political elite believed that "words always outlived the grandest handiworks of sculpture and architecture."[14]

These republican attitudes toward commemoration, for example, came into question as Congress debated how to memorialize George Washington in the early 1800s. How to honor the great man? More than 80 years later Congress finally did so in dedicating the now familiar Washington Monument. We *know* it is the Washington Monument, though nowhere on the 555-foot-tall obelisk does it indicate that the structure, considered Freudian by more imaginative critics, is such. By 1885, Americans had overcome their aversion to European-styled monuments and, in fact, had embraced permanent memorials in the aftermath of the Civil War. The Washington Monument fit with what became the style of the capital city. The Washington Monument, the Capitol building, and the Executive Mansion reflected the neoclassical architecture of the ancient world—Egyptians, Greeks, and Romans—so prominent in the eighteenth and nineteenth centuries, and in fact would influence federal architecture in the District of Columbia well into the twentieth century.[15]

Over the course of the nineteenth century, L'Enfant's vision for the capital city went from impractical to largely realized, even if his actual plan receded into history. Largely neglected during the first half of the 1800s, the envisioned park remained overgrown, a bit wild, and, according to Savage, "occasionally traversed by chained gangs of slaves being sold downriver—a palpable blot on the 'empire of liberty' L'Enfant's plan was supposed to represent." Even before the Civil War, however, city planners began transforming the District of Columbia. The new rotunda for the Capitol was the most visible and symbolic feature, but the swampy parkland also began to look more like a park. Instead of L'Enfant's equestrian statue of George Washington, the great obelisk of the Washington Monument connected to the Capitol, via an expansive park rather than the grand avenue of L'Enfant's original plan—which, to be clear, is not what one sees today as the National Mall.

Thus, according to Savage, the capital city did not neglect or forget L'Enfant's plan, but rather "compromised and altered" it in "various ways." While planners at the end of the nineteenth century resurrected L'Enfant as a city-designing genius (now that, according to them, the city had finally taken his image), Savage is right to argue that, as the twentieth century dawned, modernism and order overtook the previously haphazard approach to placing statues, parks, and other features throughout the city. "Public space" overtook "public grounds." New concepts would guide the development of what would become the National Mall.[16]

Neoclassical style even became the accepted form for monuments around the country and American memorials abroad. For decades, obelisks in particular were popular for their simplicity and frugality, if not their republicanism. There is, for example, an obelisk in Mexico City, erected in 1848, in the American cemetery; an obelisk marks the site of the 1876 Battle of the Little Big Horn; there is an obelisk at the site of the Battle of the Cowpens, erected in 1932, to honor the American forces victorious over the British in this pivotal Revolutionary War battle. Obelisks and columns erected in the nineteenth through early twentieth centuries could and still can be found just about anywhere. The American Battle Monuments Commission, formed in 1923 to coordinate American cemeteries and memorials in the aftermath of World War I, also stayed true to this style in its design of overseas cemeteries for American dead from both world wars. Commemoration of the heroes of the Union army from the Civil War caused a boom in statuary throughout Washington, DC. Statuary, considered so gauche during the Early Republic, gained enormous popularity and was in keeping with neoclassical style—anyone who has been to Gettysburg can attest to the prominence of what modernist public art critics called "the turd on a stick."[17]

On the National Mall, the Washington Monument, along with the Lincoln and Jefferson Memorials—dedicated in 1922 and 1943 respectively—stayed true to the concept of honoring great men of democracy and the ideals they purportedly cherished. No national war memorials—not 1812, not the Mexican War, nor the War with Spain or the Great War—dotted the Mall's landscape. According to art historian Harriet Senie, the Washington Monument and the Lincoln Memorial served as "lynchpins of national identity," that is, a white identity that demanded a specific narrative of the American experience. Honoring Washington also honored the Founding. Memorializing Lincoln honored the restoration of the Union after the horrific Civil War. Washington as reluctant Cincinnatus fit the national narrative of selfless service to the nation. The Egyptian-inspired obelisk reflected nothing "heroic" nor anything like the gaudy artistic depictions of Washington ascending to heaven such as the Apotheosis of Washington depicted in the rotunda of the Capitol, completed in 1865. The Lincoln Memorial portrays Lincoln as the Savior of the Union, but tellingly says little of Lincoln as the Great Emancipator. With the addition of the Jefferson Memorial, the National Mall had the perfect trifecta of sites for citizen pilgrimage to reflect on the core ideals of the Republic.[18]

As Washington, DC, grew and more initiatives came forth to establish this or that memorial, monument, or park, a variety of entities attempted to control or bring order to what was already established and the inevitable growth to follow. Before 1910, no commissions or boards existed to approve statues or the like; thus, in part, the lack of a cohesive plan for the city. Statues, for example, tended to be installed by political organizations, civic clubs, or veterans' groups.

Established in 1901, the Senate Park Commission first proposed the Mall as a cohesive spatial "system" heavily influenced by the City Beautiful Movement of the 1890s and early 1900s. This "system" involved tearing down entire neighborhoods and rooting up old trees and gardens that locals had come to enjoy in order to "eliminate distracting details on the ground and open up the city fabric to sweeping expanses of space" in the interest of replacing what had become fiercely local with something grandly national, à la L'Enfant. Now, new memorials making up a "monumental core" would be placed in accordance with spatial considerations so that neoclassical buildings, plazas, and grand monuments "fit" among open spaces. The Senate Park Commission's bold 1902 plan—also known as the McMillan Plan, for the Commission's chairman Senator James McMillan of Michigan—became a major guiding force in city planning for the District of Columbia. Not surprisingly, the Commission included famed landscape architect Frederick Law Olmsted, who proposed a series of gardens surrounding the Washington Monument and what would soon become formally known as the National Mall.[19]

Much had changed, however, by the 1930s, when land had been cleared and the Potomac dredged in accordance with the Commission's 1902 plan. By then, the automobile had replaced the horse—to risk understatement—forcing a reconsideration of walking paths for actual streets. The National Mall that is so familiar today was taking shape. Additionally, more organizations nosed their way into the ad hoc memorial approval process. In 1910, President William Howard Taft abolished the Senate Park Commission, asking Congress to replace it with the permanent Commission of Fine Arts to review any new federal construction in the District of Columbia.[20] In 1924, Congress also established the National Capital Park Commission, known today as the National Capital Planning Commission, as the planning authority for all federally owned buildings and land in and around the District of Columbia. To convolute agency oversight even further, in 1986 Congress established the National Capital Memorial Advisory Commission (NCMAC) to directly review and approve design and sites for memorials on federal property in and around Washington, DC.

Incredibly, the McMillan Plan continues to serve as a sort of doctrine to guide capital development.[21] Add to this menagerie of commissions other stakeholders, such as the National Park Service, the Architect of the Capitol, and other government and non-government agencies, all rife with vague mandates and often conflicting motives. These entities would play critical, if not controversial, roles in the design, placement, and construction of the war memorials on the National Mall. Compromise, often reluctantly, would by necessity be their informal motto.

Before these agencies could muddy the waters too much, the Marine Corps Memorial—popularly known as the Iwo Jima Memorial, replicating the immensely popular but staged Joe Rosenthal photograph of Marines raising the flag atop Mount Suribachi—controversially broke with the McMillan Plan. Designed by sculptor Felix DeWeldon, a Navy veteran of World War II, the initial bronze structure was placed on Constitution Avenue in Washington in 1945. The Commission of Fine Arts and the National Sculpture Society severely criticized the piece for its break with neoclassical memorial tradition and called the government to task for not holding an open competition for a more appropriate, if not modern, scheme. Congress and the Marine Corps stood firm on the design (veterans liked it and actually paid for it; non-establishment artists also liked it), but did agree to place the larger permanent rendition in its present location in Arlington National Cemetery in 1954.[22] The significance is that it was not allowed a permanent place on the National Mall.

Whether or not the real story behind the Iwo Jima image measures against the propaganda, as a people Americans nevertheless wanted to nostalgically honor the implied heroism and sacrifice which the image invoked. It gave a personal face to the memorial that the collective could experience, mythologizing a memory that celebrated victory and sacrifice, and thus served national identity.[23] Historian Kurt Piehler notes that the controversy surrounding the Iwo Jima Memorial signaled that the classical approach to public memorial had "increasingly fallen out of favor, both in artistic circles and among various elites in American society." Could neoclassical public art capture the horrors and sacrifices of modern war, even when victorious? Many increasingly thought not.

Modernism may have had an influence here as well. Modernist architects and artists had criticized classical monument-building in the 1930s, notably objecting to John Russell Pope's design for the Jefferson Memorial. Dedicated in 1943, the Jefferson Memorial was the last openly classical monument built in Washington for several decades. As a movement, modernism had an anti-monumental bent, and as a visual philosophy it took more interest in bringing attention to society's ills through practical design than in commemorating triumphal achievements, military or otherwise.[24]

Modernist criticism and a general weariness of the neoclassical may explain in part why no memorial was built immediately after World War II to celebrate the greatest national undertaking in American history; so, too, may the tension-filled years of the Cold War. According to Michael F. Lewis, the complex and ambiguous events of the early Cold War "made the very idea of a celebratory national consensus seem laughable, let alone the idea of building monuments to express it."[25] Korea's end was ambiguous, while Vietnam left the nation deeply divided. Building a triumphant World War II memorial amid these events was not plausible. But as these events and years passed, nostalgia for triumphal victory and a desire to honor soldiers from a clearly honorable war, along with the approaching triumph of democracy over Soviet communism in the Cold War, opened a window for a brief return to the neoclassical style of old.

Ironically, before that happened, a monument to veterans of America's worst war and its only war defeat was built on the National Mall, which then made a World War II memorial possible. The problems involved in a Vietnam memorial were immense and for the United States unprecedented—how could such a divisive war defeat be commemorated? What would be the purpose of such a memorial?[26]

The process of a permanent memorial to honor those who served in Vietnam, which culminated in Maya Lin's extraordinary design, began in 1978. An inconspicuous plaque with an "indirect and muted" inscription that at first did not even mention Vietnam and a tomb for an unknown soldier were established in Arlington National Cemetery in 1978 and 1984, respectively. Also in 1978, Vietnam-era congressmen established Vietnam Veterans Week to highlight the needs of veterans as well as to honor them, despite, as several of the congressmen noted, continued deep divisions over American involvement in the war. In 1979, veterans of the war, under the leadership of veteran Jan Scruggs, took matters into their own hands to establish a permanent memorial. Scruggs, twice wounded during his tour in South Vietnam in 1969 and suffering from post-traumatic stress disorder, claimed that seeing the 1978 Michael Cimino film *The Deer Hunter* inspired the idea for a memorial listing all the names of the American dead in the Vietnam War. Scruggs proposed the idea to Vietnam Veterans Week planners, then, failing to get any traction, established the Vietnam Veterans Memorial Fund in 1979 on his own initiative. After a slow start, Scruggs got unexpected fundraising momentum from a couple of CBS News stories on his effort, and, by 1981, he had raised several million dollars.[27]

In 1980, Congress approved a site for the structure, near Constitution Gardens on the National Mall. The Vietnam Veterans Memorial Fund lobbied hard to locate the memorial in Constitution Gardens, a wooded area bordered by Constitution Avenue, the Reflecting Pool, the Lincoln Memorial, and the Washington Monument, which until the early 1970s housed several World War I-era government buildings. Established in 1976 as part of the Bicentennial celebrations, Constitution Gardens provided a symbolic location for the controversial memorial. With the Washington Monument to the east and the Lincoln Memorial to the west, the Vietnam Veterans Memorial would sit between two of the most iconic and symbolic structures in the United States, one representing the founding of the nation, the other representing its survival. To place a memorial to the 58,000 Americans who perished in this divisive conflict within sight of Washington's and Lincoln's places of national honor spoke volumes about this attempt to reconcile the Vietnam nightmare with the national narrative.[28]

Stipulating only that the memorial had to list the names of the dead and missing, have no political message, and be "reflective and contemplative in nature," the Commission of Fine Arts opened its design competition in 1981. After intense consideration of over 1,400 submissions, the Commission's selection committee made its choice—entry number 1026. A 21-year-old Yale architecture student of Asian descent, Maya Lin, won with a design that would spark intense controversy, but which once built would become one of the most visited sites on the National Mall and be praised for faultlessly capturing the conflicted emotions around the Vietnam War. Thus, according to Savage, "the nation's first therapeutic memorial was born—a memorial made expressly to heal a collective psychological injury," caused by the trauma of Vietnam.[29]

Lin considered her design an "anti-monument," deliberately counter to the traditional neoclassical structures of commemoration present on the National Mall and throughout the District of Columbia. Heavily influenced by a class on funerary architecture at Yale, Lin was drawn to memorials that represented the dead and missing that served as a cemetery *in absentia*. Edward Lutyens's *Memorial to the Missing of the Somme* at Thiepval, France inspired Lin's concept of a processional or journey of mourning. At Thiepval, visitors approach a grand central arch from a field of cropped grass, then enter the archway, wherein the 72,000 names of the Somme missing are engraved. Through the arch is the cemetery. Missing and dead are brought together. Significantly for Lin, Lutyens placed a massive black stone slab in the center floor under the arch.

Lin also drew from sculpture from earthwork and embedded structures. Claes Oldenburg's 1967 temporary work of earthen art in New York City's Central Park, titled *Placid Civic Moment*, consisted of a hole dug, left empty, then refilled, much like a grave *sans* corpse. Richard Serra, whom Lin knew at Yale, used objects protruding from the earth, such as the triangulated steel plates of his 1971 work *Stepped Elevation* in St. Louis. For Lin, understanding death was just as important as understanding war. These works of art and design had an enormous impact on her visual and emotional goals for the Vietnam Veterans Memorial.[30]

These works guided Lin toward a design that forced the visitor to journey into the earth, into a violent opening that "in time would heal." From these influences, Lin derived her stark black wall, dug into the earth, with the two 246-foot flanks of the wall coming together as a wide V at just over 125 degrees. Lin chose a quiet area toward the western end of Constitution Gardens to locate the memorial, intending it to be a place of introspection and solitude, where one would not be distracted by the hustle and bustle of the main thoroughfares of the National Mall. Lin's Lutyens-like passage of remembrance would take visitors down the one flank, deeper into the earth, where an apex more than ten feet deep made the enormity of the cost of Vietnam tragically apparent. Each panel on the flanks listed names, nothing more. From that depth, the Vietnam Veterans Memorial would allow the visitor to egress back—to use Vietnam slang—to "The World."[31]

Many veterans' groups lashed out at the design, claiming the stark black granite panels relegated their service to a scarred gouge in the ground—"a black gash of shame." The color raised objections: Many thought it represented shame or evil, still others assumed it signified some racial overtone. Lin rejected white marble for both aesthetic and symbolic reasons. Black granite would provide better reflection and, for Lin, the color represented mourning, not shame or evil. Instead of honoring the victims of a divisive war, critics claimed the design buried Vietnam out of sight and thus out of mind, to *dis*honor the sacrifice of Vietnam's living and dead. Some shouted out in public hearings that they did not want "their" memorial designed by a "gook." Feminist critics such as Elizabeth Hess criticized the design as misogynistic, claiming it represented an open vagina awaiting the Washington Monument's colossal phallus. Lin's design had no engraved words to justify the loss or at least explain why these soldiers died in Southeast Asia. A black wall featuring only names, critics cried, only made Vietnam worse—not even an American flag was included in the original design.[32]

To bring about consensus, the Commission of Fine Arts altered Lin's design. In 1982, a compromise between the Vietnam Veterans Memorial Fund and the Commission of Fine Arts included sculpture and a flagpole. An American flag, which many critics wanted at the apex of the Vietnam Veterans Memorial, was ultimately erected near the soldiers' sculpture, placed perfectly so that visitors can see the Stars and Stripes reflect in the polished black granite panels. The absence of the American flag had indeed been a sore point for many critics. Including it gave patriotic legitimacy both to those who served and died and to the cause for which the nation sent them to fight. An inscription at its base affirmed the nation and its values, and confessed that those who served did so under "difficult circumstances."[33]

Scruggs and the Vietnam Veterans Memorial Fund had originally rejected any statuary as unnecessary—no one figure could represent all service members for the Vietnam War and by 1980 most Americans already had a version of the stereotypical Vietnam soldier firmly embedded in their minds via film and television, so their reasoning went. Sculpted by Frederick Hart, a bronze statue group called the Three Servicemen depicting three soldiers of racial and ethnic variation returning from a patrol, facing the names of their dead comrades on the Vietnam Veterans Memorial, answered critics who wanted the memorial to look more "like a war memorial." Hart saw the Vietnam Veterans Memorial as an ocean or sea, representing sacrifice; his three figures on the shore gazed out at a vast ocean of lost humanity. Others interpreted the three soldiers as meeting their own fate in joining the dead listed on the panels. The three figures work; they and the paneled wall neither take nor distract from each other. Rather, they coexist and connect the living and the dead.[34]

Once Hart's Three Servicemen had been erected, a movement grew to honor the service of women in the war. Diane Carlson Evans, who served as an Army nurse in Vietnam, and others appreciated that the eight women listed on the Vietnam Veterans Memorial were permanently joined with the thousands of men who died in Vietnam, but now they desired the same physical representation that soldiers had in Hart's sculpture. In 1984, Evans and the Vietnam Women's Memorial Project commissioned sculpture artist Roger M. Brodin to model a single figure of a nurse. The Commission on Fine Arts rejected Brodin's model, however, over concerns that the Vietnam Veterans Memorial complex was getting crowded and the National Mall itself was in danger of being overrun by the numerous memorial proposals spurred by the unanticipated success of Lin's memorial.

But, as was often the case, some beneficial national media attention in the form of CBS's *60 Minutes* and the support of numerous veterans' organizations energized interest. In 1988, Congress authorized the building of the Vietnam Women's Memorial, and the next year it approved a site in Constitution Gardens. After an open design competition, the selection committee chose a cluster of bronze figures by artist Glenna Goodacre. Using the *Pietà* as a framework, Goodacre's sculpture in the round has four figures—three nurses, titled "Caring," "Hope," and "Despair," respectively—surrounding a wounded soldier. It is at once powerful, moving, and provocative. The sculpture does not directly connect to the Vietnam Veterans Memorial as Hart's Three Servicemen does, but that was not the intent of either Goodacre or the Vietnam Women's Memorial Project. Dedicated in 1993, the Vietnam Women's Memorial is less visited than the Three Servicemen or the Vietnam Veterans Memorial. Moreover, both sculptures elicit different responses than are normally seen at the Vietnam Veterans Memorial. Visitors pose for photographs in front of the statues; there is little solemnity, unlike the hushed tones heard at the Vietnam Veterans Memorial, which is treated as hallowed ground.[35]

Even naming the memorial took some negotiating. Ultimately Lin's wall became the "Vietnam Veterans Memorial" rather than the "Vietnam War Memorial." Lin's work certainly rejected the classical for the modern, and the unexpectedly quick and dramatic popularity of the memorial, dedicated in 1982, all but erased the memory of the contentious design process.[36] But the lasting effect of the Vietnam Veterans Memorial lay in the narrative it established and the memory it imposed. Lin wanted visitors to be moved, but even she did not anticipate the extent of the emotional reaction to the Vietnam Veterans Memorial. Visitors quickly treated the memorial as a cemetery, as sacred ground on the National Mall, the nation's public space. "Silence" and "respect" characterize implicit group behavior as visitors approach the Vietnam Veterans Memorial. They behave, as Senie puts it, "reverentially, as if they were at a cemetery, largely because the presence of bodies is implied by the list of names" on the polished black panels.

To the surprise of many, like visitors to a grave, family members, friends, and strangers left items of remembrance—everything from toys to cans of beer—at the base of the panels. The National Park Service, which administers the Vietnam Veterans Memorial, began collecting the objects early on and in 1984 established the Vietnam Veterans Memorial Collection. Since that time, well over 100,000 objects have been cataloged. The Vietnam Veterans Memorial also became a gathering place for veterans, especially for reunions. Family-held mourning rituals are common sights. Rubbing of names became a phenomenon in and of itself. Images of a veteran or family member physically touching the name of a comrade or loved one are now ubiquitous but remain moving nonetheless.[37]

The success of the Vietnam Veterans Memorial unleashed an "unprecedented monument building mood" that continues now, more than three decades later. What genie had Lin unintentionally let out of the bottle? To use Doss's phrase, "memorial mania" grabbed the American public by the throat, or rather the heart, resulting in hundreds of monuments, many permanent but still many more temporary, for an amazing array of subjects. According to Doss, the rash of memorial-building represented "heightened anxieties about who and what should be remembered in America." The Vietnam Veterans Memorial opened the spigot of guilt, ignominy, and grief that had always been deeply present in the American national psyche but that Vietnam had brought perilously close to the surface. This, combined with the rise of identity politics and the new "culture wars" of the 1980s, gave diverse voices cause to "harness those anxieties and control particular narratives about the nation and its publics." "Memorial mania" catered to "individual memories and personal grievances," to "trauma" of all kinds, and to often self-serving agendas across the social and political spectrum. Doss best describes its influences: "Driven by heated struggles over self-definition, national purpose, and the politics of representation, memorial mania is especially shaped by the affective conditions of public life in America today; by the fevered pitch of public feelings such as grief, gratitude, fear, shame, and anger."[38]

"Memorial mania" infected the National Mall, as decades-old dormant projects suddenly found new life and new demands for memorials flooded each congressional session. A memorial for Franklin Roosevelt that had been authorized in 1959 and originally designed in the 1970s was finally built and opened in 1997. The Martin Luther King, Jr. Memorial (dedicated in 2011), one to Dwight Eisenhower (approved in 2015), and the United States Holocaust Memorial Museum (opened in 1993), for example, also quickly gained momentum.

The Korean War Veterans Memorial was the next war memorial established on the National Mall. Intended to recognize, in a modest manner, service in the Korean War—the first full-blown Cold War conflict—which ended in stalemate in 1953, Congress authorized the Korean War Veterans Memorial in 1988. The controversial project was dedicated in 1995 after a lengthy design process involving the American Battlefield Monuments Commission, the Commission of Fine Arts, the Korean War Memorial Advisory Board, and several other stakeholders. Known as the "Forgotten War," the Korean War is perhaps the least known and understood American conflict of the twentieth century. The sense of irony was palpable. Many agreed with the "Remember the Forgotten War" slogans supporting the memorial, but few were interested in actually remembering the details of the war.[39]

Located in Ash Woods near the Lincoln Memorial, the Korean War Veterans Memorial is directly connected to the Vietnam Veterans Memorial in design as well as line of sight, being separated only by the Reflecting Pool. It contains three disparate design elements: the Field of Service, the Mural Wall, and the Pool of Remembrance. Each on its own is a striking work of art. Combined, however, they offer a muddled message that is ironically appropriate for a war about which many Americans have only muddled awareness.

The Field of Service involves several racially diverse steel figures, representing various services and jobs of war. They are arrayed upon a triangular field, as if walking toward some unknown objective. Their faces are partially obscured; their look is deeply haunting. Running parallel to the Field of Service, the Mural Wall is akin to the Vietnam Veterans Memorial, except instead of names, images of photographs are engraved into the polished stone, exposing some detail up close, but ever so faintly revealing Korean mountains at a distance. The images do not appear to have any cohesion other than showing individuals and scenes from the conflict—the day-to-day mundane activities of war. The Pool of Remembrance sits beyond the Field of Service, behind a flagpole. An inscription reads "Freedom is Not Free," suggesting that the war was "fought for freedom, that a price was paid, and that is what needs to be remembered."[40]

Debates raged among stakeholders as to design, purpose, and control. The original design from a team of architects from Penn State University ended up in court as the various parties failed to reach consensus on the team's proposal and who "owned" it. The architectural firm of Cooper-Lecky then took over design development, while the American Battlefield Monuments Commission and the Korean War Veterans Memorial Advisory Board continued to battle the Commission of Fine Arts over major elements as well as minor details. The Field of Service, for example, was extremely contentious. The Commission of Fine Arts wanted to eliminate it from the design, while the Korean War Veterans Advisory Board wanted it to remain. The level of racial recognition among the nineteen steel figures even caused consternation among stakeholders. The bickering became indicative of the pitfalls and complexities of building a memorial on the National Mall.[41]

The timing of the Korean War Veterans Memorial raises questions, chiefly: Why was this memorial not more about the triumph in the recently won Cold War? Why not celebrate that tremendous national, indeed international, decades-long undertaking? Rather than place the sacrifice and service in the context of the Cold War, the main engraving of the memorial asks only that Americans "honor its sons and daughters who answered their country's call to defend a country they did not know and a people they had never met." True enough, but this reinforces a narrative of idealism at the expense of the realism that actually determined American vital interests in Korea and the Cold War. It is as if the memorial wants blind honor and remembrance at the expense of asking any questions, especially "why."[42]

The irony of the Korean War Veterans Memorial lies in its original intent. The Korean War Veterans Advisory Board wanted a simple memorial that reflected what, in their memory, was a simpler time. This nostalgia, like most nostalgia, could not have been more misplaced. The early Cold War years were among the most complex, dangerous, and uncertain times in not only American history, but world history. To honor "blind devotion" of soldiers who, in American national memory, knew little about who, what, where, and why they were fighting does a disservice to those who served and those who sent them into harm's way. Another principal purpose of the memorial was to restore the nation's faith in military service—a hard sell after Vietnam, but one that was recovering through the success of the All-Volunteer Force by the early 1990s. The fights over the Korean War Veterans Memorial were about depicting trauma versus heroism in a war most have forgotten.[43]

While the Korean War Veterans Memorial was being debated, compromised, and actually built, a memorial to the war that would restore the Greatest Generation and its affiliated mythology to the forefront of American memory was in its developmental stages. Following initial proposals in the late 1980s, Congress authorized the creation of a national World War II memorial in 1993. Despite congressional authorization to manage the project, the American Battle Monuments Commission quickly lost control of the development to the Commission of Fine Arts and its headstrong chairman, J. Carter Brown. Brown had been instrumental in preserving Maya Lin's basic concept for the Vietnam Veterans Memorial in 1982 and was known by many as the "Master of the Mall." At his behest, the original site near Constitution Gardens chosen in 1995 was rejected for a more radical location at the foot of the Reflecting Pool, a location that was not even considered by the National Park Service or the National Capitol Planning Commission. The Commission of Fine Arts approved the Reflecting Pool location, despite lacking the required historical, cultural, and environmental impact statements that had been completed on the other sites. The National Capital Planning Commission gave its formal nod to the site literally just hours later. As the American Battle Monuments Commission moved forward with its design plans, the National Coalition to Save Our Mall moved forward with a lawsuit to stop the memorial, charging that standard procedures had not been followed. More importantly, the National Coalition to Save Our Mall feared the memorial site would destroy the Senate Park Commission's intended vistas of the National Mall by driving "a wedge between the Washington Monument and Lincoln Memorial, breaking the connection between the nation's two most prominent symbols of democracy."[44] These concerns could not have been more correct.

The design itself sparked as much controversy as the site. In 1998, Freidrich St. Florian, an architect from the Rhode Island School of Design, won the open competition, which was judged by the Commission of Fine Arts and the National Capital Planning Commission. St. Florian's design recalled pre-World War II neoclassical monument-building, complete with triumphal arches and pillars. It fit exactly the tradition of the American Battle Monuments Commission, but St. Florian also wanted to emphasize the tremendous cost of the war. His original design, for example, included wide earthen berms on either side of the memorial, evoking a feel similar to that of the Vietnam Veterans Memorial.[45]

Reviewing agencies, notably the Commission of Fine Arts, wanted to downplay the trauma of World War II and, quite naturally for the national narrative, play up the unifying heroism of the war. Ultimately, the only indication of the scale of sacrifice is the 4,000 gold stars representing the 400,000 American dead. The stars are obscured, if not hidden, as if to deny the cost and ignore the trauma. Critics even compared the design to the work of Albert Speer for its overt triumphal nationalism that celebrated the national over the personal. Supporters wanted exactly that: a monument that collectively said "we won the war!" After several failed lawsuits, requests for injunctions, and numerous tedious but probably necessary public hearings, the National World War II Memorial was finally completed and dedicated with great ceremony and fanfare on May 29, 2004. Brown got what he wanted, but the result was a massive war memorial that overwhelmed the central core of the National Mall.[46]

Despite the troubling Greatest Generation mythology that pervades American memory, the National World War II Memorial delivers an appropriately unifying national narrative of both the event and the moment of dedication. The scene oozes collective triumphalism. It is not, as noted by Savage, a place for "reflection and reckoning."[47] Moreover, it looks as though it could have been built *before* the war by Franklin Roosevelt's Works Progress Administration. For want of a better word, it "fits." The Korean War Veterans Memorial is less collective, more personal, though it seems visitors are not exactly sure how to react to it, which is appropriate as the American public remains uncertain about the Korean War's place in the nation's memory. The design is a grand example of what can result when trying to please everyone who wants a say in what that memory should be. The Vietnam Veterans Memorial is overtly personal, almost overwhelmingly so, but brilliantly offers a collective feeling of sorrow and apology while nationally honoring the individual, without political statement—an impossible task achieved. Lin's cemetery on the National Mall worked. It is a place that gives the visitor limited reactive options: to mourn and to honor.

War memorials are meant to offer some sort of permanent reminder of war, of collective and individual sacrifice, and of a conflict's role in shaping national identity. The problem is that their desired permanence cannot be. While their physical structure may remain unaltered, society changes around them. So too does historical interpretation of the past, which may enhance a memorial's meaning or degrade it. Events may overtake the importance of a memorial and the war it commemorates; thus the meaning of the monument diminishes.[48]

Increasingly, it seems that war memorials will have to offer widely different messages to satisfy the memory needs of different constituencies. Yet achieving this consensus is difficult. While democratic on the one hand, this memorial pluralism can overshadow "authentic remembrance." Such memorials are more likely to sustain or enhance what a society wants, and even does not want, to remember at a given time.[49] Ultimately, those who establish memorials cannot know what their monuments will come to mean to future publics. Maya Lin's crystal ball could not have anticipated what her Vietnam Veterans Memorial would come to mean to the nation, just as those who created the Lincoln Memorial could not foresee the amazing events that occurred with large Lincoln sitting behind in witness. In finally honoring the World War II generation, at the time of its construction and dedication, Americans had to ask whether the National World War II Memorial was anything more than "grateful remembering, more than a tribute to beliefs that we are no longer confident that we share."[50] Americans have questioned those beliefs since Vietnam, even more so since the Iraq/Afghanistan Wars. Those values, however, may now have come to be accepted and fully meaningful again, which will give the World War II Memorial a different look for some future generation. For now, we cannot tell, but we can hope. Any memorial, war memorials on the National Mall included, will mean different things to different people at different times.

The historian Jay Winter writes that "historical remembrance is a process which occurs in space and time."[51] Memory, or, to use Winter's preferred term, "remembrance," is key to promoting distinctive national narratives in a time when identity politics govern national conversations. With so many entities competing for and demanding access to a voice in those conversations, bringing together these voices to agree upon a unifying narrative to commemorate, remember, and honor those who fought and died in a war is iffy at best. Witness the recent debates over the World War I Centennial Commission's chosen design for the National World War I Memorial to be sited at a revamped Pershing Square. Identity politics and memorial are a difficult mix, especially on a National Mall that Congress in 2003 declared "a completed work of civic art."[52]

With that said, how will the United States commemorate the Iraq and Afghanistan Wars? What will be depicted? Soldiers in an armored vehicle; some attempt to honor "coalition" partners; and, with the high rates of PTSD among veterans, a veteran in civilian clothes, sitting with *her* head in *her* hands? Who will decide? We will soon find out, as a memorial for these recent conflicts is in the works—before the conflicts have actually ended. A possible site on the Ellipse in front of the White House has been selected by the National Iraq War Memorial Council, which has also selected a design from an open competition. Video screens of varying size will show soldiers in all walks of life. It is interesting that the National Iraq War Memorial Council chose a site directly in front of the White House—no political statement there, surely. Despite a congressional mandate that ten years must have passed since the end of a conflict before a war memorial can be considered, we seem in such haste now to commemorate, so much have we fully succumbed to Doss's "memorial mania."[53] Our War Mall awaits more memorials. Let the controversies over design and the shaping of the memory continue.

## Notes

1. Kristin Ann Hass, *Sacrificing Soldiers on the National Mall* (Berkeley: University of California Press, 2013), 1–2.
2. Robert D. Benford, "Whose War Memories Shall Be Preserved?" *Peace Review* 8:2 (1996), 189–195.
3. G. Kurt Piehler, *Remembering War the American Way* (Washington, DC: Smithsonian Institution Press, 1995), 2–3.
4. Timothy G. Ashplant, Graham Dawson, and Michael Roper, eds. *The Politics of War Memory and Commemoration* (New York: Routledge, 2000), 5–6; Martin Evans and Ken Lunn, eds. *Memory and War in the Twentieth Century* (New York: Berg, 1997), xvi–xviii; Sarah J. Purcell, "War, Memory, and National Identity in the Twentieth Century," *National Identities* 2:2 (2000), 187–195.
5. Kirk Savage, *Monument Wars: Washington, DC, the National Mall, and the Transformation of the Memorial Landscape* (Berkeley: University of California Press, 2009), 10–11.
6. Erika Doss, *Memorial Mania: Public Feeling in America* (Chicago: University of Chicago Press, 2010), 59–60.
7. Jeffrey Olick, ed. *States of Memory: Continuities, Conflicts, and Transformations in National Retrospection* (Durham: Duke University Press, 2003), 3.
8. Jenny Edkins, *Trauma and the Memory of Politics* (Cambridge, UK: Cambridge University Press, 2003), 16–19.
9. Harriet F. Senie, *Memorials to Shattered Myths: Vietnam to 9/11* (Oxford: Oxford University Press, 2016), 10.
10. Hass, *Sacrificing Soldiers*, 3–5.
11. Ibid., 1.

12 Savage, *Monument Wars*, 1.
13 And did not American forces help Iraqis topple statues of Saddam Hussein in 2003?
14 Savage, *Monument Wars*, 1.
15 Senie, *Memorials to Shattered Myths*, 1.
16 Savage, *Monument Wars*, 12–15.
17 Michael F. Lewis, "Mumbling Monuments," *Commentary* (2001), 50–54.
18 Senie, *Memorials to Shattered Myths*, 2; Savage, *Monument Wars*, 107–144. See also Barry Schwartz, *George Washington: The Making of an American Symbol* (Ithaca: Cornel University Press, 1990).
19 Savage, *Monument Wars*, 12–18; Jon A. Peterson, "The Senate Park Commission Plan for Washington, DC: A New Vision for the Capital and the Nation," in *Designing the Nation's Capital: The 1901 Plan for Washington, DC,* Sue Kohler and Pamela Scott, eds. (Washington, DC: US Commission of Fine Arts, 2006), 1–48; Michael J. Lewis, "The Idea of an American Mall," in *The National Mall: Rethinking Washington's Monumental Core,* Nathan Glazer and Cynthia R. Fields, eds. (Baltimore: Johns Hopkins University Press, 2008), 1–26; "A Simple Space of Turf: Frederick Law Olmsted, Jr.'s Idea for the Mall," in *The National Mall*, Glazer and Fields, 55–68. See also *Report of the Senate Park Commission. The Improvement of the Park System of the District of Columbia*, United States Senate, Committee on the District of Columbia, 57th Cong., 1st sess. (Washington, DC: US Government Printing Office, 1902).
20 Sue A. Kohler, *The Commission of Fine Arts: A Brief History, 1910–1995* (Washington, DC: United States Commission of Fine Arts, 1996), 1–4.
21 Subcommittee on Public Lands, Reserved Water, and Resource Conservation, *Memorials and Monuments in the District of Columbia*, Committee on Energy and Natural Resources, United States Senate, 99th Cong., 2d sess., Vol. 4 (Washington, DC: US Government Printing Office, March 18, 1986), 20; Patricia E. Gallagher, "Planning Beyond the Monumental Core," in *The National Mall*, Glazer and Field, 159–174.
22 Piehler, *Remembering War the American Way*, 135–137. See James Bradley and Ron Powers, *Flags of Our Fathers* (New York: Bantam, 2000). Directed by Clint Eastwood, the film *Flags of Our Fathers* was released in 2006 and was well received by critics and historians alike.
23 See Bradley and Powers, *Flags of Our Fathers*.
24 Piehler, *Remembering War the American Way*, 135–137.
25 Lewis, *Mumbling Monuments*, 51.
26 Robert Wagner-Pacifici and Barry Schwartz, "The Vietnam Veterans Memorial: Commemorating a Difficult Past," *American Journal of Sociology* 97:2 (1991), 377.
27 Jan C. Scruggs and Joel L. Swerdlow, *To Heal a Nation: The Vietnam Veterans Memorial* (New York: Harper Collins, 1992); Senie, *Memorials to Shattered Myths*, 12.
28 Seine, *Memorials to Shattered Myths*, 12–13.
29 Wagner-Pacifici and Schwartz, *The Vietnam Veterans Memorial*, 389; Lewis, *Mumbling Monuments*, 51; Savage, *Monument Wars*, 266–267; Seine, *Memorials to Shattered Myths*, 13.
30 Doss, *Memorial Mania*, 43–44, 127–129; Seine, *Memorials to Shattered Myths*, 17–19.
31 "Vietnam Veterans Memorial: America Remembers," *National Geographic*, 67:5 (May 1985), 557; Savage, *Monument Wars*, 271–275.
32 Savage, *Monument Wars*, 276; Senie, *Memorials to Shattered Myths*, 19–20.
33 Senie, *Memorials to Shattered Myths*, 21–22.
34 Ibid., 22–24.
35 Ibid., 25–27.
36 Wagner-Pacifici and Schwartz, *The Vietnam Veterans Memorial*, 395; Lewis, *Mumbling Monuments*, 52.
37 Senie, *Memorials to Shattered Myths*, 28–33; Kristen Ann Hass, *Carried to the Vietnam Veterans Memorial: American Memory and the Vietnam Veterans Memorial* (Berkeley: University of California Press, 1998), 83–120.
38 Lewis, *Mumbling Monuments*, 52; Doss, *Memorial Mania*, 2.
39 Hass, *Sacrificing Soldiers*, 21.
40 Ibid., 26.

41 Ibid., 42–56.
42 Ibid., 26–27.
43 Ibid., 56–58.
44 Joseph Fishkin, "Anatomy of an Eyesore," *The New Republic*, September 25, 2000, 14–15; National Coalition to Save Our Mall, "The World War II Memorial Defaces a National Treasure" (2000), http://www.savethemall.org/wwii/index/html (accessed May 26, 2009).
45 Savage, *Monument Wars*, 300–301.
46 Anne Rothfeld, "National World War II Memorial," *OAH Newsletter*, February 2006, A3; "Memorial Approved for Capital Mall, But Battle Rages On," *Planning*, November 2000, 24–25; Fishkin, *Anatomy of an Eyesore*, 16; Savage, *Monument Wars*, 302.
47 Savage, *Monument Wars*, 298–299.
48 Michael Martone, "Permanent Temporary," *The Southern Review* 41:4 (2005), 878–885.
49 James M. Mayo, "War Memorials as Political Memory," *Geographic Review* 78:1 (1988), 62–75.
50 Nicolaus Mills, *Their Last Battle: The Fight for the National World War II Memorial* (New York: Basic Books, 2004), xii.
51 Jay Winter, *Remembering War: The Great War between Memory and History in the Twentieth Century* (New Haven: Yale University Press, 2006), 135.
52 Doss, *Memorial Mania*, 48; Peggy McGlone, "World War I Centennial Commission Picks Final Design for Memorial," *Washington Post*, 26 January 2016; Anna Mulrine, "New World War I Memorial: American Looks Back to Move Forward," *Christian Science Monitor*, 26 January 2016; *National Mall Plan: Summary—Enriching Our American Experience, Envisioning a New Future* (Washington, DC: National Park Service, 2010), 6.
53 Iraq War Memorial Council, http://www.nationaliraqwarmemorial.org/ (accessed May 30, 2009); Bob Barnard, "Will There Be an Iraq War Memorial?" Fox 5 News, Washington, DC, May 22, 2009 (accessed 30 May 2009), http://www.myfoxdc.com/dpp/live_video/video_stories/052209_iraq_war_memorial.

# 3

# RE-CARVING THE STONE: REINTERPRETING WORLD WAR II MONUMENTS IN BRAZIL

*Uri Rosenheck*

Societies erect monuments to capture memorable moments for future generations to behold. Through engraving time in stone and casting the past in bronze, human interaction with an inanimate material assigns meaning to a monument. The supposed essence of the monument as a vessel of eternal meaning, however, is erroneous. It is the ongoing human interaction with the monument—how people understand the artifact—that creates meaning, and this understanding is unavoidably subjected to change.

Writing on Holocaust monuments, James Young explains that "once created, memorials take lives of their own" that digress from the initial official meaning, and thus the significance of the memorial is ever-changing.[1] This chapter builds on this observation and analyzes the evolution in the meaning of World War II (WWII) monuments in Brazil. It also turns the process Young describes on its head, since, in the Brazilian case, it was the masses who created the monuments and the state that tried to appropriate and invest new meaning into them. Furthermore, this chapter argues that the monuments' geographic dispersion explains why—at least according to some Brazilian intellectuals—the commemorated soldiers have faded into obscurity and the monuments have ceased to be respected.

In January 1941, Brazil had recognized the existence of war status between itself and the Axis powers. The act was not an obvious one in light of the long and beneficial neutrality Brazil had maintained and the nature of its own dictatorial *Estado Novo* (New State), headed by Getúlio Vargas since his self-coup in 1937. Brazil's contribution to the Allies' war effort was multifaceted. It supported the Allies diplomatically and allowed the US to build air bases on its northeastern tip to supply troops in North Africa and Southeast Asia. Its navy patrolled the South Atlantic looking for Axis submarines and escorting convoys. It sent tens of thousands of *soldados da borracha* (Rubber Soldiers) to the Amazon to tap rubber and other valuable minerals crucial for the war industry. Moreover, it also sent an expeditionary force—*a força expedicionária brasileira* (henceforth FEB)—a 25,000-strong infantry division that fought in northern Italy from June 1944 to the end of the European campaign in May of the following year.

## Early monuments: Civic spirit and civilian values

After the laureate *febianos* (members of the FEB) arrived back in Brazil, the concerned regime, hearing the clapping wings of the angel of history, hastened to demobilize the FEB and send its soldiers back to their homes.[2] Upon their arrival, welcoming committees and cheering crowds greeted the novice veterans, celebrated their safe return, and mourned those who were not so fortunate.[3] On many occasions, the festivities included the inauguration of a local monument, an affixation of a plaque, or at least a comparable ceremony that started fundraising for a future monument. Immediately as the war ended, Brazil saw an influx of monuments. The dramatic rate of production of this cultural artifact left its marks on the civicscape of hundreds of Brazilian cities and towns.[4]

By the end of 1946, Brazilian communities had erected no fewer than 63 monuments, nearly one third of the 192 WWII monuments in Brazil (see Table 3.1).[5] During the following four decades, Brazilians inaugurated an average of three or four monuments annually. A comparison with other nations puts the meaning of these construction rates into perspective. Anthropologist Oz Almog proposes to establish the cultural significance of such an artifact by calculating the ratio between the monuments and the fallen soldiers they commemorate.[6] A quantitative comparison of commemoration patterns in Brazil and a few other nations clearly demonstrates the abundance of the Brazilian WWII monuments (see Table 3.2).

Beyond their mere abundance as a cultural artifact, the monuments also best interpreted what the war meant to the Brazilian public in general. Most other WWII memorials in Brazil—such as veterans' memoirs, veteran associations' museums, war correspondents' collected articles, and authorities' organized parades—offer the

**TABLE 3.1** FEB monuments, 1945–1984

| Period | # Monuments | Annual average | Percentage (%) |
| --- | --- | --- | --- |
| 1945–1959 | 105 | 7.0 | 54.6 |
| 1945–1946 | 63 | 31.5[a] | 32.8 |
| 1947–1959 | 42 | 3.23 | 21.8 |
| 1960–1984 | 87 | 3.48 | 45.3 |
| Total: 1945–1984 | 192 | 4.8 | 100.0 |

*Sources: Livros de Comemoração* in acervo da ANVFEB – Rio de Janeiro; Mattos, João Baptista de. *Os Monumentos Nacionais: A Força Expedicionária No Bronze*. Rio de Janeiro: Imprensa do Exército, 1960.

*Note*: [a]In fact, since the war ended in May 1945, the 63 monuments were built in little more than a year, rather than over two years. This increases the average to 42 monuments per year.

**TABLE 3.2** Comparative abundance of war monuments per fallen soldiers

| Country | Commemorated event | # Fallen soldiers | # Monuments | Monuments per soldier |
| --- | --- | --- | --- | --- |
| Canada | WWI and WWII | 97,000 | 1,232 | 1:79 |
| New Zealand | WWI | 18,000 | 452 | 1:40 |
| Britain | WWI, WWII, and the Revolution in Ireland | ~1,002,000 | ~40,000 | 1:25 |
| Israel | Multiple wars 1948–1990 | ~15,300 | ~900 | 1:17 |
| New Zealand | Boer War | 228 | 44 | 1:5 |
| Brazil | WWII | 465 | 192 | 1:2.42 |

*Sources*: Robert Shipley, *To Mark Our Place: A History of Canadian War Memorials* (Toronto: NC Press, 1987), Appendix B: List of Monuments, 178–187; Jeff Keshen, "The Great War Soldiers as National Builders in Canada and Australia," in *Canada and the Great War: Western Front Association Papers*, ed. Briton Cooper Busch (Montreal; Ithaca: McGill-Queen's University Press, 2003), 4; Ian Dear and M. R. D. Foot, *The Oxford Companion to World War II*, New ed. (Oxford: Oxford University Press, 2005), "Demography, Table 1: Approximate war-related deaths of major combatant nations in the Second World War," 225; Colin McIntyre, *Monuments of War: How to Read a War Memorial* (London: Robert Hale, 1990), 49, 131–132; Chris Maclean and Jock Phillips, *The Sorrow and the Pride: New Zealand War Memorials* (Historical Branch, 1990), 47, 69–70, 78; Oz Almog, "War Casualties Monuments in Israel: A Semiotic Analysis," *Megamot* (1992), 182; *Livros de Comemoração* in acervo da ANVFEB – Rio de Janeiro; João Baptista de Mattos. *Os Monumentos Nacionais: A Força Expedicionária No Bronze*, Rio de Janeiro: Imprensa do Exército, 1960.

participants' interpretation of the war, or that of the government that sent them to fight. In contrast, the monuments, and especially the early ones, reflect the interpretations of their creators: soldiers' families, neighbors, and fellow citizens.[7] Examination of the monuments' forms suggests what and who these monuments commemorate.

About a quarter of all monuments (54 monuments, or 28 percent) are statues of human figures, most of which (70 percent) are of a generic, unnamed soldier. In a sharp contrast to other nations' commemorative traditions—such as the typical and abundant "Rest on Arms Reserved" position in the Commonwealth that communicates grief and respect—Brazilian human figures on WWII monuments do not convey the hardship, suffering, and grief imposed by war. Instead, these statues are positioned as active and aggressive while advancing (32 percent), charging (32 percent), or in victorious gestures (8 percent). Maybe the relatively low number of casualties Brazil suffered in the conflict explains this focus. New Zealand's Boer War monuments follow the same pattern and reinforce this explanation.[8] Despite the combative positions and the high attention to detail demonstrated by their artists, the statues show no trace of dirt, hardship, or struggle. All soldiers are alive, healthy, and clean. They do not portray a real war, but an ideal one, and thus they celebrate Brazilian masculinity, potency, and virility.

The majority of the early monuments—70 percent of all those erected before 1950 and 50 percent of all monuments inaugurated before 1960—were obelisks.

The obelisk has a long commemorative tradition as a symbol of military prowess, triumph, death, and victory.[9] More than just a part of a global cultural pattern, WWII Brazilian obelisks also follow a Brazilian monumental tradition of using obelisks to commemorate non-military achievements.[10] Beyond global and local traditions, practical considerations such as simplicity of design, low cost, and rapidity of construction also contributed to the popularity of the obelisk. The obelisk's inexpressive design turns our attention to the monuments' inscriptions in our search for meaning.

Monuments' inscriptions frequently reference local identities at the community level. In addition, the majority of the monuments do not commemorate fallen soldiers, but are dedicated to all soldiers, dead or alive, who came from a specific locality. The monuments do not express sorrow or Brazilian *saudade* for the fallen by a bereaved community, but rather pay tribute to the living by maintaining a proud people.[11] By dedicating monuments to "the heroes of Assis," or those who "carried the civic spirit of Perdões to the War," the monuments show the local communities' part in the nation, and at the same time they also represent local patriotism that helps distinguish these localities from other municipalities thanks to their civic attributes.

Indeed, as James Mayo has argued, due to their lack of utilitarian function and their capacity to provoke sentiment, war monuments and the commemorative rituals conducted at their bases are types of memorials that well communicate values and virtues. The Brazilian monuments' inscriptions most often explain to the observer that the FEB has fought for "democracy," "liberty," and "civic spirit." Less often, the observer will learn that it also fought for "victory," "honor" (especially national honor), "national integrity," and "human values." Rarely mentioning the armed forces at all, the monuments' inscriptions communicate a civilian perception of the FEB and honor the expeditionary force not for its military achievements, but for its political and human dimensions. A closer look at one such monument will further illustrate the meanings which those who erected the monuments invested in them.

On Sunday, March 16, 1947, the people of Petrópolis, a municipality in the state of Rio de Janeiro, gathered in the centrally located square of D. Pedro for the unveiling of the town's monument commemorating its four fallen *pracinhas*.[12] The Mass in honor of the fallen soldiers in the Cathedral had already ended, and the weather seemed to cooperate, as the rain that had poured for several days halted. Despite the presence of high-ranking officers and representatives of the national authorities, the monument and the ceremony were local in many aspects. The monument's granite pillar was curved of local stone, and the life-sized bronze women at its feet symbolized—so explained the organizing committee—the town. Furthermore, while the bronze plaque named the fallen soldiers and included their images, the first, tallest, largest, and most visible part of the inscription was the town's name. The ceremony took place on the town's founding date, and after the military band played a few tunes, a civilian band played "The Petrópolitan Expedicionario Song."

The description of the monument and ceremony in a commemorative album capturing such acts of gratitude which Brazilians offered their veterans exposes the civic interpretation of the mission of the FEB. It explains that the monument paid homage to the soldiers who fell "in defense of the sacred rights embodied in democracy and liberty, against any ideology that attempts to introduce itself to the dominions of the free people who desire to live under the aegis of human principles."[13] When these values are set within the political climate at the end of the war, and the end of Vargas' authoritarian rule and the return to democracy, the monuments also tell the story of the FEB's European campaign as a catalyst for the political change back at home.

## The military regime: Cold War politics and political legitimacy

The 1964 military coup sought to dramatically change the meaning of WWII in Brazilian public memory by establishing new methods of interaction with existing monuments and representing them in other mediums. Historians such as Francisco Alves Ferraz and Dennison Oliveira have observed the militarization of the monuments by the armed forces. Ferraz points, for example, to the order of seating at ceremonies, where high-ranking officers and military personnel gradually came to occupy the first rows, replacing the veterans, who were now marginalized at the back and reduced to mere audience members.[14] Oliveira argues that the ceremony to commemorate 50 years having passed since the end of the war obscured the causes and consequences of the war, overstated the military achievements, and had a general military tone.[15]

The militarization of the monuments can also be seen in the symbolic meaning which the military assigned to the monuments in newsreels (*cinejornais*). By appropriating the FEB's prestige and putting the recognized National Monument for the WWII Dead (henceforth the National Monument) in different contexts, the military government—like previous regimes—used the newsreels for political propaganda. One newsreel from 1967, for example, depicted a Japanese prince's visit to Brazil and included the obligatory ceremony wherein foreign heads of state put flowers on the Grave of the Unknown Soldier at the National Monument. Beyond diplomatic bilateral relations, this report also included subliminal messages regarding Brazil's moral and military superiority over the former Axis state and current economic powerhouse and beacon of modernity.[16] It also, however, reinterpreted the meaning of WWII in Brazil when the narrator explained that the prince was paying homage to the brave *pracinhas* and FEB members who gave their lives for "enhancing the high reputation of the Armed Forces."[17] The following year, another newsreel showed officers from multiple American nations who had participated in the Eighth Conference of American Armies depositing flowers at the National Monument. This time, the narrator explained that the Americas were now free, with their armies united in order to prevent a "new catastrophe."[18] The comment equated the WWII hemispheric alliance with Cold War-era hemispheric counterinsurgency and anti-communist cooperation.

Another long newsreel from the early 1970s reported at length on military maneuvers in the Amazon, where soldiers trained for the "liberation" of a town held by "subversives." The report ended at the National Monument and explained that it is a symbol of Brazilian soldiers' commitment to the defense of the fatherland, and that Brazilians can rest assured that the armed forces are capable of protecting Brazil against the enemies of freedom and justice.[19] In this example, the visual language of the dictatorship's war on "subversives" was equated with Brazil's WWII battle against fascism.

In these three examples, the narrated and visual languages of the newsreels reinterpreted the mission of the FEB in WWII as a struggle for democracy, now defined as "anti-communist," against "left-wing subversion." The juxtaposition of the military in the 1960s and 70s and the WWII-era FEB served to appropriate the prestige of the FEB and legitimize the contemporary politics of the armed forces. This was achieved by repeatedly using the National Monument, which now became a visual symbol of the FEB as a whole.

As part of a broader cultural maneuver aimed at appropriating the FEB's prestige, the military regime reinterpreted monuments' meanings in other cultural arenas as well. Several Brazilian governments used philately to assign the FEB their desired meaning, and the military regime was no different. One of these stamps used the national monument in such a way. The 1972 stamp is a sheet of four stamps (see Figure 3.1), three of which represent the three branches of the armed forces—Army, Navy, and Air Force—while the fourth shows a recognizable element from the National Monument portraying three soldiers of the three branches. The conversation between the four stamps on the sheet reinterprets the monument, and the FEB it signifies, as the unifying symbol of the armed forces, and deprives it of its earlier meaning.[20]

The military regime might have been the most successful in appropriating the memory of the FEB and militarizing its memory, but it was not the only one

**FIGURE 3.1**  Homenagem às Forças Armadas: Monumento, Marinha, Exército, Aeronautica, December 28, 1972. Photo by the author

trying to do so. One attempt to reclaim the monuments occurred on February 13, 1968, when artists from the Guanabara Theatre, in an act of protest against censorship, deposited flowers on the Unknown Soldier's tomb, an element of the National Monument, "for those who in the War fell for democracy and liberty." The following day, Jamil Amiden, an FEB veteran and a deputy in the Federal House of Representatives (Câmara Federal), protested the expulsion of the artists from the monument, arguing that it was "sacred ground" and the "oracle of our democracy [and] origin of our liberty."[21] The protestors did not primarily attempt to reclaim the memory of the FEB, however. Very much like the military itself, they asked to appropriate the FEB's prestige to advance their politics. The nature of the monument as an object where flowers are offered to show respect to higher causes served them well. For generals and dissidents alike, the nature of the monument made these memorials useful objects, and the rituals at their feet proved to be a utilitarian means to an end. The shifting meanings of the monuments, and the FEB as a whole, were just the byproduct of this cultural maneuver.

## Spatial oblivion

In August 2016, a new public electronic petition called for the inclusion of the history of the FEB in students' curricula.[22] The petition reacted to the growing number of voices in the press and the academy lamenting that for years the FEB had been forgotten.[23] Monuments too had been neglected, vandalized, and even misused as parking garages.[24] The competition over the appropriation of the FEB's monuments and its memory had turned into oblivion and neglect.

One possible explanation for this transformation points to the armed forces' successful appropriation of the FEB during the military regime and their embrace of the veterans and their associations. According to this explanation, when the military regime collapsed, those groups and institutions that were associated with it fell from grace as well.[25] A spatial analysis of the monuments, however, calls into question the accuracy of these assertions.

The geographical examination of monumental commemoration patterns reveals regional commemorative differences. While Brazilian authorities planned on mobilizing soldiers from all over Brazil and sought to present the FEB as representing all of Brazil, in reality *febianos*' regional origin deviated from the national population distribution. For example, the five states of Rio de Janeiro, São Paulo, Minas Gerais, Rio Grande do Sul, and Paraná, all in the south and southeast regions, accounted for 53.5 percent of the Brazilian population but contributed 77 percent of the FEB soldiers.[26] In light of this demographic composition, it is not surprising that 93 percent of all FEB monuments can be found in the southern and southeastern regions of Brazil (see Table 3.3).

The most exceptional numbers are found, however, in the states of Rio de Janeiro, including the Federal District at the time, and São Paulo. While one third of all soldiers came from the state of Rio de Janeiro, only about 10 percent of the

**TABLE 3.3** Distribution of monuments and soldiers by region and state

| Region and state | # Monuments | % Monuments | # Soldiers[a] | % Soldiers | Ratio of soldiers to monuments |
|---|---|---|---|---|---|
| North (total) | 1 | 0.52 | 372 | 1.57 | 0.332 |
| Amazonas | 0 | 0.0 | 91 | 0.38 | 0.0 |
| Para | 1 | 0.5 | 281 | 1.19 | 0.439 |
| Northeast (total) | 10 | 5.21 | 2,945 | 12.43 | 0.419 |
| Lagos | 1 | 0.5 | 148 | 0.62 | 0.834 |
| Bahia | 3 | 1.6 | 686 | 2.89 | 0.540 |
| Ciara | 1 | 0.5 | 377 | 1.59 | 0.327 |
| Marana | 1 | 0.5 | 134 | 0.57 | 0.921 |
| Paraiba | 1 | 0.5 | 349 | 1.47 | 0.354 |
| Pernambuco | 3 | 1.6 | 651 | 2.75 | 0.569 |
| Piaui | 0 | 0.0 | 67 | 0.28 | 0.0 |
| Rio Grande do Norte | 0 | 0.0 | 341 | 1.44 | 0.0 |
| Sergipe | 0 | 0.0 | 192 | 0.81 | 0.0 |
| Center-west (total) | 3 | 1.56 | 790 | 3.33 | 0.469 |
| Goiás | 2 | 1.0 | 111 | 0.47 | 2.224 |
| Mato Grosso | 1 | 0.5 | 679 | 2.86 | 0.182 |
| Southeast (total) | 135 | 70.31 | 15,217 | 64.20 | 1.095 |
| Espirito Santo | 3 | 1.6 | 345 | 1.46 | 1.073 |
| Minas Gerais | 42 | 21.9 | 2,947 | 12.43 | 1.759 |
| Rio de Janeiro | 20 | 10.4 | 8,036 | 33.90 | 0.307 |
| São Paulo | 70 | 36.5 | 3,889 | 16.41 | 2.222 |
| Sub-total | 135 | 70.31 | 15,217 | 64.20 | 1.095 |
| South (total) | 43 | 22.40 | 4,378 | 18.47 | 1.212 |
| Paraná | 9 | 4.7 | 1,542 | 6.51 | 0.721 |
| Rio Grande do Sul | 23 | 12.0 | 1,880 | 7.93 | 1.510 |
| Santa Catarina | 11 | 5.7 | 956 | 4.03 | 1.420 |
| Total | 192 | 100.00 | 23,702 | 100.00 | 1.000 |

Sources: *Livros de Comemoração* in acervo da ANVFEB – Rio de Janeiro; João Baptista de Mattos, *Os Monumentos Nacionais: A Força Expedicionária No Bronze*, Rio de Janeiro: Imprensa do Exército, 1960; João Baptista Mascarenhas de Moraes, *A FEB pelo seu Comandante*, São Paulo: Instituto Progresso Editorial, 1947, 304.

Note: [a] The available data includes soldiers and non-commissioned officers only (*praças*). Data on officers is not available.

monuments can be found there. Additionally, while 36 percent of all monuments are in the state of São Paulo, it only sent 16.4 percent of the soldiers. Applying finer resolution to where soldiers came from and where monuments are located within the states will shed some light on this anomaly.

As Table 3.4 shows, the state capitals account for very few monuments in relation to the number of soldiers they sent to the FEB, while in the countryside the ratio is significantly higher. The commemorative difference is more dramatic between the big urban centers and the smaller towns than between regions. This dissimilarity requires an explanation.

**TABLE 3.4** Distribution of monuments and soldiers in the states of Rio de Janeiro and São Paulo and their capitals

| City and state | # Monuments | % Monuments | # Soldiers | % Soldiers | Soldier–monuments ratio |
|---|---|---|---|---|---|
| City of Rio de Janeiro | 2 | 1.04 | 6,094 | 25.71 | 0.041 |
| State of Rio de Janeiro (w/out the capital) | 18 | 9.38 | 1,942 | 8.19 | 1.144 |
| City of Sao Paulo | 6 | 3.13 | 1,000[a] | 4.22 | 0.741 |
| State of São Paulo (w/out the capital) | 64 | 33.33 | 2,889 | 12.19 | 2.735 |

Sources: *Livros de Comemoração* in acervo da ANVFEB – Rio de Janeiro; João Baptista de Mattos, *Os Monumentos Nacionais: A Força Expedicionária No Bronze*, Rio de Janeiro: Imprensa do Exército, 1960; João Baptista Mascarenhas de Moraes, *A FEB pelo seu Comandante*. São Paulo: Instituto Progresso Editorial, 1947, 304.

Note: [a] The number of soldiers native to the city of São Paulo is based on historian Cesar Campiani Maximiano's estimate communicated to the author in an email on October 3, 2009.

Exceptionality and intimacy explain the difference. Most of the *febianos* came from the small, sleepy towns of the interior.[27] These soldiers crossed the ocean and took part in a global conflict which constituted an extremely exceptional experience that touched, excited, and intrigued anyone who heard about it. That event, however, did not have the same effect when experienced in the cosmopolitan metropolises.

Second, in small towns intimacy contributes to the fact that many relate personally to such an extraordinary event; in a large city, there is no intimacy between large segments of the population. Brazilian anthropologist Roberto DaMatta articulated Brazilian social relations through the now-classic metaphor of the "house and the street." In each sphere, so argues DaMatta, different codes of behavior govern, and the two codes co-exist. In the "street" (the public space), one is regarded as an "individual," that is, an autonomous being among one's peers who is equal before the law and the state. In contrast, in the "house" one is a "person," which is a relational position that is always connected to others and regarded according to one's location in the social web.[28]

In small towns, however, these spheres operate differently. Using DaMatta's classification, anthropologist Rosane Prado argues that in small rural towns one is always a "person" tied to others in an inescapable intimacy.[29] Unlike in the busy city, in an intimate town everyone would personally know the WWII veteran. His story was not an impersonal generic one from a documentary or a history textbook. When passing in front of the FEB monument, usually located in a central place in town, the town-dweller would think about "his" or "her" *febiano*—a relative, a neighbor, a colleague, or a friend familiar from routine interactions. The memory of the FEB in these towns is a personal experience, and, as such, is stronger than the way most major city-dwellers experienced the memory of the FEB.

Most agents of memory—intellectuals, journalists, politicians, academics, authors, and even veterans—live in the big urban centers of the southeast. In their reality, the monuments are indeed scarce, the exciting nature of the FEB is in constant competition with other cosmopolitan attractions, and the FEB is monumentally undercommemorated. When these agents claim the FEB is forgotten, they project their specific reality on to the entire country. Placing the monuments in their geographical space, however, questions the validity of these assertions.

## Conclusion

WWII monuments in Brazil are abundant cultural artifacts. They communicate values and identities, and they are tools to be mobilized and appropriated in intense political conflicts. As soon as the war ended, dozens of small communities erected monuments to their soldiers, but also to their own locality. These early monuments' shapes and inscriptions reveal that their creators perceived Brazil's participation in the conflict as a civic act in the name of liberal-democratic values, something that did not characterize Brazil during the war.

As the military regime took over civil society, its generals used the FEB's prestige to legitimize their politics. This battle over consciousness and meaning included reinterpreting the mission of the FEB through interacting with WWII monuments in new ways. The militarization of the monuments and the ceremonies at their feet well served the new narrative of the armed forces—incarnated in the FEB—fighting to preserve the country's integrity against foreign ideologies and subversion by internal enemies. While the military was not the only body to use the FEB in support of its politics, it was the most successful one. This rewriting of the monuments' meaning was possible exactly because the monument is an artifact constantly subjected to reinterpretation.

The successful association of the military with the FEB led to the former's declining status after the return to democracy. The healing nation looked as far from the military as it could in its search for new identities and values. In such an atmosphere—and with the natural process of aging veterans gradually vanishing from the public sphere—some monuments too suffered from deterioration and neglect. Concerned voices lamenting the nation's forgetting its fighting sons, however, collided with the lasting physical presence of hundreds of monuments in many cities and towns. A spatial analysis of the monuments' dispersion offers a way to reconcile the two. The monuments' locations reveal that communities' collective memories of the FEB are not uniform. Replacing the national-level generalizations with finer regional perspectives, and even more so noting the differences between the big cities and the smaller rural towns, highlights the local context of the agents of memory who claim to speak for the nation. This observation also completes a full-circle questioning of the armed forces' success in appropriating the monuments and the memory of the FEB. By doing so, it reminds us that while it is indeed a human interaction that casts the bronze and carves the stone into a meaningful artifact, once embedded in the object, more than ceremoniously delivering a moving speech or playing a hymn at the monuments' feet is required to reshape their meaning.

## Notes

1. James Edward Young, *The Texture of Memory: Holocaust Memorials and Meaning* (New Haven: Yale University Press, 1993), 3.
2. Most historians agree that the Vargas regime saw the returning troops as a political threat and was concerned they would be used by presidential candidates who came from the ranks of the army to overthrow the government. See, for example, Ricardo Bonalume Neto, *A Nossa Segunda Guerra: os brasileiros em combate, 1942–1945* (Rio de Janeiro: Expressão e Cultura, 1995), 217, and Frank D. McCann, *The Brazilian–American Alliance, 1937–1945* (Princeton: Princeton University Press, 1973), 440. A counterinterpretation argues the FEB's soldiers supported Vargas, and their demobilization by the army was intended to weaken the regime. See Shawn C. Smallman, *Fear & Memory in the Brazilian Army and Society, 1889–1954* (Chapel Hill: University of North Carolina Press, 2002).
3. Such gestures and ceremonies are captured in a 1947 commemorative album that lists many similar activities. See Edelzia dos Santos et al., org., *Nosso Valente Pracinha: Documentário da Guerra* (Rio de Janeiro: Norte-editora, 1947).
4. "Civicscape" is a portmanteau of "cityscape" and "civic space" that signifies the physical and architectural representations in a designated space for civic rituals. See Daryle Williams, "Civicscape and Memoryscape: The First Vargas Regime and Rio de Janeiro," in *Vargas and Brazil: New Perspectives*, Jenes R. Hentschke, ed. (New York: Palgrave Macmillan, 2006), 55–82.
5. All information in this chapter and its tables regarding the Brazilian WWII monuments was compiled from two main sources. The first is a 1960 published survey of FEB monuments in Brazil that counted 105 monuments. The second is a handwritten compilation of a national survey of FEB monuments and memorials carried out by the FEB Veterans' Association (*Associação nacional dos veteranos da força expedicionária brasileira*, henceforward ANVFEB), which is now deposited in the association's main archives. The monuments' database compiled from these two sources contains data on 192 monuments erected between 1945 and 1984. See João Baptista de Mattos, *Os Monumentos Nacionais: A Força Expedicionária no Bronze* (Rio de Janeiro: Imprensa do Exército, 1960); *Livros de Comemoração* in acervo da ANVFEB – Rio de Janeiro.
6. Oz Almog, "War Casualties Monuments in Israel: A Semiotic Analysis," *Megamot* (1992), 22; for monuments as an abundant cultural artifact in general see Alan Borg, *War Memorials: From Antiquity to the Present* (London: Leo Cooper, 1991).
7. In this sense, the noticeable and iconic national monument in Rio de Janeiro is an exception. For a close examination of this monument see Ana Maria Mauad and Daniela Ferreira Nunes, "Discurso de uma Morte Consumada: Monumento Dos Pracinhas," in *Cidade Vaidosa: Estudos Sobre Imaginária Urbana no Rio de Janeiro*, Paulo Knauss, ed. (Rio de Janeiro: Sette Letras, 1999), 53–73.
8. For a characterization of the New Zealand war memorials see Chris Maclean and Jock Phillips, *The Sorrow and the Pride: New Zealand War Memorials* (Wellington: Historical Branch, 1990), 48–49.
9. Borg, *War Memorials*, 2–5.
10. For example, São Paulo's first monument, erected in 1814 as homage to the city's governing triumvirate; the famous 1906 obelisk in Rio de Janeiro that celebrated the city's development; and Porto Alegre's five obelisks from the 1920s and 1930s that each honored the contribution of a different ethnic group to the city.
11. The Portuguese term *saudade* is often translated as "nostalgia" or "longing." Nonetheless, it is a more complex term than this; Daniel Toro Linger describes it as "a bittersweet emotion," which has "a profound, melancholy sense of physical separation, or apartness, of being literally out of touch with a person, a place, a time." Daniel Touro Linger, *Dangerous Encounters: Meanings of Violence in a Brazilian City* (Stanford: Stanford University Press, 1992), 7.
12. Members of the FEB are often called *febianos* and, fondly, *pracinhas*.
13. Santos, *Nosso Valente Pracinha*, 152–3.

14 Francisco César Alves Ferraz, "A Guerra Que Não Acabou: A Reintegração Social Dos Veteranos da Força Expedicionária Brasileira (1945–2000)" (PhD diss., Universidade de São Paulo, 2002), 345.
15 Dennison de Oliveira, "Cultura e Poder Nas Cerimônias Militares Das Forças Armadas Brasileiras: O Caso da Vitória de Monte Castelo," *Revista de Ciências Humanas (Curitiba)*, 9 (2000), 31–55.
16 On Japan in Brazilian imagery see Jeffrey Lesser, *A Discontented Diaspora: Japanese Brazilians and the Meanings of Ethnic Militancy, 1960–1980* (Durham, NC: Duke University Press, 2007).
17 *Cine Jornal Informativo n. 66*. 1967. In Archivo Nacional (Rio de Janeiro) EH/FIL 0293. VHS 12. 0:55:00
18 *Cine Jornal Informativo n. 112*. 1968. In Archivo Nacional (Rio de Janeiro) EH/FIL 0338. VHS 15. 0:01:09 and 0:07:21.
19 *Documentario: Operação Carajás*. (1971). In Archivo Nacional (Rio de Janeiro) EH/FIL 0910. VHS 24. 0:00:39.
20 For a closer reading of the FEB's philatelic representations see Uri Rosenheck, "Philatelic Remembrances: Stamps, National Identity, and Shifting Memories of WWII in Brazil," *Latin Americanist* 60:1 (2016), 115–137.
21 Cited in Ferraz, *A Guerra Que Não Acabou*, 346. Less than a year afterward, on January 16, 1969, the military regime stripped Amidan's political rights for ten years, together with dozens of other political figures. "Novas Cassações atingiram parlamento," *O Dia*, January 17, 1969.
22 "Petição para Inclusão da FEB na Grade Curricular dos Alunos," http://www.peticao publica.com.br/pview.aspx?pi=BR89762 (accessed 15 September 2016).
23 For example, see Gerson Severo Dantes, "Heróis do passado estão esquecidos no presente" *(Acritica.com)*, Manaus, May 8, 2011, http://acritica.uol.com.br/manaus/Herois-passado-estao-esquecidos-presente_0_476952388.html (accessed 3 June 2011); Telma Silvério, "Dia da Vitória é lembrado por poucos," *Jornal Cruzeiro do Sul* 5 (2011), http://www.jornalcruzeiro.com.br/materia/295042/dia-da-vitoria-e-lembrado-por-poucos (accessed 15 September 2016). For such claims by academics see Luis Felipe da Silva Neves, "A Força Expedicionária Brasileira: 1944–1945," In *Segunda Guerra Mundial: Um Balanço Histórico*, Oswaldo Coggiola, ed. (São Paulo: Universidade de São Paulo, 1995), 295; Cesar Campiani Maximiano, *Onde Estão Nossos Heróis* (São Paulo: Editora Santuário, 1995), 102; Roney Cytrynowicz, *Guerra Sem Guerra: a Mobilização e o Cotidiano em São Paulo Durante a Segunda Guerra Mundial* (São Paulo: Geração Editorial, Edusp, 2000), 287–320.
24 For example, see "Monumento do Pracinha é transferido para o entorno do Museu da FEB após 40 anos," *O Tempo*, Belo Horizonte, May 30, 2012, http://www.otempo.com.br/cidades/monumento-do-pracinha-%C3%A9-transferido-para-o-entorno-do-museu-da-feb-ap%C3%B3s-40-anos-1.422250 (accessed 15 September 2016); O Globo com a colaboração da leitora Cynthia Fiuza, "Monumento aos Pracinhas é utilizado como garagem," *O Globo*, May 24, 2011, http://oglobo.globo.com/rio/monumento-aos-pracinhas-utilizado-como-garagem-2765582 (accessed 3 June 2011).
25 Classic examples of this process are journalist William Waack's argument that the FEB was neither militarily important nor successful and director Sylvio Back's 1990 pseudo-documentary film *Rádio Auriverde* that presented the rank and file as cannon fodder and victims of North American imperialism. William Waack, *As Duas Faces da Glória: A FEB Vista Pelos Seus Aliados e Inimigos* (Rio de Janeiro: Editora Nova Fronteira, 1985).
26 For the regional origin of the soldiers see João Baptista Mascarenhas de Moraes, *A FEB pelo seu Comandante* (São Paulo: Instituto Progresso Editorial, 1947), "Quadro da contribução dos estados, em praças, para a organização da FEB," 304; for census data see Instituto Brasileiro de Geografia e Estatística, *Anuário Estatístico do Brasil: Ano VII – 1946* (Rio de Janeiro: Serviço Gráfico do Instituto Brasileiro de Geografia e Estatística, 1947), Table "Estado da população: I. População do Brasil, na data dos recenseamentos gerais: 2. Distribuição, Segundo as unidades da federação, 1872/940," 36.

27 Joaquim Xavier da Silveira, *A FEB Por um Soldado* (Rio de Janeiro: Editora Nova Fronteira, 1989), 58.
28 DaMatta developed and demonstrated this concept in various locations. See Roberto A. DaMatta, *A Casa & a Rua*, 5th ed. (Rio de Janeiro: Rocco, 1997), esp. ch. 2: "Cidadania."
29 Rosane Prado, "Small Town, Brazil: Heaven and Hell of Personalism," in *The Brazilian Puzzle: Culture on the Borderlands of the Western World*, David J. Hess and Roberto A. DaMatta, eds. (New York: Columbia University Press, 1995), 59–82.

# 4

# MEMORIALIZING THE "UNKNOWN HEROES" OF WORLD WAR II: GERMAN DESERTER MONUMENTS

*Steven R. Welch*

Germany has the distinction of being one of the very few countries in the world with monuments dedicated to military deserters.[1] The first was created in 1985, and there are now more than 30 deserter monuments in cities across the country.[2] Throughout the 1980s and 1990s, proponents of deserter monuments often encountered fierce opposition to their proposals for memorializing deserters. The idea of honoring soldiers who deserted from the ranks of Germany's armed forces represented a direct challenge to the widespread belief that the *Wehrmacht* had fought a "normal" war and that the Nazified SS bore the responsibility for war crimes and genocide, while ordinary soldiers had maintained their honor and decency. By the turn of the century, however, the terms of the debate had perceptibly shifted. The myth of the decent *Wehrmacht* had been debunked, and the argument that deserters from Hitler's army deserved to be memorialized had gained significant support in German society, as evidenced by the passage of a law in the German parliament rehabilitating soldiers who had been court-martialled during World War II for desertion.[3] As I will argue in this chapter, the two outcomes were related: The local campaigns for the establishment of deserter monuments contributed to the broader national debate about the nature of World War II and the *Wehrmacht*'s complicity in a criminal war of annihilation. Thus, the creation of deserter monuments helped to expand and alter the boundaries of the public memory of the war in Germany.

The first section of this chapter briefly outlines the origins of the deserter-monument movement in Germany and sketches the contours of the public debates concerning deserter monuments. In the second and third sections, I examine three examples of each of the two major categories of deserter monuments, those that focus primarily on honoring German deserters from the *Wehrmacht* and those that are more broadly dedicated to honoring the principle of desertion itself. The final section of the chapter evaluates the impact and significance of the deserter-monument movement and the extent to which it has succeeded in changing the public memory of the war in Germany.

## Origins

The origins of the deserter-monument movement can be traced back to the late 1970s and early 1980s. In the immediate decades after World War II, German deserters had largely been forgotten; their experiences, whether framed in terms of victimization by the Nazi regime or acts of resistance against Nazi tyranny, were not incorporated into the "war stories" that Germans crafted in order to make sense of the catastrophic outcome of the war.[4] Literary efforts in the 1950s and 1960s by Alfred Andersch and Heinrich Böll, both of whom had themselves been deserters, to bring the deserters and the issue of desertion as a moral choice back into public view found little resonance with the German public.[5] *Wehrmacht* deserters continued to be viewed as cowards and traitors who had left their comrades in the lurch.

The call for a monument for German deserters from the *Wehrmacht* was first raised in 1978 in a newspaper article published by Ulrich Restat, a teacher of disabled children in the city of Kassel. Restat's article was prompted by the so-called Filbinger affair.[6] Hans Filbinger, the Christian Democratic Union Minister President of the state of Baden-Württemberg, was forced to resign from office in August 1978 after details of his service as a naval judge during World War II were revealed. The scrutiny of Filbinger's role in cases that ended with death sentences for German deserters also raised broader questions about the nature of the military justice system under the Nazi regime and the very high number of death sentences that had been imposed.[7] Restat provocatively called for a monument to honor deserters such as those sentenced to death by Filbinger. In November 1981, Restat, now a Green Party city councilman in Kassel, introduced a motion in support of erecting a deserter monument in Kassel, and the city council authorized a research project on soldiers from Kassel who had deserted from the *Wehrmacht*. The results of the study were published in 1985 and showed that 114 soldiers from Kassel had refused military service, 56 had been sentenced to death, and 29 had been executed.[8] In February 1985, the council voted to establish a memorial for these soldiers. After some delay, on 9 May 1987, a commemorative plaque honoring the deserters was added to the municipal memorial for the fallen soldiers of both wars in the Fuldaaue (see Figure 4.1).

The memorial plaque hangs alongside an earlier plaque dedicated to sailors who fought and died for Germany's "glory and honor." This provocative juxtaposition is designed to spark critical reflection about the nature of war and the traditional soldierly values associated with it. Veterans groups greeted the monument with harsh criticism, seeing it as a calculated insult to those soldiers who had fought with the *Wehrmacht* to the bitter end.

The Kassel memorial was the outcome of one key strand of the early deserter-monument movement. A second important strand can be located in the efforts, from the early 1980s onward, of various pacifist groups, church-sponsored associations,

FIGURE 4.1  Kassel memorial plaque. "In memory of the soldiers of Kassel who refused military service for the national socialist tyranny and were as a result persecuted and killed." From the author's personal collection

and members of the Green Party to protest against NATO rearmament policies that included the stationing of intermediate-range cruise missiles in Germany.[9] At rallies, protestors often made reference to the "unknown deserter" in order to encourage refusal to carry out military service, either through conscientious objection or through desertion. At a demonstration in Karlsruhe in October 1983, a plaster figure of the unknown deserter was unveiled. According to Rudi Seibt, one of the organizers of the action, the purpose of the unknown deserter was to convey an anti-militaristic message.[10] The primary goal of protest groups such as the *Spätverweigerer* ("late objectors to military service") was the abolition of the military. The deserter was chosen as a symbol of individual choice.

This strand of the deserter-monument movement was not concerned with commemorating the German deserters of World War II; it sought instead to highlight examples of desertion from more recent conflicts: the Vietnam War, the Soviet war in Afghanistan, and insurgent warfare in Central America. Eventually, however, discussions about current cases of conscientious objection and desertion aroused interest in the historical precedents for such cases in German history. The use of the figure of the unknown deserter led to calls for deserter monuments dedicated in the first instance to the principle of desertion rather than to any specific historical episode of desertion. This second strand of the deserter-monument movement sought to challenge the principles underpinning military values and to provoke reflection on the value of refusing military service. As the deserter-monument movement expanded and gained momentum in the 1980s, this strand often

**FIGURE 4.2** Bremen memorial to the unknown deserter. From the Archiv der Bundesarbeitsgemeinschaft der Deserteure-Initiativen (BAG DI). Published with permission of Rudi Seibt on behalf of the BAG DI

intersected with and merged with the strand aimed specifically at commemoration of German deserters from the *Wehrmacht*.

The monument consists of a one-meter-high pedestal topped with a sculpture of a soldier's head with a steel helmet and camouflage net—a NATO rather than a *Wehrmacht* helmet. The inscription reads: "To the unknown deserter. Reservists who refuse military service." Preceding the dedication of the Kassel monument by eight months, the Bremen monument (see Figure 4.2) qualifies as the first public deserter monument in Germany. It was clearly inspired by the anti-NATO protests of the early 1980s. It sought primarily to highlight the principle of desertion and to encourage conscientious objection and desertion in the case of future wars rather than to commemorate *Wehrmacht* deserters.

The two initial deserter monuments in Bremen and Kassel served both as an inspiration for further memorial actions elsewhere in Germany and as a target for conservative outrage. Throughout the 1980s and well into the 1990s, opinions about the deserters and about the desirability of deserter monuments were sharply polarized between a small activist minority in favor of rehabilitation and memorialization and a majority who held fast to the traditional view of deserters as cowards and criminals and vehemently rejected memorialization. Veterans groups, in particular, expressed anger at the very notion of deserter monuments, regarding them as defamatory attacks on their own military service. The long-serving chairman of the West German Association of German Soldiers, Jürgen Schreiber, succinctly expressed the prevailing view of most *Wehrmacht* veterans in 1992 when he wrote that "putting up commemorative plaques or erecting monuments 'for the unknown deserter' is nothing short of perfidious."[11] Other opponents argued that the deserter-monument movement was in reality simply a cover for a leftist campaign aimed at undermining the *Bundeswehr*, the West German military.[12]

Supporters of the deserter-monument movement proposed a radically new assessment of the deserter as a figure of resistance rather than a traitor. In 1987, Gerhard Zwerenz, a *Wehrmacht* veteran who had deserted to the Soviets in 1944 and who became a prolific West German author in the postwar years, commented in an article published in the *Frankfurter Rundschau* newspaper:

> As one of the last surviving deserters of the criminal Second World War I take the liberty of speaking on behalf of all the other known and unknown deserters. Desertion was the resistance of the little soldier. If there was any honor of the German soldier, then it manifested itself only in resistance or in refusal to serve. So much for the helmeted heroes who today incessantly mumble about heroism and fighting to the last minute ... It reflects credit on the nation that it has produced so many brave deserters who refused to become guilty. A state that had understanding and reason would pay pensions not to the Knights of the Iron Cross but to the deserters.[13]

On April 4, 1990, a Green Party member in the Bavarian parliament referred to deserters from the *Wehrmacht* as "the unknown heroes" of the Second World War.[14] This description represented a complete reversal of the conventional view of the deserter and suggested the need for a fundamental shift in the conceptualization of heroism itself. Central to the argument of the proponents of deserter monuments was the contention that the war launched by Germany in September 1939 was an illegal war of conquest and annihilation. Given the unjustifiable and immoral nature of the war, every act of soldierly refusal to participate in such a war represented a humane and morally justified response. Every deserter meant one fewer soldier for Hitler's illegal war. In this depiction of Nazi Germany's war as an aggressive, unjust war of annihilation, the deserter-monument movement contributed to a major public debate within Germany from the mid-1980s on the nature of the war and the degree of *Wehrmacht* complicity in war crimes.

The deserter monuments in Kassel and Bremen stirred up political controversy and inspired subsequent deserter-monument initiatives in cities and towns across West Germany (and, after 1990, across the former East Germany as well). By the mid-1990s, at least 60 initiatives had been launched. Not all were successful in achieving their aims, but the campaigns kept the issue of deserter monuments in the public eye. The founding of the Federal Association of Victims of Nazi Military Justice in October 1990 by 38 former deserters, conscientious objectors, and "subversives" also helped to sustain the deserter-monument movement. Members of the

**74** Steven R. Welch

association were active in promoting local monument initiatives that then also became platforms for advancing surviving deserters' argument that they deserved to be officially rehabilitated and reintegrated in an honorable way into the German narrative of World War II.

The Bremen and Kassel monuments also stood as examples of the two key categories of deserter monuments that subsequently emerged: those dedicated explicitly to the deserters from the *Wehrmacht* and those that make no direct reference to World War II but instead focus on the principle of desertion. Roughly two thirds of deserter monuments belong to the first category, one third to the second. In the following two sections, I examine three prominent examples from each of these categories.

## Monuments to the principle of desertion

In the city of Ulm, a group of "late objectors" organized a deserter-monument initiative in 1988. In conjunction with the artist Hannah Stütz-Mentzel, their efforts culminated in the creation of one of the most impressive early deserter monuments (see Figure 4.3).

The six-ton steel sculpture entitled *Stein des Anstoßes* was unveiled on September 9, 1989. Dedicated to the German deserters of World War II, it was originally placed

FIGURE 4.3   *Stein des Anstoßes* in Ulm. From the Archiv der Bundesarbeitsgemeinschaft der Deserteure-Initiativen. Published with permission of Rudi Seibt on behalf of the BAG DI

on the public site of a former military fortress. The work consists of 12 progressively smaller flat rectangular steel blocks mounted on a steel plate; the number of blocks corresponds to the number of years the Nazi regime was in power. The largest of the steel blocks is four meters high, the smallest ten centimeters. The smallest block is gold-plated while the remaining blocks are rusty steel. The smallest of the blocks has tipped over, starting a chain reaction that, domino-style, has begun to topple the next nine blocks; only the two largest blocks are still standing straight upright.

The sculpture's title carries a double meaning. Figuratively, the phrase *Stein des Anstoßes* denotes a stumbling block or something that gives offense; the act of desertion has traditionally been regarded as an act that transgresses against accepted codes of male behavior. In a literal sense, the sculpture depicts a block (*Stein*) that gives a push (*Anstoß*) to the other blocks, thus causing them to tumble over. Like the smallest block, the courage of the individual deserter unleashes a chain reaction that topples the military colossus. In Brigitte Hausmann's words, Stütz-Mentzel's sculpture depicts desertion as "an act with consequences, a transformation 'from below' which becomes an avalanche and can bring about a fundamental change."[15] The monument's inscription is a 1925 slogan from the anti-war author Kurt Tucholsky: "Here lived a man who refused to shoot at his fellow human beings. Honor his memory."[16] The organizers stated that the monument was designed to pay homage to the courage of deserters and conscientious objectors who rejected violence and acted on behalf of the cause of peace.

City authorities in Ulm ordered the monument to be removed from public ground.[17] From October 1989 until late 2005, the sculpture was stored in a private back garden in Ulm. The Greens in the city council repeatedly sought to obtain a public space for the monument in central Ulm, but their attempts proved unsuccessful. In March 2005, the Cultural Affairs Committee of the city of Ulm once again rejected a plan to erect the Ulm deserter monument on a public site. The Lord Mayor, Ivo Gönner (SPD), who had originally supported the idea of a deserter monument in 1989, now voiced his opposition, arguing that the city has a central monument which commemorates all victims of World War II and of National Socialism and that, in his view, was sufficient: "anything else would just mean a segmentation into victim groups."[18] At the end of 2005, however, the sculpture was relocated to a piece of ground leased by the Greens near the bus stop "*An den Schießständen*" (at the shooting ranges), a site where executions took place in the Third Reich—executions which most likely included deserters.[19]

The year 1989 also saw the dedication of a deserter monument in what was then the West German capital of Bonn (see Figure 4.4). Dedicated to the unknown deserter, the monument was first exhibited on Anti-War Day on the Friedensplatz (Peace Square, which was named Adolf Hitler Square from 1933 to 1945).[20] After just ten hours on public display, an order was issued for the monument to be removed. City officials in Bonn subsequently refused to approve a public site for the monument and in September 1991, following the fall of the Berlin Wall, it was relocated to Potsdam, which had been Bonn's sister city in the former German Democratic Republic. The monument's location on Platz der Einheit (Unity

FIGURE 4.4  Monument to the Unknown Deserter, Potsdam. From the author's personal collection

Square) in the heart of Potsdam provides a clear counterpoint in a city that owes its existence to the martial legacy of the Prussian kings. As the chief garrison city for the Prussian army and with the palaces of the former Hohenzollern rulers only a few kilometers away, Potsdam has long been synonymous with Prussia's military past. The deserter monument takes on a particularly provocative edge in this setting.

Created by the Kurdish sculptor Mehmet Aksoy, the monument is carved from gray Carrara marble and weighs approximately 12 tonnes. Measuring two meters in height, three meters in width, and four meters in length, it represents a wall, damaged by shooting, through which the silhouette of a man is disappearing. According to Aksoy, the monument seeks to depict "flight away from the blind destruction of war toward life."[21] In contrast to the Ulm monument, which places the act of desertion within a broader framework of fundamental social change, the Potsdam monument represents desertion in terms of individual refusal, with no reference to its wider social context.

For several years after its initial placement in Potsdam, it was unclear whether the monument would become permanent. During this period, there was no fixed inscription. In 1995, chalk inscriptions were written around the base of the monument that described it as a monument to the unknown deserter with the motto: "better a live coward than a dead murderer" (see Figure 4.5).

By 2000, city officials had decided that the monument would become a permanent feature of the square. The area around the monument was re-landscaped and a

**FIGURE 4.5** Chalk inscription in front of Potsdam monument in 1995. From the author's personal collection

plaque was installed which carried the dedication "For the unknown deserters," along with the same Tucholsky slogan used in Ulm: "Here lived a man who refused to shoot at his fellow human beings. Honor his memory."

The most significant deserter monument dedicated in the post-2002 period to the principle of desertion was installed in Stuttgart in August 2007. The monument had its origins in an initiative launched in 1996. The monument is located in front of the Theaterhaus in central Stuttgart; this is a temporary position until a final decision about a permanent public site is taken. The Stuttgart initiative organized a competition to determine what form the monument would take and received over 50 submissions. The sculptor Nikolaus Kernbach's "profile form" emerged as the winning design. From a large block of granite, Kernbach cut out a slightly larger than life-size piece in the profile of a standing human figure (see Figure 4.6). This figure is positioned a few meters away from the original block from which it was cut, facing directly back toward the solid rock from which it has seemingly "broken free," leaving a gaping hole. The effect is similar in some respects to Askoy's Potsdam monument. Both monuments present the deserter as an individual figure who has escaped from the stifling bonds of social conformity. Speaking at the dedication ceremony, the art historian Renate Gebessler praised the sculptor for powerfully "profiling for us this nameless, unknown deserter, his sensitivity, fragility, his constraints and the multiplicity of his motives."[22]

One of the keynote speakers at the dedication ceremony was Ludwig Baumann, a *Wehrmacht* deserter and the head of the Federal Association of the Victims of Nazi Military Justice. His presence highlighted the link between the monument and those German soldiers who deserted from the *Wehrmacht* in World War II. But the Stuttgart monument is not dedicated specifically to German deserters from that war; instead it articulates a position endorsing the principle of desertion. The monument includes a plaque with the inscription "dedicated to the deserters of all wars." This universal appeal to the principle of desertion was underscored at the dedication ceremony by the presence of another of the keynote speakers, Chris Capps, a veteran of the Iraq War who deserted from the US Army. The prominent military

78  Steven R. Welch

FIGURE 4.6  Deserter monument in Stuttgart (photo by Wolfgang Krauß; used with permission)

historian Manfred Messerschmidt also spoke at the ceremony, and while he devoted some attention to the specific experience of German deserters under the Nazi military justice system, he also made extensive comments on the contemporary situation of deserters in conflicts in the Balkans, the Middle East, and Iraq.

## Monuments to deserters from the *Wehrmacht*

In 1990, one year after the unveiling of the monuments in Ulm and Bonn, a deserter monument was dedicated in Göttingen. Installed on the facade of the building which served as the barracks for the 82nd Infantry Regiment from 1871 to 1945, its location, like those of other deserter monuments, was deliberately chosen in order to draw attention to the contrast between traditional military values and a life-affirming ethos represented by desertion.

The monument consists of a large granite slab showing a trampled Nazi flag and a cherry tree branch, under which are chiseled the words "Not out of fear of death, but rather out of the will to live," a sentence from Alfred Andersch's book *The Cherries of Freedom* (see Figure 4.7). The cherries in Andersch's book are in turn a reference to

FIGURE 4.7  Deserter monument in Göttingen. From the author's personal collection

Erich Maria Remarque's novel *All Quiet on the Western Front*, in which cherries stand as a metaphor for desertion.[23] There is also a plaque bearing the inscription: "To the deserters who for reasons of conscience refused to carry out war service for the national-socialist tyranny and as a result were persecuted, killed and slandered." The Greens in Göttingen sought to delete the phrase "for the national-socialist tyranny" in order to make the plaque representative of deserters of all wars but this initiative failed.[24] Eckart Stedeler, one of the spokespeople for the Göttingen pacifists who led the initiative, stated that the monument was intended to stimulate reflection upon "the false ideals of heroism, unconditional obedience and readiness to sacrifice oneself."[25]

Following German reunification in 1990, deserter-monument initiatives began to emerge in some cities of the former German Democratic Republic. In Erfurt, a group including members of the German union movement and local clergy met in November 1994 and launched a project with the goal of establishing a deserter monument to be dedicated on the 50th anniversary of the liberation of Erfurt in May 1945. The initiative aimed to "make a contribution to the political rehabilitation and compensation of the victims of Nazi military justice."[26] One can see in this instance how the two projects of memorialization and political rehabilitation of victims became interrelated; the call for official rehabilitation of deserters, which had emerged in the course of the initial stage of the monument movement in the 1980s, became a key motive and driving force in local initiatives throughout the 1990s.

Local Erfurt artist Thomas Nicolai was chosen as the sculptor for the proposed monument. Donations raised 21,000 German marks for the project, and material for the monument was provided by a metallurgy firm. The German Railway (*Bundesbahn*) also provided support. On March 22, 1995, the city council voted 24–17 in favor of the project, with support coming from the Greens/Forum, the Party of Democratic Socialism (PDS), and a majority of the Social Democrats.

The monument is located on the Petersberg just outside the walls of the old military citadel. During World War II, the Petersberg was the site of a military court, and the complex also contained a jail in which deserters were confined prior to execution. The Catholic priest who was the military chaplain throughout the war has written that at least 20 soldiers were executed by firing squad near the Petersberg or were guillotined at the prison in Weimar.[27]

The monument consists of eight steel pillars designed to represent a military formation. Seven of the eight pillars are identical, standing at the same angle, conveying a sense of uniform military subordination (see Figure 4.8). One of the eight pillars, however, is turned differently, representing the deserter who breaks formation. One might also interpret the pillars as a representation of a military machine whose smooth functioning is brought to a halt as a result of the "malfunction" of one of its parts. This kind of reading fits neatly with the quotation from Günter Eich that is part of the monument's inscription: "Be the sand, not the oil, in the works of the world."[28] This text follows the main inscription that reads: "To the unknown Wehrmacht deserter. To the victims of Nazi military justice. To all those who refused to serve the Nazi regime."

The most recent major deserter monument focused specifically on honoring deserters from the *Wehrmacht* was dedicated in November 2015 in Hamburg. Although deserter-monument initiatives had begun in the city as early as the 1980s,

**FIGURE 4.8**  Deserter monument in Erfurt. From the author's personal collection.

it was not until June 2012 that the city government voted unanimously in favor of erecting a monument. The following year, a competition to find an appropriate design was announced. The committee conducting the competition indicated: "We do not wish for a traditional monument that imitates the memorials to the dead or the tributes to heroes characteristic of early periods with their affirmative and purposeful dedications and forms."[29] Instead, a distinctly modern form of memorialization was sought, one that would be informed by contemporary aesthetic approaches.

The site chosen for the monument was near the Dammtor railway station in the center of the city, in close proximity to two earlier monuments: the war memorial to the 76th Infantry Division dedicated at a massive Nazi-choreographed ceremony in March 1936, and the anti-war counter-monument constructed by Alfred Hrdlicka in the years 1983–1986 (but left uncompleted).[30] The deserter monument was to be inserted into a space already characterized by the "field of tension" created by the juxtaposition of the 1936 Nazi memorial celebrating war and the counter-monument highlighting the destructiveness of war.[31] This placement of the deserter monument would guarantee a high degree of public exposure and also offer the opportunity for a critical confrontation, in particular with the 1936 monument. The spatial proximity would allow for the "visual alteration and defamiliarization (*Verfremdung*) of the Nazi monument itself and also provoke reflection on the victims of the military justice system during the Third Reich."[32]

The winner of the competition was the German sculptor Volker Lang. The "Memorial Site for Deserters and Other Victims of Nazi Military Justice" takes the form of an equilateral triangle (see Figure 4.9). Two of the walls consist of word

FIGURE 4.9    Hamburg deserter monument. Hrdlicka counter-monument in right foreground and war memorial to the 76th Infantry Division in background. Photo credit Johannes Arlt/laif

grills that reproduce the first 19 lines of Helmut Heißenbüttel's 1967 poem "Germany 1944." Heißenbüttel's text strings together fragments of quotations from 1944 from both victims and perpetrators of Nazi violence.

The text of the first word grill, to be read from outside the monument, reads:

> are you attached to life they sacrifice it with fervour for higher things
> no one forced them to do it but their heart's beat their soul's
> command are you attached to life they sacrifice it with fervour for
> higher things no one forced them to do it but their heart's beat their
> soul's command the long duration of the war has led to a general
> slackening of rigorous views on the perniciousness of supplementary
> benefits for compatriots blood now circulate rejuvenated by ever
> more blooming bodies sweet is the body's music words are a mosaic
> which means that cracks run between them these logically considered
> are gaps one must reject and eject

The text of the second word grill, to be read from inside the monument, reads:

> these vilest creatures who have ever worn the military uniform of history this
> rabble that has managed to save itself from the former era I was
> standing now at the window now on the meadow so as to impress
> upon myself now this now that impression like someone who is
> occupied with a long sequence of camera shots perhaps much
> later when all these terrible things are past someone will understand
> the torture and the scream the front in these weeks calls only
> for reinforcement and weapons and the people desire to bring the very
> last to the front to avert the threat from our frontiers one most remarkable
> thing is[33]

According to Volker Lang, the Heißenbüttel text was chosen because it documented the specific political landscape of Nazi Germany that was shaped and perverted by ideology and violence. The fragments remain anonymous and without context; the individual appears meaningless in the face of the arbitrary destructiveness unleashed by the Nazi war of annihilation. The individual deserter is the figure who rebels against this bleak and suffocating reality.

Visitors to the monument can enter the interior space through a small opening between the word grills. From inside, one has a view through the grills to both of the neighboring monuments from 1936 and 1986. An audio installation plays a recording of Heißenbüttel reciting the opening lines of "Germany 1944." One can also listen to biographical details of the 227 German soldiers known to have been executed in Hamburg for the crimes of desertion and subversion. Additional information about the military justice system and its network of courts and incarceration centers throughout Hamburg is provided on the back concrete wall of the monument.

## Impact and significance of the deserter-monument movement

As a result of three decades of activism by proponents of deserter monuments, there are now more than 30 deserter monuments in Germany. As the survey above indicates, one can distinguish between two major types of deserter monuments. Those in Kassel, Göttingen, Erfurt, and Hamburg are dedicated to the German deserters of World War II and can be understood primarily, though not exclusively, as sites of commemoration.[34] The monuments in Bremen, Ulm, Potsdam, and Stuttgart, on the other hand, make no explicit reference at all to the German deserters of World War II, but instead focus on the universal principle of desertion itself, not desertion linked to a specific historical episode. Provocation to reflection, not commemoration, is their main purpose. To be sure, the more commemorative monuments are not without their own provocative edge, which often derives from their location within or alongside earlier war memorials or military sites. But their message is more circumscribed and less universal than the monuments focused on the principle of desertion.

Both types of deserter monuments can be regarded as examples of modern counter-monuments. While they do not represent direct challenges to the way in which monuments themselves are conceptualized and understood—one of the key features of counter-monuments as defined by James Young—they do exhibit one of the other key criteria which Young has incorporated into his definition: the aim to provoke rather than to console.[35] By recognizing and honoring those German soldiers who refused to comply, the deserter monuments in Kassel, Göttingen, Erfurt, and Hamburg raise the often very uncomfortable and troubling question of the individual responsibility of those soldiers who *did* comply with the crimes committed in the name of the German nation. These monuments, thus, force a confrontation with a part of the German past that has been long avoided, ignored, forgotten, or conveniently reinterpreted in a distorted fashion. The second type of monument, exemplified by those in Bremen, Ulm, Potsdam, and Stuttgart, transcends the specific historical case of desertion from Hitler's army and attempts to challenge conventional thinking about deserters and about soldierly values in general. These monuments suggest that the traditional discourse surrounding death in war deserves to be questioned. Rather than regarding death in war as, by definition, a "noble sacrifice," these monuments insist that the conventional language of soldierly obedience, heroism, and comradeship needs to be reconsidered.

Both types of deserter monuments also qualify as counter-monuments in the sense that they have been explicitly conceptualized as critical counterpoints to the ubiquitous war memorials found across Germany (as of the late 1980s there were an estimated 100,000 war memorials in what was then West Germany; in the reunified Federal Republic the total may be around 130,000). Through their deliberate location on former military sites or within existing war memorials, as well as through their inscriptions, deserter monuments confront and seek to subvert the messages conveyed by war memorials. They are dedicated to de-glorifying war and to challenging axiomatic views about the value of the soldierly virtues of self-sacrifice and obedience unto death.

What impact has the deserter-monument movement had and what does it reveal about the refashioning of German memories of World War II? A number of commentators have argued that the movement to establish deserter monuments and to achieve legal rehabilitation of the deserters produced a significant shift in public attitudes concerning deserters. As early as 1990, Norbert Mecklenburg argued that the deserter-monument movement had resulted in "a considerable shift" in public attitudes in favor of the deserters.[36] In an article published in 2004, Wolfram Wette labeled the law of May 2002 that rehabilitated those *Wehrmacht* soldiers convicted of desertion as "something like the official certification of a shift in values." According to Wette,

> a majority in German society as well as in the German parliament paid their respect to the 'little people' who refused to serve in the wars of the unjust National Socialist regime, nullified their convictions as a whole, and in so doing granted to them "belated justice."[37]

In a newspaper interview published in March 2005, the military historian Manfred Messerschmidt expressed the view that, with regard to the deserters, "in recent years, fortunately, there has been a reorientation in opinion—but only more than a half a century after the war."[38]

Some of the proponents of deserter monuments, while acknowledging that there has been some shift in public attitudes, have been more ambiguous in their overall judgments. In 2000, Rudi Seibt, for example, expressed skepticism that a major shift had taken place among the broader German public. He pointed to the strong opposition encountered by many of the deserter-monument initiatives across the country; more of them ultimately failed to achieve their goal than succeeded. Seibt's own efforts to erect a deserter monument in Munich ran into fierce opposition from political conservatives in the Bavarian capital.[39] In the northern city of Braunschweig, proponents of a deserter monument had to deal not only with political opposition but with repeated acts of vandalism toward provisional monuments which they set up from 1989 through 1997. The saga of failure in Braunschweig has been labeled as a clear example of "a social process of repression—from the refusal to remember, to administrative stonewalling, through to open aggression."[40]

The city of Marburg offers another example of the failure of a deserter-monument initiative to prevail in the face of stiff local opposition.[41] The failures of deserter-monument initiatives in many German cities indicate that the shift in public attitudes concerning the German deserters of World War II was not uniform or comprehensive. It seems fair to conclude, however, that the deserter-monument movement has succeeded in raising public awareness of the issue of desertion—both from Hitler's armed forces and from forces involved in more recent wars—and has played a very significant role in securing legal rehabilitation of deserters and conscientious objectors through the passage of the law of May 2002, and of those accused of war treason through a law passed in September 2009.

The deserter-monument movement provides a clear example of a group of "forgotten victims" gaining belated public recognition. Just as homosexuals, Sinti and Roma, Germans compulsorily sterilized between 1933-1945, and foreign forced laborers were, over the course of two decades between 1990 and 2010, officially recognized and memorialized as victims of the Nazi regime, so too were the deserters rehabilitated and memorialized. Recognition of the deserters added a new strand to the multiple war stories that collectively constituted German public memory of the war and expanded the German memory space that had to a large extent been monopolized in the early postwar decades by the war stories of prisoners of war and expellees.

The deserter-monument movement also helped to generate, and fed into, broader public debates in Germany over the past two decades about the nature of World War II, the role of the *Wehrmacht*, and the forms of anti-Nazi resistance. It did this in at least three ways. First, one of the central arguments of the deserter-monument movement—that World War II was an illegal, aggressive, racial war of annihilation—increasingly came to be accepted by a significant portion of politicians and the general public.[42] A resolution addressed to the issue of rehabilitation of deserters and conscientious objectors passed by the Bundestag in May 1997, for example, begins with the assertion: "the Second World War was an aggressive war of annihilation, a crime for which National Socialist Germany bears the responsibility."[43]

Second, the deserter-monument movement sparked a series of historical studies that produced a significantly more critical appraisal of the German military justice system in World War II.[44] In opposition to the conventional view which insisted that the military justice system had functioned in a "normal" fashion, impartially dispensing justice in a manner similar to the military justice systems of the Western Allies, the new research depicted the military justice system as an integral part of the Nazi system of legal terror which willingly and actively contributed to the achievement of Nazi war aims.[45] This view in turn helped to further undermine the credibility of the "myth of the decent *Wehrmacht*" and reinforced the arguments of those who regarded the deserters as victims of a flawed system of military injustice.

Third, the debates stimulated by the deserter-monument movement were instrumental in having desertion increasingly recognized as a form of anti-Nazi resistance. The German Resistance Memorial Center in Berlin, opened in 1989, includes accounts of *Wehrmacht* deserters as part of its permanent exhibition. From the mid-1990s, general reference works on National Socialism and on anti-Nazi resistance started to include entries on desertion, depicting it as a form of resistance from the ranks of ordinary soldiers that deserved to be acknowledged alongside the more well-known officers' plot of July 20, 1944.[46]

The establishment of deserter monuments deserves to be regarded as a significant episode in the long-running—and still continuing—struggle in postwar Germany to confront its problematic past.[47] Through the deserter monuments, the German deserters of World War II have become publicly visible again, achieving a political and social recognition that had been denied them for decades after the war. The monuments themselves can be read as tangible signs marking a modest but nevertheless discernible shift in German public memory of World War II.

## Notes

1 In June 2001, a monument was dedicated at the National Memorial Arboretum in Staffordshire, UK, to 307 British and Commonwealth soldiers who were executed during World War I for desertion and cowardice. That memorial resulted from the efforts of the "Shot at Dawn" movement that had campaigned for years to obtain pardons for the executed soldiers. See the entry in the War Memorials Archive of the UK at http://www.ukniwm.org.uk/server/show/conMemorial.46465/fromUkniwmSearch/1.
2 In 2014, a deserter monument was dedicated in Vienna on Ballhallsplatz. Images and extensive information can be found at http://www.deserteursdenkmal.at.
3 The law exonerated the deserters, expunged their criminal records, and declared the verdicts imposed on them by the military courts to have been unjust and invalid. Gesetz zur Änderung des Gesetzes zur Aufhebung nationalsozialistischer Unrechtsurteile in der Strafrechtspflege, July 23, 2002 in Bundesgesetzblatt 2002, Part 1, No. 51, 2714.
4 On the concept of war stories see Robert G. Moeller, *War Stories: The Search for a Usable Past in the Federal Republic of Germany* (Berkeley: University of California Press, 2001).
5 Heinrich Böll, "Wo sind die Deserteure?" *Aufwärts. Jugendzeitung des Deutschen Gewerkschaftsbundes,* March 5, 1953; Alfred Andersch, *Die Kirschen der Freiheit. Ein Bericht* (Zurich: Diogenes Verlag, 1968; first published 1952), English translation by Michael Hulse, *The Cherries of Freedom. A Report* (New Milford, CT: The Toby Press, 2004); Heinrich Böll, *Entfernung von der Truppe. Erzählung* (Berlin and Cologne: Keipenhauer and Witsch, 1964), English translation by Leila Vennewitz, *Absent Without Leave* (New York: McGraw-Hill, 1965).
6 The key documents concerning the Filbinger affair can be found in R. von dem Knesbeck, *In Sachen Filbinger gegen Hochhuth: die Geschichte einer Vergangenheitsbewältigung* (Reinbek bei Hamburg: Rowohlt, 1980); see also Wolfram Wette, "Der Fall Filbinger" in his edited collection *Filbinger, eine deutsche Karriere* (Springe: Zu Klampen, 2006), 15–34.
7 Pathbreaking critical studies by Fritz Wüllner and Manfred Messerschmidt argued that German courts-martial in World War II handed down an estimated 50,000 death sentences against soldiers and civilians; approximately 33,000 of these were actually carried out. See Fritz Wüllner and Manfred Messerschmidt, *Die Wehrmachtjustiz im Dienste des Nationalsozialismus* (Baden-Baden: Nomos, 1987) and Fritz Wüllner, *Die NS-Militärjustiz und das Elend der Geschichtsschreibung: ein grundlegender Forschungsbericht* (Baden-Baden: Nomos, 1991).
8 Jörg Kammler, *Ich habe die Metzelei satt und laufe über: Kasseler Soldaten zwischen Verweigerung und Widerstand (1939–1945): eine Dokumentation* (Fuldabrück: Hesse, 1985).
9 For an account of resistance to the missile issue see Jeffrey Herf, *War by Other Means: Soviet Power, West German Resistance, and the Battle of the Euromissiles* (New York: Free Press, 1991).
10 Interview with Rudi Seibt in Munich, June 28, 2000.
11 Jürgen Schreiber, "'Heldenhafte' Deserteure?" *Soldat im Volk* 41:3 (1992), 30.
12 Franz W. Seidler, *Fahnenflucht. Der Soldat zwischen Eid und Gewissen* (Munich and Berlin: Herbig, 1993), 477.
13 Zwerenz's article appeared on April 1, 1987 in the *Frankfurter Rundschau*. This passage quoted from Seidler, *Fahnenflucht*, 481.
14 Stenographic record of Bavarian Landtag, 11/126, April 4, 1990, p. 8643.
15 Brigitte Hausmann, *Duell mit der Verdrangung? Denkmäler für die Opfer des National-sozialismus in der Bundesrepublik Deutschland 1980 bis 1990* (Münster: Lit Verlag, 1997), 56.
16 The quotation appeared originally in a piece entitled "Die Tafeln" published in *Die Weltbühne* 21 (1925), 601. Like Andersch, Tucholsky has functioned as an inspirational figure in the deserter-monument movement. Tucholsky's assertion in 1931 that "soldiers are murderers" sparked a debate and court case in the early 1990s. See Michael Hepp and Viktor Otto, eds., *Soldaten sind Mörder: Dokumentation einer Debatte 1931–1996* (Berlin: Ch. Links, 1996) and Otto Gritschneder, "'Soldaten sind Mörder.' Das Tucholsky-Zitat

von 1931 im Lichte einer Entscheidung des Bundesverfassungsgerichts von 1994," in *Recht ist, was den Waffen nützt: Justiz und Pazifismus im 20. Jahrhundert*, Helmut Kramer and Wolfram Wette, eds. (Berlin: Aufbau-Verlag, 2004), 317–320.
17 Ulrike Puvogel and Martin Stankowski (eds.), Gedenkstätten für die Opfer des Nationalsozialismus. Eine Dokumentation, 2nd edition (Bonn: Bundeszentrale für politische Bildung, 1995), 99.
18 Bernd Dörries, "Ein Stein des Anstoßes, verborgen im Garten," *Süddeutsche Zeitung*, March 22, 2005, 11.
19 Interview with Domino Winter, April 2006, available at http://www.uni-kassel.de/fb5/frieden/themen/Pazifismus/deserteure.html.
20 Ibid., 503.
21 Mehmet Aksoy quoted in the pamphlet *Deseteur Denk-mal!* published by the Bonner Friedensplenum, in BAG DI, Ordner 4.
22 Address by Reante Gebessler in Dokumentation über die Einweihung des Deserteur denkmals am 30. August am Theaterhaus Stuttgart (Stuttgart, 2007), 13, available at http://www.deserteurdenkmal-stuttgart.de.
23 Norbert Haase, "Die Zeit der Kirschblüten … zur aktuellen Denkmalsdebatte und zur Geschichte der Desertion im Zweiten Weltkrieg." In Verräter oder Vorbilder? Deserteure und Ungehorsame Soldaten im Nationalsozialismus, edited by Fietje Ausländer (Bremen: Temmen, 1990), 152-154.
24 Press release from Eckart Stedeler, May 5, 1990; in BAG DI, Ordner 3.
25 Quotations from *This Week in Germany*, September 28, 1990, 6, published by the German Information Center.
26 *Dokumente einer Erfurter Denkmal für den unbekannten Wehrmachtdeserteur* (Erfurt: DGB-Bildungswerk Thüringen e.V.), 4.
27 "Erinnerungen eines Standortpfarrers," in ibid., 6.
28 Günter Eich, "Wacht auf, denn eure Träume sind schlecht!" in *Gesammelte Werke*, 1st ed., vol. 2 (Frankfurt am Main: Suhrkamp, 1973), 322.
29 Stellungnahme des Senats zu dem Ersuchen der Bürgerschaft vom 14. Juni 2012, "Deserteursdenkmal—Opfer der nationalsozialistischen Militärjustiz in Hamburg—Neue Formen des Gedenkens, vernachlässigte Aspekte, Fortentwicklung des Gesamtkonzeptes für Orte des Gedenkens an die Zeit des Nationalsozialismus 1933–1945 in Hamburg," Bürgerschaft der freien und Hansestadt Hamburg, 20. Wahlperiode, Drucksache 20/7833 April 30, 2013, 4, available at http://www.hamburg.de/gedenkort-fuer-deserteure/4974406/entstehung-gedenkort-fuer-deserteure/.
30 For a succinct overview of the two Dammtor memorials see Peter Reichel, *Politik mit der Erinnerung. Gedächtnisorte im Streit um die nationalsozialistische Vergangenheit* (Munich: Hanser, 1995), 83–88.
31 Gedenkort für Deserteure und andere Opfer der NS-Militärjustiz, *Dokumentation des Gestaltungswettbewerbs* published by the Freie und Hansestadt Hamburg (Hamburg: Druckerei Siepmann GmbH, 2014), 7, available at http://www.hamburg.de/gedenkort-fuer-deserteure/4974406/entstehung-gedenkort-fuer-deserteure/.
32 Stellungnahme des Senats zu dem Ersuchen der Bürgerschaft vom 14. Juni 2012, 5.
33 English translation from Helmut Heissenbüttel, *Texts*, selected and translated by Michael Hamburger (London: Marion Boyars, 1977), 100. Selection is from "Germany 1944" in New Treatises on Human Understanding. Hamburger's English translation is reproduced on the back wall of the Hamburg deserter monument. It deviates only slightly from the printed translation provided in the 1977 book.
34 Other significant monuments dedicated to Wehrmacht deserters include those in Buchenwald concentration camp (2001), Cologne (2009), and, most recently, Hanover (2015).
35 James E. Young, "The Counter-Monument: Memory against Itself in Germany Today," *Critical Inquiry* 18 (1992), 267–296, here 277.
36 Norbert Mecklenburg, "Hilfloser Antimilitarismus? Deserteure in der Literatur," *Krieg und Literatur/War and Literature* 11:3 (1990), 139.

37 Wolfram Wette, "Deserteure der Wehrmacht rehabilitiert. Ein exemplarischer Meinungswandel in Deutschland (1980–2002)," *Zeitschrift für Geschichtwissenschaft* 52 (2004), 505–527, quotations from 525.
38 Manfred Messerschmidt interviewed by Joachim Käppner, "'Dieses Gefühl von Schuld'. Das Los der Deserteure: Manfred Messerschmidt über den Terror der Militärrichter gegen die eigenen Soldaten," *Süddeutsche Zeitung*, March 22, 2005, 11.
39 Interview in Munich, June 28, 2000.
40 Albrecht Fay, "'Den Deserteuren ein Denkmal: Sie schaden dem Krieg!' ein schwieriges Stück Gedenkstättenarbeit," (2002); originally available at http://bs.cyty.com/kirche-von-unten/archiv/gesch/fs90heintze/Fay-Deserteuren.htm.
41 See Roland Müller's piece at the site of the Geschichtswerkstatt Marburg, available at http://www.geschichtswerkstatt-marburg.de/ddenkmal/index.htm.
42 As the website of the National Socialist Documentation Center in Cologne notes, "The image of the Second World War has changed dramatically over the previous twenty years. The realization that this war did not represent a 'normal' war but rather a criminal and racial war of annihilation has in the meantime gained widespread acceptance." See https://museenkoeln.de/ns-dokumentationszentrum/default.aspx?s=1897
43 Quoted from Deutsche Bundestag, May 14, 1997, Drucksache 13/7669 (neu), 3. For further examples see the comments by Uwe Lambinus (SPD) in the minutes of the plenary proceedings of the Bundestag, December 2, 1993, p. 17080 and the motion by Bündnis 90/Die Grünen from December 9, 1993, Deutsche Bundestag, Drucksache 12/6418, 12.
44 These include: Wüllner, *NS-Militärjustiz*; Norbert Haase, *Gefahr für die Manneszucht: Verweigerung und Widerstand im Spiegel der Spruchtätigkeit von Marinegerichten in Wilhelmshaven (1939–1945), Veröffentlichungen der Historischen Kommission für Niedersachsen und Bremen. XXXIX, Niedersachsen 1933–1945*, vol. 6 (Hanover: Verlag Hahnsche Buchhandlung, 1996); Lothar Walmrath, *"Iustitia et disciplina": Strafgerichtsbarkeit in der deutschen Kriegsmarine 1939–1945* (Frankfurt am Main and New York: P. Lang, 1998); Manfred Messerschmidt, *Die Wehrmachtjustiz 1933–1945* (Paderborn: Schöningh, 2005); and Walter Manoschek, ed., *Opfer der NS-Militärjustiz: Urteilspraxis, Strafvollzug, Entschädigungspolitik in Österreich*, 1st ed. (Vienna: Mandelbaum, 2003).
45 See Steven Welch, "'Harsh But Just'? German Military Justice in the Second World War: A Comparative Study of the Court-Martialling of German and US Deserters," *German History* 17 (1999), 369–399.
46 Wolfgang Benz, Hermann Graml, and Hermann Weiss, eds., *Enzyklopädie des Nationalsozialismus* (Stuttgart: Klett-Cotta, 1997); Wolfgang Benz, ed., *Lexikon des deutschen Widerstandes* (Frankfurt am Main: S. Fischer, 1994); Peter Steinbach and Johannes Tuchel, eds., *Lexikon des Widerstandes, 1933–1945* (Munich: Beck, 1994).
47 For confirmation that the process of challenging and rewriting public narratives of the war is by no means over, one need look no further than the recent remarks made by Björn Höcke, state leader of the Alternative for Germany Party in Thuringia, in a speech in Dresden on January 17, 2017. Höcke lamented that Germans were "the only people in the world to plant a monument of shame in the heart of its capital," referring to the memorial to the murdered Jews of Europe located near the Brandenburg Gate in the center of Berlin. It seems likely that Höcke would have an equally critical attitude toward deserter monuments. See Amanda Taub and Max Fisher, "Germany's Extreme Right Challenges Guilt over Nazi Past," *New York Times*, January 18, 2017, https://www.nytimes.com/2017/01/18/world/europe/germany-afd-alternative-bjorn-hocke.html.

**PART II**
# Negotiated memories of war

# 5

# EMPERORS, BONES, AND DISSONANT MEMORIES: JAPANESE COMMEMORATION OF THE BATTLE FOR PELELIU ISLAND

*Stephen C. Murray*

In April of 2015, Emperor Akihito of Japan and his wife, Empress Michiko, traveled 2,000 miles south of Tokyo to visit the Palau Islands for two days.[1] This was only the second time the emperor had traveled to Japan's former colony in the archipelagoes of Micronesia in the Central Pacific, his first visit having been to Saipan ten years previously (see Map 5.1). Akihito did not come to partake in the scuba diving, fishing, or cultural tours favored by most visitors to Palau. Instead, he came for a very specific historical purpose: To travel to Peleliu Island, site of one of the fiercest battles of the Pacific War, to pay his respects to all those—Japanese, Americans, and Palauans—who lost their lives on Peleliu and elsewhere in Palau during 1944–1945.[2]

Most Palauans felt deeply honored to host the emperor of the nation that had so greatly affected their islands and ways of life during its 30 years of colonial dominance from 1914 to 1945. (Emperor Hirohito, the father of Akihito, occupied the throne of Japan from 1926 to 1989 and was the commander in chief during World War II, but he never visited his Pacific island empire.) One might expect that Akihito's trip—coming 70 years after the end of the Pacific War, as he himself observed—was meant as a symbolic coda to the conflict, intended to bring to a final conclusion the sorrows shared by Palauans and the Japanese alike as a result of a horribly destructive war. But, to the contrary, an important purpose of the emperor's visit was to publicize, maintain, and even expand Japanese efforts to memorialize the nation's losses in the defeat on Peleliu.

On April 13, 2015, Palau's *Tia Belau* newspaper described the warm toasts exchanged at a banquet between the president of the Republic of Palau (ROP), Tommy Remengesau, Jr., and Emperor Akihito. Remengesau recalled the generous financial aid the ROP had received from the Japanese government since the 1980s, their mutual interest in marine conservation, and the shared cultural values that included respect for the wartime dead. In reply, the emperor mentioned having heard about how well Japanese colonial migrants and Palauans had worked together,

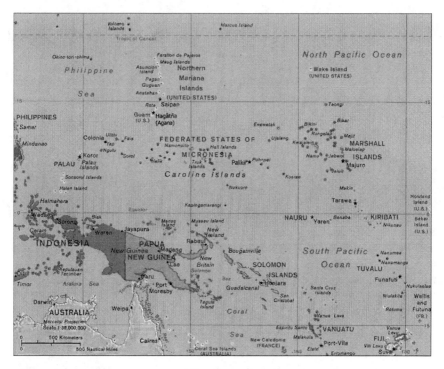

**MAP 5.1** Micronesia in the Central Pacific region. Courtesy University of Texas Libraries

and how the Japanese military had helped safeguard the lives of Palauan natives during the conflict. He then thanked the Palauan people for taking care of the monuments that Japan had raised to honor its troops, and for assisting in the recovery of the remains of fallen Japanese soldiers. Remengesau also spoke about a seemingly peripheral subject: He committed to opening 200 caves on Peleliu that the Americans had sealed closed during the battle, entombing their Imperial Army defenders. In fact, opening these particular caves was at the heart of the emperor's reasons for making a formal visit to Palau.

## Colonialism and war

Japan called the island colony it ruled in the Central Pacific the Nan'yō, meaning "South Seas."[3] Located just 550 miles east of the Philippines, Palau (see Map 5.2), with its relatively large land mass and excellent harbors, was designated capital of the Nan'yō, and during the 1930s a bustling, attractive town emerged on the island of Koror. The Imperial Navy valued the Nan'yō for its strategic advantages in case of a conflict with the United States or Britain, but Japan also eagerly exploited its natural resources, built modern infrastructure, and encouraged large-scale immigration by settlers from Okinawa and the home islands.

The major military airfield in Palau was placed on the island of Peleliu in 1937, thoroughly disrupting the patterns of life for the 825 natives on the island. When the Pacific War began, Palau was safely beyond the reach of American forces for the first two years. Only after Palau suffered a highly damaging air raid by American carrier-borne aircraft in March of 1944 did the Imperial Japanese Army (IJA) send its 14th Division to construct defenses against possible amphibious assaults by the Americans. The town of Koror was evacuated as 30,000 troops, approximately 14,300 Asian civilians, and almost all the 5,600 Palauans (including the inhabitants of Peleliu) moved to Babeldaob Island, the archipelago's largest island. Rural and forested, it allowed the troops and civilians to spread out and seek cover from air attack. Meanwhile, approximately 11,000 soldiers and forced laborers, including at least 300 Palauan men, spent five months fortifying Peleliu, excavating some 200 new caves to complement the 300 natural caves within its fractured limestone ridges. When the United States did invade Peleliu and neighboring Angaur Island in mid-September 1944, this new Japanese tactic of avoiding US firepower by going underground proved hellishly effective. The battle for the five square miles of Peleliu lasted almost 11 weeks, as the invaders were forced to engage and destroy the enemy one by one in every cave. Peleliu earned a reputation as one of the bloodiest, most difficult invasions of the Pacific War. Of the 11,000 defenders, only 300 were captured alive. The Americans suffered 1,600 deaths. The natural and human landscapes of Peleliu were devastated.[4]

For almost a year, from September 1944 to August 1945, the Americans used Peleliu's airfield to fly regular air patrols over Babeldaob and Koror, to suppress the Japanese forces marooned there. These patrols bombed and strafed the 30,000 soldiers and sailors and the 20,000 Asian civilians and Palauans indiscriminately. The Palauans were forced to build simple huts deep in the jungle and to garden under trees or at night. Fishing was extremely dangerous since men in the lagoons had no cover. In one incident, six Palauan fishermen were killed by two US planes that caught them on the open lagoon. As the Japanese military's rations began running out in early 1945, starving troops and Asian civilians begged or stole food from Palauan gardeners and fishermen. A persistent Palauan folk belief is that, to preserve food for itself, the army intended to massacre all Palauans in a cave on Babeldaob's west coast.

Ultimately, 5,000 military men died on Babeldaob and very likely an equal number of the helpless Asian civilians; 80 percent of these 10,000 deaths were caused by starvation and the diseases associated with malnutrition. Approximately 110–180 Palauans died as a result of the hostilities.[5] Palauan memories of the war, then, encompass the shared experiences of 17 months of constant warfare, of the destruction of their villages, and of terror and hunger that only stopped when Japan capitulated in mid-August 1945.

In his banquet toast, Emperor Akihito revealed his understanding of the Nan'yō years and the war's impacts on Palau. Although the Palauans received him with honor and warmth, many of their perspectives on the past were at odds with those of their guest. The islanders view the Japanese colonial period, the war, and how

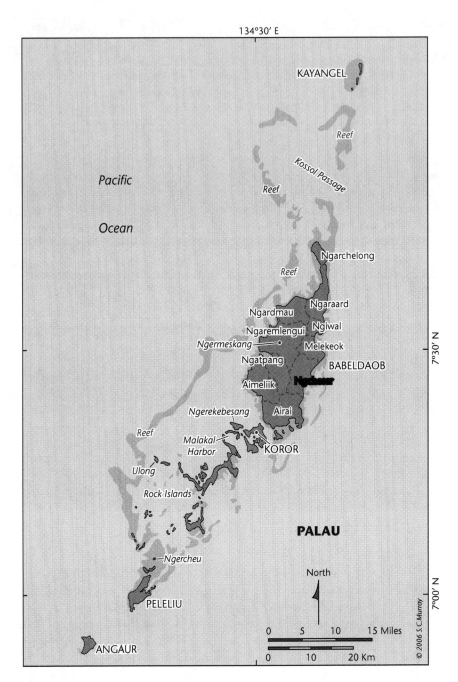

MAP 5.2 The Palau Islands. Map by S.C. Murray. Courtesy University of Alabama Press

Japan remembers both in far more complex and critical ways than were apparent at the welcoming dinner.

Akihito toasted Palauans and Nan'yō settlers working together, and the islanders had indeed appreciated their brush with such badges of modernity brought by the Nan'yō as electricity, modern transport and medical care, and consumer goods. But they remember also how their elders suffered within an official racial hierarchy that dubbed them third-class people, ranking behind the home-island Japanese as first, and Okinawans and Koreans as second. Palauan children were given only three meager years of schooling; a select few received five. The Nan'yō's economic development was designed to benefit Japan, not the local population. Heavy Japanese immigration to the Nan'yō swamped the native populations and cultures. By 1940, immigrants outnumbered the 5,600 Palauans by nearly five to one, and the colonial government claimed vast tracts of native lands for their use.[6]

The emperor hailed the military's "safeguarding" of Palauans by removing them to the relative safety of Babeldaob, and said it was "truly painful" that native casualties were caused by "air raids, food shortages, and plagues." Akihito's listeners from Peleliu knew that in truth their families had fled in their canoes to nearby island refuges after the first carrier raid in March 1944. Here they lived precariously for five months without Japanese assistance, until they were ordered to board Imperial Army boats that dropped them off in Ngermeskang, a deserted village on Babeldaob, shortly before the American invasion. Some elders of Peleliu say the Japanese moved them not from humanitarian impulse, but from fear that those who had worked on the island's fortifications would reveal their knowledge of them to the Americans. Palauans also understand that although the American air siege of Babeldaob was brutal and negligent in its treatment of civilians, the "air raids, food shortages, and plagues" could have been prevented if the Japanese commander, Lt. General Inoue Sadae, had acknowledged his hopeless position and simply surrendered to the overwhelming American forces after the loss of Peleliu in November 1944. We should also consider how many deaths would have occurred among Babeldaob's desperate populations if the war had lasted into late 1946 or beyond, as Allied planners had expected.[7]

## The politics of Japan's war memory and its postcolonial clashes

Today, Japan's seemingly unrepentant views on the war, especially when criticized by victimized neighbors like China and South Korea, can suggest that the nation's public opinion is monolithic and defensively nationalistic. Actually, the question of how to remember the nation's imperial past is a topic of vigorous and frequent argument by politically engaged groups positioned across the country's political spectrum. These often heated debates have been led not by the national government but by organizations within civil society; by citizens' groups of disparate political beliefs that organize to pressure the various levels of government to support their causes. One of the largest and most influential is Nihon Izokukai, the Japan Association of War-Bereaved Families, a conservative organization that objects to "categorical" apologies to other nations and has sought pensions for veterans' families and government support for various forms of war commemoration. Nihon Izokukai has been active on Peleliu since the late 1960s, collecting the remains of Japan's war dead. By comparison, the centrist Japan Teachers' Union argues that school textbooks should be forthright in acknowledging Japan's responsibility in fomenting war. Further to its left lie pacifist organizations that want the government to compensate Japan's many victims and offer unambiguous apologies abroad.

At the extremes of the right wing, however, crouch reactionary groups nostalgic for the days of Hirohito's empire. Many promote a return to the prewar worship of the emperor as a god at the center of a militarized, emperor-based national polity (*kokutai*) symbolized by the practice of state Shinto. This theocratic variant of Japan's indigenous religion was banned by the United States during the Occupation, and is today contrary to Japan's postwar constitution, which separates religion from the state. The Right denies atrocities like the Rape of Nanjing or the abuse of prisoners of war. Proposals to build a public museum dedicated to peace and showing accurately the devastation caused by Japan's war machine will invariably attract fierce opposition from factions on the right, which will try to eliminate or force compromises in exhibits. Such contentious interpretations of Japan's past have been exported to Palau, where they are manifested in monuments and their inscriptions, in Shinto shrines, in ceremonies, in touring and souvenir hunting, and in disputes over gathering human remains.[8] For example, David Cloud reported in the *Los Angeles Times* of May 3, 2015 that during the emperor's visit to Palau, a right-wing group that followed him from Japan gave out hand-fans pleading for a shrine to be built in honor of Colonel Nakagawa Kunio, commander of the troops who defended Peleliu. They also managed to organize some Palauans to shout "Banzai!" at the emperor's motorcade. These embarrassments were not reported in either the Palauan or Japanese press, both of which covered the visit extensively.[9]

After World War II, the United States was awarded control of Micronesia as a Trust Territory under the auspices of the United Nations. Japanese residents were repatriated, and the Americans essentially closed the islands to the outside world for 20 years. The people of Peleliu had returned to their island in 1946 to find it devastated by the lengthy battle and by the vast naval airbase that the Americans constructed, which consumed nearly two thirds of the island. The five prewar native villages had disappeared entirely, along with residents' homes, subsistence gardens, fishing canoes, and infrastructure such as piers and stone paths. Even the great lagoon's fisheries were diminished. The islanders struggled to rebuild what they could of the prewar life, but were hampered by an American administration that discouraged reconstruction of the old villages, sowed confusion over ownership of lands, yet offered no capital or meaningful economic stimulus.

Starting in the mid-1960s, small numbers of visitors were allowed into Micronesia. Among the first of these was Funasaka Hiroshi, a sergeant of the Imperial Army who survived the invasion of Angaur, and by 1965 owned a large bookstore in Tokyo. He wrote that everywhere he went on Peleliu and Angaur he was confronted by "bones, bones, bones," the remains of unburied Japanese troops.

Funasaka became a leader of the Izokukai and other Japanese civic groups who came to Palau for commemorative purposes, or what the Palauans called "the Ireidan" (Japanese for "association for consoling souls," pronounced *ee-ray-don*). The most resolute of the Ireidan have never wavered in their determination to achieve two paramount goals: to recover the remains of their fallen countrymen, and to erect memorials to honor their sacrifices. Through its Ministry of Health, Welfare, and Labor (HW&L), the government in Tokyo also became involved in the retrieval of remains. For decades now, expeditions that are sometimes private and sometimes combine private Ireidan and HW&L employees have scoured locations not just on Peleliu but throughout the South and Central Pacific.

Initially, most Ireidan who went to Palau were either families of men who died on Peleliu and Angaur, or survivors of the siege of Babeldaob. Palauans deeply sympathized with both Japanese and American visitors who came to mourn or to search for remains. The islanders have strong traditions of their own concerning the importance of proper burials and the marking of grave sites. Peleliu especially attracted bone-gathering expeditions because many thousands of remains were concentrated and well preserved in the mountain caves. American forces had left bodies in caves where they fell, and they remained undisturbed since Palauans avoided the ridges out of fear of the restless spirits of the unburied dead. The Japanese parties would collect the bones and cremate them with appropriate ceremonies intended to console the souls of the dead and bring them peace (see Figure 5.3).[10]

When Japanese Ireidan appeared in the mid-1960s needing lodging, food, and other services, while offering possible connections to repatriated relatives and Japan's thriving economy, many on Peleliu saw them as an economic opportunity. The visitors gravitated toward those islanders who viewed Japan most favorably and spoke the best Japanese; these were usually families who counted a father or grandfather among the immigrants to the Nan'yō. Some Palauans who lacked these connections complained about being shut out of business opportunities. But as the numbers of Ireidan increased into the 1970s, and more and more bones were removed, many residents of Peleliu grew worried that when the bones ran out, this important source of income would vanish as well. Islanders also viewed the situation through the prism of their customs, as part of which a person who dies while in a village not his own will be buried by a family in that host village. The burial creates strong and lasting social bonds that the two families take very seriously. The Americans had initially buried their dead on Peleliu, and their decision to exhume and relocate the bodies in 1948 caused the islanders genuine grief. They felt the same toward the Japanese dead. When the Peleliu government passed an edict prohibiting further removal of remains, sharp altercations with anguished Japanese families erupted. The Palauans argued that the men had died on Peleliu and should remain there, in accordance with local custom. The Ireidan responded, "Let us take the bones! Their blood will always remain behind!"[11]

Government officials in Tokyo attempted to ease the standoff by inviting the chiefs of each of Peleliu's five traditional villages to visit Japan. They were given 22 days of VIP treatment, the climax of which was an audience with a powerful

**FIGURE 5.1** Author Stephen C. Murray (left) and Steven Nakamura at the Shinto shrine erected on Peleliu's Bloody Nose Ridge by the right-wing group Seiryusha in 2002. It has recently been expanded. Photo by the author

member of the national legislature, the Diet. But before he could urge the chiefs to rescind the edict, their spokesman, Saburo Ngirablai, used this unprecedented encounter with a powerful agent of the former colonial overlord to ask a pointed question: "Did you Japanese and Americans get an invitation from us to come fight on our island of Peleliu? You destroyed everything and then went away and left us with nothing." Taken aback, the politician admitted that the war came to Palau because of Japan's actions. The subject of collecting bones was left unresolved. Over the years, Peleliu's local legislature and governors have generally permitted their removal, but sometimes prohibited it. No official policy regarding sealed caves has been enacted, but many Palauan officials have been reluctant to open them, whether due to customary practices regarding holding the dead of other communities, or for reasons of economics or historic preservation. Emperor Akihito's visit can be fully appreciated only within this context of disagreements over the proper treatment of Japan's war dead.[12]

## Japanese monuments: Competing messages in stone

As family members, comrades in arms, and the central government pressed on in their search for human remains, they also raised markers to commemorate the dead. In Palau there are no committees to review and approve the size, design, or messages on public or private monuments. Their creators from Japan find greater freedom to celebrate particular historical and political beliefs on the island than is available on the fractious political terrain back home. No matter where they are raised, inscriptions on monuments are intended to commemorate, not to analyze historical events. Yet those on Peleliu are notable for the very different positions they assume toward Japan's past and the meaning of the battle for Peleliu. I discuss here several representative Japanese memorials.[13]

The first two monuments erected in Palau were placed in the native cemetery on Peleliu in the village of Ngerchol in 1967, one by Funasaka and the other by the Japanese national government. Their inscriptions are typical of the early memorials. Funasaka's says: "We pray for the repose of the defending soldiers in Peleliu who bravely fought for noble peace, and we give thanks for their contribution." The government's stone next to it says, cautiously, "A memorial for all the Japanese who died here." Funasaka's support for the war and his claim that the army men died fighting for peace would jar those who consider Japan an aggressor in World War II, but these are common sentiments among Japanese of conservative leanings. Neither of these early texts is translated into English or Palauan, nor does either express repentance or concern for any of the others, like islanders or Americans, who also lost their lives in the war. This will change with later memorials. Today, this cemetery holds scores of prayer sticks and dozens of markers of all sizes recalling the battle for Peleliu from the defenders' perspective.

On the slopes of the island's limestone hills, which the US Marines famously dubbed "Bloody Nose Ridge," lies another stone marker placed in 1989 by an association formed to promote the memory of the infantry troops who defended Peleliu, and their commanding officer, Colonel Nakagawa Kunio. Like other monuments in the hills, it is frequently ringed by artifacts that visitors find nearby: helmets, mortar shells, canteens, rifle magazines. It is notable for the staunch admiration it shows for the fighters, implying strong support for Japan's engagement in the war, and for various points made in its brass-lettered inscriptions, one in English, the other in Japanese. The English text cites how, "against the overwhelming American landing forces," the defenders "fought the most fierce and courageous battle to the very last soldier" for more than two months. The Japanese text also cites the "superior war power" of the United States, but adds that at the end of the battle Col. Nakagawa committed suicide, and the surviving soldiers turned to guerrilla warfare.

What gets remembered here, and in which language, is revealing. Both versions cite American military might as the cause of the IJA's defeat. This is a recurring theme among defenders of Japan's militarism (and also among Nazi apologists). Government propaganda had assured soldiers and civilians alike that Japanese fighting spirit would negate America's enormous productive advantages. In his memoir of the battle for Angaur, Funasaka describes the despair he felt over the limitless resources the United States could hurl at him and his comrades. On the Peleliu monument, the story of Col. Nakagawa's suicide is suitable for a Japanese audience but would likely be misunderstood by foreigners, so it is left out of the English translation. So too is the dubious assertion about guerrilla fighting: American accounts of the battle consider the Japanese stragglers just an occasional nuisance.

Importantly, in the Japanese version the fallen troops are called *eirei* (*ay-ray*). Within the idiom of Japanese war memory, no term signals one's political stance toward the war more clearly. Used as official terminology during the war, *eirei* means "spirits of the glorious, heroic war dead." It is highly controversial today and implies, as Herbert Bix writes, "a positive attitude toward the imperial state and a negative evaluation of the postwar values inscribed in the constitution," in which, among other reforms drafted by the Occupation, Japan renounces war. Newspapers avoid the word, and its appearance on a memorial in Japan would excite loud objections from the political center and left.[14]

On his visit to Peleliu, Akihito paid his respects at two memorials.[15] One, placed by the American Army's 81st Infantry Division that fought on Peleliu and Angaur, stands at the former cemetery in which all American dead were interred until 1948. In a discomfiting reminder of the enervating rivalry that distracted the US Army and Navy (to which the Marines belonged) even during total war, its text honors the dead of the army division, yet makes no mention of the Marines who lay beside them.

Akihito also visited the largest war memorial on the island, a joint project of the governments of Japan and Palau from 1985. This Peace Park Memorial was well chosen, in that it alone among Peleliu's monuments explicitly honors all three peoples who suffered the war in Palau, with inscriptions in each of their languages—English, Japanese, and Palauan. The English reads, "In memory of all those who sacrificed their lives in the islands and seas of the West Pacific during World War II and in dedication to world peace." In message and language, this is the most inclusive of the monuments, and one that occupies safe middle ground in war memory.[16]

From the extreme right of Japan's political spectrum comes a secretive ultranationalist organization that has been active in Palau for perhaps 35 years, yet whose principles and purposes in the islands are little known. Seiryusha, meaning "clear stream organization"—perhaps a reference to Japan's Hirohito-era belief in its racial purity and superiority—has been led since inception by Namekawa Yuji, a businessman and resort owner in Japan. Funasaka Hiroshi, who survived Angaur, was a member and leader of Seiryusha. The organization is sympathetic to state Shinto—the prewar form of the religion, now unconstitutional, that considered the emperor as divine and the embodiment of the sacred Japanese state. Palauans familiar with the organization have described it as "radical Shinto," "imperialist," and "politically extreme." Namekawa has been very active in recovering remains, and generous in his gifts to Peleliu and Angaur to assure access. He clashed angrily with agents of Japan's HW&L Ministry over whether the bone collecting should be led by the government or by dedicated private organizations like his. Seiryusha built Shinto shrines on Peleliu and Angaur in the 1980s, and revived for its own use the Nan'yō Jinja, the great Shinto shrine dedicated in Koror in 1940, where state Shinto rites had routinely been performed. A tablet which the organization placed there celebrates Japan's imperial past and asserts that, after the "setback" of World War II, the nation is once again expanding into the South Seas and reviving the "proper historical purposes" of the great shrine. In 2003, I witnessed there an extravagant Shinto ceremony sponsored by Seiryusha. No Palauans were present. The same ceremonies are repeated annually at the shrines on Peleliu and Angaur. In 2002, Seiryusha replaced its original Peleliu shrine with a much larger one (Figure 5.1), provocatively located right next to the modest stone dedicated to the US Marine Corps in 1984, which it overwhelms.[17] In recent years, Seiryusha has changed its name to Nan'yō Kōryū Kyōkai (NKK), or the Japan–Nan'yō Cultural Exchange

Association—in order to better hide its political intentions, as was pointed out to me by a Japanese scholar.

Close to the small museum that the residents of Peleliu have built, which contains mostly artifacts from the battle, lies the memorial espousing the strongest anti-war statements on the island. Raised by an organization from Hiroshima, its message exhibits the pacifism and anti-nuclearism characteristic of the Japanese Left. One portion of its English text particularly stands out to readers familiar with the vocabulary of Japanese war memory: "Learning lessons from the calamity we suffered and the sense of guilt we feel toward other nations concerned in World War II, we have pledged in our Constitution never again to conduct aggression toward foreign countries." This is notable both for its forthright acceptance of "guilt" for the war and for its admission that Japan was the aggressor, both notions that are anathema to the Right. Although neither term appears in the Japanese version of the inscription, this contains its own unique hot-button admission—that Japan has pledged never to invade (*shinryaku*) other nations. My colleague Professor Iitaka Shingo suspects that the writers dropped "guilt" from the Japanese text in order to avoid criticism over a statement intended for global distribution. He also noted that the Right would reject *shinryaku* in favor of *shinsyutsu*, meaning "to advance into." But substituting the latter for the former in Japanese schoolbooks is just the sort of whitewashing that ignites protests from China and South Korea. Dating from 1999, the anti-war theme of this Hiroshima stone, and sites such as the Peace Park that acknowledge *all* the human losses from war, represent for Peleliu an evolution away from the militaristic and imperialistic messages of the earlier Japanese markers and shrines. As we shall see, however, their frankness and regret represented the high-water mark of a tide that turned rather quickly.[18]

## Hosts and guests: Uneasy relationships

What do the people of Peleliu make today of all these ceremonies, stones, shrines, and contending versions of the past concocted by the many outsiders who still invite themselves to the island? Naturally, their wartime memories of loss strongly color their attitudes toward the foreigners and their memorial activities. Many, especially elders, blame Japan for the hubris shown in foolishly waging war against a nation that so easily crushed the empire, and in the process so thoroughly destroyed their own ancestral home and way of life. They still resent the miserly reparations that Japan and the United States finally paid them 25 years after the war. The two powers labeled them "ex gratia" payments, meaning they were made from goodwill, not from any legal or moral obligations.[19] The tale that all Palauans narrowly escaped massacre on Babeldaob remains stubbornly alive in native memories. The islanders are keenly aware that most Ireidan from both Japan and the United States ignore them. "We're invisible in the US books," a chief told me, while Peleliu's local historian observed: "We have never had a voice."

Partly in response to the disregard they detect from outsiders, Peleliu's residents tend to dismiss the monuments to both sets of combatants that dot their landscape.

"Those are their stones, not ours" and "They write for themselves, not us" are common opinions. Palauans too are still searching for missing relatives from the war. The week the emperor arrived in Palau, a local newspaper printed a letter from a Senator of the Republic, Joel Toribiong, to the Japanese ambassador, saying that his uncle had been recruited to fight alongside Japanese soldiers in Indonesia. The uncle never returned, and the senator was asking the ambassador and the emperor to help the family in its search for his remains.[20] (Seiryusha erected a stone memorial at the Nan'yō Jinja that lists 19 Palauans who died overseas during the war in service to Japan; their remains were never recovered.) When a visit to Palau by Emperor Akihito was first proposed in 2003, an elder woman of Peleliu complained to me: "He's not coming here to thank us for taking care of the Japanese when they were here. He'll just come to pray for the souls of those who died and thank them for fighting in the war." Another resident of the island observed that although Japan and the United States have helped Peleliu since the war, "Both always come here for their own reasons."[21]

The numbers of Ireidan peaked in the 1980s, when women's groups numbering up to 50 would travel to Peleliu annually. In contrast to today's day-trip tourists from Koror (Fig. 5.2 shows a group of such visitors) or aloof bone hunters focused on their own pilgrimages, these women spent four or more days on the island and came to know personally many of the islander women, who still spoke Japanese. The Palauan women made return visits to Japan as Palau gradually became wealthier through American aid and the growth of tourism from Japan, Taiwan, Korea, and now China.[22] The relationships established during the women's visits provided the best

FIGURE 5.2  Tour guide Nakagawa Tsukane explains the battle of Peleliu to Japanese visitors, 2003. Behind them stands an American amphibious landing vehicle. Photo by Siegfried Nakamura

opportunities of the 70-year period for the two sides to express their memories and judgments of the war, to broaden understandings, and to grieve over mutual losses. But time passed, and the elders of Peleliu say that as the Ireidan aged and stopped coming, their children lacked interest in continuing regular visits. Today, the great majority of Palauans speak English as their second language, not Japanese, and their concern for the war years does not match that of their parents and grandparents.

While visits by Ireidan had declined noticeably by the 1990s, many of those who did come were motivated by fervent right-wing political beliefs and a zeal for continuing the search for human remains. A visitor who became a regular bore one of the most infamous names of the World War II era—Tōjō Yūko, the granddaughter of the former premier and executed war criminal General Tōjō Hideki. A strident ultranationalist who denied that Japan's wars constituted aggression, she visited Peleliu at least five times between 1999 and her death in 2013. She and Namekawa, the leader of Seiryusha, helped turn attention to the many caves that US forces had dynamited shut during the battle, which had become the likeliest source for new discoveries of bones. On one occasion, Tōjō sparred with Palau's Historic Preservation Office, which wanted the caves left closed as historic resources belonging to Palau.

A clash of deeply held opinions on the war occurred in Palau when Tōjō encountered a thoughtful survivor of the Imperial Army's annihilation during the invasion of Angaur. Kurata Yoji had immigrated to the islands in 1941 at the age of 14 and fought as a private on Angaur, where, like Funasaka, he survived because he was wounded and captured. He moved to Palau in 1996, and worked as a naturalist and environmentalist. Tōjō Yūko was particularly interested in excavating an antitank trench on Peleliu that the Marines might have used as a mass grave for slain Japanese. Kurata told me how that trench had been dug by Japanese troops using hand shovels. "We dug our own graves," he said somberly. He told Tōjō that the bones on the battlefields are hard to identify and that it would be impossible for all of them to be found. "It's time to focus on things other than the war—like the natural environment and the welfare of the island people," he argued. Unmoved, she continued to pressure Palauan authorities to let her open sealed caves on Peleliu.[23]

When I first explored the ridges of Peleliu in 1967, 23 years after the invasion, I was astonished to find the caves littered with skeletons, skulls, rifles, bayonets, hand grenades, gas masks, ammunition, mortar rounds, canteens, cooking gear, helmets, and personal equipment of every description. I turned a stiff leather boot upside down and was startled by the foot bones that rattled out on to the floor of the cave. Today, these same caves are cleared of bones, and most are also emptied of all relics of portable size. Once caves are opened, they are mercilessly looted; neither Palau nor Peleliu's local government has the resources to protect them. American battle histories make it clear that the attackers routinely used explosives to close up the entrances to caves that held Japanese troops, whether dead or alive. So there is no question that still-sealed caves on Peleliu hold significant quantities of human remains. Far less certain are their possible numbers, given the doubtful figures

FIGURE 5.3  Photos displayed in the lodge of tour guide Nakagawa Tsukane on Peleliu, 2003. The skulls and bones in the upper photo were collected for cremation by a Japanese government expedition of March 2002 that included Tōjō Yūko, granddaughter of General Tōjō Hideki. The other photo is of Nakagawa as a young cadet pilot during World War II. Photo by the author

claimed for remains supposedly collected and cremated over the past half-century—7,600 out of 10,200 defenders by one Japanese estimate, leaving 2,600 yet to be found. An obvious problem is that almost all of the 7,600 were found and counted by untrained amateurs, many of them students or families of the dead, often in expeditions that lacked official supervision.[24]

Palau's national government has usually left matters regarding the hunt for bones in the hands of the Peleliu state government. (Peleliu Island is one of 16 states of the Republic.) But in 2011 the nation lost its main power-generation plant to fire. As it had done before, Japan came to the rescue, with two large grants totaling $26 million in 2012 and 2013 to build a replacement plant. Palau found itself freshly beholden to its primary Asian ally just as the Liberal Democratic Party (LDP) returned to power, with Abe Shinzō as Prime Minister, in late 2012. Abe's very conservative, nationalistic government supports expanding the searches for Japan's war dead in the Pacific. Gratitude for the generous aid provided, and the deeply felt honor of the possibility of hosting the emperor and empress, would leave Palauans struggling to identify what their small islands could reciprocate with, within the give and take of international diplomacy.

The understanding in Palau is that Abe made very plain what Japan expected. He strongly urged President Remengesau to speed up the opening of Peleliu's sealed caves. When Remengesau traveled to Japan in 2014 to formally invite the emperor to the island, he duly committed to expediting efforts to retrieve military remains. The governor of Peleliu, Temmy Shmull, made the identical promise in February 2015, in anticipation of the emperor's April visit. (Shmull served as Minister of State in a previous Remengesau administration, so he is sensitive to

Palau's relations with Japan.) Amid much publicity, and with Remengesau and Shmull taking part in the digging, a sealed bunker and its attached cave were opened on Peleliu's invasion beach just two weeks before the emperor arrived. The remains of six IJA troops were found. Thus we come to understand why, in his banquet toast, Remengesau spoke of long-dead soldiers and underground caverns, and why he repeated his pledge to repatriate all "bone-remains" on Peleliu, especially those within sealed caves.[25]

At the same time, the larger role played by the emperor of Japan in furthering his nation's policies during his visit to Palau comes into clearer focus. Given the constraints on his activities imposed by Japan's constitution, Akihito is usually careful to avoid overt political acts and gestures. So his willingness in Palau to let the imperial house get involved in the contentious diplomatic issue of sealed caves seems anomalous, particularly since the matter has been promoted with such ardor by the extreme Right, which he tries to keep at arm's length.[26] Perhaps, just as Japanese who raise monuments in Palau enjoy greater freedom of expression there than they find back home, Akihito felt he came under less scrutiny in Palau. Although the Japanese press covered his visit heavily, they focused on his prayers for the war dead and the reactions of islanders and former immigrants, saying nothing about the sealed caves. That subject was left to the Palauan press, which publishes in English.

## Conclusion: Pasts not dead

Most Palauans were deeply honored by the imperial visit, yet many would judge Akihito's characterization of the Nan'yō era and the war years as incomplete (e.g., easy prewar friendships in mutually beneficial labor; food shortages and deaths caused solely by American air patrols). In contrast to statements he has made to other nations, Akihito failed to accept responsibility or apologize for Japan's role in bringing the devastation of war to Palau. This silence derived from the long-established fiction preferred by Japan that the aid it provides the Republic is given as gifts, not reparations. Gifts require reciprocation, such as agreeing to open caves; reparations, however, require shouldering one's moral and financial obligations for harm inflicted upon defenseless noncombatants, and offering sincere and explicit atonement.[27] But directly voicing objections to the emperor's visit would be an unconscionable breach of Palauan manners. Senator Toribiong's letter about his missing uncle is instead a classic, subtle islander riposte: It criticizes no one expressly, but reminds all sides that while Palauans also lost relatives in the war, they have not made state visits to Tokyo to press demands for help in recovering their remains, even though Palauan families deserve the same assistance from Japan that it expects from Palau.

Japan's memorial activities in Palau continue steadily, even after 50 years of tireless efforts to console both the living and the dead. Governments in Tokyo have typically sought to diminish or avoid the awkward topics arising from World War II, eager to forget the conflict and seal shut the doors to the past. It seems contradictory, then, that the attraction of Palau's battlefields has remained so exceptionally powerful, a warping of space and time that invokes a place and an era that most Japanese have suppressed or never heard of. Japan has shown itself willing to deploy as necessary its great reserves of soft power, including large grants of aid and a visit from a widely admired emperor, to persuade small island nations to cooperate in its quest to gather the bones of its lost soldiers and salve the nation's painful war memories.

Aside from the human need to put loved ones and comrades to rest, what accounts for the obsession with the physical retrieval of bones? The historian John Dower provides, I think, another part of the answer. He observes that after 1945 Japan faced the agonizing question of what the living could possibly say to the dead about a war so disastrously lost. An indispensable step, to which few could object, would be to erase the shame of having the bones of so many loyal soldiers abandoned and scattered across the far reaches of Asia and the Pacific. The dead had to be found and properly buried. The concentration of undisturbed bones in Peleliu's caves would make the island an irresistible site.[28]

Japanese monuments raised in Palau exhibit the thrust and parry of domestic disputes over Japan's role in the war and how it should portray its past today. Their texts often speak directly, freed from the constraints imposed back home. Further liberties—and protections— appear in translations that reach certain readers but bypass others. Over time, a kind of evolution is discernible: Voices moderated, shifting from declarations of the dead as heroes in what is assumed to be a righteous war to messages that were more inclusive and intended for wider audiences, with regret for losses among all the nations involved. The Hiroshima stone and the Peace Park Memorial at which Akihito prayed, with its three messages of concern for all those who died in Palau, carry inscriptions meant not just for the domestic audience, but also for the increasingly important ones in East Asia, and for the oft-forgotten islanders.

Yet these sentiments of conciliation and sympathy toward civilian victims and former foes have been subject to the oscillating currents of Japanese politics. In the 1990s, the Liberal Democratic Party initiated a "movement for historical revisionism" that has constantly inflamed tensions over the history and memories of World War II in Japan.[29] Consistent with this movement, the most recent of Peleliu's major commemorative structures is the imposing Shinto shrine erected in 2002 by Seiryusha. It is a defiant gesture, meant to stoke yearning for the bellicose and expansionist imperial state, repudiate Japanese stones standing nearby that admit guilt or aggression, and, in its scale and location, poke a thumb in the eye of the United States Marine Corps. (On the day that Japan surrendered in 1945, Koreans attacked and burned Shinto shrines all across the peninsula as the chief symbols of Japanese colonial oppression.[30])

Activists of the Japanese Right have the ear of the current Abe LDP government, and would be expected to urge its officials to press the Palauan people to agree to open the remaining caves on Peleliu. Recovering the remains of Japan's fallen soldiers stirs such deep emotions that Emperor Akihito proved willing to lend his prestige to the cause. Under its current government, Japan is pursuing singlemindedly what it, as a former participant in war, most seeks from the battlefield on Peleliu.

However, the argument made by Palau's Historic Preservation Office is a valid one: All the sealed caves are historic resources that belong to the nation of Palau. The natural caves among them provided shelter to the earliest Palauans who discovered the islands, possibly 3,500 years ago. Buried in the floors of these caves lies the prehistory of the Palauan people—the animal bones, plant pollens, and human tools and debris that can tell today's residents what their islands were like and how their ancestors lived when they first encountered the pristine archipelago. Recent professional excavations on Peleliu found that, despite disruptions caused by the fighting, natural caves yielded much valuable evidence about the earliest human habitation.[31] The sealed caves do not contain the history of only one people, the doomed defenders of Japan's empire; they contain the histories of two, one of whom owns the island within a history that stretches back for millennia. The caves should be opened, if at all, only by qualified archeologists under close supervision of Palauan authorities. On Peleliu, more than 70 years after the end of the Pacific War, the sifting of the floors of caves, and of the unresolved wartime past, is bound to continue.

## Notes

1 The author wishes to thank Merirei Blunt and Des Matsutaro of Peleliu, Palau, for their valuable assistance.
2 *Japan News*, April 9, 2015.
3 Three chains of small islands comprised the Nan'yō: the Carolines included Palau and Yap in the west and Truk and Ponape (now Chuuk and Pohnpei) in the east; the Marshalls lay further east still; and the Marianas, chief of which was Saipan, were found to the north. Guam, although part of the Marianas chain, was a US possession from 1898.
4 Derrick Wright, *To the Far Side of Hell: The Battle for Peleliu, 1944* (Tuscaloosa: University of Alabama Press, 2005); Joseph H. Alexander, *Storm Landings: Epic Amphibian Battles in the Central Pacific* (Annapolis, MD: Naval Institute Press, 1997), 104–125; Stephen C. Murray, "The Palauan *Kirikomi-tai* Suicide Bombers of World War II and the Siege of Babeldaob: A Reconsideration," *Pacific Asia Inquiry* 4:1, 30–57; http://www.uog.edu/pai; Stephen C. Murray, *The Battle over Peleliu: Islander, Japanese, and American Memories of War* (Tuscaloosa: University of Alabama Press, 2016), 73–97.
5 Murray, "Palauan *Kirikomi-tai*," note 3, 52–54; Murray, *Battle over Peleliu*, 98–117; interviews with surviving Japanese immigrants to Palau appear in *Japan Times*, April 6, 2015.
6 Murray, *Battle over Peleliu*, 21–72; Mark R. Peattie, *Nan'yō: The Rise and Fall of the Japanese in Micronesia, 1885–1945*, Pacific Islands Monograph Series No. 4 (Honolulu: University of Hawai'i Press, 1988), 62–197; Francis X. Hezel, S.J., *Strangers in Their Own Land: A Century of Colonial Rule in the Caroline and Marshall Islands*, Pacific Islands Monograph Series 13 (Honolulu: University of Hawai'i Press, 1995), 146–241.
7 For the wartime experiences of Micronesians, particularly the Palauans, see Lorenza Pedro, "The Effects of Foreign Culture and School on Angaur, Palau, 1899–1966" (Master's Thesis, Micronesian Area Research Center, University of Guam, 1999); Karen L. Nero, "Time of Famine, Time of Transformation: Hell in the Pacific, Palau," in *The Pacific Theater: Island Representations of World War II*, Geoffrey M. White and Lamont Lindstrom, eds. (Honolulu: University of Hawai'i Press, 1989), 117–148; Karen R. Walter, "Through the Looking Glass: Palauan Experiences of War and Reconstruction, 1944–1951" (PhD dissertation, Department of History, University of Adelaide, 1993); Murray, "Palauan *Kirikomi-tai*"; Murray, *Battle over Peleliu*, 73–117; Lin Poyer, Suzanne Falgout, and Laurence M. Carucci, *The Typhoon of War: Micronesian Experiences of the Pacific War* (Honolulu: University of Hawai'i Press, 2001). Arguing the merits of the IJA's doctrine

prohibiting its troops from surrendering and urging suicide instead is beyond the scope of this chapter. In the case of Palau, whatever the true feelings of the 30,000 troops on Babeldaob about facing slow, agonizing, and pointless death by famine and sickness, the 20,000 civilians and islanders had taken no pledge to die rather than surrender. At a minimum, General Inoue should have released all the civilians to the Americans. He released no one. Yet neither he nor any other officer of the 14th Division's leadership committed suicide after he suffered the humiliation of surrendering all Palau to the US Navy on September 2, 1945.

8 Franziska Seraphim, *War Memory and Social Politics in Japan, 1945–2005*, Harvard East Asian Center Monographs 278 (Cambridge, MA: Harvard University Asia Center, 2006); Kerry Smith, "The Shōwa Hall: Memorializing Japan's War at Home," *The Public Historian*: Special Issue "Beyond National History: World War II Recollected," 24:4 (2002), 35–64; Xiaohua Ma, "Constructing a National Memory of War: War Museums in China, Japan, and the United States," in *The Unpredictability of the Past: Memories of the Asia-Pacific War in US–East Asian Relations*, Marc Gallicchio, ed. (Durham, NC: Duke University Press, 2007), 155–200.

9 On the emperor and the *kokutai* see Herbert Bix, *Hirohito and the Making of Modern Japan* (New York: Harper Collins, 2000), 10, 53–55, 313–315. For recent overviews of Japanese war memory, commemoration, and the problems they create, see Sven Saaler, "Bad War or Good War? History and Politics in Post-War Japan," in *Critical Issues in Contemporary Japan*, Jeff Kingston, ed. (New York: Routledge, 2014) 137–148; Jeff Kingston, *Contemporary Japan: History, Politics, and Social Change Since the 1980s* (Malden, MA: Wiley-Blackwell, 2011), 185–205; and Jeremy Black, *Rethinking World War Two: The Conflict and its Legacy* (London: Bloomsbury, 2015), 169–208. Black's discussion in chapter 7 (pp. 193–208) of how public memory of World War II might evolve in the future is thought-provoking. Akihito has won admiration at home and globally for his courageous efforts to forge reconciliation in Asia over the wartime depredations of Japan during his father's reign. Besides Saipan and Palau, he has visited Iwo Jima and paid his respects and apologized to victims in China, Southeast Asia, Okinawa (which his father could never visit because Okinawans believed his government had sacrificed them needlessly when the war was already lost), and the Philippines. In 1990, Akihito became the first prominent Japanese to apologize publicly to Korea for the suffering Japan inflicted upon the peninsula as a Japanese colony from 1910 to 1945. The Japanese public supports Akihito's initiatives and, in Jeff Kingston's words, wants the government to do more to "acknowledge war responsibility and atone for it." Japanese conservatives, however, deplore the apologies for the country's previous military aggression and the "masochistic view of history" they think such repentance embodies. The most complete and sincere apologies from the national government were issued by opposition parties on the rare occasions when they wrested power from the dominant right-leaning Liberal Democratic Party (LDP). For Akihito's efforts see Kingston, *Contemporary Japan*, 209–213, 217.

10 Murray, *Battle over Peleliu*, 145–69; Shingo Iitaka, "Remembering Nan'yō from Okinawa: Deconstructing the Former Empire of Japan through Memorial Practices," *History & Memory* 27:2 (2015): 126–151, esp. 127; Peattie, *Nan'yō*, 314–316; Hiroshi Funasaka, *Falling Blossoms* (English translation of *Eirei no Zekkyō*), translated by Hiroshi Funasaka and Jeffrey D. Rubin (Singapore: Times Books International, 1986), 3.

11 Murray, *Battle over Peleliu*, 152.

12 Ibid., 118–169.

13 Ibid., 156–169.

14 Bix, *Hirohito and the Making of Modern Japan*, 658; Seraphim, *War Memory and Social Politics in Japan*, 82–83; Murray, *Battle over Peleliu*, 159–161; Funasaka, *Falling Blossoms*, 9, 12–13, 28–29, 40, 54.

15 *Japan News*, April 9, 2015.

16 Murray, *Battle over Peleliu*, 174, 163.

17 Ibid., 165–169. See photo, 169.

18 Before leaving the island in 1944–1945, the 81st Infantry Division of the US Army built three monuments to honor its fighting alongside the Marine Corps, and then its completion of the battle after the Marines were withdrawn. That the Peleliu base, once captured, proved of very limited use to the United States made the battle an especially painful memory for American veterans. Not until 40 years later, in 1984, did a private organization put up the first memorial dedicated to the Marines. Other private American parties have since put up several plaques dedicated to small units or individuals. Their inscriptions compare with the earliest of those from Japan: They lack translations, and they celebrate the heroism of the nation's fighters while offering no thoughts for peace, or the foe, or the people whose home island was so heavily scarred. American visitors have never matched their Japanese counterparts in numbers or in range of activities. "Things are not balanced on Peleliu," commented Chief Renguul Donald Haruo. "Where is the US on Peleliu? The US needs more of a presence." American Ireidan and war buffs who spend several days on the island usually stay in homestays run by islanders who speak English and have experience with visitors from the West. See Murray, *Battle over Peleliu*, 170–189.

19 Murray, *Battle over Peleliu*, 135–138.

20 *Tia Belau*, April 6, 2015.

21 Murray, *Battle over Peleliu*, 209, 211–213.

22 Palau's exceptional reefs attract scuba divers from around the world. Typically, one third of its tourists come from Japan and the vast majority visit for marine recreation, not battlefield tourism. The Republic of Palau, also known as Belau, became an independent nation in 1994, but signed a compact of free association with the United States, which provides generous financial support in return for certain military options. Today, Palauans number approximately 25,000.

23 Murray, *Battle over Peleliu*, 180–182. See the memorable photo of the aged Kurata attending Akihito's visit to the Peleliu Peace Park in the *Japan Times* of April 9, 2015, http://www.japantimes.co.jp/news/2015/04/09/national/history/tribute-of-emperor-empress-has-extra-meaning-for-battle-of-peleliu-veteran/#.WF1PAja7q70.

24 *Asahi Shimbun*, February 21, 2015; Seraphim, *War Memory and Social Politics in Japan*, 183.

25 *Tia Belau*, March 26, 2015; *Island Times*, February 24, 2015. Japan's two grants of $4 million and $22 million for power generation are documented respectively in the Palauan newspaper *Island Times*, issues of March 5, 2012, http://pidp.org/pireport/2012/March/03-06-09.htm, and April 25, 2014, http://pidp.org/pireport/2014/April/04-28-15.htm.

26 Kingston, *Contemporary Japan*, 210–211.

27 Murray, *Battle over Peleliu*, 135–138.

28 John W. Dower, *Embracing Defeat: Japan in the Wake of World War II* (New York: W. W. Norton & Co./The New Press, 2000 [originally published 1999]), 485–521. For a corresponding preoccupation with gathering remains of American air crews shot down in Palau, see Wil S. Hylton, *Vanished: The 60-Year Search for the Missing Men of World War II* (New York: Riverhead Books, 2013). Among knowledgeable Japanese, the shame of defeat, and the need to retrieve the military dead, would be augmented by awareness that a shockingly high proportion of Japanese troops who died from 1941 to 1945—at least 60 percent, or one million men of a total of 1.74 million—perished not from combat but from starvation and the diseases associated with malnutrition. IJA doctrine expected its armies to live off the land in "self-sufficiency," but this proved impossible in tropical jungles, on tiny islands, and in other occupied territories where Imperial forces' brutality and pillaging caused famine and economic collapse. When hundreds of thousands of Japanese fighting men throughout the Pacific were cut off by American forces from resupply, and abandoned by Tokyo (as happened to those on Babeldaob in Palau), these men met what they themselves termed *injuni*, "a dog's death," dying of beriberi or dysentery, or starving in droves. As Lizzie Collingham recognizes, this seldom discussed abandonment of its own fighting men was one of the worst atrocities perpetrated by Imperial Headquarters during the entire war. Micronesian battlefields such as Saipan,

Guam, or Peleliu may therefore be especially attractive to Ireidan because at these sites their men actually died fighting. See Lizzie Collingham, *The Taste of War: World War Two and the Battle for Food* (London: Penguin Books, 2012 [Original edition 2011]), 273–316; John W. Dower, *War Without Mercy: Race and Power in the Pacific War* (New York: Pantheon Books, 1986), 298; Murray, "Palauan *Kirikomi-tai*"; Black, *Rethinking World War Two*, 88–89.
29 Saaler, "Bad War or Good War?" 141.
30 Ian Buruma, *Year Zero: A History of 1945* (New York: Penguin Press, 2013), 263.
31 Murray, *Battle over Peleliu*, 224–226.

# 6

# DIVIDED NATION, DIVIDED MEMORIES

*Brendan Wright*

For those with a bleak sense of irony, the history of the Korean War (1948–1953) provides ample fodder.[1] Indeed, in attempting to make sense of the conflict, one is forced to navigate the dizzying array of contradictions that defined the Korean War: A postcolonial civil war that rapidly evolved into an international war; a war for national unification that wound up hardening the peninsula's division; a conflict waged by two staunchly nationalistic camps whose survival was wholly dependent upon their superpower patrons; finally, an archetypical Cold War conflict that has managed to survive more than three decades after the fall of the Berlin Wall. These ironies, however, are dwarfed by the sheer tragedy of the war's brutal violence. Estimates vary, but most place the total war dead anywhere between two and four million—the majority of which were civilians.[2]

Statistics, however, fail to communicate the scale, character, or psychological burdens of this fratricidal catastrophe. War was pitilessly waged at the village level, leading to politicidal bloodletting between rightists and leftists. In communist-controlled areas, landlords, police officers, and Christians became the targets of dispossession, revolutionary show trials, and executions. Throughout the southern mainland and Cheju Island, rightists roamed from village to village, repeatedly massacring civilians suspected of harboring communist sympathies.[3]

The United States was likewise a major author of this carnage against civilians. At different points in the war, the US command created free-fire zones which resulted in numerous examples of unarmed refugees being bombed, strafed, or mowed down with machine guns. Meanwhile, in an effort to sap the resolve of its communist foe, the US bombed the North into virtual oblivion, resulting in the deaths of hundreds of thousands—if not millions—of North Korean civilians.[4]

For all of its horrors, the Korean War solved nothing, ending in an inconclusive armistice agreement on July 27, 1953 that the South Korean President Syngman Rhee refused to sign. In place of a border, a landmine-infested 250km by 4km corridor—referred to without irony as the "Demilitarized Zone"—continues to serve as a buffer between the two Koreas. The war's ambiguous conclusion has led it to be conventionally eulogized as a stalemate.

While there is certainly merit to this verdict, in South Korea—where the civil war between rightists and leftists was most ferocious—it was an unambiguous victory for the counter-revolutionary forces of the political right. Indeed, if in 1945 political power in South Korea was briefly in the hands of the political left, by 1953 a hardline anti-communist state composed of landlords, Christians, far-right nationalists, and ex-colonial collaborators held the reins of power. In the wake of this settlement, the anti-communist state shaped the official memory of its recent fratricidal conflict under the penumbra of the ongoing national division. This basic political fact is crucial for understanding the character and evolution of the memory of the Korean War in South Korea from 1953 until the present. However, while dominating the landscape of memory, the anti-communist state has never achieved a complete monopoly over the nation's historical imagination. Over the past six decades, writers, artists, activists, and other actors have fashioned a series of alternative war memories. While diverse, what has united these memories is a yearning to recover, work through, and perhaps transcend the war's unresolved contradictions and tragedies—a project that remains unfulfilled.

This chapter traces the relationship between these two respective mnemonic lenses of the Korean War past in South Korea from 1953 to the present. In the first section, I summarize the politics of memory surrounding the war during the authoritarian years (1953–1980). Throughout these years, official memory of the war was dominated by the "June 25" (*yugio*) anti-communist war narrative. However, though dramatically curtailed by the rigid anti-communist system, alternative narratives which focused on the war's devastating impact on the population proliferated throughout these decades. The dominant emphasis in these accounts was on the rehabilitation of the family.

In the second section, I examine shifts in the Korean War memory landscape from 1980 until the present. In this epoch, the state's hegemony over the production of the Korean War waned, leading to the breaking of taboos and a broadening of the national dialogue surrounding the nation's division. Previously repressed voices and ideas came to the surface, leading to a major re-examination of the war. However, the continued presence of national division and the threat of the northern regime have ensured that residual features of anti-communism retain their dominance.

## Manufactured memory in postwar South Korea

In the immediate aftermath of the Korean War, official memory of the conflict in South Korea was "subordinated to the hegemony of the nation state" and "manufactured" according to the state's political agenda.[5] Over time, this version of the past has been enveloped by the term "June 25."[6] What were the contents of this official memory, and how was it dispersed? First, memory of the Korean War was intertwined with state identity. From 1948 onward, the official ideology of South Korea was anti-communism. As its name suggests, the key feature of the state's ideology was opposition to the North Korean regime.

The "June 25" narrative worked to reinforce this perspective through three interrelated tropes. The first was through a chronological claim. By naming the conflict after June 25, 1950, the day on which the Soviet-backed People's Army (*Inmin'gun*) invaded South Korea, the state made a stark claim about the origins, and therefore the culpability, of the nation's fratricidal division. Most crucially, this was an act of erasure. Indeed, following the US-backed decision to hold a separate election on the southern half of the peninsula to establish a separate state, the already fragmented southern population was plunged into a civil war between the South Korean Workers Party (*Namnodang*) on one side, and the South Korean government and its right-wing paramilitary supporters on the other. Estimates vary, but this two-year conflict killed as many as 100,000 South Koreans, with the majority of these deaths at the hands of government forces.[7] By indicating that the Korean conflict began on June 25, 1950, the state sought to bury this history of internecine violence, and its role in causing a sizable portion of it.

Closely related to this was an effort to delegitimize the northern regime by emphasizing the communist foe's lack of nationalist credentials. The cornerstone of this tactic was to paint the government and its leader, Kim Il-Sung, as agents of international communism. Explicit in this charge was the idea that communists were something other than Koreans. Because Korean national identity was premised on shared ethnic heritage, communists were seldom described as fellow Koreans. Instead, they were identified with slurs such as "commie/red" (*ppalgaengi*) or "impure person" (*pulsun punja*), while the northern government was ubiquitously referred to as a *koeroe chŏnggwŏn* ("puppet regime").[8] Similar to the "June 25" framing, this effort to de-Koreanize Korean communism worked to obscure the civil component of the Korean War. In painting communism as something alien to Korean society, the state effectively portrayed the war as a foreign attack, thus omitting internal causes of the country's division or of the appeal of revolutionary socialism, such as struggles over land reform or the southern state's rehabilitation of real and alleged Japanese collaborators.

Finally, buttressing the above discourse was a narrative which framed the war as part of a broader international defense against communism. There was, of course, a great degree of truth to this: 21 United Nations countries came to the defense of South Korea following the North Korean invasion of June 25, 1950.[9] However, the state's emphasis on this international dimension reveals a key contradiction in South Korea's anti-communist nationalism: while the South Korean state presented itself as the guardian of the Korean people (*minjok*), its survival throughout the period of war and division (1945–1953) was entirely dependent on outside powers—particularly the US. Intriguingly, the state framed the UN intervention as a source of legitimacy. Indeed, the government of Syngman Rhee propagated the idea that the Republic of Korea was the "Son of the UN" and, from 1950 onward, October 24 was designated "United Nations Day" in South Korea.[10]

The basic contours of this official memory remained essentially unaltered throughout the authoritarian years, and were etched into the nation's physical landscape and disseminated throughout its cultural institutions. In the war's aftermath, the Rhee government named streets after famous generals and monuments were built to honor anti-communist "martyrs" and "patriots." In the years of military rule under Park Chung-Hee (Pak Chŏng-hui, 1961–1979), this practice accelerated with the construction of multiple monuments, sites, and graves dedicated to the remembrance of South Korean and UN soldiers.[11] The state's war narrative, meanwhile, was inculcated into the nation's youth through the public education system. Through textbooks and curriculum, students were encouraged to become loyal anti-communist citizens, with courses such as "anti-communist ethics" (*pangong totŏk*) taught from the late 1950s onward. Depictions of the North Korean invasion and the ensuing carnage provided crucial fodder in the state's arsenal. Students were taught that the North Korean government was a puppet regime that had caused the nation's national division. Further, textbook chapters on the war contained lurid descriptions of communists entering villages and massacring entire families. Typically, these accounts ended with UN or South Korean soldiers coming to the aid of survivors, thus indicating that the state and its allies were the ultimate guarantors of the lives of citizens.[12] These accounts of the war were taught to South Korean children well into the 1980s.

It is impossible to gauge the cumulative effect of this narrative. But there can be little doubt that it was formidable. First, much of postwar South Korean society—particularly the populations that lived under the North Korean occupation during the war—was thoroughly anti-communist. Second, the state imposed a rigid, and at times arbitrary, censorship regime which dramatically curtailed public discussion and artistic expression. Beneath all this was a deep reservoir of social stigma associated with having a "red" background or "pro-communist" (*yongkong*) sentiments. The result was that throughout the Rhee and Park years, there were few sustained challenges to the state's hegemony in the production of the Korean War past.

### Early counter-memories

However, in the much denser forest of cultural memory, the state failed to hold a monopoly over the population's historical imagination. In both metaphorical and concrete terms, the "civil" component of the war was fratricidal, with families either separated or torn apart by the ideological and social schisms of the post-liberation period. The enormity and complexity of this traumatic history meant that the state's official account of this tortuous past could hardly appease the deep scars of the divided nation. Throughout these years, literature provided a vital, if circumscribed, role in navigating and working through these problematic memories.

The timbre, politics, and content of these works varied throughout the decades, but a common theme running throughout what is often referred to as "division literature" was the war's legacies for families and communities. A profound novel from the era was Park Wan-Suh's (Pak Wan-sŏ) *The Naked Tree* (1970). A psychologically complex and semi-autobiographical coming of age novel about a young woman who lived through the chaos of war in Seoul (which changed hands four times during the war), Park's portrayal of the war's effect on the family was devastating, and in many respects transcended the stifling contours of anti-communist ideology.

Most intriguing in my reading was Park's depiction of the war as something simultaneously ominous and abstract, yet also intimate. Rather than representing the war through the lenses of political or military conflict, the war's meaning is channeled through the psychological scars of the narrator, Kyŏng-a. Following the brutal deaths of her two brothers near the end of the novel, for example, the narrator exclaims:

> I packed and unpacked, torn between my desire that the war would come to kill off everyone and my fear that the war could rush upon me at any moment. Having inherited the contradiction ... I let myself be torn apart.[13]

Kyŏng-a's confusion is compounded by the violence that the loss of her two brothers does to the once harmonious relationship between her and her mother. In a commentary on the gendered layers of the war's aftermath, Kyŏng-a and her mother's bond is damaged by her mother's anguish over the fact that she has lost all of her boys and has to survive with only her one daughter. Kyŏng-a's only respite from the guilt and resentment caused by this knowledge is to sit alone under the trees, where she "cultivates a hatred" for her mother.[14]

If Park's novel provided a vivid depiction of the intimate devastations of the war and a social critique of how hierarchies within Korean society amplified these legacies, other novelists cautiously expanded the terrain of war memory by subtly humanizing North Korean communists. For those unfamiliar with Cold War South Korean history, this point may seem underwhelming. However, in a political and cultural landscape dominated by demonic caricatures of the communist "other," the very act of humanizing North Koreans may be interpreted as a form of resistance in itself. A very early postwar novel to do this was Hwang Sun-wŏn's 1954 work *The Descendants of Cain* (*K'ainŭi Huye*). While clearly an anti-communist novel, focused on the 1946 North Korean land reform's parasitic effects on a village community, the book is interesting in retrospect due to its tempered portrayal of the villagers who turned to communism. Rather than being presented as Soviet stooges, those who turn to communism in the novel often do so for reasons of class. Further, though the protagonist is from the *yangban* (the elite class), the landlords are often portrayed as feckless or as having behaved exploitatively in the past. Although the novel provided a brutal critique of the North Korean regime, it also provided readers a window into the social conflicts of the post-liberation era that were largely obscured within the state's official account of the war.[15]

Meanwhile, in his 1956 short story, "Palbari," Hwang cryptically communicated the ambivalent memories on Cheju Island in the wake of the so-called "Cheju Incident."[16] Here, a young woman lives as an outcast following a rumor that she had shot and killed her brother over his involvement with communist guerrillas.

Reflecting on the villagers' conflicting views on the young woman's deed, Hwang writes: "for a while, people had praised her for what she had done, but inwardly they found it repulsive and they avoided her."[17] In this passage, we can see Hwang covertly conveying the differences between outward and inward sentiments about the recent civil war. Though having ostensibly committed a "patriotic act" by killing a communist, the young woman is shunned for her betrayal of her family, thus indicating a more textured communal memory of the period's violence.

Other works in the 1960s and 1970s subtly subverted the "June 25" script by collapsing the distinctions that existed between North and South Korea. This was done at the political as well as the social level. An interesting novel which addressed the former of these was Ch'oe In-hun's 1960 work *The Square* (*Kwangjang*). Written immediately after the fall of Syngman Rhee's regime (1948–1960), when there was a brief period of liberation, the novel provocatively portrayed both the communist North and the capitalist South as fundamentally flawed and dehumanizing societies. For example, the author paints South Korean political society as a place in which "garbage and excrement have just piled up."[18] Indeed, the novel contained within it a harsh criticism of anti-communism and the national security state. At one point in the work, the protagonist, a young man named Myŏng-jun, is wrongfully accused of being a communist and is beaten and tortured by the police. The detective casually informs Myŏng-jun that he could "easily kill a Red bastard" like Myŏng-jun and dump his body where no one could find it.[19] Eventually, the corruption and unsafe conditions in the South lead Myŏng-jun to flee to the North. Though Ch'oe's treatment of the North is equally harsh (eventually Myŏng-jun departs for a third country, but commits suicide on the way), in terms of its willingness to critique South Korea and the harshness of the state's anti-communist ideology, *The Square* was quite radical.

In other works, an imagined solidarity between the people of North and South Korea, based upon a shared geography and bloodline, was invoked to humanize North Koreans. Kim Wŏn-il's 1978 *Evening Glow* (*Noŭl*), for example, addressed the problematic nature of the war for families with elders who sided with the communists. In one passage, a father is trying to explain to his son why their grandfather sided with the communists. The father is philosophical about the nature of Korea's division:

> Wherever there is a split, people always claim that their own side is right. It was the same with us. They thought what they believed was right and we did the same. So we blamed each other and fought ... In fact, they are exactly the same as us, brothers from the same ancestors. The simple truth is that they are our brother of the same blood. They just live separated from us in a communist-dominated part of the land, that's all.[20]

It is interesting to reflect on this passage in comparison with the state's appropriation of the idea of a shared Korean bloodline: While the state used ethnicity to prove that the North was something other than Korea, Kim used it to construct an imagined solidarity between the two Koreas.

Perhaps the most radical rethinking of the civil war to emerge from literature during the Rhee/Park decades was Hyŏn Ki-yŏng's haunting *Uncle Suni* (*Sun-i Samch'on*, 1978). The novella addresses a family's attempts to make sense of the character Aunt Sun-i's suicide and the calamitous incident 30 years earlier which caused her mental health issues.[21] Sun-i's death forces the family to recount a 1948 massacre of hundreds of villagers in Pukch'on-ri at the hands of the government forces, which occurred during the so-called "Cheju Incident." Though technically a fictional account, Hyŏn's narrative contains a number of depictions of the events on Cheju Island that are now regarded as historically accurate. For example, in reference to government policy toward villagers on the island, one of Hyŏn's characters argues: "I have no doubt that the order was to execute all civilians."[22]

The work also challenges the government's official position that all of the targets of the "scorched earth operations" were red guerrillas. Rather pointedly, the book's narrator critiques the absurdity of the anti-communist state's position that many of the people killed on the island were "unarmed red guerrillas," instead, arguing that they were simply refugees fleeing the government forces' rampage—a fact now confirmed by historians and government fact-finding teams.[23]

Finally, the book addressed what was, and perhaps still is, the greatest taboo of Korea's civil war past: the frequent rape of young women by government suppression forces. In one passage, the book references how the paramilitary anti-communist youth groups sent to the island would "sexually assault young women whenever they saw one."[24] As notions of female purity and entrenched anti-communist/pro-military ideology prevented virtually all public discourse regarding the widescale rape of women during the Korean War, it is difficult to understate the importance of Hyŏn's intervention. However, the author would pay a severe price for his moral and artistic courage: Following *Sun-i Samch'on*'s publication, Hyŏn was arrested and tortured by the Joint Investigation Headquarters and his book was banned for a number of years.

Throughout the Rhee and Park years, there were few overt political challenges to the state's accepted version of the civil war, or attempts to punish the perpetrators responsible for crimes against civilians. However, there was one notable, and heartbreaking, exception. This episode involved the so-called "Bereaved Family Associations" (*yujokhoe*) in 1960–1961. Composed primarily of the families of real and imagined "leftists" who were executed by government forces throughout the civil war, the *yujokhoe* petitioned the moderately liberal—but short-lived—Second Republic (1960–1961) for financial compensation, the punishment of perpetrators, truth commissions, the right to collectively bury and mourn the victims, and money to build monuments to honor their loved ones. These committees were formed from the bottom up and organized themselves in an interlocking manner throughout the Chŏlla, Kyŏngsang, and Cheju Provinces. Initially these groups had some legal success: Investigations were launched throughout the country in the spring of 1960, which led to confirmation that close to 10,000 civilians had been massacred (though the true number is certainly higher).[25] Furthermore, in a few cases, perpetrators were brought to trial and punished for their misdeeds.[26] Most provocatively, through their public speeches, collective memorial readings, petitions to the government, and advertisements sent out in newspapers, the *yujokhoe* offered a deep rethinking of the Korean War past. In these performances, the once maligned victims were portrayed as martyrs to the cause of a future unified democratic state, while the Rhee regime was cast as a "dictatorship" (*tokche*) that "massacred innocent people like flies" and a betrayer of the Korean *minjok*.[27] To my knowledge, this was the most radical challenge to the "June 25" narrative and the political machinery behind it.

However, this brief challenge ended in catastrophe for the *yujokhoe* membership and their relatives. When General Park Chung-Hee rose to power on May 16, 1961, through a military coup, he immediately arrested and prosecuted the *yujokhoe* leadership. Members were tortured and convicted on the grounds that they were disseminating "pro-communist" (*yongkong*) sentiments. The trials are now recognized to have been a legal sham.[28] Additionally, the monuments that were built to honor the victims were smashed throughout the country, while the collective graves were bulldozed and desecrated. In a few incidents, the victims' bones were dug up by security forces and incinerated. As a final insult, survivors were sent a bill for the service of a state cremation.[29] This episode left lasting scars on the families of these victims and it would be more than three decades before they could once again openly mourn their loved ones. The grim fate of the *yujokhoe* vividly illustrates the very real constraints on historical memory in Cold War South Korea, and the brutal consequences that existed for those who overtly challenged the legitimacy of the state.

## Democratization and the shifting mnemonic landscape (1980–2007)

On October 26, 1979, Park Chung-Hee was assassinated by the chief of the Korean CIA, Kim Chae-kyu. By December 12, political power was firmly in the hands of another general, Chun Doo-hwan, who would remain in power until 1988. Chun's rule was marked by human rights abuses and increasing protests which eventually led to what is referred to as the "June Democratic Uprising" in 1987. In May 1980, the Chun regime committed a US-backed massacre of hundreds of protesting students and workers in the southern city of Kwangju. Though the government officially claimed that the protest was a "riot" instigated by North Korean agents, the incident led many young students and intellectuals to rethink the nature of the South Korean state, its relationship to the United States, and the tortuous past which had produced the divided nation's malaise.[30] Inquisitions into Korea's period of division and its subsequent fratricidal bloodletting were an integral part of this process.

The most thorough rethinking of the Korean War past came from those associated with Minjung ideology. A nebulous vanguard of intellectuals, students, and radicals, the Minjung saw modern Korean history as a failure—one of "absence and distortion" predicated upon Korea's importation of American values and its political system.[31] In order to rectify their history, Minjung activists sought to compose a counter-memory of the post-liberation period. This process entailed a search for a national narrative which escaped the stifling state-centric anti-communism of the authoritarian years, and focused on the Korean masses for authenticity.[32] Cho Chŏng-nae's *Taebaek Mountain Range* (*Taebaek Sanmaek*) was the representative Korean War novel of this decade. The massive novel was serialized from 1983 until 1989, and focused on the local struggles between right and left in the southwestern village of Pŏlkyo from 1946 to 1953. Cho openly declared that he wished to capture "the vital energy of the *minjung*" with his work.[33] The primary way in which Cho accomplished this was to portray the left-wing "Partisan" campaigns as genuine expressions of nationalism, while painting the Korean peasantry as agents of revolution. *Taebaek Sanmeak* was widely read and has been almost universally acclaimed by critics as a great Korean War novel. However, a formal complaint was launched against Cho, leading to his investigation under the National Security Law. Though Cho was never charged, the investigation did not end until 2005.[34]

In 1987, South Korea held its first free and fair democratic election. A split in the democratic opposition meant that Chun's chosen successor, General Roh Tae-woo, became the sixth president of South Korea. However, in 1993, the nation's first civilian president, Kim Young-sam, was elected to office. Kim Young-sam's rule was followed by ten years of progressive government, respectively led by Kim Dae-Jung (1998–2003) and Roh Moo-hyun (2003–2008). These two decades were marked by a rise of civic engagement, a democratization of culture, grassroots and political attempts at engagement with the North, limited reunions of divided families, and a rethinking of the traumatic past. What can be said of all this? The contemporary landscape of memory is markedly kaleidoscopic and contested, but a general shift can be demarcated. Indeed, I posit that democratization has helped diminish, though certainly not dislodge, the hegemony of the "June 25" script.

There are four domains in which we may recognize this change: the legal; the monumental; the literary; and the visual arts. In the case of the first, the most meaningful shift has occurred for the families and descendants of "leftists" massacred throughout the Korean War. With formal democratization, *yujokhoe* once again formed throughout the country, demanding restitution for past wrongs. The results of these endeavors have been mixed, but compared with the doomed struggles of 1960–1961, notable successes have been achieved. In 1996, the Special Measures Act on the Restoration of the Honor of Those People Involved in the Kŏch'ang Incident (*Kŏch'ang Sakkŏn tŭng Kwalyŏnja ŭi Myŏngyehoebok e kwanhan T'ŭkpyŏljoch'ibŏp*) was passed and, in 2000, the Special Act on the Fact-Finding Investigation into the April 3 Cheju Incident Victims and the Restoration of their Honor (*Cheju 4.3 Sakkŏn Chinsang Kyumyŏng mit Hŭisaengja Myŏngyehoebok e kwanhan T'ŭkpyŏlbŏp*) came into law.[35] These acts provided the blueprint for the 2005 Truth and Reconciliation Commission of South Korea (*Chinsil Hwahae rŭl wihan Kwagŏsa Chŏngni Wiwŏnhoe*, TRCK), which launched a nationwide investigation into state-authorized killings during the Korean War.

American behavior during the war has also come under greater scrutiny. Most famous have been the revelations surrounding the "No Gŭn-ri Incident," an episode in which US soldiers killed hundreds of unarmed civilians.[36] The incident at No Gŭn-ri, however, was merely the "tip of the iceberg," as the intellectual Kim Dong-Choon presciently noted in 2002.[37] Indeed, the South Korean Truth and Reconciliation Commission recently uncovered 96 cases of US violence against South Korean civilians during the war, which led to the deaths of approximately 3,672 civilians—though the number is almost certainly higher.[38] Numerous criticisms have been made regarding the shortcomings of these commissions, and few of their recommendations have been adopted by governments.[39] However, they have officially restored the honor of thousands of victims, offered compensation for a select number of victims, and provided future historians and activists with an archive of knowledge to continuously re-examine this still opaque past.

Dramatic changes have also occurred within South Korea's monumental landscape. Most significant has been the rise of "peace parks" dedicated to honoring the above-mentioned victims of state and US Army violence. Prominent examples include the Cheju 4.3 Peace Park (*Cheju 4.3 P'yŏnghwa Kongwŏn*), the Kŏch'ang Incident Memorial Park (*Kŏch'ang Sakkŏn Ch'umo Kongwŏn*), and the No Gŭn-ri Peace Park (*No Gŭn-ri Pyŏngwa Kongwŏn*). Though lying far outside the capital region, and therefore peripheral to dominant spaces of public memory consumption, these sites comprise an important collection of tangible spaces for challenging the "June 25" ethos in three crucial ways. First, through their victim-focused mode of representing the war, they expose the limitations of the notion that the South Korean state and its US patron are the guardians of the South Korean population. Second, in legitimizing their suffering through the language of liberalism, human rights, and transitional justice, these sites offer a global repertoire, free from the narrow confines of nationalist discourse, for exploring this history of trauma. Finally, they offer a temporal redefinition of the conflict. Here, the unresolved nature of the war is not simply a geopolitical fact, but also a social reality that has structured the lives of victims. Indeed, a common feature throughout of all of these parks is the lived aftermath of these atrocities for survivors, and the dogged, decades-long struggles for clarification and restitution waged by these communities.[40] With this, the voices of victims and survivors have become part of the contested and ongoing dialogue regarding the Korean War past and its manifestation in the political present.

Throughout these decades, literature has continued to play a vital role in expanding the boundaries of permissible discussion by raising probing questions and providing a more objective standpoint for understanding the conflict. Much of this has entailed a deepening of the themes and concerns of the previous generation of writers. Yi Ho-ch'ŏl's 1996 work *Northerners, Southerners* was an impressive literary achievement which successfully provided an objective and humanized portrayal of North Korean soldiers during the Korean War. Based on his own experiences as a North Korean soldier and then as a prisoner of war in South Korea, Yi's account captured the absurdity of the war with a brutal and unsentimental realism.[41] The period has also witnessed a rise in "scar literature," which has provided lurid and complex portrayals of the war's effects on the lives of its survivors. O Chŏng-hŭi's 1986 short story "Spirit on the Wind" (*Param ŭi nŏk*), for example, chronicles the wretched life of its protagonist, Ŭn-su, who is driven to excessive wonderings by a repressed memory of her mother being brutally murdered by a pick-ax-wielding man during the war. Reflecting upon the embodied nature of her repressed past, the orphaned Ŭn-su asks: "did this mean that instead of memories there remained only sensations of a part of her life that had been buried fast and deep like a rock ever since her early years, which themselves she could not remember?"[42]

Authors have also exploited the genre to raise difficult moral and political critiques of the country's ongoing division and the ethical stakes entailed in reconciliation. Hwang Sok-Yong's 2000 serialized novel *The Guest* (*Sonnim*) is representative of this mode.[43] The novel focuses on the history and aftermath of the infamous and still murky 1950 "Sinchon Massacre" in South Hwanghae Province, North Korea. Hwang's work is masterful and complex, and in light of our analysis thus far, two features are worth noting. The first is that it furthers the anti-communist state-as-perpetrator discourse previously opened up by the *yujokhoe* and their sympathizers. In Hwang's novel, the Sinch'ŏn Massacre, officially viewed by North Korea as an American atrocity against North Korean civilians, is represented as an act committed by anti-communist patriots.[44] Here, the civil war that was waged at the village level is laid out in stark and intimate terms, as Christians and communists engage in a pitiless cycle of massacre and retaliation. In this account, the former group, represented through the narrator's older brother Yohan, is revealed to be particularly savage. Indeed, the author's narrative of the massacre climaxes in a killing spree led by Yohan that culminates in the ruthless murder of two young female musicians with a pick-ax.[45] What is so radical in this retelling is not merely the fact that anti-communist "patriots" are portrayed as murderers, but also that North Korean communists are represented as victims. As the official processes of truth and reconciliation often involved victimized families proving their ideological purity, Hwang's portrayal of the ideological "other" as a victim worthy of mourning offers a deep challenge to the still formidable ideology of anti-communism.

The novel's political/ethical orientation, however, is ultimately toward inter-Korean reconciliation. Crucially, the state is denied the privilege of facilitating this shift. Rather, it is the ghosts of the victims and perpetrators and surviving family members that are granted the greatest agency in this endeavor. Indeed, in its structure, which mimics a shamanistic ritual, its emphasis on healing at the level of the family, and its use of ghosts as the authoritative voice for revealing the "truth" of the Korean War past, Hwang's work grants the most power, and therefore a moral obligation, to the Korean people themselves in overcoming the scars of war and division.

Hwang's purpose in writing the book was revealed by the author himself. Hwang noted that by giving the book the title *The Guest*, which was a euphemism for smallpox in Korea, he was raising the idea that communism and Christianity were infectious diseases imported from the West.[46] Thus, there is an intriguing tension at work: On the one hand, Hwang unflinchingly portrays the Sinch'ŏn massacre as an inter-Korean affair, while on the other, the ideologies behind it are presented as foreign contagions. Like his Minjung predecessors, Hwang describes

Korea's internal disintegration as a consequence of Koreans' failure to modernize internally. Genuine reconciliation, therefore, is premised upon the removal of outside power, principally that of the United States of America.

While literature has raised the most probing inquisitions into the Korean War past, it is film that has become the dominant media for historical consumption. In this arena, representations of the conflict have proliferated, leading to a more layered depiction. An intriguing early example was Chŏng Chi-yŏng's 1990 film *Nambugun*. Based on the experiences of Yi Tae, a South Korean journalist/partisan, the film provided a realistic and objective picture of the wartime experiences of the South Korean partisans.[47] Beyond offering a humanized depiction of South Korean communists, the film was particularly bold in its empathetic portrayal of the partisan experience in South Korea by chronicling it as a history of hope, suffering, and profound loss.[48]

Similarly, the above mentioned *Taebak Sanmaek* was turned into a major motion picture in 1994, giving viewers another vivid portrayal of the southern civil war's complexities. While Chŏng's *Nambugun* did not explicitly moralize the conflict, Im Kwŏn-taek's interpretation of Cho's novel was unambiguous in its condemnation of the parasitic role of ideology in destroying the Korean nation. Toward the end of the film, one of the main characters remarks, "we did nothing but slaughter people"—a less glamorous but arguably more accurate depiction of the war than one will find in nationalist accounts.[49]

The success of the 2004 war film *T'aegŭkki Hwinallimyŏ*, however, is perhaps most illustrative of the profound revision that the war has undergone in South Korea.[50] Vividly portraying the violence of war, the film attracted an estimated 11.74 million Koreans, an astonishingly high number given the country's modest population (an estimated 48 million at that time). Differing from typical war blockbusters, however, the film is notable for its pathos and its critique of the southern regime. The film's plot, which tells the story of two brothers (Yi Chin-tae and Yi Chin-sŏk) who are conscripted into the South Korean army, serves as an allegory for the conflict's dehumanizing and fratricidal character. Over the course of the conflict, Chin-tae's vanity and hatred of communists slowly engulf him, causing him to lose his humanity, as well as the love and admiration of his younger brother. Though the brothers are reconciled in the film's climax, this comes at the expense of Chin-tae's life. In structuring the film around the sufferings of the two brothers, the movie, in both symbol and reality, evokes the larger familial tragedy that the Korean War was, and continues to be, for the Korean people.

It is the movie's characterization of the Republic of Korea (ROK), however, that is its most revealing aspect. In the early portions of the war, South Korean conscripts are demonstrated to be poorly fed, uninterested in the survival of the South Korean state, and suffering from an extreme lack of cohesion. Later in the film, ROK troops are depicted torturing POWs, largely for their own amusement. In what is arguably the film's most heartbreaking scene, anti-communist forces brutally murder Chin-tae's fiancée, Yŏng-sin, for confirming her allegiance to the communist Workers' Party of Korea in order to get food for her family. While a work of fiction, the implications of *T'aekŭkki Hwinallimyŏ* ought not to be lost on the reader: By the mid-2000s, once taboo subjects formed the core of one of the most popular movies in the country's history.

## Conclusion: The recomposition of anti-communist hegemony and the continuing struggle over the Korean War past (2007–present)

For those hoping that a rethinking of the Korean War past would lead to reconciliation between the two Koreas, the past decade has been a bitter disappointment. With the sabotage and collapse of the "Sunshine Policy," the hopeful period of the early 2000s now seems like a mirage. On the geopolitical front, deterioration has defined the arc of the past ten years, as we have witnessed a series of cross-border confrontations and threats, and a radical erosion of inter-Korean solidarity. With some justification, the North Korean regime and its increasingly formidable nuclear arsenal have been painted as the culprits for this impasse. However, these developments must be measured carefully within the context of a rising China, increased armament across East Asia, a surge of right-wing power in South Korea and Japan, and the United States' expansive and erratic post-9/11 behavior on the world stage.[51] At the time of writing, North Korea was poised to launch its sixth nuclear test, with the recently elected US president Donald Trump verbally vacillating between threats of war and suggestions that he would be "honored" to sit down with the North Korean leadership.[52] Meanwhile, the now departed South Korean defense minister openly declared in the fall of 2016 that the ROK has detailed plans for the assassination of Kim Jong-un.[53]

The domestic situation in South Korea has, until recently, been likewise discouraging. The conservative regime of Lee Myung-bak (2008–2013) rapidly terminated the work of the Truth and Reconciliation Commission, leading to an incomplete, and at times compromised, final set of reports.[54] Likewise, the tenure of Park Guen-hye (2013–2017) has seen the first banning of a political party since 1987, curtailment of artistic expression, a sustained assault on organized labor, and deep corruption leading to political paralysis. Most worrying, perhaps, is the recent move by the government to take over the production of textbooks and remove incidents such as the Kŏch'ang massacre from historical education.[55] Indeed, the repression under Park has been severe enough to receive the condemnation of international agencies such as Amnesty International and has led some scholars to conclude that Korea has entered a period of "post-democratization."[56] With Park's recent impeachment, the reins of power have now been handed to the nominally "progressive" government of Moon Jae-in, who has suggested that he will adopt a less confrontational approach to the North than his predecessors. The impact of this development, however, remains unclear, as the situation is fluid, and currently threatening to spin out of control.

Developments have not been entirely unidirectional, though. The breaking of the taboos surrounding state-sponsored massacres has led to numerous acts of catharsis and intercommunal reconciliation at the local level.[57] Meanwhile, a transnational historical redress culture has blossomed throughout the Pacific Rim, and a sustained rethinking of the Korean War past, beyond stable national frameworks, has been vital to these endeavors.[58] The political power of these latter groups remains scant. However, the groups' transnational structure and ethos, and their unprecedented inclusion of female voices, may represent the most formidable counterweight to the hyper-militarized masculinity that has often dominated political discourse on the peninsula.[59] Historians, of course, make for poor prophets. Nevertheless, it is upon these political and cultural fault lines that future struggles over the Korean War past will likely shift.

What has been presented above is hardly an exhaustive depiction of the nation's memorialization of the Korean War past. Rather, I have merely sketched the dominant currents and shifts of focus in South Korea's ongoing reckoning with its still present and unresolved past. It is, of course, a cliché to say that the past is never settled. But, in the case of the divided peninsula, the full weight of this predicament smothers its population with a rare and encompassing urgency. In 2007, Hwang Sok-yong lamented that "the scars of our war and the ghosts of the Cold War still mar the Korean peninsula."[60] Despite the gains made in the post-authoritarian years, it is not clear that Koreans are any closer to a lasting reconciliation. It is difficult to decipher whether the culprit for this malaise lurks in Korea's tortuous past or in its murky present. As Theodore Adorno remarked, "we will not have come to terms with the past until the causes of what happened then are no longer active. Only because these causes live on does the spell of the past remain, to this very day, unbroken."[61] The current fractures of historical memory on the Korean peninsula are a profound reflection of this predicament. A full reckoning with the peninsula's civil war and violent past, therefore, is contingent upon a working-through and overcoming of the division system itself. As the ghosts of the Korean War past continue to haunt the peninsula's present, this remains an urgent task. The above collection of citizens, artists, and activists has thus far been unable to transcend Korea's tragic condition. However, they will provide an essential compass for future efforts to navigate through this avalanche of historical debris.

## Notes

1 There is no agreement on how to periodize the conflict. Conventional demarcations place the beginning on June 25, 1950, the day that North Korean troops crossed the 38th parallel to invade the ROK. I place the beginning in 1948, the year that the two separate Koreas were established and separate elections led to civil war in the South.
2 Similar to the issue of dating, there is no agreement regarding the total amounts of deaths during the war. Contemporary scholarship lists the total amount of battle deaths at roughly 1.2 million, but this is merely conjecture. Estimates of total deaths range from 2.5 to 4 million. See Bethany Lacina and Nils Petter Gladitsch, "Monitoring Trends in Global Combat: A New Dataset of Battle Deaths," *European Journal of Population* 21 (2005), 154.
3 See, for example, Kim Dong Choon, *The Unending Korean War: A Social History*, trans. Sung-ok Kim (Larkspur: Tamal Vista Publications, 2009), 143–212; Kim Hak-chae, "Hanguk Chŏnjaeng chŏnhu Min'ganin haksal kwa 20 segi ŭi naejŏn" [Pre- and

Post-Korean War Civilian Massacres and Civil Wars of the Twentieth Century], *Asea yŏn'gu* [Asian Research] 53:4 (2010), 82–118; Kwŭn Kwi-suk, "Taeryang Haksal ŭi Sahoe Simni: Cheju 4.3 sakkŏn ŭi Haksal Kwajŏng" [The Socio-Psychological Processes of Genocide: The Stages of Massacre of the Cheju 4.3 Incident], *Han'guk Sahoehak* [Korean Sociology] 36 (2002), 171–200; Pak Myung-lim, "Chŏnjaeng kwa Inmin: T'onghap kwa Punhwa wa Haksal" [War and the People: Integration, Differentiation, and Massacre], *Asea Munhwa* [Asia Culture] 16 (200), 97–167.

4 Kim Taewoo, "Limited War, Unlimited Targets: US Air Force Bombing of North Korea during the Korean War 1950–1953," *Critical Asian Studies* 44:3 (2012), 467–492.

5 Yoo Im-ha, "Breaking the Seal of Memory: A New Perspective on Memory of the Korean War in Korean Novels after the Post-Cold War Era," *The Review of Korean Studies* 9:2 (2006), 136.

6 As former TRCK member Kim Dong-Choon has noted, memorializing the conflict under the heading of "June 25"—the day that North Korean troops crossed the 38th parallel—has allowed various South Korean governments to attribute all the war's causalities and devastation to a "communist conspiracy." According to Kim, "textbooks for primary and middle school students have been written, national holidays selected, museums subsidized, and speeches of politicians delivered" to evoke North Korea's historic guilt. Kim Dong-Choon, "Beneath the Tip of the Iceberg: Problem in Historical Clarification of the Korean War," *Korea Journal*, Autumn (2002), 63.

7 Like the total number of casualties, it is impossible to decipher the exact number of civilians killed during the cycles of guerrilla warfare and counterinsurgency campaigns in the 1948–1950 period. Estimates from the "Cheju Incident" (discussed below) range from 30,000 to 60,000. Civilian deaths during the suppression campaigns associated with the Yŏsun Mutiny are generally believed to be in the tens of thousands. However, as the Rhee government did not keep statistics and used a blanket category to label "communists," it is difficult to determine. See Cheju 4.3 Sakkŏn Chinsang Kyumyŏng mit Hŭisaengja Myŏngye Hoebok Wiwŏnhoe [The National Committee for the Investigation of the Truth about the Cheju 4.3 Incident], *Cheju 4.3 Sakkŏn Chinsang Chosa Pogosŏ* [Cheju 4.3 Incident Investigation Report] (Seoul: Cheju 4.3 Sakkŏn Chinsang Kyumyŏng mit Hŭisaengja Myŏngye Hoebok Wiwŏnhoe, 2003); The National Committee for the Investigation of the Truth about the Cheju 4.3 Incident, *The Cheju 4.3 Incident Investigation Report* (Cheju City: Cheju 4.3 Peace Foundation, 2014); Yŏ-sun Sakkŏn Chinsang Chosa Wiwŏnhoe [Commission for the Investigation of the Truth of the Yŏsun Incident], *Yŏsun Sakkŏn Sunch'ŏn Chiyŏk P'ihae Silt'ae Chosa Pogosŏ* [Investigation Report on Actual Damages from the Yŏsun Incident in the Sunch'ŏn Region] (Sunch'ŏn: Yŏ-sun Sakkŏn Chinsang Chosa Wiwŏnhoe, 2010).

8 Kang Sŏng-hyŏn. "Ak'a' wa 'Ppalgaengi' ŭi T'ansaeng: 'Chŏk Mandŭl ki 'wa 'Pigungmin' ŭi Kyebohak," [Ak'a and the Birth of the "Ppalgaengi": The Making of the Enemy and the Genealogy of the Non-Citizen], *Sahoe wa Yŏksa* [Society and History], 100 (2013), 235–254.

9 Countries that came to the defense of South Korea under United Nations command included the United States of America, the United Kingdom, Philippines, Thailand, Canada, Turkey, Australia, New Zealand, and Ethiopia, among others.

10 Lee Jeong-eun, "International Human Rights Regime and Domestic Politics in South Korea: An Analysis of the Human Rights Agenda between 1948–1960," *The Review of Korean Studies* 11:3 (September 2008), 70.

11 Chŏng Ho-gi, "Chŏn Chaeng Sanghon ui Chiyu Kongkan e Taehan Sisan ui Chŏnhwan: Han'guk esa wi Chŏn Chaeng Kinyŏmmulŭl Chungsim ŭro" [Shifting Views on Places for the Healing of War Wounds: A Focus on Korean War Memorials], *Minchuchuŭi wa Ingwŏn* [Democracy and Human Rights] 8:3 (2009), 188–196.

12 Han'guk Kyuyok Munhwa Hyŏp'oe [Korean Cultural Education Association], *Aeguk Tokbon* [Patriot Reader] (Seoul: Ujongsa, 1955), 83–86.

13 Park Wan Suh, *The Naked Tree*, trans. Yu Young-nam (Ithaca: Cornell East Asia Series, 1995), 150.

14 Ibid., 148.
15 Hwang Sun-wŏn, *The Descendents of Cain*, trans. Suh Ji Moon and Julie Pickering (Armonk: M.E. Sharp Publishing, 1997).
16 Hwang Sun-wŏn, *Lost Souls: Stories*, trans. Bruce Fulton and Ju-Chan Fulton (New York: Columbia University Press, 2010), 318. Once described as a communist riot, the "Cheju Incident" is now recognized as a series of massacres against civilians primarily committed by government forces from 1948 until 1954. The largest concentration of killings occurred during the 1948–1949 winter suppression campaign. Bruce Cumings, *The Origins of the Korean War, Volume 2: The Roaring of the Cataract, 1947–1950* (Princeton: Princeton University Press, 1990), 250–259; John Merrill, "The Cheju-do Rebellion," *Journal of Korean Studies* 2 (1980), 139–197; Kwŏn Kwi-suk, "Taeryang Haksal ŭi Sahoe Simni: Cheju 4.3 Sakkŏn ŭi Haksal Kwajŏng" [The Socio-Psychological Processes of Genocide: The Stages of Massacre of the Cheju 4.3 Incident] (2004). *Han'guk Sahoehak* [Korean Sociology] 36, 171–200; Pak Ch'an-sik, *4.3 ŭi Chinsil* [The Truth of 4.3] (Cheju City: Cheju 4.3 P'yŏnghwa Cheadan [Cheju April 3 Peace Foundation], 2010).
17 Hwang, *Lost Souls*, 318.
18 Choi In-hun, *The Square*, trans. by Kim Seong-kon (London: Dalkey Archive Press, 2014), 42.
19 Ibid., 54.
20 Kim Wŏn-il, *Evening Glow*, trans. Agnita M. Tennant (Fremont: Asian Humanities Press, 2003), 158.
21 While the title of the work is translated as "Uncle Suni," the eponymous character is in fact female. It is possible that Hyun did this as a commentary on the fact that after the Cheju massacre the island's male population was decimated, so many women took over as heads of the household. It was also common for islanders to refer to each other as "samch'on" (uncle) following the string of mass killings. Thanks to my colleagues Minna Lee and Jerome de Wit for their insights on this matter.
22 Hyun Ki-young, *Sun-i Samch'on*, trans. Lee Jung-hi (Seoul: Asia Publishers, 2012), 105.
23 Ibid., 137.
24 Ibid., 121. See also Kim Seong-Nae, "Sexual Politics of State Violence: On Cheju April Third Massacre of 1948," in *Traces 2: Race Panic and the Memory of Migration*, M. Morris and Brett de Bary, eds. (Hong Kong: Hong Kong University Press, 2002), 259–292.
25 In total, the commission revealed 8,522 victims. The largest number came from the Kyŏngbuk (2,200) and Kyŏngnam (2,892), most of whom were victims of the National Guidance League killings or the mass executions at Taegu Prison. On Cheju, the commission uncovered 1,878 deaths. Meanwhile, the commission confirmed 1,552 deaths in the Honam regions. Beyond the deaths, the report also documented extensive property damage, affecting more than 10,000 homes, and the loss of thousands of livestock throughout the country. "Sakkŏn tangsi Pudaejang mit Kwallyŏnja Kyumyŏng" [Commander at the Time and Those Involved with Incident Identified]," *Cheju Sinbo*, June 13, 1960; "8 Ch'ŏni nŏmnŏn Haksalcha/Puljirŭ ko Yak'tal Nanhaeng/3 Pu Haptong Chosatan kwa T'ŭkpyŏl Choch'ibŏp Chejŏng ŭl Ch'okku/Yangmin Haksal Kukhoe Chosatansŏ" [More than 8,000 Slaughtered/Violently Burned and Plundered/3 Member Investigation Team and Enactment of Special Law Urged]," *Han'guk Ilbo*, June 21, 1960.
26 Kim Chong-wŏn and Yi Hyŏp-pu, two men involved in large-scale massacres throughout Kyŏngsang Province, were convicted of arson and murder. However, both had their convictions overturned by the military junta of Park Chung-hee in 1961.
27 Brendan Wright, "Raising the Korean War Dead: Bereaved Family Associations and the Politics of 1960–1961 South Korea," *The Asia-Pacific Journal* 13:40, No. 2 (October 12, 2015), 9.
28 Chinsil Hwahae rŭl wihan Kwagŏsa Chŏngni Wiwŏnhoe [Truth and Reconciliation Commission], *Chinsil Hwahae Wiwŏnhoe Chonghap Pogosŏ IV: Ingwŏn Ch'imhae Sakkŏn* [Truth and Reconciliation Commission Comprehensive Report IV: Incidents of Human Rights Abuses] (Seoul: Chinsil Hwahae rŭl wihan Kwagŏsa Chŏngni Wiwŏnhoe, 2010), 270.

29 Chinsil Hwahae rŭl wihan Kwagŏsa Chŏngni Wiwŏnhoe [Truth and Reconciliation Commission], *Che 2-Chang Chiptan Hŭisaeng Kyumyŏng Wiwŏnhoe: Ulsan Kungmin Podo Yŭnmaeng Sakkŏn* [Committee for Examining Incidents of Large-scale Sacrifice, Section 2: Ulsan National Guidance League Incident] (Seoul: Chinsil Hwahae rŭl wihan Kwagŏsa Chŏngni Wiwŏnhoe, 2007), 999–1001.
30 Shin Gi-wook and Hwang Kyung Moon, eds., *Contentious Kwangju: The May 18th Uprising in Korea's Past and Present* (Lanham: Rowman and Littlefield, 2003).
31 Namhee Lee, *The Making of the Minjung: Democracy and the Politics of Representation in South Korea* (Ithaca: Cornell University Press, 2007), 39.
32 Ibid., 61.
33 We Jung Yi (2013), "Family Apart: The Aesthetic Genealogy of Korean War Memories," PhD dissertation, Cornell University, Ann Arbor; ProQuest UMI, 2013 (Publication Number. 3574751), 103.
34 "11 Years of Torture for Novel 'Taebaek Sanmaek'," *The Hankyoreh*, March 30, 2005. http://english.hani.co.kr/arti/english_edition/e_editorial/22271.html.
35 The Kŏch'ang Incident occurred in the winter of 1951, when veteran counterinsurgency commanders from the Cheju campaign ordered the systematic slaughter of more than 700 civilians—the majority of whom were women, children, or elderly people—throughout the township of Sinwŏn. Though the victims were initially accused of aiding and abetting southern communist partisan (*ppalch'isan*) forces, subsequent investigations have exonerated and restored their honor.
36 Sarh Conway-Lanz, "Beyond No Gun-Ri: Refugees and the United States Military in the Korean War," *Diplomatic History* 29:1 (January 2004), 49–81; Charles Hanley et al., *The Bridge at No Gun Ri: A Hidden Nightmare from the Korean War* (New York: Henry Holt and Company, 2001).
37 Kim, "Tip of the Iceberg," 60.
38 Chinsil Hwahae rŭl wihan Kwagŏsa Chŏngni Wiwŏnhoe [Truth and Reconciliation Commission], *Chinsil Hwahae Wiwŏnhoe Chonghap Pogosŏ III: Min'ganin Chiptan Hŭisaeng Sakkŏn* [Truth and Reconciliation Comprehensive Report III: Incidents of Large-Scale Civilian Sacrifices] (Seoul: Chinsil Hwahae rŭl wihan Kwagŏsa Chŏngni Wiwŏnhoe, 2009), 176–202.
39 Problems associated with the commission include, but are not limited to, a large passage of time between the incident and the investigation; destruction of evidence; poor advertising for the committee; lack of compensation for victims; lack of subpoena power; and no punishment for the still living perpetrators, to name a few. Scholars have also pointed out theoretical and moral problems with the truth and reconciliation process itself. Chŏng, Ho-gi, "Chinsil Kyumyŏng ŭi Chedohwa wa Tach'ŭngjŏk Chaejomyŏng: Min'ganin ŭi Chiptanjŏk Chugŭm ŭl Chungsim ŭro" [Institutionalization of Truth, Clarification, and Reconsideration from a Multifaceted Perspective: A Focus on Mass Deaths of Civilians], *Chenosaidŭ Yŏn'gu* [Genocide Research] 6: 83–109; Han Sŏng-hun, "Kwagŏ Ch'ŏngsan kwa Minjujuŭi Sirhyŏn: Chinsil Hwahae Wiwŏnhoe Hwaltong kwa Hwŏngo Sahang ŭi i Haenggi Chŏngŭi rŭl Chungsim ŭro" [Transitional Justice and the Realization of Democracy: A Focus on the Truth and Reconciliation Commission's Activities and the Implementation of Recommendations for Transitional Justice], *Yŏksa Pip'yŏng* [History Criticism] November (2010), 116–141.
40 Han Sŏng-hun, "Kinyŏmmul ŭl Tullŏssan Kiŏk ŭi Chŏngch'iwa Chiptan Chŏngch'esŏng: Kŏch'ang Sagŏn ui Wiryŏngbi rŭl Chungsimŭro" [The Politics of Memory and Collective Identity Surrounding Monuments: A Study of the Kŏch'ang Incident Memorial Stone], *Sahoe wa Yŏksa* [Society and History] 78 (2008), 35–63; Kang, Eun-Jung, Noel Scott, Timothy Jeonglyeol Lee, and Roy Ballantyne. "Benefits of Visiting a 'Dark Tourism' Site: The Case of the Cheju April 3rd Peace Park, Korea," *Tourism Management* 33:2 (2012), 257–265; Kim, Min-hwan. "Chŏnjang i toen Cheju 4.3 P'yŏnghwa Kongwŏn: P'oktong Non ŭi 'arŭn Kŏrim' kwa Punyŏl toen Yŏndae" [Cheju 4.3 Peace Park as Battlefield: The "Absent Presence" of the Riot Interpretation and Divided Solidarity], *Kyŏngje wa Sahoe* [Economy and Society] (2014), 74–109; Kim Minhwan and Paekyŏng

Kim, "Haksal kwa Naejŏn, Kongganjŏk Chaehyŏn kwa Tamnonjŏk Chaehyŏn ŭi kangŏk: Kŏch'ang sakkŏn ch'umo kongwŏn ŭi konggan punsŏk" [Spatial and Discursive Conflicts over the Representation of Massacres and Civil War: An Analysis of the Spatial Configuration of Kŏch'ang Incident Memorial Park], *Sahoe wa Yŏksa* [Society and History] 100 (2008), 5–31. Seunghei Clara Hong, "Silenced in Memorium: Consuming Memory at the Nogŭnri Peace Park," *Cross Currents: East Asian History and Cultural Review*, E Journal 14 (March 2015), 178–203.
41 Yi Ho-chol, *Northerners, Southerners: A Novel*, trans. Andrew P. Killick and Sukyeon Cho (Norwalk: Eastbridge Publishing, 2004).
42 O Chŏng-hŭi, "Spirit on the Wind," in *The Red Room: Stories of Trauma in Contemporary Korea*, trans. Bruce Fulton and Ju-chan Fulton (Honolulu: University of Hawai'i Press, 2009).
43 Hwang Sok-yong, *The Guest*, trans. Kyung-Ja Chun and Maya West (New York: Seven Stories Press, 2007).
44 For an analysis of the North Korean state narrative, see Han Sŏng-hun, "The Ongoing Korean War at the Sinch'ŏn Museum in North Korea," *Cross Currents: East Asian Culture Review*, E Journal 14 (March 2015), 152–177. Ryu Young-ju, meanwhile, focuses on the prospects for, and limitations of, reconciliation in Hwang's text: Ryu Young-ju, "Truth or Reconciliation: *The Guest* and the Massacre that Never Ends," *Positions: East Asia Cultures Critique* 23:4 (Fall 2015), 633–663.
45 Hwang, *The Guest*, 218–220.
46 Ibid., 7–8.
47 Chŏng Chi-yŏng, *Nambugun* (Seoul: Nam Productions, 1990).
48 Indeed, the film ends with Yi's comrades surrounded and slowly killed off by counterinsurgency forces, reduced to virtual starvation, in turn leading to betrayal and capture.
49 Yi Kwŏn-taek, *T'aebaeksanmaek* (Seoul: Taehung Pictures, 1994).
50 Ji-hoon Hun and Je-gyu Kang, *T'aegŭkki Hwinallimyŏ*, DVD, Directed by Je-gyu Kang (South Korea: Showbox, 2004).
51 For an objective, and historically informed, account of the recent increases in hostility across the DMZ, see Nam Kim, "Korea on the Brink: Reading the *Yŏngp'yŏng* Shelling and Its Aftermath," *The Journal of Asian Studies* 70:2 (May 2011), 337–356.
52 Julian Borger, "I'd Be Honored to Meet with Kim Jong-un under 'Right Circumstances'", *The Guardian*, May 1, 2017. https://www.theguardian.com/us-news/2017/may/01/donald-trump-kim-jong-un-meeting-north-korea.
53 Richard N. Hess, "The Coming Confrontation with North Korea," *Project Syndicate*, September 20, 2016. https://www.project-syndicate.org/commentary/north-korea-confrontation-coming-by-richard-n--haass-2016-09. It is not clear how serious the threat of preemptive assassination is, and it is plausible that it is a public relations move by the Park Administration, as the US still has operational control over the South Korean army. Yi Yŏng-in, "Mi Paegakkwanŭn Taebung Sŏnjet'Agyŏng Kyehoek ŏpta" [The White House Has No Plan for Pre-Emptive Strike on North Korea], *The Hankyoreh*, September 25, 2016. http://www.hani.co.kr/arti/international/america/762607.html.
54 Kim Dong-choon and Mark Selden, "South Korea's Embattled Truth and Reconciliation Commission," *The Asia-Pacific Journal* (March 1, 2010). An illustrative example of this concerns the official report on the "National Guidance League Killings". In the summer of 1950, the South Korean security forces executed thousands of self-confessed "communists" who had been promised amnesty if they joined the League. In June 1950, over 300,000 had joined, the majority being illiterate peasants who likely were coerced or bribed into joining. It is estimated that anywhere between 20,000 and 100,000 League members were killed, though some place the number even higher. However, the commission was only able to confirm 5,129 deaths. Chinsil Hwahae rŭl wihan Kwagŏsa Chŏngni Wiwŏnhoe [Truth and Reconciliation Commission], *Chinsil Hwahae Wiwŏnhoe Chonghap Pogosŏ III: Min'ganin Chiptan Hŭisaeng Sakkŏn*, 158.
55 Kim Chi-hoon, "7-chong Han'guksa Kyogwasŏ Chŏjadŭl 'T'ekyoyukpu Kwŏn'gonŭn up'yŏnhyang T'ŭjipchapki'" ["Ministry of Education Has Right-Wing Bias" Say

7th Edition Korean History Textbook Authors], *The Hankyoreh*, October 22, 2013. http://www.hani.co.kr/arti/ISSUE/108/608142.html.
56 Jamie Doucette and Se-Woong Koo, "Pursuing Post-Democratisation: The Resilience of Politics by Public Security in Contemporary South Korea," *Journal of Contemporary Asia* 46:2 (2016), 198–221. "South Korea Ban on Political Party Another Sign of Shrinking Space for Freedom of Expression," *Amnesty International*, December 19, 2014. https://www.amnesty.org/en/latest/news/2014/12/south-korea-ban-political-party-another-sign-shrinking-space-freedom-expression.
57 Heonik Kwon, "Legacies of the Korean War: Transforming Ancestral Rituals in South Korea," *Memory Studies* 6:161 (2013), 161–173.
58 An intriguing example of this type of work is the multimedia "Still Present Pasts" exhibit: http://stillpresentpasts.org/. Korean and international feminists have also worked to break the impasse on the peninsula: https://www.womencrossdmz.org/. Activists fighting the construction of the US naval base at Gangjeong Village, meanwhile, have invoked the history of the Cheju massacre to argue against the militarization of the island: see http://savejejunow.org/history/.
59 See, for example, Shelia Myoshi Jager, "Monumental Histories: Manliness, the Military, and the War Memorial," *Public History* 14:2 (Spring 2002), 389–392.
60 Hwang, *The Guest*, 8.
61 Theordor Adorno, "What Does Coming to Terms with the Past Mean?" in *Bitburg in Moral and Political Perspective*, Geoffrey Hartmann, ed. (Bloomington: Indiana University Press, 1986), 129.

# 7
# WAR TOURISM AND GEOGRAPHIES OF MEMORY IN VIETNAM

Christina Schwenkel

> War is at once a summary and a museum . . . its own.
>
> *Paul Virilio*

In December 2015, the travel section of the *New York Times* advertised a ten-day historical tour of Vietnam entitled "Lingering Legacies of a War." The itinerary, spanning the country from north to south, offered nothing particularly novel—visits to the demilitarized zone, the Cú Chi tunnels, and the Reunification Palace have long been popular destinations for war buffs and tourists interested in the history of a conflict that continues to mark the landscape. Even the planned meeting with Vietnamese veterans to hear their personal recollections of the battlefield is standard fare for groups of returning US veterans and their family members, and reveal how easily scarred bodies and scarred landscapes merge in these mediated tourism scripts. What was unique with the *Times* journey, however, was both the cost and the targeted audience: The price for the package tour started at a whopping US $6,195 for double occupancy, excluding international and domestic airfare. This shift to a more upscale "war tourism" industry that markets state-sanctioned memories of the war in Vietnam to a more affluent niche signals an important departure from past itineraries and tourist practices. To demonstrate such changes, I map the specific nodes or centralized places for the consumption of war heritage on to the geography of the country, highlighting popular attractions in southern, central, and northern Vietnam. This comparative approach, based on long-term ethnographic research that started in 1997, demonstrates how each node offers visitors a unique, mediated sensory experience of the war—with distinctive sights, sounds, and smells, for instance—shaped by dominant historical imaginaries for that region.

The marketing of the war in Vietnam to non-nationals is not a new phenomenon, but emerged concurrently alongside the development of a nascent tourism industry in the early 1990s.[1] In those years, state tourism officials began to develop a market around the construct of the "Vietnam War," as it is known in the West (it is called the "American War" in Vietnam).[2] A diverse set of state and nonstate actors set about deploying iconic expressions, artifacts, images, and knowledge linked to the wartime experiences of American military forces and their allies, as sensationalized in US popular memory. This meant, for example, representing the pro-communist forces in the South as "VC" (Viet Cong, considered by many in Vietnam to be a derogatory epithet), rather than as troops of the National Liberation Front. American popular culture thus deeply penetrated and helped give shape to Vietnam's postwar landscape of war attractions.[3]

The commodification of the war at that time had two intersecting components that worked in tandem with one another: It was both centralized, insofar as sites were curated and managed by state tourism officials, and concurrently decentralized, often providing lucrative opportunities for marginal and stigmatized actors in the informal economy, such as veterans of the army of the Republic of Vietnam.[4] This meant that the historical information presented to visitors could be more diverse than typically expected, offering an alternative perspective on the war that, while unsanctioned, was tolerated by ambivalent officials and welcomed by skeptical foreigners who were keen to hear "the other side" of the story.[5] Such findings are important as they call into question the casual observation that war sites in Vietnam are simply places for the "whitewashing" of history. For the one-time visitor this may appear to be the case, and it certainly holds true that important voices and experiences that contradict the official narrative are omitted or *disremembered*.[6] However, through the use of sustained ethnography, it is possible to go beyond the surface of crafted appearances into the more complex workings of the industry to see that war heritage sites are not only more dynamic than typically acknowledged, but also have the potential to be controversial spaces for competing truths and memories.[7]

The war tourism industry in the 1990s was developed and sold predominantly to American visitors and other international tourists.[8] It was also deeply embedded in a low-budget or "backpacker" economy, that is, it mostly (but not exclusively) attracted a younger generation of adventure travelers for whom the war was but a spectacle featured in film, video games, and other cultural representations.[9] As diplomatic relations between the United States and the Socialist Republic of Vietnam improved, culminating in a formal normalization of diplomatic relations in July 1995, expectations that US citizens, and especially war veterans, would return to Vietnam in large numbers inspired the re-Americanization of Vietnam's postwar landscape, as I describe in more detail below. Such predictions did not materialize as expected, however. Officials grossly underestimated the complex emotions, if not stigma, attached to the past, leading to a vigorous campaign that "Vietnam is a country and not a war." Recent years have seen the number of American tourists climb more quickly, however, as travel to Vietnam has become increasingly normalized.[10]

At the same time, visitor demographics have changed tremendously since the early years. Given the rise in the standard of living for certain strata of the population, it is now more common to find Vietnamese visitors, usually in groups, at some sites where they were previously absent. One also finds more non-European tourists, mostly from other Asian and ASEAN (Association of Southeast Asian Nations) countries. Inadvertently, then, war attractions have become sites of intersecting and oft-conflicting memories, experience, and knowledge about the past that transcend official narratives of history. For this reason, rather than thinking of such destinations as spaces of commodified entertainment that induce social amnesia devoid of critique, I find it more fruitful to recognize the critical memory work that can, and indeed does, take place in fraught spaces of return (e.g., to the battlefield) and encounter (e.g., between former adversaries) that are imbued with profound emotions and diverse meanings.[11] This approach does not deny that many formative memories remain buried and sensitive, if not outright verboten. Where there is memory, there is always forgetting, and many Vietnamese have learned how to live *unhistorically*, that is, how to remember and forget certain pasts in particular times and places.[12] However, rather than view war attractions as unmediated sites for the transfer of state heroic narratives of the war—which are certainly present and dominant—it is also important to recognize the extent to which memory is co-constituted. In other words, tourist scripts and individual experiences, both local and global, intersect and bump up against one another to complicate, and at times undermine, state-managed memory. Attention to the jaggedness of memory work allows us to think of memory-making not simply as a uniform state project (e.g., production of a *national* history) but also as an uneven, transnational process subjected to a range of interventions.[13]

As the demographics of tourism have changed to also attract a new class of consumers, such as those targeted by the *New York Times*, so too have the opportunities to market the war expanded. To demonstrate such shifts and how they reflect changing narratives and sensory engagements with history as new destinations are added to itineraries, I examine the recently launched "Path of History: Bomb Shelter Tour" at the five-star Metropole Hotel in Hanoi. This elite tour offers an aestheticized and yet unsettling subterranean experience of the air war without having to dirty one's hands and knees as occurs while crawling through narrow tunnels at other popular attractions. To show the distinctiveness of this shelter visit, I first turn to the classic sites that gave shape to the industry in the 1990s and that continue to attract crowds of sundry visitors. I begin with the best known destination in southern Vietnam: the Cú Chi tunnels. This tour focuses on the subterranean activities of the so-called Viet Cong during the "American War." In it, the invisible and feared enemy is made known, his or her secrets of survival ultimately unveiled through a multisensory, embodied experience of life underground. The following section travels up the coast to the former demilitarized zone (DMZ) close to the 17th parallel that once divided the country. Here, abandoned American bases and battles against the dreaded "NVA," or North Vietnamese Army,[14] occupy the central experience and narrative of the "Vietnam War."

Up to this point, the geography of war tourism has been largely based on American experiences and imaginaries of war (e.g., GI fear of the VC), regardless of the perspective given (American War or Vietnam War). To some extent, this slippage also occurs in the last section of the chapter, on the air raid shelter in Hanoi where hotel guests and employees sat out strikes, including the infamous Christmas bombing in 1972. And yet, this private tour marks a radical departure from the other state-run war sites: here the marketing of the war and the hotel are mutually imbricated. Under the corporate management of the Metropole, the exclusive tour for hotel guests only reveals how the US bombing of Hanoi has become a marketing tool to sell the most expensive accommodation in the capital city by showcasing *celebrity* experiences of the "Air War". And yet, like at state-regulated sites, here dominant narratives are made more complex with the insertion of other voices and memories.

## The "American War": Tunnel tours

Underground tourism in subterranean spaces—tunnels, trenches, bunkers, and bomb shelters—remains an understudied topic within the broader rubric of "dark tourism."[15] And yet, in Vietnam, it is central to the war tourism experience and has largely come to define it. The Củ Chi tunnels, 60 kilometers northwest of Ho Chi Minh City in a bucolic setting among rubber trees, remain Vietnam's most popular war attraction to this day. Once a region of intense fighting between US/Republic of Vietnam (RVN) forces and the National Liberation Front, this hallowed battleground has been remade into a much anticipated tourist space for a multisensory "Viet Cong" experience. Part of the allure of the tunnel tour lies in its promise to divulge the crafty wartime secrets of the undetectable enemy, but to do so in a way that is palatable and gripping—without the pain, as Kennedy and Williams have argued.[16] It also has to be done in a way that is relatively safe, free of the discomforts that guerrillas regularly faced, though not without losing an exhilarating sense of adventure and risk. The tunnel tour is not for the cautious or claustrophobic, but tourists are reassured that passageways have been sprayed for venomous creatures. The dilemma for tourism officials is thus how to stage the war as an authentic embodied experience without making it *too* real. All the while, the adjacent war cemetery and martyr temple serve as a candid reminder that such sites of touristic pleasure remain spaces of death and trauma for many others.[17]

The Củ Chi tunnels emerged as an international tourist attraction in the early 1990s. Before then, most of the extensive 200-kilometer network of winding passageways, which in some places dropped up to 10 meters below ground, had been left to decay. After the war, a few passages and chambers were preserved as a memorial, which attracted government officials, schoolchildren, and eventually foreign visitors. Forecasting an increase in the number of international tourists, state tourism authorities set out to modify a select number of the preserved tunnels to accommodate their perceived taller and broader physiques. Originally, the narrow tunnel system had been designed for the slighter stature of Vietnamese guerrillas, which would allow them to quickly slip through tight and undetected entryways on the forest floor. Most US soldiers, on the other hand—with the exception of the GI "tunnel rats" who went in after the Viet Cong—could not fit.[18] Today, few of the original underground passages remain, but one that does is used as a demonstration to illustrate bodily difference: after a local guide, dressed as a guerilla, descends through the tight entrance, a non-local spectator is invited to try to follow suit. Most of what tourists encounter today are reconstructions, though they are touted as "original" (Figure 7.1).[19]

The "Củ Chi Tunnel Historical Remains," as they are called today, comprise a large area (an estimated 830,000 square meters) that is managed by the central tourist administration of Củ Chi District. The complex is divided across two hamlets, Bến Đình and Bến Dược, each of which maintains a set of tunnels—one for international tourists and another for domestic visitors. As such, each location offers a different encounter with history, depending on the perceived desires of the visitors: Foreigners are thought to want the "real thing"—that is, a more authentic and embodied experience of the war—while Vietnamese tourists, who are less interested in consuming the past as commodity, come to enjoy the serene surroundings.[20] Low-budget tours that start in the "tây ba lô" or backpacker area of Ho Chi Minh City (around Phạm Ngũ Lão St) take busloads of mostly European and North American tourists on day trips to the tunnels for a mere couple of dollars, not including a steeper, but affordable, entrance fee (applicable only to foreigners). Upon arrival, they are greeted by a young guide, dressed in the trademark dép lốp, or tire sandals, who will accompany visitors through a day in the life of a typical "VC fighter." Note that the use of American jargon remains constant, positioning the visitors as outsiders (GIs) peering in on clandestine guerilla activity. Engrossed in the performance, tour groups are scarcely aware of the crowds of urban Vietnamese seeking respite from the city on the other side of the park.

The tour begins in a small theater where visitors are briefed on the design and construction of the tunnels before watching a black-and-white documentary on the everyday lives of Củ Chi combatants. This prepares the group and arouses curiosity for what lies ahead as they set out for the trek into the once defoliated jungle

FIGURE 7.1   Guide posing in "original" tunnel, 2004. Photo by the author

under a canopy of eucalyptus regrowth. The first stop is a "VC weapons exhibit". Here guests observe defense strategies adapted from traditional hunting techniques, such as the dreaded swinging door, a device that, when stepped on squarely in the center, flips up to close on to the lower leg, impaling it with sharpened, if not poisoned, bamboo spikes. A mural depicting scenes of wounded US soldiers caught in the clutches of such lethal entrapments demonstrates the efficacy of the rudimentary defense system, while celebrating victory over the United States. Visitors then walk single-file along dusty trails past bomb craters, a destroyed tank, and a number of tunnel access points, as distant machine-gun fire pierces the quietude of the forest, contributing to a contrived sensation of moving through a former battle zone. They soon arrive at the pinnacle of the tour, where the more intrepid travelers descend below ground to slowly crawl 100 meters through dimly lit and stifling passages that drop three meters beneath the earth's surface. Anxious and undecided tourists are informed of the existence of emergency exits every 30 meters if they are unable to proceed into the deeper and narrower tunnel sections.

After emerging, the multisensory experience continues. Panting and perspiring, the dirt-speckled guests are invited into the underground kitchen chamber for tea and a sampling of "guerilla food": boiled cassava dipped in salted crushed peanuts. As the journey continues, more secrets to underground survival are divulged, showcasing the clever ingenuity of the combatants, including how smoke from the kitchen was dispersed through a series of small air holes, giving the illusion of lingering jungle mists; how pilfered American soap was used to throw off the scent of the dreaded war dogs; and how dead US bombs were sawn open and used for ammunition. These demonstrations regularly elicit awe from viewers. The tour then comes to a close at the shooting range, where war enthusiasts and curious tourists pay one dollar a bullet to fire a Soviet AK-47. The commingling of US popular culture (including joking references to Rambo by guides from Ho Chi Minh City who fought alongside Americans) and heroic accounts of VC perseverance produces a "cacophonous script" about the American War that mixes entertainment and education.[21] Such narratives are typically, although not exclusively, consumed by younger tourists ("backpackers") who are familiar with Vietnam mostly through mediated images, such as Hollywood films, but also through stories from their families. As I show in the next section, this demographic shifts when the attraction becomes the Vietnam War as experienced on deserted US bases.

## The "Vietnam War": Base tours

Military bases have long been popular tourist sites, combining historical education, commemoration, and a smattering of militarism, as Geoff White has argued of the USS *Arizona* at Pearl Harbor in Hawai'i.[22] Tourism to US military installations in other countries, such as the Clark and Subic bases in the Philippines that developers have transformed into popular sites of commerce and leisure,[23] gives new meaning to the term "rest and recreation." Clearly, for bases to become tourist destinations, they need to be decommissioned, and, in the case of Vietnam, abandoned.

After the war, several major US base camps, such as the Củ Chi Army Airfield (under which ran some of the tunnels), were taken over by the Vietnamese military, and remain off-limits to visitors to this day. Other installations that no longer served a purpose, such as those along the southern edge of the former DMZ, were dismantled and left to scavengers. Over time, these spaces—despite having "little to see" (a common tourist complaint)—were remade into war attractions in a process that I call the re-Americanization of the landscape.[24] In the 1990s, as Củ Chi tourism officials were working to accommodate a growing number of international visitors to the tunnels, their counterparts in the province of Quảng Trị set about organizing a day tour around locations that resonated strongly in American historical memory. Such places, and the vernacular language used to identify them, would be familiar and ostensibly appeal to American tourists, especially returning veterans with geographical and historical knowledge of the region.[25]

There is perhaps no other province that bears the catastrophic effects of the war more than Quảng Trị. Bomb craters, deforestation, unexploded ordnance, overgrown ruins, martyr cemeteries, and deserted bases tell the tragic story of a violent history that continues to impact the present—as well as pique the morbid curiosity of tourists. Quảng Trị is well known in American history for its strategic airfields and base camps that experienced some of the heaviest combat during the war. Positioned along Highway 9, just south of the DMZ, US military installations within firing range of northern artillery were subjected to regular attack from enemy forces, leading to heavy casualties. The area thus remains a deeply meaningful, if not sacred, landscape in American war memory, and a priority destination for returning US veterans. Cognizant of its significance (and its representation in popular culture), discerning authorities launched the popular "DMZ tour" in the mid-1990s; it continues to this day, but not without important changes.

Compared with Củ Chi, the 12-hour DMZ tour is less of an historical spectacle and it attracts a broader spectrum of visitors. Low-budget Western travelers comprise the majority of tour participants, while those with more means who feel compelled to make a personal journey typically rent a car and proceed on their own.[26] The tour begins each morning at 6am in the neighboring imperial city of Huế, a tourist hub. The war attractions are grouped into two clusters—Highway 9 (east–west) and Highway 1 (north–south). Along the latter route, tourists make brief stops at the bombed ruins of a Catholic church that guides refer to as a "skeleton cathedral," followed by the Hiền Lương Bridge, which traverses the Bến Hải River that marked the temporary border at the 17th parallel. They briefly cross into the foreboding territory of "the North" to visit the Vịnh Mốc tunnels, where they edge their way through subterranean pathways—higher in height than at Củ Chi, so no crawling necessary—built by villagers to escape the fierce and persistent air strikes. Until the mid-2000s, this was the only space of contact between domestic and international travelers, and the relative lack of Vietnamese visitors encountered on the daylong journey revealed the extent to which *American* memory of the *Vietnam* War shaped the excursion.

The marketing of the war permeates the tour. After lunch at the 'DMZ Hotel,' the second leg continues west along Highway 9, passing a barren piece of land that once housed the marine base, Camp Carroll. The bus then travels to the 'Rockpile,' a 230-meter-high limestone formation that served as a firebase and observation point. The script at this point deviates little—pointing to a distant mountain range, a guide identifies 'Hamburger Hill,' which most tourists recognize from the Hollywood film. It is not uncommon, however, for guides to integrate stories learned from US veterans, presenting a more complex history than that intended by state narratives. Scripted narrations are likewise obfuscated at the last stop on Highway 9, the Khe Sanh marine base, close to the border with Laos. In recent years, this popular destination has undergone substantial renovation to attract a wider range of visitors, including Vietnamese tourists and veterans. Khe Sanh is thus a fruitful place to observe the dynamic forces at work in the war tourism industry, including its shifting demographics.

Nestled among Robusta coffee trees, Khe Sanh Combat Base is a highly anticipated stop on the DMZ tour. In Vietnamese memory, Khe Sanh is identified as "Sân bay Tà Cơn," or Tà Cơn airport. This linguistic variation shows the distinctive memory work that takes place at the deserted base: While foreigners visit "Khe Sanh," domestic tourists go to "Sân bay Tà Cơn." The site of one of the most decisive (and debated) battles in the war's history,[27] Khe Sanh is also the best known in American popular memory. The camp's lengthy 77-day siege by enemy forces in 1968 became "daily fare for American television viewers," fueling its legendary status and its historical value as war heritage.[28]

In 1998, when I first visited the base, there were few material remains from this history, except for traces of the airstrip, rounds of spent ammunition, and rusted scrap metal from US aircraft strewn about the large open space. A one-room building housed a small display of war artifacts and photographs, most without captions. Local vendors sold exhumed relics—"base waste"—as souvenirs to curious tourists, including rusted forks, spoons, razors, coins, medals, lighters, and dog tags, most of which, I observed over repeated visits, were fake.[29] "Don't wander off the path," guides warned groups of European and American visitors in the early years of the tour, pointing to the lingering threat of mines that continue to claim Vietnamese lives.

A decade later, a marked shift toward the "Vietnamization" of the landscape of war heritage had occurred, with important implications for both the tourism industry and the complex work of memory. At Khe Sanh, officials renovated and enclosed the grounds, expanding the exhibits and consolidating them into a newly built museum that foregrounded Vietnam's victory over the US military (Figure 7.2). This view presented the government's official interpretation of the war and the historical value it assigned to the former marine base. The official naming of site as the "Historical Remains of Tà Cơn Airbase" (Di tích Sân bay Tà Cơn)—notably, not Khe Sanh—served to attract a more diverse group of visitors traveling to the remote location. As domestic tourism grew, so too did the numbers of Vietnamese visitors, including veterans—also from the military of the former RVN,

FIGURE 7.2   Khe Sanh Museum, 2011. Photo by the author

sometimes as tour guides, like at Củ Chi. The number of US veterans and their family members likewise increased as Vietnam became known as a safe and welcoming destination. This meant that low-budget, Western tourists were no longer the main actors on the scene. Perhaps most remarkable, as a result of encounters between these different groups, Khe Sanh/Tà Cơn emerged as a place for spontaneous, collective commemoration across all sides of the war, if not empathetic understanding, as witnessed in the emotional entries written in comment books.[30] The combat base thus serves as a reminder that war attractions can become malleable sites of memory-making beyond state control, even allowing for the possibility of reconciliation.

## The "Air War": Bomb shelter tours

The historic Hotel Metropole in central Hanoi houses one of the newest war attractions in a region of the country (northern Vietnam) that experienced the war first-hand through protracted aerial bombing. Unlike the other tours in Quảng Trị and Củ Chi, the Path of History® bomb shelter tour is managed by a private entity (the French-run Sofitel, under the Legend signature brand) and is incorporated into a trademarked network of the world's most famous hotels, a designation maintained by a global hospitality association.[31] Notably, it is not open to the public, only to hotel guests (and the occasional inquiring anthropologist).[32] The tour thus marks a shift from *mass* war tourism to a more *exclusive* consumption of war memory. Although it relies on a similar technique of promising visitors an aesthetic and multisensory embodied experience, it does so in a way that presents the war through the privileged eyes of foreign—mostly American—guests in Hanoi during the air strikes. As such, the bomb shelter tour offers a selective history of celebrities-in-wartime that, while displacing the daily violence faced by Hanoians, has become a key marketing strategy in an ever more competitive, upscale tourism industry.

Built in 1901, the Metropole was the most exclusive colonial-era hotel in the city and remains so today. A luxury establishment, room rates typically run between 200 and 300 US dollars, always pricing higher than comparative five-star accommodations. Guests are attracted by the architectural splendor of the building, its nostalgic colonial charm, and the long list of famous guests (including Charlie Chaplin on one of his honeymoons, as I would learn). The Metropole—renamed Thống Nhất, or Unification Hotel, after the defeat of the French in 1954—was one of two hotels authorized to house foreigners during the war (the other being the adjacent Dân Chủ, offering cheaper and more basic lodging, e.g., to guests from socialist countries). The Thống Nhất was the place where sympathetic critics, activists, journalists, and writers (from capitalist countries) stayed during the air raids—public figures who are now at the center of the hotel's publicity campaign and claims to heritage. After the first bombs were dropped on Hanoi in 1964, an underground bunker was constructed with reinforced concrete to protect these high-profile guests, along with hotel employees.

After the end of the war in 1975, the Thống Nhất was used by diplomatic embassies, including that of Australia, while the air raid shelter was transformed into a storage area. With the overhaul of the hotel in the late 1980s after economic reforms were launched (and the return of the name Metropole), the shelter was sealed and subsequently forgotten. Two decades later, in August 2011, while renovating the outdoor Bamboo Bar, workers came across the well-preserved sanctuary (containing empty bottles of Australian wine, the story goes). After excavation and repair, the space was opened to the public in May 2012. Today, there are two daily tours offered to small groups of guests, each lasting 45 minutes.

The bomb shelter tour begins in the Path of History hall, beyond the lobby and past the shopping arcade that displays prominent brands such as Louis Vuitton and Bali. Here, tour participants (on my tour, a group of five older North Americans and Australians) are introduced to the guide—a woman who had survived the air war as a child—who is referred to as an "Ambassador of History," thus ascribing her a higher status than guides on other war tours. The Ambassador of History first explains how recognition of the Metropole's "legendary past" enabled its listing as one of the most eminent "heritage hotels" in the world, leading to the creation of the trademarked Path of History® corridor, found only at select establishments around the globe. This permanent exhibit traces the evolution of the hotel over 100 years through photographs and artifacts, although most of it focuses on the air raids and celebrities who spent time in the bunker. The most famous guest, the Ambassador of History reveals while pointing to her picture, was Jane Fonda, who stayed in the hotel during the summer of 1972 and was evacuated to the shelter along with her husband, Tom Hayden, and their infant son. Guests are then informed that Joan Baez visited the hotel twice: once for 12 days in 1972 during the notorious Christmas bombing—which inspired her album and hit single "Where Are You

Now My Son?"—and a second time in 2013, when she returned to Vietnam, stayed at the Metropole, and paid another visit underground. A guest roster displayed prominently on the wall lists Susan Sontag as a visitor in 1968, as well as Filipina journalist Gemma Cruz Araneta, who stayed at the hotel for a month in the same year (and escaped several times to the shelter), as documented in her autobiographical account named *Hanoi Diary*. All of these images—and more!—can be viewed on Channel 22 in the comfort of one's hotel room, the Ambassador mentions to our group.

After viewing the exhibit, with anticipation mounting, the tour then proceeds to the entrance of the restored shelter, which is next to an opulent pool and poolside bar. Guests descend 12 steps, don green helmets to protect their heads, continue down another set of stairs, and pass through a thick steel door to find themselves four meters underground in a long, narrow room that is close to two meters high (Figure 7.3). This allows for a less confined, more spacious exploration of subterranean architecture than is possible at the other underground attractions.

Like bunkers worldwide, there is a distinctly modern, monolithic character to the Metropole's air raid shelter.[33] This is clearly articulated in the Ambassador's technical synopsis of the 39-square-meter fortification that was built over 64 days under two meters of soil and solid concrete to shelter 50 people in eight small compartments (rather than one large room), each one separated by a thick door of

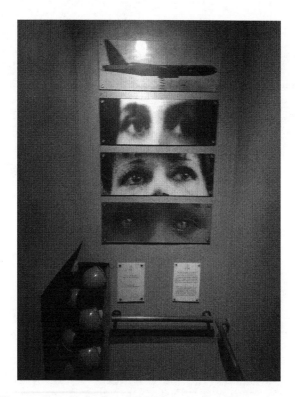

**FIGURE 7.3**  Descent into the bunker, 2015. Photo by the author

War tourism in Vietnam  141

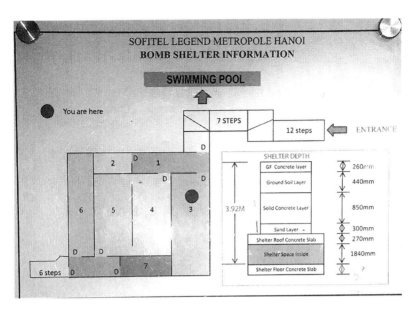

FIGURE 7.4  Bomb shelter overview, 2015. Photo by the author

wood or steel (Figure 7.4). (Upon prodding, the Ambassador admits that hotel guests had priority over staff, but there were rarely so many visitors at one time.) In a typical day of air attacks, people would descend up to five times when the sirens rang out, and would stay underground for up to 30 minutes. A ventilation system maintained a constant flow of air through the shelter and an electrical system provided dim light during raids, if the power was still on (usually not, she added). Walking through the clammy rooms—groundwater intrusion being one of the challenges designers faced—guests pass the main staircase that connects to the lobby, which has been left in its original state and is not in use today. As with Củ Chi and the DMZ, this war attraction is also shaped by the desire to consume authenticity.

Sound is a defining feature of the bunker experience, one that invites an encounter with the real. The highlight of the tour unfolds in the space where Joan Baez took refuge and recorded the thunderous explosion of bombs amid the wailing of sirens during the Christmas bombing. This soundscape was incorporated into her 1973 album. Lyrics from the song are posted on the concrete wall next to a meditative portrait of Baez taken in the shelter in 2013 (Figure 7.5). At the Ambassador's insistence, guests follow suit by closing their eyes and reflecting on the aerial assault as she plays the unsettling recording. The damp smells of mildew and the tight rigidity of the fortified space add to the uncanniness of the experience, inviting guests to envision the terror of evacuees and the catastrophic destruction unleashed on the city above.

The tour ends at the trendy poolside bar. After emerging from the cavernous depths, visitors are greeted with a glass of fresh tamarind punch, reminding them of

**FIGURE 7.5** Joan Baez's return to the shelter. Photo by the author

the warm hospitality extended to guests even in the midst of air strikes.[34] The bomb shelter tour thus cleverly works to market the hotel, and the distinguished service for which it is known, by deploying the air war as a promotional tool. And yet, like at Củ Chi and Quảng Trị, the subterranean attraction is a dynamic site for the production of a wide range of memories that surpass the intended tourist script. Running counter to the story of how the rich and famous survived the air war in the security of the reinforced shelter, in our visit the Ambassador of History shared her own life experiences as a child, prompting reflection on the inequitable distribution of resources during the war, which put celebrities before citizens. For instance, she recounted her evacuation to the countryside, where children dug "frog bunkers" (hầm con ếch) out of mud. "We were poor and didn't have cement then," she explained, comparing her makeshift refuge with the thick fortifications at the Metropole. While celebrities were protected beneath two meters of concrete and soil (see Figure 7.4), children in the frog bunkers were shielded by layers of bamboo and other forest materials. Back in Hanoi, her family dug trenches up to two meters below their beds, the wooden frames serving as protective covers. And unlike the helmets worn by Fonda and Baez, Vietnamese children donned straw hats that they wove themselves to shield them from shrapnel. "When I think back," the Ambassador said pensively, "their effectiveness was probably more psychological than actual." As in the other war tours, here the guide's experiences serve as a critique not only of the state and its historical narratives, but also of capitalism and its valuing of some lives over others.

## Conclusion: The future of war attractions in Vietnam

At the time this chapter was written, Barack Obama had just returned from an official visit to Vietnam, the third by a standing US President since the reunification of the country in 1975. In contrast to Bill Clinton's symbolic state trip in 2000, during which he addressed the importance of reconciliation and attention to the aftermaths of war (though he stopped short of mentioning Agent Orange), Obama's trip seemed to signal a clear break with the past, as indicated by the agreement to lift the arms embargo that had remained in place since the war. Vietnam, it seemed, finally no longer referred to a war, but to a country (and a valued ally in the South China Sea conflict). How then can we speculate on the future of these war attractions—will they one day become obsolete and irrelevant as Vietnam's beaches and newly built resorts become an even greater tourist attraction?

Urban youth have long distanced themselves from the past as they try to build more prosperous, innovative futures.[35] One scholar has even argued, based on surveys, that tourism to war sites seems to be on the wane.[36] My ethnographic observations over the *longue durée* seem to suggest otherwise, however. Warzone tourism appears to be growing in distinctive ways, as I have shown above. New or renovated sites offer broader perspectives beyond official narratives, as groups of visitors across the spectrum of class and nationality diversify the kinds of memories expressed in spaces of "difficult heritage."[37] Such trends do not show signs of abating; if anything, the absurdly priced *New York Times* "Lingering Legacies" tour affirms this direction away from budget travelers. As mass construction continues apace throughout the country, new attractions may be discovered or older ones threatened and preserved; some—like the air raid shelter—may be recognized by UNESCO. This suggests that the marketing of war heritage is a work in progress, rather than an abandoned project.

Looking at war attractions ethnographically across time and space, it is possible to see how places of history and memory-making in Vietnam are not simply static or controlled, but in fact dynamic and contested. At all of the tours discussed above, regardless of whether state- or market-driven, upscale or not, there was a plurality of meanings generated at the site and a transgression of sanctioned narratives. Geographically, each tour offered a different perspective on the war: the VC experience of the American War in southern Vietnam; the GI experience of the Vietnam War in the central region; and the experience of celebrity evacuees during the air war in northern Vietnam. There are, of course, many other viewpoints that are sorely lacking here, such as the experience of troops of the RVN. And yet, at each place, the interjection of personal memories—from US visitors to RVN veteran guides—pushed tours to deviate from crafted scripts, showing them to be more malleable than is often recognized. Moreover, the insertion of US popular culture references—Rambo, Hamburger Hill, Jane Fonda, and Joan Baez, respectively—suggests an important transnational component to the diversification of memory, one that also included the Philippines with mention of Gemma Cruz Araneta. As consumers of these war memories continue to change, so too will the narratives—and the sites themselves—transform in unexpected ways. Might this then signal the gradual loss of state control of memory? The question perhaps is not *if* these sites and their sensationalized histories will be relevant in the future,[38] but *how* and the extent to which visitors will continue, even if spontaneously, to demand inclusion of other, still suppressed memories.

## Notes

1 Joan C. Henderson, "War as a Tourist Attraction: The Case of Vietnam," *The International Journal of Tourism Research* 2:4 (2000), 269–280; Laurel B. Kennedy and Mary Rose Williams, "The Past without the Pain: The Manufacture of Nostalgia in Vietnam's Tourism Industry," in *The Country of Memory: Remaking the Past in Late Socialist Vietnam*, Hue-Tam Ho Tai, ed. (Berkeley: University of California Press, 2001), 135–163.
2 Christina Schwenkel, *The American War in Contemporary Vietnam: Transnational Remembrance and Representation* (Bloomington: Indiana University Press, 2009).
3 Such as the Zippo lighters for sale in Ho Chi Minh City, the Apocalypse Now nightclub in Hanoi, and the excavated "dog tags" in the DMZ: see Christina Schwenkel, "Recombinant History: Transnational Practices of Memory and Knowledge Production in Contemporary Vietnam," *Cultural Anthropology* 21:1 (2006), 3–30.
4 Schwenkel, "Recombinant History," 18–20.
5 Ibid.
6 One of the most controversial omissions is the Huế massacre, which remains hotly contested in Vietnam, but is presented in all its gruesome details in Western guidebooks. Scott Laderman, *Tours of Vietnam: War, Travel Guides, and Memory* (Durham, NC: Duke University Press, 2009), 87–122.
7 See, for example, Christina Schwenkel, "The Ambivalence of Reconciliation in Contemporary Vietnamese Memoryscapes," in *Four Decades On: Vietnam, the United States, and the Legacies of the Second Indochina War*, Scott Laderman and Edwin Martini, eds. (Durham, NC: Duke University Press, 2013), 103–131.
8 At the time, the domestic tourism market was almost nonexistent and to the extent that it did exist, Vietnamese citizens were not as interested in visiting war sites, or as financially able to do so. Those who did visit sites had very different motivations and itineraries (Schwenkel, *The American War*, 94–97). As domestic tourism has grown, so too has tourism to war sites. See Schwenkel, "The Ambivalence of Reconciliation," 118–119.
9 This observation is also affirmed in Laderman, *Tours of Vietnam*.
10 Although there is still trepidation among certain groups, including Vietnamese Americans. As Minh Uong points out in a recent *New York Times* article in response to his wife's "crazy" suggestion that they take a family vacation to Vietnam: "I know a lot of Westerners are discovering Vietnam . . . but it wasn't at the top of my list as a vacation destination. Maybe that's because I was born there." Minh Uong, "Memories of What I Left Behind," *New York Times*, December 20, 2015.
11 For example, impression books placed at sites have become expressive literary devices for working through the past and for debating history, as well as for honoring those who have died on location: see Schwenkel, "The Ambivalence of Reconciliation," 124–126.
12 Friedrich Nietzsche, *On the Advantage and Disadvantage of History for Life*, trans. Peter Preuss (Indianapolis: Hackett Publishing, 1980 [1873]), 9.
13 Schwenkel, *The American War*, 9–13.
14 Officially, the People's Army of Vietnam, or PAVN.
15 Malcolm Foley and John Lennon, *Dark Tourism* (New York: Continuum, 2000). For an exception, see Paul Virilio, *Bunker Archaeology*, trans. George Collins (New York: Princeton Architectural Press, 1994).
16 Kennedy and Williams, "The Past without the Pain: The Manufacture of Nostalgia in Vietnam's Tourism Industry."
17 Including for many American visitors. On one tour in 2000, a Vietnam veteran held my hand tight as we descended into the tunnels and shots rang out in the background (the shooting range). For him, visiting the tunnels was more a therapeutic act than it was entertainment. On returning US veterans' complex relationship with Vietnam, see Schwenkel, *The American War in Contemporary Vietnam*, 25–49.
18 Tom Mangold, *The Tunnels of Cu Chi: A Harrowing Account of America's Tunnel Rats in the Underground Battlefields of Vietnam* (New York: Presidio Press, 2005).
19 Schwenkel, "Recombinant History," 14.

20 Ibid.
21 Hue-Tam Ho Tai. "Hallowed Ground or Haunted House: The War in Vietnamese History and Tourism," *Contemporary Issues*, vol. 3 (Cambridge, MA: Fairbank Center for East Asian Research, Harvard University, 1994), 8. See also Henderson, "War as a Tourist Attraction."
22 Geoffrey White, *Memorializing Pearl Harbor: Unfinished Histories and the Work of Remembrance* (Durham, NC: Duke University Press, 2016).
23 Vernadette Vicuña Gonzalez, *Securing Paradise: Tourism and Militarism in Hawai'i and the Philippines* (Durham, NC: Duke University Press, 2013).
24 Schwenkel, "Recombinant History," 7.
25 Terms used to identify locations would be less familiar to the average Vietnamese person outside of the immediate region. For example, there are Vietnamese tours to Quảng Trị, not the DMZ, which is a marketing tool to attract foreigners interested in the Vietnam War. Destinations on the Quảng Trị tour include sites important in official Vietnamese memory of the American War, including the Trường Sơn National War Cemetery.
26 The DMZ tour is more expensive than the trip to Củ Chi, though prices have decreased significantly in recently years, from 25 US dollars in the 1990s to 12 dollars, and then bottoming out at 8 dollars by the mid-2000s.
27 The Khe Sanh battle marked the beginning of the 1968 Tet Offensive, which even in Vietnam remains "a subject that arouses controversial views" within the Communist Party and among historians. Lien-Hang T. Nguyen, *Hanoi's War: An International History of the War for Peace in Vietnam* (Chapel Hill: University of North Carolina Press, 2012), 111.
28 Stanley Karnow, *Vietnam: A History* (New York: Penguin Books, 1983), 553.
29 Christina Schwenkel, "War Debris in Postwar Society: Managing Risk and Uncertainty in the Former DMZ," in *Interactions with a Violent Past: Reading Post-Conflict Landscapes in Cambodia, Laos, and Vietnam*, Vatthana Pholsena and Oliver Tappe, eds. (Singapore: National University of Singapore Press, 2013), 135–156.
30 Schwenkel, "The Ambivalence of Reconciliation," 125–126.
31 Its website explains: "The Most Famous Hotels in the World is the global research organization of the hospitality industry. Specialized in history marketing it safeguards the history of over 400 Select Member Hotels, presenting the largest totally independent collection of famous, legendary and historic hotels." https://pathofhistory.com/about-famoushotels/.
32 I confirmed in advance my participation in the tour, which was permitted only after I explained my interest and background in researching war attractions in Vietnam.
33 Virilio, *Bunker Archaeology*, 37.
34 The message being conveyed was that Vietnamese hospitality knows no boundaries. The Ambassador of History reaffirmed this through a story about another famous guest at the hotel during the campaign at Điện Biên Phủ, which led to France's defeat: The spouse of the French commander, Christian de la Croix de Castries, stayed at the hotel during the battle and was "well cared for by the staff," even though she was "the wife of the enemy."
35 Christina Schwenkel, "Youth Culture and Fading Memories of War in Hanoi, Vietnam," in *Everyday Life in Southeast Asia*, Kathleen M. Adams and Kathleen Gillogly, eds. (Bloomington: Indiana University Press, 2011), 127–136.
36 Matthew O'Lemmon, "Analysis of the Legacy of Conflict among International Tourists in Vietnam," *International Journal of Tourism Anthropology* (forthcoming).
37 Sharon Macdonald, *Difficult Heritage: Negotiating the Nazi Past in Nuremberg and Beyond* (London and New York: Routledge, 2008).
38 The continued attraction of World War I and World War II sites shows that temporality and the passage of time and memories are not the deciding factors here (see White, *Memorializing Pearl Harbor*). In fact, in recent years there has been a resurgence of interest in sites associated with the Great War. See Caroline Winter, "Tourism, Social Memory and the Great War," *Annals of Tourism* 36:4 (2009), 607–626.

# PART III
# Expeditionary wars and national pride

# 8

# "CURSE YOU RED BARON!": WORLD WAR I AVIATION'S IMPACT ON POPULAR VISIONS OF FLIGHT

*Guillaume de Syon*

"I'd rather you drank than built those airplanes," said an airshow spectator to pioneering aviator Louis Blériot around 1907. Ten years later, French ace Georges Guynemer (1894–1917) told a journalist that the public adulation he received when traveling had robbed him of his own persona. The change in attitudes toward the nature of flying would be expected as the new technology gained in public acceptance. For all the innovations it elicited, World War I aviation's impact on popular memory stands in reverse proportion to its historical importance. While it progressed immensely over the four years of the conflict, aviation remained at best a peripheral weapon, an arm not mature enough in the minds of tacticians and strategists to make a clear difference in the conflict. In parallel, it developed into a myth that thrived during the conflict: Aviation fit the mold of technological supremacy, but also offered a tie-in to earlier forms of warfare thanks to the uniqueness of the flight experience. Despite the stark realities pilots experienced in World War I, myth and memory contributed to clouding the reality of air warfare, but such shifts found their origin in the conflict itself, not afterwards.

Like the other combat experiences of the Great War, aviation underwent what George Mosse has identified as the process of trivialization.[1] In place of the fear of flight which so many trainees experienced, or the fact that aerial losses were staggering at all stages of the conflict, picture postcards, board games, magazine articles, and even toys all transformed aviation into a glorious adventure, one in which the individual still had his place. In turn, this influenced postwar interpretations of the conflict in film, as well as in literature and comic books, to name but a few popular media. To understand this process of trivialization, it is necessary first to summarize some of the traditions which pilots experienced, most of which went unreported on the home front. This will allow for a contrast that explains better how memories of the war in the air actually masked the war, sometimes thanks to the aviators who benefited from the myth themselves.

## Pilot realities

When World War I began, aviation was viewed at best as a kind of support for the artillery, replacing balloons. Within months, the belligerents discovered the value of aerial reconnaissance and, by October 5, the first instance of air combat had been recorded, when a French "Voisin" aircraft shot down a German observation plane. The sudden value that flyers began to acquire stood in stark contrast to their ephemeral fame in prewar years.

The life of a pilot before 1914 amounted to a kind of ongoing struggle to survive. As the memoirs of such flyers as Roland Garros make clear, not only were technical problems part of everyday life, but their impact affected whether one became a loser in the eyes of the crowd, or a local star signing autographs.[2] Endorsements meant survival and paying one's mechanics to keep the machine ready to fly at the request of various festival organizers. Winning a major prize could bring about additional contracts and even the purchase of a new machine. The "air show," although including obvious patriotic dimensions, however remained a form of rough entertainment where pilots were akin to the travelers of a circus spectacle. Even on the eve of the war, that attitude remained strong.

The beginnings of trench warfare in the fall of 1914 called for new means to break the stalemate. Pilots faced a dual challenge: to be taken seriously, and to learn to make it back alive. As Georges Bellenger (1878–1977) reminisces, air service was regarded as "customarily undisciplined," and any flyer was little more than "a mechanic with no strategic knowledge."[3] Attempts to convince the high command of the value of aviation for observation purposes would cost Bellenger his career, as exemplified in this exchange between him and General Henri Berthelot (1861–1931) about aerial photographs that were more precise than the officer's battlefield map:

> What? You dare tell me that my map is inaccurate? . . . [Yours] is wrong: here is a point where you measure 200 meters between our positions and the Germans'. I say there is only 50 meters . . . and your photos won't make me change my mind![4]

Within days, however, a new attitude began permeating the attitudes of the general staff, and the appearance of enemy aircraft over Paris accelerated that shift. Though the "fifth arm" was still considered a fifth wheel, steps were taken by 1915 to increase its size exponentially. Thus, by conflict's end, a force that numbered a few hundred at the start of the war now exceeded 25,000 aircraft.

Manning these planes was an evolutionary process. Aside from volunteers, pilots were recruited from the ground forces either for their ability, or because they did not fit there. The physical examinations soldiers had to undergo were often re-evaluated to allow men too weak to serve in the infantry to have a role elsewhere.[5] Among the volunteers, some hoped to forget the dreariness of daily life on the ground by transferring into the air force. As Roland Dorgelès

(1885–1973), the future author of *Les Croix de bois*, put it to aviation columnist Jacques Mortane:

> Were you to pull me out of this moral hell so that I may get into aviation, you would render a great, unforgettable service . . . On our end, it's always mud, disgusting holes, stale water, cold grub . . . Help me, my friend, get me out of here.[6]

What was unbeknown to Dorgelès, however, was that were he to be chosen for flight school, he would be trading mud for the horror of flying and the risk of free fall. Few, in fact, made it past that stage.

Indeed, it is in the selection and training of pilots that one discovers the peculiarities of the pilot myth. True, young pilots eagerly sought out the leather attire, cold gear, and helmet, all of which signaled belonging to a "different" type of "phratries."[7] Yet the attraction ended quickly. Flying school in fact was very much akin to an infantry training ground where dreamers awoke to hard living conditions, abusive instructors, and dealing with mechanics protective of "their machines." As René Fonck, the top French ace, reminisced later on:

> For a month I lived through both hope and fear of a first flight . . . Neither pilots nor their help wanted us too close to their machines. They feared our unworthy hands, knowing too well to what wire the life of a man sometimes clung.[8]

This sacralization of the machinery seemed to see it as akin to a baby that one was to be allowed to hold for the first time. What such jealousy masked, however, was the fact that not enough aircraft and instructors were available to respond to the demands of the front, and thus to train new pilots successfully. It followed that most pilots, even the "naturals" who felt at ease on their very first flight, would either experience or witness crashes of unlucky or untrained comrades.

The accelerated training rate explains this. Airfields where pilot formation was carried out usually kept a drawing horse to go and fetch airplane wrecks several times a week, a rate that increased depending on the demands of the front. Marcel Jeanjean (1893–1973), who immortalized pilot life in many caricatures, put a smiling face on the whole matter. But a closer reading of his memoirs shows the tragic implications of such choices. Jeanjean claims that he and those of his cohort required 80 days of training to master aerial combat. Historian Edmond Petit's examination of the Farmann training school where Jeanjean trained reveals a reality closer to 30 days divided equally between theory, pilot's-license training, and military certification.[9] Past that realm, an additional training period would usually occur during which the standard attribute of military life, "hurry up and wait," punctuated the days of the young pilots. By then, many had washed out, or were required to carry out further training.

Jules Abel, who learned to be a reconnaissance pilot in 1916, remembers two accidents during his schooling. One killed an instructor and his newly minted pilot;

the other featured a heavy Voisin aircraft on final approach that had trouble completing its landing after a smaller Blériot machine landed atop its superior wing.[10] Abel's journal contrasts with most postwar accounts by depicting the challenges that surrounded learning to fly. Fighter pilots appeared less inclined to discuss their early trials, and when they did, they tended to trivialize them. On the other hand, Abel's assignment suggests he felt no shame in recording (at least privately) the somber aspects of flight training. Furthermore, Abel's honesty helps confirm the far better living conditions pilots experienced once at the front. Though close to the lines, they rarely had to face the daily onslaught of mud, a characteristic of the infantryman's experience.

What a reading of the memoirs makes clear, however, is the importance of the aircraft mechanic on the ground. Roland Garros, one of the few prewar "clowns" to join the air force, notes time and again the importance of the men who kept his machines flyable. Aside from Garros', their acknowledged participation in the glory of an aerial victory is limited, and in some cases practically nonexistent. Yet it is the logistics of flying that made the air ace possible.

Therein lies the third element that one may extract from reconsidering older accounts: It is in fact the severity of air combat that made clear the difficulty of surviving more than a few air patrols. As Bernard Mark has noted in his biography of ace Georges Guynemer, the list of fallen aviators by 1917 was staggering, and the horror of air combat genuine. In fact, the routine of death was still something petrifying, as the ace described one of his first victories in the following terms:

> And the German falls and catches fire. Our last bullet had killed the pilot whom I saw collapsed in the fuselage while the observer, realizing the consequences of the tragedy, raised his arms to heaven in desperation.[11]

The lack of parachutes (these did not appear until later in the war) accentuated the terror associated with air combat.

The myth of the supreme fighter in the air masks a tension all flyers experienced when killing an enemy. On the one hand, pilot Jean Morvan's nonchalant remark that "we murder the wanderer who is daydreaming" reflects a cold technical reality.[12] But so does Brindejonc des Moulinais' empathic description of the art of the kill: "It's a pity to murder decent guys, and it's a real joy to burst the skin of a coward who escapes under the first shot."[13] Flyers were described as returning covered in oil but also blood spots from flying too close to one of their kills. The horror of dying in flight and disappearing into the ground forced a re-examination of the dangers of aerial combat, for newly minted flyers often did not last an hour. As Robert Wohl has noted more soberly, the rookies actually fed the myth of the war ace by becoming his killing fodder.[14]

Considering this evolution of the visions of the warrior pilot, it becomes clear that the construction of the myth of the flyer was cast as much in the field as on the home front. In a 1915 war pamphlet, journalist Paul Vergnet notes that aviators had already been able to prove their bravery before the war and thus quickly justified "the hopes the French Army had put in them." The author went on to confuse prewar and combat exploits, and juxtaposed the feats of daredevils with those of the first aces. Flyers were willing to indulge in this adulation for, as John Morrow notes, they established their own code of silence. The few who broke it either were criticized by their peers, or published their work anonymously.[15] Thus, the removal of the air war experience from its context became an early foundation of air war memory caused in part by the flyers themselves, though also by the perceived martyrdom of the war aces.[16]

## The ace

The horrors of air combat, though extremely stressful to its survivors, nonetheless offered individuals an opportunity to distinguish themselves and face a death that bore more similarities to medieval chivalry than to trench warfare. Early aces quickly developed their own individual style of flying and even modified their aircraft themselves.[17] Early in the conflict, victors of an aerial duel were known to have dropped a wreath in the area where their adversary had crashed. By 1916, as the conflict wore on, fighter pilots began to appear whose function was not simply patrol but rather full-scale hunting, thereby transforming the use of aircraft from reconnaissance to bombing. Because the practice of air combat was so novel, it was perhaps the only realm of the Great War where those in combat actually could claim and share expertise with limited interference from elders in command centers, especially if they had scored multiple shoot-downs.

Historians differ on when the actual "war ace" identification really began, partly because an aerial victory in the first half of the conflict was already grounds for celebration. Early successes on the German side, for example, netted the pilot an engraved silver cup.[18] By 1917, as air combat increased and rationing on the ground grew worse, the cups were made of iron and given out every five, and later nine, victories. The actual "War Ace" designation originated on the French side of the conflict, and was awarded for five aircraft shot down. Quickly, aces acquired cultural values that combined their hunting aggressiveness with a dutiful youth.

Several aerial practices from the Great War passed into memory despite their falling into disuse. An accidental maneuver by German war ace Max Immelmann offers such an example. Accidentally discovered, perhaps in an attempt to escape the enemy, the maneuver consisted of a sudden and steep climb following an attack on an enemy aircraft. When the climb was no longer possible, the pilot rolled his machine sideways and faced downwards to initiate another pass. Still in existence in a modified form, the so-called "Immelmann turn" continues to exist in civilian aerobatic competitions, though few spectators know of its origins. Some historians doubt that Immelmann actually accomplished the maneuver that bears his name, because the type of aircraft he then flew would have likely broken up under the stress of the sudden yaw. Regardless, Immelmann, like many other fighter pilots, discovered new maneuvers in combat, since aerobatics were not formally taught in flying schools until 1917. The resulting gap contributed to the creation of a mnemonic aura that further anchored the myth of the fighter pilot,[19] and, consequently, that of the ace.

When Immelmann died in combat in late June 1916, one of his comrades, ace Oswald Boelcke, was removed from the front for "safekeeping." Yet he proceeded to write an entire series of rules of engagement that became a kind of early pilot "bible." Many of these rules were common to successful fighter pilots across the trenches, ranging from firing only at close proximity to emphasizing a rear attack with the sun behind one's back. The latter maneuver, carried out in both World Wars, became grounds for an official warning motto on the Allied side: "Beware of the Hun in the sun."[20]

Boelcke's own death in combat, and those of others, further cemented the martyrdom element of flying. Instead of the thousands of dead registered every week on the ground, the public could focus on the heroic deeds of flyers and hope that their footsoldiers too were distinguishing themselves. In all cases, what comes to dominate is masculinity, whether in the air or on the ground. The only role given to women in all war accounts is in those spaces devoted to motherhood. A recent historical study of the place of mothers in aviators' lives suggests the need for young men to share their deeds with their loved ones, but also to shield them from the horrors of war, thereby contributing to the myth of the war experience. In turn, this facet of gender relations allows the public to focus on grieving with the mother without the fear of having one's masculinity questioned.[21] In such a context, soldier and poet Siegfried Sassoon's poem "The Hero" gains new importance. Whereas Sassoon's piece describes the death of a soldier whose cowardice is hidden from his grieving mother, the fact that the character has been "blown to bits" is too horrible to describe to the old woman and thus masks all aspects of his demise, moral and physical.[22] The same factors affected descriptions of the deaths of pilots. Whether falling to their deaths or ripped apart by bullets, the details of a flyer's actual demise were generally hidden from the public, especially when it came to aces. For example, the death of ace Georges Guynemer, whose body was likely destroyed in artillery fire between the trenches where it had fallen, was reported with an emphasis on how death had struck him suddenly, keeping him forever young. This would help create a kind of secular sainthood tinted with religious overtones in the postwar biographies that followed. The mechanisms of propaganda had played a role, but their effectiveness relied on a positive public perception of the event or the hero.[23] In the case of specifically identified aces, the process worked, though there was an edge when flyers and soldiers met on the ground.

Though the popular image of the warrior–aviator was generally positive, the overwhelming presence and suffering of ground troops and the recording thereof affected the image of the pilot after the war. Students of war literature note how memoirs of flyers often overlooked difficult facets of their trade to paint an almost nostalgic portrait of air combat. Even writers of the ground troops' experience, such as Henri Barbusse in France or Ernst Jünger in Germany, praised the aviation experience either for its fierce attacks or for the "new warrior" who controlled the flying machine.[24]

The violence in the air also changed the attitudes of many soldiers on the ground. Whereas many envied the clean quarters of the pilots and their many perks (such as trips back to the home front), few wished to join them, and infantrymen often emphasized instead a respect for a technical mastery difficult to understand. Novelist Gabriel Chevalier (1895–1969), who remained an infantryman throughout all four years of the conflict, described the end of a French flyer at the mercy of five German fighters: "For a few seconds, with a sinking heart, we were thrown into the void with him. Such combat had appeared supernatural to us earthmen with heavy muddied legs."[25] This seeming contradiction between respect and disdain is partly the result of limited contact between pilots and infantrymen, but also of a cultivated elitism associated with aviators' search for their own service identity (since most had initially served in other branches of the military).[26]

## The literary takeover

As noted above, the discovery of the ace concept suited the media as well as propaganda services. The top ace on the German side was Manfred von Richthofen, nicknamed the Red Baron because the planes he flew sported a sharp red color. His fame, already established by the time of his death in April 1918, continued in Germany with the hasty publication of his autobiography, *Der Rote Kampfflieger*, written in response to public thirst for his story.[27] Unlike other such accounts, however, Richthofen's emphasizes the necessity of killing as a sport, as well as the importance of the pilot rather than his equipment.[28] The coldness of the account still reflects individualism in an age of mass slaughter, which may explain why the public welcomed such an account. By 1939, it had sold more copies than Erich Maria Remarque's *All Quiet on the Western Front*.[29] In France, a similar process of hero-mythbuilding occurred. One flyer interned in neutral Switzerland after landing there by accident received multiple requests from a French publisher who begged him to write an account of his aerial fights and related adventures. Introspection was not the point. All that mattered was action, thus hiding the difficulties of everyday life as a pilot.[30]

The Red Baron's fame remained despite the fact that he was not the public's favorite pilot. His myth grew immeasurably in the United States through the publication of Floyd P. Gibbons' romanticized biography of the top ace.[31] This would in turn feed the frenzy of pulp and comic fiction, and this further contributed, as George Mosse notes, to sublimating heroic death.[32] Popular culture absorbed elements of it in the narratives of several writers, such as William Faulkner.

Enrolled into the Royal Air Force in 1918, William Faulkner saw no combat, as the hostilities ceased before he was declared fit to take flying lessons. Faulkner would not learn to fly for another decade, and then as a civilian. He nonetheless incorporated substantial elements of aviation lore into several of his works, notably praising the British-built Sopwith Camel aircraft, which he never actually flew.[33] Though some of Faulkner's early works included references to aces and to aviation technology, it was American ace Elliott White Springs' 1926 publication of his *War*

*Birds: Diary of an Unknown Aviator* that brought new fascination for the aviation genre. It may also have inspired Faulkner's own description of aerial combat in his 1929 novel *Sartoris*. Both share a disillusion with the war effort, and the characters portrayed show several similarities.[34] Regardless, the emphasis on metaphor also presented the public with an aesthetic of the war that, despite the pessimistic content, still came across in a very positive light. This further growth in the myth of the fighter pilot masked but did not erase the other facet of World War I aviation: bombing.

## Strategic bombing

Because aviation's potential remained misunderstood for much of the war, the aerial campaigns associated with it were often haphazard operations. Some were cancelled despite being successful, as was the case when the French initiated strategic bombing missions in 1915. Still, the very fear of bombing from above added to what became the first fully mechanized war, resulting in unheard-of levels of destruction. Consequently, bombing was deemed a dirty business, not only because of the rules of war, but also because of what it asked of the bombers. French top ace René Fonck abhorred such missions, possibly because it clashed with his desire to see the enemy he wished to kill.

An exception to the ambiguity of strategic bombing involved Zeppelin airships, which hit Antwerp in 1914 before setting their sights on Paris and London. The impact of such strategic targeting was immense for civilians, who, though accepting the notion of artillery fire, did not expect death from above.[35] The results of such campaigns in memory ranged from powerful images in art and literature to the establishment of a pattern of arguments about the value of strategic bombing. Common to all, the terrorized reaction of targeted civilians was a herald of things to come. The precision of the bombing was of lesser importance to writers and artists than the bombs hitting at random, emphasizing how little control victims had over their fate.[36] The haphazard nature of such warfare stayed with German artist Otto Dix, an artilleryman in the war, whose etching *Lens Being Bombed* makes clear how the airplane depicted affected civilians. The machine is clearly visible, yet it is fading away, while the contorted faces of running victims fill the lower part of the artist's work.[37]

Memories of aircraft dropping bombs loom large, despite the fact that raids were infrequent and some of the damage inflicted on strategic targets was often the result of artillery. Paradoxically, though Germany began fielding giant airplane bombers in 1917 to replace Zeppelins, Londoners remembered Zeppelin raids far more, as their journals and newspaper reports suggest. Indeed, a kind of pre-memory had already been created in British popular culture through H. G. Wells' *War in the Air* (1908), which chronicled airship combat. In this example of early science fiction, Wells constructed a story in which a young balloonist accidentally stumbled upon a fully prepared German airship fleet that eventually attacked the United States.[38] Combined with a phantom scare the following year that claimed Germans had landed troops near Dover via airship, Wells' novel helped the legend grow once actual bombing raids began.[39] Rather than crouch in their basements, Londoners eagerly sought to catch a glimpse of the slow, rumbling giant airships. By 1917, they would no longer attempt this, since the impact of the bombings was now understood and faster-moving aircraft had replaced airships. Still, the imagery remained strong. Army recruiting posters emphasized the barbarity of airships, showing one after its load had killed a little girl. Following the war, traces of "Zeppelinitis" could be found in both high and low literature, from parodies of the airship scare in vaudevillian theater to the personal correspondence of D. H. Lawrence.[40] Moreover, plays, postcards, even miniature models imprinted public memory of bombings with the image of the airship.[41]

The result of these limited, yet psychologically important strategic bombing campaigns was two-fold. First, they would influence military thinking about the value of strategic bombing all the way to the present day, notably with regard to its fear-inducing impact on civilians.[42] Second, they set the public stage for a preparation for war that raised awareness of the risk of massive bombings in the 1930s. In that sense, Dix's etching also serves as a herald to Picasso's *Guernica*, which portrayed the outcome of the aerial bombing of a city in the Spanish Civil War.[43] In the case of airships, even the reversal of the Versailles Treaty clauses banning their construction in Germany did not preclude numerous public and media comments in the interwar years opposing their presence as civilian machines. What some have termed "the long shadow" of airships tainted even the most stupendous achievements of long-distance transport Zeppelins, only to be displaced later by the pictures of the *Hindenburg* disaster.

## Postwar productions of memory

Following World War I, the myth of the fighter pilot underwent multiple transformations, yet the central theme of individual moral struggle remained present. Several factors either displaced or built on the early memories manufactured in the Great War. These factors de-emphasized the negative popular memory of bombing, while further contributing to the picture of the adventurous fighter pilot. In recasting aviation, however, public portrayals relied on the image's malleability, for it fit not only the ideals of popular culture in democratic societies, but those in Fascist ones too.

The sacrifice of the wartime pilot, though acknowledged and commemorated in all the nations involved in the conflict, found a special echo in the advent of Fascism as a new political movement that would spawn dictators. In Italy, the Futurist art movement provided the cultural impetus to the political movement by praising modernist elements, notably the advent of high speed as reflected in airplanes and automobiles. However, as a movement rejecting religion, Fascism replaced faith with myth. Aviation became both a cleanser of ideals and a modernizer of society.[44] World War I in the air increased such perceptions, as the new weapon spawned warriors who faced horrors different from those on the ground.

The fact that several sympathizers with Italian Fascism, such as Gabriele D'Annunzio, had been fighter pilots in the war also served to anchor the use of military flying in the mindset of totalitarianism. Culturally, then, aviation as a liberating force could also be turned into an affirmation of new political authority, regardless of its successes and shortcomings. Because it was a novel technology, the interpretations of its value could go in several directions, and include a positive memory in democracies.

In the United States, the myth of the fighter pilot found its expression in multiple realms, including youth literature. There, a tradition of books for boys predated the Great War, and several series either picked up on the war in the air, or were launched on its very basis. Some shared very precise technological details, gleaned from the pages of *Scientific American*, while others emphasized air combat fantasies aboard secret aircraft. Excluding the horrors of warfare while capitalizing on its heroic fiber, all had in common the moral appeal of the flyers, who were often prodigal adolescents. Furthermore, they emphasized flight as a modernist wonderment, illustrating what Joe Corn identifies as "The Winged Gospel." Available in public libraries and affordable for middle-class families, these books all placed emphasis on smart, educated boys with a knack for mechanical things. In the fantasy world, they already can fly, and their moral agenda includes siding with the British. But at no point does it involve more than scouting ethics in the service of the war effort.[45]

## The role of film

Alongside novels and children's literature, film helped to perpetuate the popular memory of aviation in World War I. Documentaries filmed during the conflict attracted producers as well as audiences because aerial combat could still portray human elements often absent in films of ground warfare, which could do little but portray the dreariness of the trenches. Such films as the German *War Fliers on the Western Front* presented to an ever anxious public visions of a clean, honorable war that contrasted starkly with that below. Shown in movie theaters as part of the news releases, such brief documentaries also charted the progress of aviation.[46] Though such documentaries ceased with the war's end, and feature films on the war did not attract public interest, these aerial scenes likely inspired film-makers who sought to recreate them in a safer environment. Yet the myth of the wartime pilot was not one automatically associated with glory; it depended on a dialog between artists and witnesses. *Wings* (1927), for example—which was the first movie to garner an Academy Award for Best Picture (1928)—and *The Dawn Patrol* (1930) both relied on the experiences of John Monk Saunders, a member of the American Signal Corps' aviation section. However, as Leslie Midkiff Debauche notes, these experiences were filtered by Hollywood writers. The expectation of romance and female interaction with the heroes is mitigated by a tone of sadness that removes the valiant emphasis one would expect when discussing pilots.[47] In fact, the first wave of postwar aviation movies reflects an ambivalence toward the air war experience, as defined in the likes of *Wings*, *The Dawn Patrol*, and *Hell's Angels* (1930.) Such movies, often filmed with the assistance of the armed forces or veteran pilots, glamorized the idea of military flight after Charles Lindbergh, fresh from crossing the Atlantic, had spread the aviation gospel in the United States. In so doing, anecdotal stories of the air war became doctrine. In *Wings*, for example, a German pilot declines to engage an adversary whose guns have jammed. Although such chivalry was seen occasionally, it disappeared as the conflict lengthened. Yet viewers exposed to the exemplary attitude portrayed came to spread the word of a special warrior code unique to flyers. Much as the single Christmas Truce of 1914 among ground troops became a widespread myth (with the claim that this truce was enacted in each year of the war), so too did aviation myths spread.

Logically, the movie genre of the interwar years should culminate in Jean Renoir's masterful *The Grand Illusion* (1937), in which two downed pilots spend their time in captivity devising ways to escape. The film is filled with irony (the dialog includes a sardonic complaint about what the aviators must wear to avoid freezing at altitude) and excludes aerial scenes in favor of presenting the lives of aviators on the ground, including the chivalric welcoming of the vanquished to the officers' bar. Not once is the downing of the aircraft revealed to the spectator. Flying combat is but a detail in what is offered as a deeply moral tale about both the futility of war and the passing of a generation.

In fact, as Dominic Pisano's documentation makes clear, the tropes of the Great War aviation movie, including the tormented characters committed to action and values in the context of air combat iconography, made way for themes of duty, cooperation, and courage that heralded the World War II movie genre.[48] Far less ambiguous, at least in the interwar phase, comics echoed movie portrayals. But they did so in a far more positive light; one intended to inspire youth.

## Comics and cartoons

Perhaps the strongest example of trivialization of World War I came in the form of the American comics in the interwar years that supplemented the "boys' books" discussed previously. In many ways, they echo youth literature, but they emphasize the adventurous tradition that helped shape a generation's perceptions of World War I flying.[49] Though successful, they soon lost ground to another flying tradition, that of superheroes, whose initial appeal in the 1930s gained ground in World War II and grew considerably afterwards. In parallel, the tradition of the "funnies" (short, 3–5-frame strips) also gained ground with both the public and artists, for narrators could switch storylines easily. Such was the case with *Peanuts*, a strip about children that sported an intelligent dog named Snoopy. In some cases, strip creator Charles M. Schulz removed Snoopy from everyday interaction with children to place him atop his doghouse (imagined for the occasion as a British-built Sopwith Camel), with the canine fantasizing about a secret life as a wartime pilot.

Inspired by his son's fascination with World War I airplane models and recalling such movies as *The Dawn Patrol*, Schulz first "fielded" Snoopy as a pilot in 1965, during the half-centennial commemorations of the conflict.[50] Though the storyline returned regularly, it shifted. As Schulz acknowledged, romantic memories of World

War I collided with the harsh realities of the Vietnam War, and forced a shift in the theme away from the quest to fight the Red Baron (who is never seen) to questions about loneliness and disaffection.[51] Nevertheless, popular culture adopted the strip's subtheme, echoing such lines as "Curse you Red Baron!"—something Snoopy utters when apparently routed in combat.

The storyline's resounding success inspired not only toys and plastic models that echoed stereotypes of World War I Germany (such as a dragster car with a spike helmet), but also a pop band's song "Snoopy vs. the Red Baron."[52] The Snoopy-as-pilot phenomenon is part of a multifaceted expression of the air war in public memory. The comic tradition that reflected aviation had grown after World War I, but it would spread in several directions, from humor to historical narratives, beginning in the 1950s.

The most widely distributed European comic convention came from the Franco-Belgian tradition. In response to educational imperatives, historical narratives appeared alongside whimsical ones. When the former represented World War I themes, the majority of them featured air combat stories. Based on actual events, the themes were shaped both to emphasize the adventures of an ace and to stress a moral element. In a story about French ace Georges Guynemer, for example, his training days emphasized his multiple mistakes and only alluded to his first victory in the second-to-last frame. The moral message of patient endeavor despite adversity matched the requirements of the French censorship board, an equivalent to the American Comic Code Authority. This body called for uplifting stories that would not offend youth and would mold their attitudes toward authority, duty, and morals. In passing, a few anecdotes based on aces' recollections might be included to make the comic strip more educational.[53]

By the 1970s, the entirely positive narratives had run their course, and, partly in response to the 1968 student uprisings that questioned education, the Vietnam War, and the establishment, a new wave of comic traditions surfaced. They took a new realistic approach that emphasized the horrors of war, and thus was geared more toward adolescent and adult readers. In this new tradition, however, aviation was de-emphasized in favor of trench warfare. When aviation appeared, its portrayal was more lucid. While still inspired by real events and persons, authors would spin a tale that moved away from heroism in favor of considering the moral challenges of the war, a reflection of changing European attitudes toward conflict. This shift reflected the coming of age of some of the readership, but was not to everyone's liking, since the comics offered an entertaining alternative to the tradition of the novel. The result was a back-and-forth between trivialization and memorialization of the air war.

The British series *Charley's War*, for example, emphasized human interaction between air combat missions. It inspired more recent accounts, this time entirely fictitious, but whose storylines seem less important than the extremely precise drawings of air combat scenes—such evolution came as a direct response to readers' demands.[54] Thus, while the public became more aware of the challenges flyers faced in the Great War, the popular historicization of the event emphasized the technical wonderment around early flying machines rather than the concerns and disillusionment pilots may have felt.

Some authors did include such concerns as part of a wider questioning about the motivations of war. In these stories, the airplane is but a support for the individual flyer searching for meaning in his potential sacrifice and his own transformation. Such scenes can prove very powerful to readers, but the support—the aircraft—could easily be replaced with a trench, a tank, or a submarine. The airplane's peripheral value casts it as one of a multitude of technologies of death.

The result of these new paths in comic tradition is a confusing one that perpetuates memory at the expense of history, for authors adopting this path confuse reality. Indeed, by humanizing the pilot, the mythical element of the wartime flyer disappears. In one account, Manfred von Richthofen's memoirs are reinterpreted to make him come across as a sick man who loves the very act of killing (as opposed to deriving pride from his work). Second, by equating the experience of warfare on the ground with that in the air, comic artists paint over the diverse experience of combatants. While pilots did indeed face high risks, the danger was daily at most, not hourly, like that which infantrymen experienced. The representation of suffering, done through drawings that emphasize cold colors and very vaguely drawn aircraft, also reflects the move away from any glorification of war.[55] The pilot hero is an accidental one, trying to make it through one more day. This new representation, an echo of the early World War I movies, is not shared universally, but reflects a shift in public history that began in the 1990s.

## Exhibits, airshows, and nostalgia

Until the 1990s, airshows and museum exhibits tended to emphasize the glorious elements of flying in World War I. Visitors to major exhibits could expect pristine-looking aircraft with technical information, and airshows, especially in the United States, would emphasize the whimsical element found in movies and comics. Among the many privately funded airshows, the Old Rhinebeck Aerodrome in New York State, led by Cole Palen until his death, featured an airshow with restored World War I aircraft. Much like World War II popular airshows and related "encampments" (where re-enactors present technical information and uniform material associated with the conflict), the historical element may emphasize some technological legacies, but the context is lost to a kind of nostalgic memory. Thus, when museums began proposing exhibits that emphasized the context of the air conflict, they encountered popular resistance.

The first full-scale exhibit to emphasize the tension between memory and history opened in 1992 at the Smithsonian Institution's National Air and Space Museum in Washington, DC. Organized by a team of curators (a departure from earlier practices) in consultation with outside experts, the exhibit purposely showed aircraft as part of the wider and more complex chain of everyday life in the war. From a bomber looming over a rebuilt trench to mannequins of women working on a factory floor, most sections of the exhibit were defined in relation to the ground, not apart from it. Even when machines were shown on their own, as was the case with one fighter aircraft, video testimony of an ace expressing how scared he had been in combat tempered any romantic association visitors might make when viewing the aircraft. The exhibit concluded with a video clip suggesting that the first strategic bombings through Zeppelin airships portended a tradition that would continue into the present, be it through bombers or missiles.

The exhibit's reception reflected a division between viewers who had gone through an intellectual experience and those, more oriented to the emotional, who felt some of it was unrelated to World War I, and thus a failure. Therein lay a tension between professionally oriented history and a popular culture still intent on viewing a museum exhibit as a temple to the past rather than a forum for reflection.[56] With the Enola Gay atomic bomb exhibit controversy three years later, the final video clip was actually removed to assuage public criticism of too intellectual an approach to the analysis of air warfare.

Regardless of the tensions the exhibit raised, it also sowed the seeds for new directions in exhibiting the air war. Museums changed their approaches when redesigning World War I exhibits, and chose to emphasize the socio-cultural experience of aviation in order to question the myth openly. In so doing, these exhibits brought back the fact that technology, in Paul Fussell's words, actually "reversed the idea of progress."[57] Thus, the National French Air and Space Museum and the Canadian War Museum both staged exhibits in 2014 and 2015 that posited a tension between popular culture and the difficult realities of air warfare in World War I. A quarter of a century has passed since the World War I exhibit at the National Air and Space Museum opened. The positive reception given to the more recent shows suggests that the historicization of World War I has now entered a new phase in which popular culture has begun to absorb some of the historical realities of air warfare, rather than emphasizing its myths alone.

## Notes

1 George L. Mosse, *Fallen Soldiers. Reshaping the Memory of the World Wars* (New York: Oxford University Press, 1990), 126–144.
2 Roland Garros, *Mémoires* (Paris: Hachette, 1966), 28–34. On autographs, see for example, "De Paris à Londres par les airs," *La vie au grand air*, 27 August 1910.
3 Georges Bellenger, *Pilote d'essais du cerf-volant à l'aéroplane* (Paris: L'Harmattan, 1995), 226, 236.
4 Ibid., 256.
5 Edmond Petit, *La vie quotidienne dans l'aviation en France au débit du XXe siècle 1900–1935* (Paris: Hachette, 1977), 110–111.
6 "L'aéronautique militaire française, 1914–1918," *Icare* 85 (September 1978), 111.
7 Petit, 112.
8 René Fonck, *Mes combats* (Paris: Flammarion, 1920), xx.
9 Petit, *La vie quotidienne*, 115.
10 Jules Abel, "Journal de Jules Abel 1916–1918," *Icare* 213 (June 2010), 22.
11 Bernard Marck. *Le dernier vol de Guynemer*, xx.
12 Letter of Jean Morvan to Edmond Petit, cited in Petit, *La vie quotidienne*, 120.
13 Petit, *La vie quotidienne*, 123.
14 Robert Wohl, *A Passion for Wings: Aviation and the Western Imagination, 1908–1918* (New Haven: Yale University Press, 1994), 249.

15 John Morrow, "The War in the Air," in *A Companion to World War I*, John Horne, ed. (Malden, MA: Blackwell, 2010), 164–165.
16 Agnès Chablat-Beylot, "Du 'chevalier de l'air' à l'ange de la mort," in *Guynemer, un mythe une histoire*, SHAA, ed. (Paris: SHAA, 1997), 89–101.
17 Wohl, *A Passion for Wings*, 210.
18 Dominic Pisano et al., *Legend, Memory and the Great War in the Air* (Seattle: University of Washington Press, 1992), 36.
19 Peter Fritzsche, *A Nation of Fliers: German Aviation and the Popular Imagination* (Cambridge, MA: Harvard University Press, 1992) 86–96.
20 John H. Morrow, Jr., "The Air War," in *The Cambridge History of the First World War, Vol I: Global War*, Jay Winter et al., eds. (New York: Cambridge University Press, 2014), 360.
21 Stefanie Schüler-Springorum, "Flying and Killing: Military Masculinity in German Pilot Literature, 1914–1939," in *Home Front. The Military, War and Gender in Twentieth-Century Germany*, Karen Hageman and Stefanie Schüler-Springorum, eds. (New York: Berg, 2002), 212.
22 Siegfried Sassoon, "The Hero," in *The Old Huntsman and Other Poems* (London: Heinemann, 1918), www.bartleby.com/135/index2.html.
23 Bernard Wilkin, "Aviation and Propaganda in France During the First World War," *French History* 28:1 (2014), 47–50.
24 Henri Barbusse, *Under Fire* (New York: E. P. Dutton, 1917), 136.
25 Gabriel Chevalier, *La peur* (Paris: Stock, 1930), xx.
26 Michael Paris, "The Rise of Airmen: The Origins of Air Force Elitism, c. 1890–1918," *Journal of Contemporary History* 28 (1993), 123–141; Wilkin, "Aviation and Propaganda in France During the First World War," 64.
27 Manfred von Richthofen, *Der Rote Kampfflieger* (Berlin: Ullstein, 1917), accessible at www.gutenberg.org/files/24572/24572-h/24572-h.htm.
28 Wohl, *A Passion for Wings*, 226–227.
29 Fritzsche, *A Nation of Fliers*, 82; Nicolas Beaupré, "Aviateurs et écrivains de la Grande Guerre (France, Allemagne)," in *La Grande Guerre des aviateurs*, Gilles Aubagnac and Clémence Raynaud, eds. (Paris: EMCC, 2014), 24.
30 Beaupré, "Aviateurs et écrivains de la Grande Guerre," 20–21.
31 Floyd P. Gibbons, *The Red Knight of Germany: The Story of Baron von Richthofen, Germany's Greatest War Bird* (Garden City, NY: Doubleday, 1927).
32 Mosse, *Fallen Soldiers*, 61–62.
33 Robert Harrison, *Aviation Lore in Faulkner* (Amsterdam: John Benjamins, 1985), 21–85.
34 Richard T. Dillon, "Some Sources for Faulkner's Version of the First Air War," *American Literature* 44:4 (January 1973), 629–637.
35 Wilkins, "Aviation and Propaganda in France During the First World War," 55–58; cf. Guillaume de Syon, *Zeppelin! Germany and the Airship, 1900–1939* (Baltimore, MD: The Johns Hopkins University Press, 2002), 94–95.
36 See for example, Jules Romain, *Men of Goodwill* (New York: Knopf, 1939), vols. 15–16, Verdun, 411–414, 418.
37 Otto Dix, *Der Krieg* (Berlin: Nierendorf, 1924), www.moma.org/collection_ge/object.php?object_id=63263.
38 Lawrence Goldstein, *The Flying Machine and Modern Literature* (Bloomington: Indiana University Press, 1986), 63–72.
39 See, for example, Alfred Gollin, *The Impact of Air Power on the British People and their Government, 1909–14* (Stanford: Stanford University Press, 1989); David Clarke, "Scareships Over Britain: The Airship Wave of 1909," *Fortean Studies* 6 (1999), 39–63; Brett Holman, *The Next War in the Air: Britain's Fear of the Bomber, 1908–1941* (Farnham: Ashgate, 2014).
40 Goldstein, *The Flying Machine and Modern Literature*, 72–74.
41 Guillaume de Syon, *Zeppelin!*, 91–99.
42 The best summary on the matter remains Tami Davis Biddle, *Rhetoric and Reality in Air Warfare: The Evolution of British and American Ideas about Strategic Bombing* (Princeton: Princeton University Press, 2002).

43 Pablo Picasso, *Guernica*, www.pablopicasso.org/guernica.jsp (accessed 30 August 2016).
44 Fernando Esposito, *Fascism, Aviation and Mythical Modernity*, trans. Patrick Camiller (New York: Palgrave, 2015), 305–325.
45 Fred Erisman, *Boys' Books, Boys' Dreams and the Mystique of Flight* (Fort Worth, TX: Texas Christian University Press, 2006), 65–79.
46 Michael Paris, *From the Wright Brothers to Top Gun: Aviation, Nationalism and Popular Cinema* (Manchester: Manchester University Press, 1995), 34–35.
47 Leslie Midkiff Debauche, "The United States Film Industry in World War One," in *The First World War and Popular Cinema: 1914 to the Present*, Michael Paris, ed. (New Brunswick, NJ: Rutgers University Press, 2000), 157.
48 Dominic Pisano, "*The Dawn Patrol* and the Air Combat Film Genre: An Exploration of American Values," in *Hollywood's World War I: Motion Picture Images*, Peter C. Rollins and John E. O'Connor, eds. (Bowling Green, OH: Bowling Green State University Press, 1997), 59–78.
49 Pisano et al., "*The Dawn Patrol*," 26–27.
50 "Snoopy and the Red Baron," http://schulzmuseum.org/12183-2/; M. Thomas Inge, ed., *Charles M. Schulz: Conversations* (Jackson, MS: University Press of Mississippi, 2000), 50.
51 Rheta Grimsley Johnson, *Good Grief: The Story of Charles M. Schulz* (New York: Pharos, 1989), 79–80.
52 The Royal Guardsmen, http://www.classicbands.com/royalguardsmen.html.
53 Luc Révillon, *La Grande Guerre dans la BD* (Paris: TTM, 2014), 98–102.
54 Ibid., 176–178.
55 Ibid., 204.
56 See, for example comments published in letters to the editor in *World War I Aero 160* (May 1998), 123–125.
57 Paul Fussell, *The Great War in Modern Memory* (New York: Oxford University Press, 1975), 8.

# 9

# THE BRITISH PUBLIC AND THE FALKLANDS WAR

*Davide Borsani*

## On the eve of the conflict

In June 1979, the weekly magazine *The Economist* published a leaked copy of the full text of Sir Nicholas Henderson's valedictory dispatch as British Ambassador to Paris before retiring. Actually, it was much more than a dispatch. It was a frank analysis of the causes and consequences of the British decline in Europe and all over the world, from both economic and diplomatic perspectives. In his conclusions, Henderson invited the British government to take a leading role in stimulating "a sense of national purpose" in order to reverse a "sense of defeat and national humiliation," so that the national spirit could be rekindled once more through the flame of patriotism. In fact, in the previous two decades, Sir Nicholas noted, the French government had pursued a similar policy under the Gaullist leadership, with great success for the whole country.[1] The dispatch provoked quite a stir among the British public, and Henderson was criticized for having gone beyond his diplomatic responsibilities.[2] This criticism, however, was not shared by the newly elected Conservative Prime Minister, Margaret Thatcher, who, impressed by Henderson's arguments, not only prevented his retirement, but appointed him as Ambassador to the United States—the most coveted post for a Western diplomat.[3]

At the end of the 1970s, Great Britain was experiencing a deep economic, political, and social crisis. It was no coincidence that many European officials started to call the country "the sick man of Europe," the nickname used in the nineteenth century by the Great Powers to stress the chronic declining state of the Ottoman Empire.[4] Economically, the country's slow but inexorable decline that had begun at the outset of the twentieth century had been exacerbated by the two world wars and the gradual dissolution of the old imperial trade routes.

During the bipolarizing Cold War years, the Keynesian reforms made under the leftist Labour governments and eventually accepted by the right-wing Tories failed to solve the economic malaise. Rather, two global economic and energy crises in the

1970s added more complications. When Mrs. Thatcher came to power in May 1979, the country was overwhelmed by a surge in inflation, recurring strikes, and social disorders. The postwar consensus had definitely collapsed.[5] Not even the first monetarist policies of so-called "Thatcherism," which took its ideological roots from the rediscovery of the free market and a greater emphasis on individualism, had positive effects. Due to a high rate of unemployment in 1981, two out of three Britons expressed dissatisfaction with the Conservative government.[6] But Mrs. Thatcher did not reverse the course undertaken: "The lady" was "not for turning," as she famously said in Brighton in 1980.[7] Yet even then, as the diplomat Sir Sherard Louis Cowper-Coles recalled, there was still a horrible sense of the inevitability of decline, and, in Europe, everyone was talking about the British problem.[8]

Moreover, economic failures coupled with diplomatic crises prominently emerged after the imperial debacle suffered at Suez in 1956. The fact that the British colonial power eventually had to give in to diplomatic pressure from the United States, its closest ally, left a lasting sense of humiliation for the British public and lawmakers. After more than two decades, that collective memory was still able to influence national strategies and perceptions. What the former US Secretary of State Dean Acheson had said in 1962 was still valid at the beginning of the 1980s: "Great Britain has lost an Empire and has not yet found a role."[9]

Indeed, the country's reputation and prestige collapsed due to the 1956 imperial throwback and nothing raised it again.[10] After Suez, the British government chose to pursue a more modest international posture by downsizing its presence overseas while, contradictorily, reclaiming its historical ability to diplomatically influence the course of the events at a systemic level. On the one hand, the search for an acceptable version of the "Little England" concept coincided with the attempt to jump on the US "bandwagon," on which Britain actually relied for the preservation of its power. On the other, the choice to withdraw from many of the overseas territories of the formal Empire, the huge military cuts, and the lack of a clear perception of the country's international role further decreased its credibility. Moreover, it undermined the possibility—despite the partial exception of the Kennedy–Macmillan years (1960–1963)—of exerting a substantial influence in the bipolar environment governed by the United States and the Soviet Union. These contradictions produced public confusion at home and a general sense of powerlessness in dealing with global dynamics, which eventually saw London as an illustrious spectator or, in the best case, as a "junior partner" to the United States.[11] With the glorious age of the British Empire having definitely been left behind, the perception of decline seemed to be unstoppable.

The Thatcher government conformed to this stance during its first two years. The 1981 Defense White Paper was intended to further overseas disengagement. It recommended additional military cuts by selling to Australia, as a symbolic provision, the "pride of the fleet," the aircraft carrier HMS *Invincible*.[12] The White Paper also reviewed the defense posture at the very distant Falkland Islands, situated in the South Atlantic some 6,700 miles from the British mainland and disputed by Argentina since the nineteenth century. The document proposed to withdraw the only naval ship deployed there, the icebreaker HMS *Endurance*. These possible measures exhibited once again the British government's bad habit of overstating its diplomatic power and credibility to compensate for a clear lack of material and psychological resources. Even though it was willing to, London could not transfer sovereignty over the islands to Argentina because of the unquestionable dissent from the inhabitants, averse British public opinion, and the need for consistency in supporting internationally the right of self-determination of people.[13] However, Buenos Aires interpreted the hypothetical withdrawal of the icebreaker as a political move that evidenced a British lack of interest in the fate of the Falklands and the inability to defend them. The misunderstanding exposed the islands to Argentinian designs, which emerged the following year.

## The patriotic awakening

Trying to take advantage of British economic, strategic, and political uncertainties, the Argentinian dictatorship led by General Leopoldo Galtieri suddenly decided to invade the Falklands. The attack occurred without a formal war declaration. In Britain, the occupation immediately ignited the patriotic flame advocated by Ambassador Henderson only three years earlier. The invasion first left the British humiliated, but very soon awoke a shared sense of unity. A few hours after the attack, many Britons rallied in front of the Argentinian Embassy in London to express their full dissent and rage by singing songs containing phrases such as "Don't cry for me, Argentina, we're going to nuke you" or the most famous "Rule Britannia," which would become the popular hymn of the war.[14] This was not an isolated demonstration. A strong feeling of patriotic redemption was noticed in mid-April in a survey conducted by the British institute MORI. It showed that 83 percent of the British public claimed sovereignty over the Falklands as being close to their hearts; more importantly, the same percentage wanted a military task force sent to the South Atlantic to get the islands back. Only 6 percent expected defeat.[15]

The press was overwhelmed by the patriotic wave and yet fed it as well. On the day that the British task force, led by the aircraft carrier *HMS Invincible*, set sail towards the South Atlantic, the moderate newspaper *The Times* ran the headline "We are all Falklanders now," supporting a vigorous reaction to the Argentinian action. An editorial warned that the "national will to defend itself has to be cherished and replenished if it is to mean something in a dangerous and unpredictable world . . . We are an island race, and the focus of attack is one of our islands, inhabited by our islanders." The right-wing *Daily Mail* announced the resurrection of national spirit and patriotism in terms of "the spring sun shining and the daffodils in full bloom." Even the center-leftist newspaper *The Guardian* initially followed suit, stating that the "cause this time is a just one." Later, however, it changed its stance, maintained the pointlessness of costly military action, and underlined the intractable future facing the Falklanders even if the Union Jack were to fly again over the islands.

A significant contrary voice regarding the Argentinian invasion was that of the *Daily Mirror*, a newspaper politically close to leftist movements. On April 5, in an editorial titled "Might isn't right," the *Mirror* clearly opposed any "military revenge," arguing that, even if the war were won, its overall costs—during and after—would be excessive in relation to the odds at stake. By contrast, the best-selling tabloid *The Sun* advocated strong military action throughout the crisis, using highly patriotic and jingoistic tones: "We'll smash 'em" was the banner headline on April 6.

This stance was paradigmatic of the British popular viewpoint. Consider that, in 1982, *The Sun* was selling about 4 million copies per day, with a readership estimated at more than 12 million people (including 9.3 million lower working-class readers), much more than its editorial rivals—*The Times'* readership was deemed to be less than 1 million and the *Daily Mirror*'s circulation was 200,000. Over the course of the conflict (April–June), *The Sun*'s readership numbers remained almost unchanged. Consequently, its circulation serves as a good indicator of the level of British patriotism ignited during the war. Finally, in spite of the Prime Minister's annoyance at this, the BBC chose to present a more even-handed narrative in its television correspondences and analyses, failing to identify itself with the more common rhetoric surrounding "our boys."[16]

The Argentinian invasion astonished Mrs. Thatcher. From the very beginning of the conflict, she naturally assumed the popular role of Churchillian war leader.[17] No appeasement was considered. Repelling Argentina and re-establishing British rule in the Falklands was, thus, the only viable option. As she proclaimed in the House of Commons after the invasion: "We cannot allow the democratic rights of the islanders to be denied by the territorial ambitions of Argentina."[18] The Prime Minister instinctively perceived the Falklands War as a war of principles—she felt that she could not allow an autocracy to settle a territorial dispute by force against a democracy committed to political freedom and the rule of law. After all, according to the 1980 islands census, all but around 5 percent of the Falklanders considered themselves British and wished to stay British. In Mrs. Thatcher's vision, principles, national posture, and reputation were at stake.

Additionally, Britain had now to champion those fundamental values for which the Western "free world" was already standing against totalitarian communism in the preeminent international Cold War framework. As Mrs. Thatcher recalled in her memoirs: "It was essentially an issue of dictatorship versus democracy."[19] The leader of the Labour opposition, Michael Foot, acknowledged that Britain had "a moral duty, a political duty" to defend the democratic rights of the inhabitants,[20] and David Owen, the leader of the Social Democratic Party, stated in the House of Commons that the government had "the right to ask both sides of the House for the fullest support" in resolving the "return of the Falkland Islands and the freedom of the islanders to British sovereignty. [The government] will get that support."[21]

Consequently, a vital interest—namely, honor—was at stake, this time not as an Empire, but as a democratic nation. In 1956, Great Britain had suffered a tremendous diplomatic defeat and, after more than 25 years, as Mrs. Thatcher recalled, "we had come to be seen by both friends and enemies as a nation which lacked the will and the capability to defend its interests in peace, let alone in war."[22] The Prime Minister understood that the Falklands War had the potential to represent a reputational lever to change that perception at home and abroad, reversing the country's declining posture while increasing its prestige and credibility. As the British historian David Reynolds has indeed maintained: "Better than any Prime Minister since Macmillan, Thatcher understood that prestige was a form of power."[23]

Accordingly, in 1982, the Prime Minister fought for the British democratic soul, not for "a vestigial speck" of formal Empire.[24] She was an ideological patriot, not a nostalgic neocolonialist.[25] In the end, the defense of the Falklands was not an anachronism of an outdated European colonialism, as Argentina maintained. Rather, documents show that Mrs. Thatcher and the British government had already been prepared to decolonize the islands, but not to hand them over without the consent of the islanders.[26]

Mrs. Thatcher's leadership and representation of the war had been accompanied by her intransigence in the face of any substantial attempt to reach a diplomatic compromise with the Argentinians that would have allowed them to exercise any effective role in administrating the islands. The British public largely rewarded the Prime Minister's attitude.[27] At the end of the short and victorious war, *The Economist* and the MORI Institute found that four out of five Britons declared themselves satisfied with the government's handling of the affair. On the eve of the Argentinian invasion, the Labour Party was leading in the voting intention polls, but, after the war broke out, the popularity of the Conservatives rose. Ultimately, public support for the government came to surpass that for the opposition: In June, when British military forces restored the Falklands to British control, the Tories led by 25 percent.[28]

This was the genesis of the so-called "Falklands factor," which rested on three pillars: the ideological pillar (successful defense of democratic values against a dictatorship and its aggressiveness); the military pillar (quick and overwhelming victory in an old-fashioned conventional conflict); and the diplomatic pillar (restoration of national pride, credibility, and prestige). In the 1983 general election, the Thatcher government enjoyed the fruits of victory. Supported by some tenuous signs of economic recovery, the Conservative Party went from a majority of 44 seats in the House of Commons to a majority of 144. In Mrs. Thatcher's words:

> The so-called "Falklands factor," beloved of political commentators and psychologists, was real enough. I could feel the impact of the victory wherever I went. It is often said that elections are won and lost on the issue of the economy, and though there is some truth in this, it is plainly an oversimplification. In this case, without any prompting from us, people saw the connection between the resolution we had shown in economic policy and that demonstrated in the handling of the Falklands crisis. Reversing our economic decline was one part of the task of restoring Britain's reputation; demonstrating that we were not the sort of people to bow before dictators was another.[29]

As for domestic politics, the Thatcher government definitely seized the initiative. What is clear today is that the patriotism rekindled during the conflict, in turn sustained by moderate economic improvement, gave the government important breathing space and a strong basis on which "Thatcherism" was able to consolidate its power.[30] So, the stage was now set to address Britain's political, social, and economic unrest of the previous decades. With strong popular support, Mrs. Thatcher pursued an agenda that reversed the perception of inevitable British decline. As she claimed in one of her most famous speeches, thanks to the Falklands War, "the nation has begun to assert itself. Things are not going to be the same again . . . We have ceased to be a nation in retreat."[31] She added:

> we rejoice that Britain has rekindled that spirit which has fired her for generations past and which today began to burn as brightly as before. Britain found herself in the South Atlantic and will not look back from the victory she has won.[32]

While the British public largely aligned with the Thatcher government, it was not unanimous. Among the few critical voices was the famous historian Eric Hobsbawm, a self-proclaimed Marxist. In an article written for the magazine *Marxism Today*, Hobsbawm acknowledged that during the war he saw "lots of people on the Left within the movement, even on the extreme Left who had the same [patriotic] reaction as people on the Right." But, reflecting on the long-term effects, he regretted that the victory allowed "the ruling and hegemonic classes," represented by the Tories, to "have an enormous advantage in mobilizing [patriotism] for their purposes," such as counterposing it, especially in its jingoistic form, "to social liberation."[33]

*The Guardian* also appeared quite disappointed with the popular nationalist implications of "Thatcher's war," noting:

> Patriotism has worked its old magic with the working class and trade unionists; skilled workers and young people have rallied to the flag and the Conservative Party . . . Yet something has happened to break the dreary routine of party politics and economic difficulties. Patriotic instincts have been aroused and they potentially transcend the dividing lines of class and ideology. A spirit of nationalism has been aroused and it will linger on beyond the quieting of the guns.[34]

The "Falklands factor" had substantial foreign-policy repercussions as well. The victory had not only made Mrs. Thatcher a leading figure abroad, but also changed the country's image as a whole, shaping both the way in which other international—particularly European—powers saw Britain's international role and how the Britons perceived themselves. On the one hand, even if the cuts proposed by the 1981 Defense White Paper were largely canceled after the war (including the selling of the *Invincible* and the withdrawal of the *Endurance*), Britain remained a medium-sized military power without the necessary capabilities to enter the superpowers' global game. On the other, the perception of a Great Britain that looked really "great again" increased the country's international credibility and assertiveness.[35] The British thus could re-enter the international club of those half-dozen countries that really mattered, and the country's voice could once again be heard on great questions.

In fact, as we have been taught by one of the major twentieth-century scholars of international politics, Hans J. Morgenthau, it is entirely possible for states to build up a credible foreign policy on the reputation of power rather than on its real substance.[36] Thanks to the Falklands victory, the Thatcher government succeeded where its predecessors failed. David Reynolds would later call it "the diplomacy of bluff."[37] In practical terms, the increased prestige allowed Mrs. Thatcher to play a considerable role in ending the Cold War by establishing a close relationship with the General Secretary of the Soviet Communist Party, Mikhail Gorbachev, and acting, if needed, as a sort of mediator between the Soviet Union and the United States.[38] As for the Anglo-American "special relationship," Mrs. Thatcher's Britain now enjoyed a level of influence in Washington—and on US President Ronald Reagan—not seen since the Kennedy–Macmillan years.[39]

## The Falklands War legacy

More than 30 years on, reflecting on the Falklands War's longstanding impact on Great Britain is not a purely academic exercise. The war's memory has shaped the country in the three decades since and will probably continue to do so indefinitely. First, Britain's successful prosecution of the Falklands War facilitated its international role well beyond the 1980s. The fact that, in the post-Cold War era, Great Britain appeared more comfortable on Mars, alongside the United States, rather than on Venus, by the side of the Europeans, has its roots in the 1982 victory.[40] Indeed, in the years following the Falklands War, the British armed forces emerged not only as a catalyst in public imagery for strengthening patriotic sentiments, but also as a reassuring means for rallying support for limited overseas military engagements.

As the military historian Sir Hew Strachan argues, initially the 1982 Falklands campaign looked like a strategic blip. But in retrospect, it paved the way for a series of short, sharp, expeditionary wars including the First Gulf War, Kosovo, and the intervention in Sierra Leone. Consciously or otherwise, according to Strachan, the victory in the South Atlantic might have affected British appetite for those kinds of engagements.[41]

Military operations in Afghanistan after the 9/11 terrorist attacks and the controversial 2003 Anglo-American invasion of Iraq came later. Yet even such a very critical observer of the 1982 war and the Thatcher years as Anthony Barnett has acknowledged the bipartisan influence of the Falklands victory on the British post-Cold War overseas strategic posture. In 2012, he wrote the following, regarding the transformation of the "Falklands factor" into what he called the "Falklands syndrome":

> Today the Falklands needs to be read as the start of a new kind of militarism . . . The Falklands Syndrome is now a norm, a baton every Prime Minister has to run with . . . Thatcher never expected to give such an order [i.e., sending

British troops into combat]. John Major inherited the need to do so from her, as British troops were already stationed to go into Kuwait in 1991. And Tony Blair was looking forward to the prospect of it. Today, David Cameron is at ease with issuing such orders; it has become "part of the job."[42]

Nevertheless, due to more than a decade of military involvement in the Middle East, the strategic dimension of the Falklands memory has seen a major backlash, which seems to radically challenge any future support (or appetite) on the part of the British public for new overseas military engagements. In 2013, British Minister of Defence Philip Hammond dreaded the emergence of an Afghan, but also Iraqi, syndrome: "when an engagement turns out to be longer and more costly than originally envisaged, there is often a public reaction to that."[43] Consider now the genesis of the "Falklands factor," which arose from a swift and overwhelming victory in defense of a simple moral cause against a clear enemy (a state). The result was uncontested and immediately visible in the public's eyes. It is possible to conclude that the Afghan–Iraqi syndrome, echoing the Vietnamese quagmire, is its exact opposite. British forces faced elusive opponents and changing rationales, and the conflicts had no certain outcomes. In the end, the Middle East wars divided the British public and weakened national unity.

As Strachan maintains, in this respect the long wave of the Falklands campaign ended in Afghanistan and Iraq, which differed greatly from the 1982 war.[44] Military historian Sir Max Hastings concluded that the wars in Afghanistan and Iraq dramatically changed the impact of the Falklands legacy on British grand strategy. These wars indeed proved much harder than beating Argentina was. As a consequence, public opinion has become increasingly risk-averse and bitterly skeptical about any new overseas engagements and, above all, the sacrifice of British lives on faraway battlefields.[45]

However, it would be entirely misleading to assume that the Falklands memory has been entirely buried by the Afghan and Iraqi conflicts. On the contrary, what is true for overseas engagements is not so for the principled dimension. Actually, those democratic values that led Mrs. Thatcher to hold steady against Argentina in 1982, such as freedom and self-determination of people, are still very relevant for today's British public. Britons see the possession of the Falklands as a territorial transliteration of the righteousness of their ideology and commitments.

The recent history of the Falklands dispute provides a clear explanation. Over the past decade, as the 30th anniversary of the conflict approached, Argentinian governments led first by Néstor Carlos Kirchner and then by Cristina Fernández de Kirchner raised the tone of their claims, asking Britain to transfer sovereignty over the islands to Argentina once and for all. They repeatedly insisted that London return to the negotiating table to discuss the issue. British governments, in response, have refused to renegotiate the issue with Argentina since the 1982 invasion. Rather, London has preferred to strengthen its military posture in the Falklands in order to deter a new attack.

Recently, David Cameron's Conservative government took a firm and clear position against the Argentinian insistence on renegotiation, emphasizing the need to defend those principles for which Britain fought in 1982. In a 2013 article for

*The Sun*, Mr. Cameron said that Argentina could continue to publicly claim sovereignty over the islands, "but as long as the Falklanders want to stay British, we will always be there to protect them. They have my word on that."[46] He had previously stated that "no democracy could ever do otherwise."[47] The current British Prime Minister, Theresa May, has reiterated the commitment.

It was no coincidence that just a few months after the 30th anniversary of the war, in March 2013, the inhabitants of the Falkland Islands held a referendum on their sovereignty in the name of the principle of self-determination. On March 10 and 11, the Falklanders answered a very simple question: "Do you wish the Falkland Islands to retain their current political status as an Overseas Territory of the United Kingdom?" As Argentina's Ambassador to the United Kingdom, Alicia Castro, said in advance, the result was "100% predictable." Indeed, the option "yes" absolutely won—99.8 percent of the voters wished to stay British.

The British public also strongly supports the Britishness of the Falklands, whose inhabitants are still seen as compatriots, kith and kin of the home nation. According to a survey conducted by the YouGov institute in 2012, the majority of Britons (62 percent) believe that their country's sovereignty over the islands is still an important issue.[48] A survey by *The Guardian* found that a clear majority across all social classes supports defending the Falklands and values what they represent. Of course, right-wing voters are most strident in their determination to protect the fruits of the 1982 victory. But, even among the leftists, there is a 55–60 percent majority in favor of defending the Falklanders at all costs. A 60–70 percent majority of all age groups support standing firm on sovereignty. Only among the youngest voters, those aged 18–24 (none of whom were born when the war took place), is there strong support (49 percent) for negotiations with a view to a handover.[49]

Major British newspapers periodically run a convincing explanation of this phenomenon. Labeled the "Falklands consensus," the phenomenon's cornerstones are patriotism, morality, and pride. *The Sun* and the right-wing press have remained loyal to the patriotic line adopted in 1982.

By contrast, the most interesting development has been the conversion of the *Daily Mirror* and *The Guardian*. For example, the former has become convinced of the need to protect the Britishness of the Falklands. According to the columnist Tony Parsons,

> It doesn't matter what you think of Thatcher, or how she milked the Falklands for the rest of her career. The servicemen who went to the South Atlantic in the spring of 1982 were fighting for a cause no less righteous than their fathers who fought older battles [during the Second World War].

Parsons went on:

> Our history shows, that the British know when it is time to go home. Our history also proves that you can never bomb, bully or blast the British into submission. From Hitler to the [Irish Republican Army] to General Galtieri to al-Qaeda, this is something our enemies always fail to grasp about the British.[50]

In March 2016, another columnist, Susie Boniface, titled an article: "Dear Argentina—bugger off, the Falklands are OURS."[51] Even *The Guardian* has been fully converted to the Falklands cause. In March 2012, an editorial admitted:

> This newspaper was opposed to a military solution 30 years ago ... in part because the cost and the risk were deemed too high, and in part because it did not believe the Falklands would be viable even if we won ... That was wrong ... As a result, Britain has to shoulder a defence burden that is less than crippling but more than nominal.[52]

The echo of the Falklands still reverberates in Great Britain's international status. At the time of the 25th anniversary of the war, in 2007, British commentator Nile Gardiner wrote that in 1982 the "British lion had roared again and the world took note. There are lessons in this victory for today's British leaders." The first of these lessons was that the "same courage and determination to defend British interests displayed by Margaret Thatcher a quarter century ago are necessary today to maintain Britain's place on the world stage." Second, the country would need "the same kind of sacrifice and visionary leadership that shaped the British nation in the weeks following Argentina's invasion." Third, "Britain was victorious in the Falklands War because it was free to shape its own destiny and willing to use military power to aggressively defend its interests." Last but not least, the "world needs a confident, powerful Britain that stands as a warrior nation in the defense of freedom and Western civilization."[53]

Despite some hyperbole, Gardiner's words are meaningful in terms of how the British public sees the role of the Falklands in its foreign policy. The archipelago is not only an overseas territory inherited from an imperial past and disputed by another country, but also remains one of the main symbols of British influence abroad. So, the defense of the islands, being commonly considered as a moral and just cause, appears as a "litmus test," symbolizing British international resilience and ability to defend its values and interests.

## Conclusion: A shared memory

From the British perspective, the 1982 Falklands War was waged in support of what the government and public deemed to be a just cause. The military action had a clear and moral intention in defending three core democratic values: the principle of self-determination of people; the rule of law; and political freedom. It was conducted as a legitimate defense against deliberate aggression by a dictatorship which neither exhausted all peaceful alternatives in regard to its claims nor openly declared war. In the end, the British government was thought to have inflicted proportionate damages and costs upon the enemy in regard to the odds at stake. The short, "little" Falklands conflict thus became very popular among the British.

The fact that war veterans and witnesses are still relatively young plays a role in shaping the memory of the war.[54] But the main reasons why Britons still remember the 1982 conflict in the way they do are eminently ideological and cultural. It is no coincidence that public memory of the Falklands War provides a common heritage for the whole nation, without any exclusive custody granted to the then-ruling Conservative Party. Indeed, the memory still contributes to forming national identity and, as the historians Oliver Daddow and Jamie Gaskarth argue, the British public's "attitude to the status of the Falkland Islands" reflects "Britain's identity over and above any ethical or power concerns."[55]

The war memory thus can be considered as a bipartisan legacy capable of reaching both the right and the left of the political spectrum. It recalls, wittingly or not, a sense of national unity in the public consciousness—the same unity that contributed in the 1980s to push the country out of trouble. In other words, the "Falklands consensus" still evokes the patriotic flame rekindled in 1982, fueled at that time by a charismatic leader who was able to rally divergent factions around a single flag and lead them towards a shared goal. As the British historian Michael J. Turner stated, "it was Thatcher's determination to resist aggression that lived longest in the public mind."[56] This is an influential lesson for today's governments.

Nevertheless, the power of Falklands memory to serve as a patriotic social "glue" should not be overestimated. International and domestic conditions have completely changed since the 1980s. The Argentinian threat to the Falklands is mostly absent now, despite some provocative rhetoric. As a consequence, in the current political landscape, the "Falklands consensus" has very little electoral power compared with the 1980s "Falklands factor" and cannot concretely influence the psychological and political climates.

"We are all Thatcherites now," Mr. Cameron told the BBC in commemorating Mrs. Thatcher after her passing in 2013.[57] Actually, more than being "all Thatcherites," the British seemed to be "all children of the Falklands War." The entire country owes a great deal to the Anglo-Argentinian conflict for having rebuilt a torn national consciousness. Political leaderships clearly acknowledge this.

One of the best indicators of this has been former Prime Minister Tony Blair's change of heart. In May 1982, speaking as a candidate for the House of Commons constituency of Beaconsfield after the British armed forces had already started military operations, he said: "I believe that, given the starkness of the military options, we need to compromise on certain things. I don't think that ultimately the wishes of the Falkland islanders must determine our position."[58] In contrast, in March 2007, in a bid for popularity during the last days of his premiership, he stated:

> I have got no doubt [the war] was the right thing to do . . . It was perfectly obvious there was only one way you were going to get it back, and that was by military action . . . But for reasons, not simply to do with British sovereignty, but also because I think there was a principle at stake which is that . . . a land shouldn't be annexed in that way and people shouldn't be put under a different rule in that way.[59]

Finally, as *The Economist* observed in 2012, it is reasonable to conclude that the victorious Falklands War, particularly its emotional impact, "still shapes the politics" and "still inspires pride and nostalgia" in Britain. "Quietly and enduringly, it left its mark" on the country.[60]

## Notes

1 *The Economist*, June 2, 1979; also in Her Majesty's Ambassador at Paris to the Secretary of State for Foreign and Commonwealth Affairs, *Britain's Decline: Its Causes and Consequences*, Diplomatic Report No. 129/79, WRF 020/1, Confidential, March 31, 1979, Margaret Thatcher Foundation document number 1109611.
2 *The Telegraph*, March 15, 2009.
3 Isabelle Tombs, "Nicholas Henderson, 1975–79," in *British Ambassadors and Anglo-French Relations 1944–79*, Rogelia Pastor-Castro and John W. Young, eds. (London: Palgrave Macmillan, 2013), 187–212.
4 Mark Clapson, *The Routledge Companion to Britain in the Twentieth Century* (London and New York: Routledge, 2009), 318.
5 Tony Judt, *Postwar: A History of Europe since 1945* (New York: The Penguin Press, 2005), 538.
6 Ipsos-MORI Institute, *Political Monitor: Margaret Thatcher—Satisfaction Ratings (Poll rating trends)*, April 2013, www.ipsos-mori.com/researchpublications/researcharchive/3158/Margaret-Thatcher-19252013.aspx.
7 John Blundell, *Margaret Thatcher: A Portrait of the Iron Lady* (London and New York: Algora Publishing, 2008), 93.
8 Max Hastings, *The Falklands Legacy*, BBC documentary, broadcast in April 2012.
9 Robert C. Self, *British Foreign and Defence Policy since 1945. Challenges and Dilemmas in a Changing World* (London and New York: Palgrave Macmillan, 2010), 6.
10 Peter Wende, *L'Impero britannico. Storia di una potenza mondiale* (Turin: Einaudi), 256.
11 See Paul Sharp, *Thatcher's Diplomacy. The Revival of British Foreign Policy* (London and New York: Macmillan Press/St. Martin's Press, 1999), chapter I: "The Pursuit of Influence."
12 Hastings, *The Falklands Legacy*.
13 See for an introduction about the dispute: Lowell S. Gustafson, *The Sovereignty Dispute over the Falkland (Malvinas) Islands* (New York: Oxford University Press, 1988); Roberto C. Laver, *The Falklands/Malvinas Case: Breaking the Deadlock in the Anglo-Argentine Sovereignty Dispute* (The Hague: Martinus, 2001); Angel M. Oliveri López, *Key to an Enigma: British Sources Disprove British Claims to the Falkland/Malvinas Islands* (London: Lynne Rienner Publisher, 1995); Barry M. Gough, *The Falkland Islands/Malvinas. The Contest for Empire in the South Atlantic* (London: The Athlone Press, 1992).
14 Robert Harris, *Gotcha! The Media, the Government and the Falklands Crisis* (London: Faber and Faber, 1983), 45.
15 *The Economist*, April 17, 1982.
16 See Harris, *Gotcha!*; Valerie Adams, *The Media and the Falklands Campaign* (London: Macmillan Press, 1986); D. George Boyce, *The Falklands War* (New York: Palgrave Macmillan, 2005), 148–170.
17 As the British scholar Malcolm Smith highlighted, "Churchillian rhetoric and standing alone against the dictators created an international myth of continued great power status, to co-exist with the myth of the people's war at home." See Malcolm Smith, *Britain and 1940: History, Myth and Popular Memory* (London and New York: Routledge, 2000), 8.
18 Margaret Thatcher, *House of Commons Speech (Public Statement)*, London, April 3, 1982, Margaret Thatcher Foundation document number 04910.
19 Margaret Thatcher, *The Downing Street Years* (London: HarperCollins, 1993), 198.
20 Quoted in Anthony Seldon and Daniel Collings, *Britain under Thatcher* (New York: Routledge, 2013), 21.

21 See *House of Commons Debate*, April 3, 1982, Vol. 21, Cc. 633–68.
22 Thatcher, *The Downing Street Years*, 173.
23 David Reynolds, *Britannia Overruled: British Policy & World Power in the 20th Century* (Harlow: Longman, 1991), 256.
24 See Alan Knight, "Latin America," in *The Oxford History of the British Empire. The Twentieth Century*, Vol. IV, Judith Brown and William Roger Louis, eds. (Oxford and New York: Oxford University Press, 1999), 623–642.
25 "Hers was, in essence, an ideological nationalism which linked the right ideas about how all people should live with the history and the genius of a particular people." See Sharp, *Thatcher's Diplomacy*, 172 and Niall Ferguson, *Always Right. How Margaret Thatcher Saved Britain* (Odyssey Editions, 2013), Kindle edition, 299.
26 See Lawrence Freedman, *The Official History of the Falklands Campaign, Vol. 1: The Origins of the Falklands War* (London and New York: Routledge, 2005), 85–123; Charles Moore, *Margaret Thatcher: The Authorized Biography, Vol. I: Not For Turning* (London: Penguin, 2013), 659.
27 The controversial sinking of the Argentinian ship *ARA General Belgrano* on May 2 actually aroused some criticism at home, but it had no significant impact on the general public support for the government's war handling.
28 *The Economist*, June 28, 1982.
29 Thatcher, *The Downing Street Years*, 265.
30 Peter Kerr, *Postwar British Politics: From Conflict to Consensus* (New York: Routledge, 2001), 170.
31 Quoted in Philip Lynch, *The Politics of Nationhood. Sovereignty, Britishness and Conservative Politics* (London: Macmillan Press, 1999), 57.
32 Quoted in Klaus Dodds, *Pink Ice. Britain and the South Atlantic Empire* (London and New York: I.B. Tauris, 2002), 172.
33 Eric Hobsbawm, "Falklands Fallout," *Marxism Today*, January 1983, 13–19.
34 *The Guardian*, June 16, 1982.
35 Mrs. Thatcher, quoted in *The Times*, June 15, 1982.
36 Hans J. Morgenthau, *Politics among Nations. The Struggle for Power and Peace* (New York: Alfred A. Knopf, 1948), 51–58.
37 Reynolds, *Britannia Overruled*, 257.
38 See Robin Renwick, *A Journey with Margaret Thatcher. Foreign Policy under the Iron Lady* (London: Biteback, 2013), 163–179.
39 See Reynolds, *Britannia Overruled*, ch. X.
40 For the metaphor, see Robert Kagan, *Of Paradise and Power: America and Europe in the New World Order* (New York: Random House, 2003), 74–75.
41 See *The Economist*, March 31, 2012.
42 Anthony Barnett, *Iron Britannia: Time to Take the Great out of Britain* (London: Faber Finds, 2012), introduction to the 2nd edition.
43 Quoted in *The Telegraph*, June 14, 2013.
44 *The Economist*, March 31, 2012.
45 Hastings, *The Falklands Legacy*.
46 Quoted in *The Sun*, March 10, 2013.
47 David Cameron, *Radio Address: Falklands Christmas Message*, London, December 23, 2011.
48 YouGov, *Falklands/Malvinas Survey Results*, April 2012.
49 *The Guardian*, March 20, 2012.
50 *The Daily Mirror*, February 11, 2012.
51 *The Daily Mirror*, March 29, 2016.
52 *The Guardian*, March 30, 2012.
53 Nile Gardiner, *The Falklands War 25 Years Later: Lessons for British Global Power* (Washington, DC: The Heritage Foundation, June 12, 2007).
54 See Tony Pollard, "Islands of No Return: Memory, Materiality and the Falklands War," in *Heritage and Memory of War: Responses from Small Islands*, Gilly Carr and Keir Reeves, eds. (New York: Routledge, 2015), 177–193.

55 Oliver Daddow and Jamie Gaskarth, "Blair, Brown and New Labour's Foreign Policy, 1997–2010," in *British Foreign Policy: The New Labour Years*, Daddow and Gaskarth, eds. (Basingstoke: Palgrave Macmillan, 2011), 1–28.
56 Michael J. Turner, *Britain's International Role, 1970–1991* (New York: Palgrave, 2010), 219.
57 Quoted in *The Telegraph*, April 17, 2013.
58 Quoted in *The Sunday Telegraph*, May 9, 1982.
59 Quoted in *BBC*, March 23, 2007.
60 *The Economist*, March 31, 2012.

# 10

# REMEMBERING THE SOVIET–AFGHAN WAR IN RUSSIA

*Roger R. Reese*

Remembering war is not only personal but also societal in nature, and it generates multiple and often conflicting viewpoints. When a war is perceived as having been victorious or in some way successful it tends to generate widespread and long-lasting attention in popular literature and professional history. When a conflict is perceived as having been lost or unsuccessful, societies tend to push the memory of it to the background. In cases where historians and popular literature shy away from examining unpopular wars, it is usually the veterans who seek to keep the memory of their war alive, and to provide justification for their sacrifices. Such is the case with remembrance in Russia of the Soviet–Afghan War, an unpopular conflict held in low regard by many.

The Russian interpretation of the Soviet–Afghan war (December 1979–February 1989) has so far gone through three distinct phases in a fairly short time. The first phase was orchestrated by the Soviet state, which officially portrayed the war as a noble cause in which Soviet soldiers defended a vulnerable developing socialist state from capitalist aggression. The state held up the soldiers as paragons of virtue to be emulated by their youthful peers. The second phase began in 1986 under Gorbachev's period of glasnost, when people could challenge the official rhetoric, and reached its fullness in the 1990s during the Yeltsin era. In this phase, the war was portrayed as a crime due to its sacrifice of the lives and well-being of Soviet youth for nothing. The war was viewed virtually as criminal, and its veterans in turn as criminals. The third and current phase began in 2001 with the 9/11 terror attacks on the United States, followed by the US invasion of Afghanistan. Russians are now more likely to interpret the war as a worthy but unfortunate necessity for the purposes of national security, which ended badly. Now, nearly four decades after the introduction of troops into Afghanistan, the Afghan war and veterans thereof are seen in a far more favorable light than they were in the period of the mid-1980s through 2001.

French historian Henry Rousso proposes that there are four "carriers" of memory: official carriers; organizational carriers; cultural carriers; and scholarly carriers.[1] Identifying these carriers in the case of Russia's Afghan War helps us understand who has constructed and reconstructed the collective memory of that war and how they have done so. The *official carriers* include, in Rousso's words, "ceremonies, monuments, and regular or irregular celebrations organized by national or local government." For Russia, no official carriers were operating until very near the end of the second phase. These consisted mostly of locally organized ceremonies in which government officials participated, but which they did not usually organize. Only in the third phase did the national government become involved, and then only sporadically and reluctantly.

Rousso's *organizational carriers* consist of groups of people who "join organizations for the purpose of preserving and unifying the personal memories of group members." Strictly speaking, in Russia, no organizations exist for this purpose; rather, the many veterans' organizations exist for the practical purpose of securing and delivering material aid to veterans and their families. But it is inevitable that group members will reminisce and share their memories with each other. *Cultural carriers*, according to Rousso, "express what appear to be highly individualistic views of the past in a variety of media, including literature, film, and television. Usually their message is implicit rather than explicit." In Russia, journalists have become the dominant cultural carriers. Finally, Rousso's *scholarly carriers* "reconstruct the facts and propose ways of interpreting them." Russia has yet to produce scholarly work on this subject, which means that an interpretive framework has yet to be added to textbooks and school curricula.

When he says that "Historians play the role of intermediaries in shaping collective memory,"[2] Rousso helps us understand the limitations we face when studying Russia's memory of the Soviet–Afghan War—because Russian historians have not yet begun their research on the war, the people have no intermediary. There are no established texts to work toward, around, or away from. Therefore, at present, veterans of the conflict and journalists, and interactions between the two, are particularly important in shaping the interpretation of the war, as it is they—not historians or officialdom—who have so far have done the most to keep alive the memory of the war—and this primarily through grassroots, rather than official, commemoration.

Despite my division of the interpretation of the war into three distinct phases, I make no claim that everyone held a similar shared understanding in these phases. I quote Rousso one final time to drive this point home: he astutely observes that "It is impossible to state precisely what the collective memory of an event is, because there is always a zone of obscurity, of individual difference, which no model can reduce and no sociology can penetrate."[3] This chapter, then, merely charts the hows and whys of the ebb and flow of interpretation and expressions of Russia's memory of the Afghan War.

On December 25, 1979, the Soviet Union introduced ground troops into the Democratic Republic of Afghanistan (DRA) two days after Soviet special forces killed the communist ruler of Afghanistan, Hafizullah Amin. The Soviet army and government had been supplying Amin and his Khalq faction of the communist People's Democratic Party of Afghanistan with armaments and advisors for several years, but had grown disenchanted with his policies, both domestic and foreign. Most especially, there were those in the USSR, particularly Politburo member and KGB chief Iuri Andropov, who feared that Amin might switch sides and align with the West. The Soviet Union pre-empted such a move, as unlikely as it was, by allying with the other main faction of Afghan communists, the Parcham, led by Babrak Karmal, who replaced the murdered Amin and his followers. Karmal welcomed the Soviet forces.

## The first phase: 1979–1986

Unlike in free societies, where governments have to compete with the media and public opinion to define the nature of a war and to establish an interpretive framework, the Soviet government, which controlled the press and public communications, was able to set a single interpretive trope before its people. The fact that the Soviet government was engaging in regime change through murder was hidden from the Soviet population at the time. Instead, from the outset, the Soviet intervention in Afghanistan was conveyed in a positive light to the Soviet people as necessary to assist the young communist Afghan government against bandits and to preempt imminent capitalist invasion. Soviet soldiers were said to be doing their "internationalist duty" to preserve peace and to raise the quality of life of the average Afghan.

What is especially striking about the early years of the first phase was that the government, despite its total command of the media, chose not to use it to mobilize public opinion in favor of the intervention. Perhaps the government was disdainful of public opinion or simply felt that it was unnecessary given that the investment in the war was intended to be small and short-lived. The result was that for the first couple of years, very little reportage emanated from Afghanistan.[4] Slowly, references to heroism in connection to the conferring of awards began to appear, but mostly in the military press, which was not widely read in civilian circles. In the course of the next several years and into 1985, the newspapers carried stories of Soviet soldiers building schools, clinics, and hospitals, and of their befriending the local populations. That there was violence and killing was downplayed and under-reported, but not completely hidden.

The violence that was admitted to was ascribed to "bandits," also labeled *dushmany*, a term harkening back to the Soviet "pacification" of the anti-Russian, anti-communist Muslim Basmachi tribe in Central Asia in the early 1920s. The reference to the Basmachi campaign was an appeal to Soviet historical memory in hopes of establishing contemporary relevance.[5] In the 1920s, the Basmachi opposed the extension of the October Revolution to Soviet Central Asia; this idea was now projected on to the Afghani *dushmany*, who needed to be dealt with because they were against the Afghan communist April Revolution of 1978. The Soviet government slapped the label "counter-revolutionary" on both the Afghans and Basmachi, making them fair game for the Red Army.

Soviet draftees sent to Afghanistan were told that they would be defending the southern border of the USSR and helping to defend and preserve the Afghan revolution. Many went convinced that they truly were going there to help the Afghan people live better lives. As time went on, the Soviet media embellished the story to include the idea that the soldiers were defending Afghanistan from NATO, which wanted the country so it could put rockets there to shoot at the USSR.[6]

A *Pravda* article from 1983 illustrates the basic narrative that lasted until Gorbachev's glasnost began in 1986, which was intended to gain popular support for the war now that it had gone on much longer than anticipated. The article describes the anti-government forces as counter-revolutionaries and Basmachi. The descriptions of events and motives are cast in ideological and Cold War terms. There is no mention of Islam or religion-inspired terrorism.[7] Not only were these "counter-revolutionaries" in the pay of the capitalist West, but also, on Afghanistan's western border, Iran was said to be stirring up trouble. *Pravda* reported that Iran was attempting to exert control in Afghanistan through the Shiites with the goal of exporting its Islamic revolution. Still, the Afghans receiving Iranian aid were labeled just as counter-revolutionaries.[8]

In 1984, the press began to adopt Cold War rhetoric, referring to the conflict in Afghanistan as an "undeclared war," which continued unabated only because the United States was arming the counter-revolutionaries. Without American interference, the counter-revolution would have collapsed early on. The insurgent leaders were viewed as proxies of Iran or the Western powers. The Soviet press portrayed them as corrupt and self-serving, but not as Islamic extremists.[9] Soon, in addition to Iran, the United States, Britain, and Pakistan, the press added China, Saudi Arabia, France, and Japan to the list of the enemies arming the counter-revolution. The supposed extent of foreign interference was used to help explain the endurance of the April Revolution's enemies and the Red Army's failure to crush them.[10]

Following the line that the USSR was just there to help, military correspondents described Soviet soldiers as selfless and ready to sacrifice themselves for the lives and well-being of the Afghan people.[11] One war correspondent claimed that "Soviet soldiers were the first outsiders whom the Afghans saw as friends, rather than enemies."[12] The fact that some Afghans neither liked nor trusted Soviet soldiers was acknowledged, but this was attributed to the lies spread by insurgents in the pay of Iran and the United States. Journalists held back from using the specific language of war and instead referred to the suffering of the Afghan people as the result of crimes and vandalism perpetrated by bandits.[13] When fighting was mentioned in news accounts, Soviet casualties were seldom mentioned or even alluded to. Every encounter with *dushmany* ended in their rout by the Soviet Army. Because of this approach to the war on the part of the Soviet media, new recruits were psychologically unprepared for the war that awaited them.[14]

Even when the press began to use the term "war," the idea that this would result in the deaths of young Soviet men was purposely ignored. When soldiers' bodies were shipped back home for burial, the entire event was downplayed. Local officials were not allowed to mention that the soldiers were killed in Afghanistan or to put that place of death on their tombstone. Headstones simply listed birth and death dates. Similarly, local newspapers were not permitted to print obituaries of soldiers killed in Afghanistan.[15] In seeking to hide the cost of its involvement in Afghanistan in the short term, the Soviet state acted as though it did not want the memory of the army's activity in Afghanistan to be remembered as a war in the long term.

In early 1984, *Komsomolskaia Pravda* published a letter to the editor designed to promote the image of the Soviet soldier doing his "internationalist duty" as not only honorable, but also superior to that of Soviet civilians of his generation. The author of the letter spoke on behalf of "Soviet people who are honorably doing their duty, often risking their lives for the sake of the Afghan people's shining future." He was proud that "My comrades know the value of labor and understand the measure of their responsibility to the homeland. Having served in the army for 18 months or more, they have become courageous, hardened and steady fighting men." This was contrasted with the soft, privileged teens and young adults back in the USSR: Unlike the self-centered contemporary Soviet youth, "We are a harmonious and united collective that has been tested in many operations and lives according to the principle 'one for all and all for one.'" The author closed by saying that the soldiers "[a]re protecting you and the entire country," and "will devote all their strength and knowledge to helping the Afghan people build a shining future." This "spontaneous letter" from a soldier shows the soldiers as ideal Soviet socialist citizens, valuing the collective over individualism, doing their internationalist duty, and selflessly protecting the country while asking for nothing in return.[16] This story was not only intended to shape public opinion in the moment, but also set the line to which soldiers were supposed to adhere when discussing the war once they were home.

## The second phase: 1986–2001

The second phase of interpreting the meaning of the war began in 1986 in Mikhail Gorbachev's second year as General Secretary of the Communist Party. Gorbachev initiated a policy of glasnost, meaning openness, which was essentially a drawing down of the Soviet censorship apparatus and an opening up of freedom of expression—a process that was completed in 1989 with the lifting of all censorship. As a result, the public was allowed to openly question the nature of the Soviet military activities that were resulting in so many casualties. Not only was information far more readily available within the USSR, but now Soviet citizens had access to information from the rest of the world. These were both preconditions for a change in perception of the war.

As one would expect, much of the news garnered from Western news sources contradicted the Soviet version. In short order, doubts about the "humanitarian" nature of the war in Afghanistan began to surface. In 1986, an anti-war movement sprang up, which included many veterans of the conflict. The main point of contention was that few were satisfied with the official explanation for the invasion and the failure of the Communist Party and Soviet government to provide adequate justification for the casualties. The party line about helping the Afghans defend the April Revolution began to be questioned. As a result, growing numbers of Russians either thoroughly doubted or rejected outright the first, state-inspired interpretation of the war.

In the Gorbachev years, the Soviet people themselves began to compare the war in Afghanistan to the United States' war in Vietnam—something the Soviet government strongly objected to because the Soviet regime had scored great propaganda points by depicting the Vietnam War as unjust, imperialistic, and an embarrassing loss for the United States. The populace now rejected the initial justification for the war and felt no need for victory; they just wanted out. Simultaneously, to the dismay of the Communist Party and the Soviet Army, news coverage of the combat and carnage increased. Once home, soldiers no longer followed the party line about being in Afghanistan to build a bright future for the Afghans. Instead they spoke freely about the chaos and mayhem perpetrated by the Soviet Army. People were horrified when they learned about the atrocities committed by and against Soviet soldiers. In the face of rising popular doubt regarding the war, the Soviet regime clung to its original interpretation of the conflict and sought to preserve the image of it as both a noble cause and an ennobling experience for the soldiers.[17]

Under pressure from and wanting to improve relations with the West, in 1986, having ascertained that the military had no realistic plans for winning the war, Gorbachev instructed the army to draw up plans for an orderly exit, over the objections of some in the high command. Even before the withdrawal of Soviet troops began and peace talks opened in Geneva, the Soviet state shifted the focus of its interpretation of the war to justify the Soviet Union's introduction of troops into Afghanistan and added that the withdrawal was not a sign of defeat. In February 1986, in an interview with the French Communist Party newspaper *L'Humanité*, Gorbachev reiterated that the war "broke out as the result of foreign interference."[18] He pointed to the United States and Pakistan as the interfering culprits. In November 1986, the USSR Ministry of Defense clearly stated that the Soviet military contingent was "in the country at the request of the Afghan government."[19]

When the first regiments were pulled out of Afghanistan in 1986, *Pravda* printed what can be viewed as a summary of the preceding years' party line on the Soviet involvement in a "welcome home" statement to the soldiers. It included the paragraph below, which is representative of the overall tone:

> In Afghanistan, you saw for yourselves that the class enemy fiercely hates everything in which we take pride: freedom and equality, culture and democracy, the happiness of all working people, and the international brotherhood of peoples. If that enemy had its way, it would sow the same hatred and malice, the same bitterness and tears, on our land that it has brought to our southern neighbor. Soviet people experienced this for themselves during the Great Patriotic War.[20]

Labeling the opposition a "class enemy" validated the war in ideological terms. Soviet propagandists meant to strike an emotional chord by comparing the plight of the Afghans and the World War II experience of the Soviet people. One of the initial regiments to be withdrawn from the war traced its heritage to World War II, which the Minister of Defense highlighted, writing: "The grandchildren of those who won the regiment fame as a guards unit during the Great Patriotic War are maintaining the unit's tradition with honor and pride."[21] This comparison equated the soldiers' service in Afghanistan to that of the soldiers in the Great Patriotic War and also inferred a similar righteousness of the cause for which they fought.

Comparing and equating the *Afgantsy* to World War II veterans unexpectedly stirred negative reactions among some of those veterans. One World War II veteran wrote a letter to the editor of *Literaturnaia gazeta* in 1987 which read:

> It is fundamentally incorrect to put the soldiers who served in Afghanistan on the same footing as participants in the Great Patriotic War. During the 1,418 days and nights of the Patriotic War, we fought against fascism and destroyed it. What can that have in common with Afghanistan? Nothing. So why have they been given equal rights with us?[22]

A letter such as this would never have been published before glasnost because it goes against the party line that internationalist duty in Afghanistan was the equivalent of service in the Great Patriotic War. The underlying motive for this letter was not to boost the pride of Great Patriotic War veterans in their sacrifices at the expense of the *Afgantsy*, but to defend the rights of Great Patriotic War veterans to first claim on the limited resources supposedly guaranteed to veterans. We can see that in one sense, at the street level, a struggle for the memory of the Afghan War started not over objective judgments of the war, but from competition for veterans' benefits. With internationalist duty being equated to service during the Great Patriotic War, it was natural for *Afgantsy* to have assumed that they would be rewarded on an equal basis with World War II servicemen. The contest for benefits then became a contest over memory.

Until the Afghan War, however, only veterans of the Great Patriotic War were legally considered veterans with rights to benefits. It was several years before the Soviet government made the decision to revise the rules to grant *Afgantsy* state benefits, and at first these were only for soldiers wounded and disabled in the fighting. Rather than write a new law, wounded *Afgantsy* were simply designated "disabled veterans of the Great Patriotic War" on the appropriate medical and government forms. Not until 1995 would participants in the Afghan War be officially called veterans. The appropriate laws designated them "veterans of combat operations outside of Russia."[23]

One World War II veteran wrote to *Pravda* to complain that "The praise and excessive decorations for the internationalists are an attempt to gloss over our failure. But they're going too far, extending unmerited and unprecedented benefits to all of them."[24] World War II veterans, who were still waiting for their benefits, could see the line for housing and medical care getting even longer and feared being displaced by younger veterans. The idea of unmerited rewards not only referred to doctors and nurses who were not soldiers, but likely insinuated that because the war was ending in defeat, shame, and humiliation, these veterans were less deserving and should join the line at the rear, if at all. By this logic, it was in the interest of the World War II veterans to portray the Afghan War as a lost war, counter to the state's version.[25] Due to glasnost, the state had to deal with competing narratives of the war—a unique and uncomfortable situation indeed.

In popular culture, it became accepted that the war was a lost cause. People questioned the virtue of its origins. Numerous films, documentaries, and novels about the war—all of them critical—debuted in 1988. Writers for the Soviet Army newspaper *Krasnaia zvezda* criticized them all for their anti-war views and for depicting the worst of soldiers and veterans, for themes of criminality, for stating the wounded were not taken care of, and so on.[26] The 1988 film *Pain*, for example, portrayed the war as futile and thus indicated that the losses and suffering of the soldiers had been unnecessary. The movie was withdrawn from theaters in Moscow and Minsk under pressure from the Soviet Army. Despite this censorship, inevitably the tide of public opinion flowed against the army and the government as the competing narrative voiced by veterans made a mockery of the earlier heroic image pushed by the regime.

A battle over how the war should be depicted then began in print media. Critical articles by war correspondents with first-hand experience began to appear, against the wishes of the military. The editor of the popular and highly regarded magazine *Ogonëk* had to fight the army to get articles by his prize reporter, Artem Borovik, printed.[27] The Ministry of Defense responded with a series of pro-war books aimed at Soviet youth, anchored on the Soviet state's original interpretation of the war as noble, just, and heroic. The Ministry of Defense would hold to this tack until the collapse of the USSR. These books had titles such as *Stars of Courageous Fighters in the Land of Afghanistan*, which told of soldiers' heroic exploits; *Star over the City of Kabul*, which lauded the exploits of pilots; and *Password—"Revolution,"* which highlighted the army's work to modernize Afghanistan. The last book to be published by the armed forces before the collapse of the failing Soviet regime, *The War in Afghanistan*, combined all the aspects of the above works with a heavy overtone of self-justification.[28]

As the drawdown of Soviet forces continued in 1988, the press reported with increasing frequency a litany of ill treatment of veterans, specifically regarding the deliberate denial of their rights, as veterans, to benefits. The primary reason benefits such as priority receipt of housing, medical care, and disability pensions were slow in coming was that veterans of the Great Patriotic War were entitled to the same things, but the resources to fulfill them were completely inadequate. Compounding the frustration of all veterans was the total absence of a single bureaucratic institution to coordinate veterans' benefits. The state placed responsibility for meeting injured soldiers' needs at the local level, where it was divided between Party, Komsomol (the Young Communist League), and local government organizations, which led to endless paperwork and the shifting of responsibility between agencies. Once the *Afghantsy* were finally granted veterans' benefits, the subsequent nonfulfillment of these benefits, as reported by journalists, became the primary vehicle of public remembrance of the war.[29]

As the war was winding down, the ideas that the war was being lost and that the introduction of troops had been a mistake from the beginning became topics of public discussion in 1987. It was revealed that the government had asked academic experts about the advisability of intervention and that in January 1980, just a few weeks after the introduction of Soviet troops into Afghanistan, these experts had expressed the opinion that it would be a mistake. They predicted that Soviet intervention would only consolidate the "anti-Soviet front of states surrounding the USSR from West to East," that Soviet influence with Muslim states would suffer, that it would hinder détente, and that it would negatively affect Soviet relations with China.[30] By 1987, all of these predictions had been proved correct.

Subsequently, in 1988, Gorbachev publicly labeled the war a "bleeding wound." The narrative then shifted away from talk of Soviet success despite foreign intervention to placing blame on the communist government of Afghanistan for its many mistakes that made the war unwinnable and a continued Soviet presence pointless. Soviet commentators blamed the April Revolution's failure to achieve its goals on the PDPA due to unwise policies that offended traditional Islamic society and factional fighting among communists themselves.

At the end of 1988, as the Soviet withdrawal was just weeks away from being complete, an article in the government's official mouthpiece *Izvestiia* formally put the blame for the lost war on the Afghans, downplayed the role of foreign intervention, and recast the opposition's identity by adopting the Western terminology *mujahideen*, no longer referring to them as bandits, criminals, *Basmachi*, or *dushmany*. The article asserted that the Afghan communists had generated the opposition against them with their crude and heavy-handed attempts to modernize the country, but went on to admit that the intervention of Soviet troops at the invitation of the Afghan government was well-intentioned and meant to be short-term; however, "the overall effect of the presence of Soviet troops and their participation in combat operations proved clearly negative." Soviet troops, as outsiders and infidels, helped the opposition recruit fighters.[31] This would be the only semi-formal admission that the USSR was partly at fault for the woes of the Afghan War.

It was important to the Gorbachev regime that the Afghan communists be responsible for the failure of the revolution, otherwise it would have looked like the capitalist West was superior and had defeated the Soviet Union. The basic initial interpretation that the USSR had been invited in and was there to help, meaning the war was still justified, was intended to stand. However, just months later in 1989, the popularly elected Congress of People's Deputies officially declared the war to have been a mistake, saying that "as a result of a thorough analysis of the available data, the Committee [on International Affairs] came to the conclusion that the introduction of Soviet troops into Afghanistan deserves moral and political condemnation"[32]—thus dealing a serious blow to Gorbachev's version of events, the Soviet Army, and the initial interpretation.

After the collapse of the USSR, the truth behind the Soviet intervention finally came out. As part of Yeltsin's consolidation of power, he discredited the previous communist regime by making available secret documents about the Soviet Union's involvement in Afghanistan from start to finish. These documents, first published in one of the country's most respected journals of history, *Voprosy istorii*, revealed the political machinations behind the intervention. The revelation made a mockery of the humanitarian motives originally espoused, and questioned the war's legitimacy.[33] The popular disgust and dismay with the war in the last years of the USSR became entrenched during the Yeltsin era, 1991–2000. The war was commonly portrayed and accepted as a humiliation of the vaunted Red Army. Popularly, it was considered a waste of time and a negative symbol of the discredited and decaying Brezhnev regime and the overall Soviet political and social system. A thoroughly negative image of the war thereby emerged to compete with the more ambivalent version that still offered justification.

In an effort to establish democracy in Russia in part by discrediting the Soviet system, the Yeltsin government encouraged people to expose every fault and crime of the communist system, including those associated with the Afghan War. Thus, soldiers' stories revealing the torture and murder of prisoners were widely circulated and readily published. In their reminiscences, fairly or not, they criticized their officers for being drunken cowards, corrupt, and stupid. They exposed the depravity of the hazing that went on among the soldiers with the officers' approval. The widespread use of drugs became common knowledge. Soldiers even reported self-mutilation and desertion as not uncommon behavior. A consensus emerged that the worst thing was that all of this had been for nothing.[34] The soldiers' firsthand accounts exposing the Soviet people to the horrific nature of the war, combined with a feeling of senselessness, largely defined the second phase of the memory of the war.

During the 1990s, the war was seldom discussed in the media. When it was, it often came in news stories that involved criminal activity of *Afgantsy* or scandals involving their veteran associations.[35] In a seeming contradiction, prominent veteran officers were quite often seen in a very positive light. Paratrooper battalion commander Alexander Lebed became a security adviser to Boris Yeltsin and later ran for president of Russia, with a fairly strong approval rating. Alexander Rutskoi, a former air assault regiment commander and Hero of the Soviet Union, served a term as Yeltsin's vice-president. Boris Gromov, who commanded Soviet forces in Afghanistan in the final years and led their withdrawal in 1989, becoming famous for being the "last man out of Afghanistan," was elected governor of Moscow province in the 1990s.

Their election campaigns trumpeted their service in Afghanistan as trials of strength in the face of daunting odds. Rather than justifying the invasion, the occupation, and their men's sacrifice in the war, these and other prominent leaders accepted the negative interpretation of the war. At a news conference during the commemorations of the tenth anniversary of the Soviet withdrawal, Gromov said: "The mistake was not withdrawing from Afghanistan but in not pulling out much earlier. The war drained the Soviet economy and contributed to the collapse of our great state."[36] Gromov's political organization *Otechestvo* (which grew out of his veterans' organization, the All-Russia Public Movement of Veterans of Local Wars and Military Conflicts) reflected the feelings of many in Russia at that time when it proclaimed: "We condemn the Afghan war but we bow before the courage of those who served in it."[37]

Aleksandr Liakhovskii, a former advisor to the communist Afghan army, wrote the first noteworthy treatment of the war in 1995, entitled *Tragediia i doblest' Afgana*, which set the tone for the army's apologists. Liakhovskii insisted that the Soviet Army never had a chance to win because it was sent in to Afghanistan without the proper means, support, training, and mentality to conduct a low-intensity conflict. It was a Cold War army, trained and equipped to fight NATO in Europe. The forces in Afghanistan also never received the number of troops they needed to fulfill all the missions expected of them. Instead the high command kept its focus on Europe and treated Afghanistan as an unimportant sideshow. He reinforced the idea that this was an unwinnable war which the army should not be blamed for not winning.[38]

The Russian State Duma approved a resolution congratulating the Afghan War veterans on the tenth anniversary of the evacuation of Soviet forces and commending their courage and loyal devotion to duty.[39] The Duma resolution was of little comfort to many veterans, who understood that society continued to reject them along with the war. When asked his opinion of the Duma's resolution by a reporter, a veteran exclaimed, "The best present the government could get for the tenth anniversary of the withdrawal would be if we all disappeared." Alexander Kovalev, head of the Moscow regional association of Afghan veterans in 1999, agreed, saying, "If it were not for veterans' organizations, society would certainly try to forget about us. The authorities don't like us because we remind them of the hundreds of thousands of people they sent to war."[40] For the most part, in the 1990s, Russian society and academia wanted to just ignore that part of history.

A notable exception to the general trend of avoiding discussion of the war was the February 1999 issue of *Rodina*, a popular history magazine with a definite patriotic outlook, which marked the tenth anniversary of withdrawal from Afghanistan by dedicating the entire issue to a retrospective on the war. The issue consisted of 35 articles and photo essays, primarily by veterans, but also interviews with veterans who ranged in rank from private soldier to general. The overall tone of the collection was positive but simultaneously regretful; it reflected to a large degree the ideas and feelings that were circulating in Russia at the time and showed a melding of ideas from the first and second phases of interpreting the war. There was a consensus that the war was a mistake made by Soviet politicians, but that the USSR had legitimate (and historic) reasons to be concerned about the security of its southern borders. All authors who touched on it agreed that it was a mistake to introduce troops into Afghanistan, but that it was not an invasion; the Soviet Army came in at the invitation of the legal government of the country. Once in, the army had no option but to do its duty, no matter what officers and men thought of the politics behind it.[41]

Some common themes that surfaced were that the soldiers did their duty and fought courageously. The authors and interviewees continued to hold fast to the idea, popular in the first phase of the interpretation of the war, that they were sent there to help stabilize the legitimate government and defend the southern border. They were still proud of their many good humanitarian works. The veterans now accepted the second-phase idea that the war was unwinnable, but this was due to the ineffectiveness of the communist Afghan government, so the Soviet Army was blameless for the ultimate failure of the Afghan communist state. Furthermore, soldiers believed that they had not been prepared for the counterinsurgency war into which they had been thrust. Because the war was an unwinnable mistake, soldiers lamented that the suffering of the men and the deceased soldiers' families had been for nothing. One soldier concluded his piece by articulating what many soldiers only hinted at: "Soldiers are just pawns in someone else's big game, they never start it."[42]

Conspicuous by their absence are criticisms of how the army waged the war or any mention of atrocities. Also missing are the experiences of veterans who did not successfully adapt after the war, developing "Afghan Syndrome"[43] (the Soviet designation for what is best described as post-traumatic stress syndrome), and who ended up as criminals or drug addicts, or committed suicide. No complaints were made against the Yeltsin government for neglecting the memory of the war and not giving the veterans the respect they were due. We see then that this issue of the journal divides the public memory into halves: the one that admits that the war was not a good thing but insists that it was not all bad—that it was not a victory, but neither would it be accepted as a defeat; and the other that rejects any redeeming value in the experience.

As the *Rodina* retrospective illustrates, since 1989, it has been mostly the veterans who have kept the memory of the war alive and have tried to shape the memory along lines acceptable to them. They were, and still are, far from united with regard to how the war should be interpreted. Veterans' organizations and societies began to emerge at both the local and the national levels in the years after the war. Former soldiers created these societies not only to keep the memory of the war alive, but also to serve a practical function, that is, to provide assistance to families of *Afgantsy* and of deceased veterans, to aid with the education of the children of the deceased, to aid in the medical treatment of the wounded and invalids, to help veterans find work, to subsidize those out of work, and to pay for funerals. They also sought to fight the poor image of veterans in society.[44] Beyond what the veterans could do themselves, the associations lobbied for their own and their families' benefits at the local, regional, and national levels. By the tenth anniversary of the withdrawal, every Russian province had an Afghanistan veterans' organization that served to unite the many local associations and represent them to the national organizations.[45]

## The third phase: 2001–present

The terrorist attack on the United States on September 11, 2001 and the subsequent US invasion of Afghanistan in October was the catalyst for the most recent reinterpretation of the Soviet–Afghan War in Russia. From that point forward, some people—often veterans—adopted the interpretation of the war as the first step in the global war on terror. The Mujahideen are now portrayed as the first wave of Islamic extremists, the Chechens the second, the Taliban and Al-Qaeda the third, and Islamic State (ISIS) the most recent. The United States' and NATO's military involvement in Afghanistan was used to retroactively legitimize the Soviet effort. Former senior Soviet/Russian *Afgantsy* officers did not condemn the American invasion and agreed that the Islamic terrorists needed to be dealt with.[46] Subsequently, some aspects of the first phase of the interpretation of the war have been resurrected, such as the need to defend Russia's southern border and the belief that the Soviet Union entered the war with good intentions. *Afgantsy* are now depicted as having been defending Russia against Islamist terrorists. There are two important differences between the first two phases of understanding the war and the third phase. The first is the lack of an official government interpretation, and the second is the emergence of a new audience—the first post-Soviet generation to come of age, some of whom are of course children of *Afgantsy*.

Now that the social and economic chaos of the transitionary Yeltsin years is behind them, and most veterans have entered middle age and are subject to feelings of nostalgia, ordinary Russians, particularly young people who have no attachment to the Soviet past, are more accepting of a favorable presentation of the war. In this changed environment, local and regional veterans' associations still work tirelessly to meet the daily needs of veterans and their families, but they are also more aggressive in keeping the memory of the war alive and giving it a positive image. Besides serving as focal points for purposes of remembrance, the associations naturally serve as meeting points for veterans where they can reminisce and lend emotional support to each other. They hold ceremonies on the dates of the entrance of Soviet forces in December and on the day of the withdrawal in February, often in collaboration with local governments. The Russian Army is often invited to send soldiers to participate in these ceremonies. Like World War II veterans' organizations, they compile memory books listing the dead from their locale, with short bios for each entry.[47] The success of these organizations is reflected in St Petersburg's association of *Afgantsy* called Afganvet, which, after years of effort, put on a museum exhibition about the war in 2009.[48]

In most ways, the memory of the war is more effectively kept alive at the local level rather than the national one. In 2009, for example, to mark the 20th anniversary of the end of the war, the province of Tiumen issued a commemorative medal for all of its Afghan War veterans, which it numbered at over 2,000. The Smolensk provincial government followed suit, issuing a medal for its veterans on the war's 25th anniversary.[49] Emulating a practice first used to memorialize soldiers of the Great Patriotic War, in January 2015, a middle school in the small town of Nekouz held an elaborate ceremony to honor the memory of one of its graduates, Lieutenant Dmitrii Churilov, who was killed while serving in Afghanistan in 1987. Children sang patriotic songs and read poems. This was followed by a short speech given by an army officer, and the dedication of a display case with memorabilia relating to Lt. Churilov and the war. He was throughout lauded as a defender of the Motherland and a soldier, faithful to his duty and his oath, in the same terms as veterans of the Great Patriotic War.[50]

For its part, the Russian Army has conflicted relations with its Soviet Army past. In order to inherit the glorious history of the Great Patriotic War, the armed forces accept continuity between the Soviet era and contemporary Russia, but this then forces them to accept the complicated legacy of the Afghan War as well. What exactly that legacy is they have yet to decide. Whenever the Ministry of Defense takes a stand on the content of "patriotic education" of Russian youth, it consistently recommends the study of the Great Patriotic War, and that war only.[51]

The Russian Army came close to expressing an official interpretation of the war in a General Staff study written in the early 1990s. The book is strictly an analysis of the strategy and tactics which the army used in the war and is not a historical analysis of the conflict. Below, one sees the defensive tone taken by the General Staff and its desire to distance itself from the decision to go to war, yet without accusing the Soviet state of wrongdoing.

> The Limited contingent of Armed Forces of the Soviet Union entered the territory of Afghanistan in the last days of December 1979, "with the mission of rendering international aid to the friendly Afghan people and establishing advantageous conditions to prevent possible actions by the governments of neighboring countries against Afghanistan." Thus, with these extremely vague goals and limited military planning time, the Soviet peoples were cast into a bloody war that would last for nine years, one month, and eighteen days. The war took the lives or health of 55,000 Soviet citizens and did not result in the desired victory for the government.
>
> At the same time, the unsatisfactory political and military-strategic results of the war should, in no way, reflect adversely on the quality of the Limited Contingent of Soviet Forces, especially in the area of operational art and tactics.[52]

The army had the book ready for publication with the intention of public sale in 1995, but could not find a Russian press willing to publish it.

As noted above, the Soviet Army, before the collapse of the USSR, made direct favorable comparisons between the Great Patriotic War and the war in Afghanistan, something the post-Soviet Russian Army hesitates to do. On an intellectual level, this puts the Russian Army at odds with the veterans. Still, when asked, local garrisons graciously provide honor guards to participate in Afghan War commemorations in towns and cities across the country.

On the 20th anniversary of the Soviet withdrawal, in 2009, the State Duma again passed a resolution honoring the soldiers' service and sacrifice in the war, saying of the soldiers that they "were faithful to the warrior's duty, who displayed heroism, bravery and patriotism." The resolution subtly justified the war in post-9/11 terms with the statement that the Soviet Army had repulsed "international terrorism and the narcotics trade" and had averted "a breeding ground for a new war" which would have threatened Russia's southern border.[53] The idea that the Soviet Army was fighting international terrorism and a war on drugs was a distinctly twenty-first-century addition to the narrative and has become a persistent theme in current popular justifications for the war.[54]

By 2010, the public had reconsidered its understanding of the war. According to an All-Union Center for the Study of Public Opinion (VTsIOM) poll that year, about half (47 percent) of respondents called the mission a "questionable undertaking of the Soviet government."[55] In previous years, the percentage of those skeptical of the war likely would have been far greater. Still, the view that it had been a mistake to intervene in Afghanistan persisted, with the mistake clearly laid at the feet of the Soviet politicians, not the military.[56] There are, however, those few who do not accept that the war was a mistake.

A story published in *Krasnaia zvezda* in December 2014, about the *Spetnaz* (Soviet special forces) group that assaulted the Afghan Presidential Palace in December 1979 and killed President Hafizullah Amin and his family to pave the way for a new, more compliant government to take over, contradicted the idea that the war was about the defense of the southern border and forestalling Islamic terrorism.[57] When this article was posted online it generated 116 comments from readers, about ten times the normal response rate. Many condemned the raid, which ended in the murder of the legitimate president of a sovereign country and his family, as a criminal act. Others lamented that it led to the long war and the loss of so many lives. No one approved of the motives behind the raid but some readers defended the Soviet Army's role; in their opinion, it was just obeying the orders of the political leaders.

The issue of national-level formal and official public recognition of the value of *Afgantsy* and their war remains. Efforts to bring the memory of the war to the public on an official basis continue to compete with the memory of World War II. As noted above, the veterans of the Great Patriotic War are on guard against their glory being infringed upon and their benefits being diluted to serve the interests of the Afghan veterans. Gaining consistent public recognition has been an uphill battle for the *Afgantsy* because the history of World War II has become entrenched in the school curriculum and popular culture, and is the focal point of numerous national holidays such as Victory Day (May 9), National Unity Day (November 7), the Day of Memory and Sorrow (22 June), and Defenders of the Fatherland Day (23 February). On the eve and the day of each of these holidays, and of the great battles of the war such as the battles of Moscow, Stalingrad, and Berlin, the media is filled with stories about World War II and interviews with veterans. The stories are overwhelmingly laudatory. The press usually only prints stories about the war in Afghanistan on the anniversaries of the invasion and the withdrawal—more often the latter. In these stories, most of which include interviews with veterans, there is always ambivalence and some degree of regret, indicating that the legacy of the war among the public is still mixed.[58] Glory is associated with the Great Patriotic War, and tragedy with the Afghan War. Perhaps because of that, *Afgantsy* tend to gather in large numbers to meet their fellow veterans and commemorate the war on Victory Day, rather than on Defenders of the Fatherland Day, which is only a week after the anniversary of the withdrawal.[59] Thanks to Russian President Vladimir Putin, in 2007, for the first time, some *Afgantsy* were included in the Victory Day parade in Moscow alongside veterans of the Great Patriotic War.[60]

It is not known how the two factions of veterans viewed this sharing of Victory Day. The *Afgantsy* may have enjoyed the attention, but clearly they had to understand that it was not their parade, nor was their war being celebrated.

In conjunction with the various military anniversaries, the media invariably reports on the plight of veterans. These focus on the government's failure to provide the promised and necessary benefits to veterans and their families.[61] When one compares stories of World War II veterans with those of *Afgantsy*, it can be seen that journalists write these stories in such a way that World War II veterans come across as being more deserving and more slighted. They are older and frailer, and the combat they saw was more intense. *Afgantsy* are younger, and often appear to be healthy. Veterans of the Great Patriotic War may have served for several years, while a tour in Afghanistan usually lasted a year and a half at most. World War II combat is portrayed as relentless, without a break, whereas combat in Afghanistan was seen as episodic, coming in intense but short bursts. The atrocities of the Red Army in Europe have been denied. The atrocities perpetrated by the Soviet Army in Afghanistan have not been. Above all, World War II veterans are seen as winners, fighters in a great and worthy cause against a powerful, aggressive enemy, whereas *Afgantsy* are victims of a lost and maybe even shameful war against a third-world country.

Veterans of both wars are a financial burden for the Russian government. The government inherited the promises made by the former Soviet regime and promised even more generous benefits to the veterans, which it cannot afford. Those promises often went unfulfilled in the Soviet era, as noted above, and successive Russian governments under Yeltsin, Putin, and Medvedev/Putin have done no better. In 2009, the State Duma reported that only 18 percent of *Afgantsy* who applied for help with social services had been successfully accommodated.[62] The complaints of veterans, especially invalids and widowed mothers of killed sons, about their unrealized entitlements continue to be an important element in maintaining the memory of the Afghan War in the public consciousness.[63]

Immediately after the war, while the USSR was still intact, requests to erect monuments to the war were usually rejected.[64] Under Putin, monuments to the war began to spring up around Russia, sponsored by local governments and both private and veterans' organizations. Many of these memorials lumped the Afghan War in with commemorations of all of the USSR's and Russia's losses in "little wars" such as that in Chechnya, along with losses of soldiers who served as military advisors in Cuba, Vietnam, Laos, Algeria, Korea, and Egypt. It took until December 27, 2004 for the first and as yet only national monument to be erected to the war.[65] Because it is set in Moscow's Poklonnaia Gora, literally standing in the shadow of the massive memorial to the Great Patriotic War and its accompanying history center, its emotional and intellectual impact as a site of memory and mourning stands to be diminished.

Before the disintegration of the USSR, February 15—the day the Soviet withdrawal from Afghanistan was complete—was designated as "The Day of the Internationalist Warrior." Subsequently it was renamed "The Day of Remembrance of Russians who Served Abroad." Unlike the grand festivities marking the end of World War II in Europe, such as the big Victory Day parade in Moscow, there were no parades and only modest, sporadic, locally organized commemorations, and these usually only in towns or cities that have a monument to the war and a local Afghan veterans' association.[66] On the 25th anniversary of the withdrawal, however, there was a flower-laying ceremony on the Afghanistan war memorial at Poklonnaia Gora in Moscow. A special exhibition dedicated to the war was also held at the Central Museum of the Great Patriotic War.[67]

A story that received wide coverage in April 2012, which illustrates the softening of views on the war, was that of the recovery of the remains of a soldier, Alexei Zuev, who had been missing since 1982. In a three-page article in *Pravda*, which was picked up by other national and regional newspapers, readers were informed that the International Committee for Afghan War Veterans' Affairs had existed since 1992 and was instrumental in tracking down missing *Afgantsy* or their bodies. A public ceremony was held for Zuev at the Afghanistan war memorial in Moscow before his body was sent home for burial. This was the first public ceremony of its type and the first mention of this organization in the press.[68] When the same committee had returned two soldiers' bodies in 2003, the story, a mere four lines long, was buried in the back pages of *Pravda* and not reprinted elsewhere.[69]

After more than 20 years, much of the press coverage reflects the ambivalence that Russian society continues to feel about the war. In 2014, *Argumenty i fakty*, a nationally prominent journal, published a long article about the grief an elderly mother still felt for her son who had been killed in Afghanistan. He died heroically and was awarded the nation's highest military honor, that of Hero of the Soviet Union. She had turned her home into a museum of his life, replete with childhood photographs, clothes, and his certificate of membership in the Komsomol. She recounted that when she was told of his death, the army captain said, "Don't cry, you have a hero." She replied: "What do I need with a hero? I need a son!" Her daughter asked, "Why is he dead, why?" This is a question that families who lost men in the Great Patriotic War would never ask. By publishing this very human and tragic episode of war on the 25th anniversary of the withdrawal, *Argumenty i fakty* was making the statement that the war was still considered by most to have been unnecessary, which made the losses unjustified, and reminding readers that the loss felt by family and friends has not abated.[70]

No longer are *Afgantsy* stereotyped as gangsters and drug addicts. Most news stories are now spun in the genre of human interest. They include interviews with veterans in which their service in Afghanistan is portrayed as fulfilling a duty to the state, but not one that destroyed them. Their time in Afghanistan is contrasted with their current lives, which are depicted as basically normal. The veterans have families and careers and are simply ordinary citizens, not extraordinary. Other stories involve friends' recollections of those who died. These accounts recall the comradeship and heroism that the war brought out in the soldiers, as though it ennobled rather than debased them.[71] The public and the *Afgantsy* no longer want to dwell on the horror and atrocities experienced. As they age, the *Afgantsy* increasingly try to reassure themselves that the war which was thought to have been necessary at the time really was so—despite its outcome.[72]

*Afgantsy* are slowly receiving the recognition they so crave, but the goal of having their war officially legitimized eludes them. Hoping to have the war officially cast in a far more favorable light than previously, in early 2014 the head of the Union of Afghan War Veterans asked Putin's government to revise the Supreme Soviet's 1989 condemnation of the war, saying that the condemnation was "politically and legally groundless."[73] The Minister of Defense deemed the request to be "inappropriate."[74]

## Conclusion

All great historical events, and wars especially, are subject to reinterpretation and revision over time, typically at the hands of historians. The case of the Soviet–Afghan War is unique in that the memory of the war continues to mutate and to be contested in Russia among veterans, surviving family members and friends of the deceased, and the wider public, but not among professional historians, who have so far shied away from serious study of the conflict. We have seen that the interpretation of the war has shifted from one extreme to another and then back to the center within the lifetimes of those who fought it, in a process that evidences the political manipulation of history and the malleability of memory.

First, the Soviet regime represented it as a necessary and honorable endeavor; then the Yeltsin government encouraged a negative appraisal; currently, the Putin government studiously avoids official recognition of any particular interpretation and engages with the war as little as possible. Of particular interest is how the clash between World War II veterans and *Afgantsy* over the interpretation of the Afghan War, based on a contest for scarce resources allocated to veterans and the generational fault lines that it exposes, has contributed to the popular understanding of both wars. For Russians, establishing the meaning of the war has been further complicated by the fall of the Soviet regime and disintegration of the USSR, and the consequent need for the country as a whole and the military as an institution to deal with the legacy of communism while trying to create a new nation and army with a new identity. Thus, Russia is left without a dominant narrative, and probably will be until either the history profession or a future government weighs in on the question. As for consensus, one has no right to ever expect such.

## Notes

1 Henry Rousso, *The Vichy Syndrome: History and Memory in France since 1944*, trans. Arthur Goldhammer (Cambridge, MA: Harvard University Press, 1991), 219–220.
2 Ibid., 260.
3 Ibid., 272.
4 Albert Plutnik, "The People Always Crave Peace and Tranquility," *Izvestiia*, May 9, 1988, 3, in *Current Digest of the Soviet Press* (hereafter rendered *CDSP)* vol. XL, no. 19, June 8, 1988, 11–12.
5 Aleksandr Izrailevich Zevelev, "Mezhdunarodnyi imperializm—vdokhnovitel' Basmachestva," *Voprosii Istorii* 12 (1980), 82–91; A. A. Kotenev, "O razgrome Basmacheskikh band v sredenei azii," *Voenno-istoricheskii zhurnal* 2 (1987), 59–64; Helene Aymen de Lageard, "The Revolt of the Basmachi According to Red Army Journals (1920-1922)," *Central Asian Survey* 6:3 (1987), 1–35.

6 Vladislav Tamarov, *Afghanistan: Soviet Vietnam* (San Francisco: Mercury House, 1992), 1–2; Roger R. Reese, *The Soviet Military Experience: A History of the Soviet Army, 1917–1991* (London: Routledge, 2000), 167–168; Jennifer Gould, "Women Veterans Fight for Rights," *Moscow Times*, December 18, 1992; Olesia Tomashova, "'Chechnia—rasplata za oshibki Afganistana.' Bivshii *afganets* o sluzhbe i zhizni," *Argumenty i fakty*, February 14, 2014.
7 V. Baykov, "Who Is Arming the Afghan Counterrevolution?" *Pravda*, May 7, 1983, 4, in *CDSP*, vol. XXXV, no. 18, May 1983, 19.
8 A. Davelkanov, "What Is the Soviet Attitude toward Iran?" *Izvestiia*, August 3, 1983, 5, in *The CDSP*, vol. XXXV, no. 31, August 1983, 6.
9 V. Skrizhalin, "Alms for Killer," *Krasnaia zvezda*, February 29, 1984, 3, in *CDSP*, vol. XXXVI, no. 6, 1984, 26; "Security Restored," *Pravda*, April 26, 1984, 5, in *CDSP*, vol. XXXVI, no. 17, May 1984, 19; G. Ustinov, "Their Excellencies Partners," *Izvestiia*, May 13, 1984, 5, in *CDSP*, vol. XXXVI, no. 19, May 1984, 25–26.
10 G. Ustinov, "Who's Fanning the Flames?" *Izvestiia*, October 4, 1984, 5 in *CDSP*, vol. XXXVI, no. 41, October 1984, 11.
11 V. Skrizhalin, "The Bridge," *Krasnaia zvezda*, August 11, 1984, 3, in *CDSP*, vol. XXXVI, no. 32, August 1984, 4.
12 V. Skrizhalin, "Let There Be Peace under the Olive Trees," *Krasnaia zvezda*, January 17, 1984, 3, in *CDSP*, vol. XXXVI, no. 3, February 1984, 19.
13 "Why the Undeclared War in Afghanistan Is Being Waged," *Pravda*, February 14, 1985, 4 in *CDSP*, vol. XXXVII, no. 7, February 1985, 4.
14 Jan Claas Behrends, "'Some Call Us Heroes, Others Call Us Killers.' Experiencing Violent Spaces: Soviet Soldiers in the Afghan War," *Nationalities Papers: The Journal of Nationalism and Ethnicity* 43:5 (2015), 719–734.
15 P. Studenikin, "I Didn't Send You to Afghanistan," *Pravda*, August 5, 1987, 3, in *CDSP*, vol. XXXIX, no. 31, September 2, 1987, 5–6.
16 Sgt. Viktor Yankin, letter to the editor, "Soviet Soldier in Afghanistan Hits Attitudes at Home," *Komsomolskaia Pravda*, February 10, 1984, 4, in *CDSP*, vol. XXXVI, no. 8, February 1984, 14.
17 *Afghanistan Weighs Heavy on my Heart: The Reminiscences and Diaries of Soviet Soldiers who Fought in Afghanistan*. trans. Mark Buser and Gail Ann Broadhead (New Delhi: Lancer International, 1992), 9–10.
18 "M. S. Gorbachev Answers Questions from the Newspaper *L'Humanité*," *Pravda*, February 8, 1986, 1–2, *CDSP*, vol. XXXVIII, no. 8, February 1986, 8–10.
19 "In the USSR Ministry of Defense," *Pravda*, November 6, 1986, 2, in *CDSP*, vol. XXXVIII, no. 45, Decembe 1986, 18.
20 "To our Internationalist Fighting Men Who Are Returning from the Democratic Republic of Afghanistan," *Pravda*, October 14, 1986, 1, in *CDSP*, vol. XXXVIII, no. 41, November 1986, 9, 23.
21 D. Meshchaninov and G. Ustinov, "Glorious Sons of the Fatherland," *Izvestiia*, October 16, 1986, 5, in *CDSP*, vol. XXXVIII, no. 41, November 12, 1986, 23.
22 Kim Selikov, "On a Difficult Path," *Literaturnaia gazeta*, October 14, 1987, 14, in *CDSP*, vol. XXXIX, no. 48, December 30, 1987, 5.
23 Natalia Danilova, "The Development of an Exclusive Veterans' Policy: The Case of Russia," *Armed Forces & Society* 36:5 (2010), 903–905, 909.
24 V. Artemenko and P. Studenikin, "The Same Blood Type," *Pravda*, September 28, 1988, 3, *CDSP*, vol. XL, no. 39, October 26, 1988, 25.
25 The fears of the World War II veterans are not unfounded. In 2014, a bill was introduced into the State Duma that would put Afghan War vets on par with veterans of the Great Patriotic War for receipt of benefits. It was specifically noted that previously *Afgantsy* were only entitled to 19 square meters of living space, whereas Great Patriotic War veterans were allotted 38 square meters. This action was not well received by a number of World War II veterans. See "'Afgantsev' mogut priravniat' k veteranam VOV v plane 'got i zhil'ia," *Izvestiia*, April 25, 2014.

26 V. Dashkevich, "Careful! This Was Paid For in Blood," *Krasnaia zvezda*, October 21, 1988, 2; P. Tkachenko, *Krasnaia zvezda*, November 5, 1988, 3, in *CDSP,* vol. XL, no. 44, November 5, 1988, 9–10, November 30, 1988, 10–11.
27 Artyom Borovik, *The Hidden War: A Russian Journalist's Account of the Soviet War in Afghanistan* (New York: Atlantic Monthly, 1990).
28 I. M. Dynin, *Zvezdy slavy boevoi: Na zemle Afganistana* (Moscow: Voenizdat, 1988), A. P. Zhitnukhin and S. A. Lykoshin, *Zvezda nad Gorodom Kabulom* (Moscow: Molodaia gvardiia, 1986); Valerii Sukhodol'skii, *Parol'-Revoliutsiia* (Moscow: DOSAAF, 1986); N. I. Pikov, E. G. Nikitenko, Iu. L. Tegin, and Iu. N. Shedov, ed., *Voina v Afganistana* (Moscow: Voenizdat, 1991).
29 R. Ignatiev, "Stamped 'Secret'," *Izvestiia*, July 15, 1988, 6, in *CDSP*, vol. XL, no. 28, August 10, 1988, 24–25.
30 Aleksandr Prokhanov, *Literaturnaia gazeta*, March 16, 1987, 10, in *CDSP,* vol. XL, no. 11, April 13, 1988, 13.
31 A. Bovin, "A Difficult Decade," *Izvestiia*, December 23, 1988, 5, in *CDSP,* vol. XL, no. 51, January 18, 1989, 10–11.
32 N. I. Pikov et al., *Voina v Afganistana*, 3.
33 A. S. Grossman, ed., "Sekretnye dokumenty iz osobykh papok: Afganistan," *Voprosy istorii* 3 (1993), 3–33.
34 Anna Heinämaa, Maija Leppänen, and Yuri Yurchenko, *The Soldiers' Story: Soviet Veterans Remember the Afghan War*. trans. A. D. Hann (Berkeley: University of California Press, 1994), 67, 87–88, 102, 105. The litany of mayhem and despair is also reflected in *Afghanistan Weighs Heavy on My Heart* trans. Buser and Broadhead; Svetlana Alexievich, *Zinky Boys: Soviet Voices from the Afghanistan War* (New York: W. W. Norton, 1992); and Vladislav Tamarov, *A Russian Soldier's Story* (San Francisco: Ten Speed Press, 2001).
35 Olga Kryshtanovskaia, "Russia's Mafia Landscape," *Izvestiia*, September 21, 1995, 5 in *CDSP*, vol. XLVII, no. 38, October 1995, 2; Oleg Shchedrov, "The Last Soviet War," *Moscow Times*, February 13, 1999.
36 Gareth Jones, "Afghan Vet: Earlier Pullout Was Needed," *Moscow Times*, February 13, 1999.
37 Susan B. Glasser, "Afghan Vets Fear a 'Sea of Bloodshed,'" *Moscow Times*, September 20, 2001.
38 Aleksandr Liakhovskii, *Tragediia i Doblest' Afgana* (Moscow: Iskona, 1995).
39 Gareth Jones, "Afghan Vet: Earlier Pullout Was Needed," *Moscow Times*, 13 February 1999.
40 Oleg Shchedrov, "The Last Soviet War," *Moscow Times*, 13 February 1999.
41 *Rodina*, no. 2 (1999): Aleksandr Liakhovskii, "K polozheniiu v 'A': Kak prinimalos' reshenie o vvode sovetskikh voisk," 38–44; Lev Rokhlin, "'Ia ne boialsia voevat'. . .," 65; Aleksandr Popov and Iurii Borisenok, "Vy ukhodili nepobezhdennymi . . ." 104–06; Makhmut Gareev, "Posle Draki . . .;" Boris Gromov, "Povinit'sia i poklonit'sia . . . ," 125–26.
42 *Rodina*, no. 2 (1999): Nikolai Ivanov, "V Kabule—dozhd . . . ," 67–71; Frants Klintsevich, "Ne propast' poodinochke . . . ," 108; quote by Aleksandr Antonov, "'Shtorm-333': Kak shturmovali dvorets Amina," *Rodina,* 55.
43 "Soviet Union and Russia Lost 25,000 Military Men in Foreign Countries," *Pravda.ru*, February 15, 2011.
44 Sergei Andreev, "Nazad, za rechku," *Izvestiia.ru*, February 12, 2009.
45 In 2014 there was talk in the State Duma of putting the Ministry of Defense in charge of all veteran-related affairs. Dmitrii Runkevich and Elena Malai, "V RF mozhet poiavit'sia agentstvo po delam veteranov," *Izvestiia*, July 9, 2014.
46 Glasser, "Afghan Vets Fear a 'Sea of Bloodshed.'"
47 Mariia Zavodovskaia, "V Tiiumeni veteran-afgantsy pochtili pamiat' odnopolchan na mitinge," *GTRK "Region-Tiumen'"* December 26, 2014, "V Penze proshel miting, posviashchennyi 35 godovshchine vvoda sovetskikh visk v Afganistan," *Vesti.ru*, December 29, 2014; "V Arkhangel'skoi obalsti uvekovechat pogibshikh 'afgantsev'," *Novosti*

*Arkhangel'ska*, May 5, 2006; A. A. Voitenko, *Oni ne vernulis' iz boia* (Ekaterinburg: Bank kul'turnoi informatsii, 2003).
48 Sergei Andreev, "Nazad, za rechku," *Izvestiia*, February 12, 2009.
49 Kseniia Dolgikh, "Tiumenskim afgantsam vruchili iubileinye medali," *Tyumen.rfn.ru*, December 21, 2009; Denis Zadokhin, "Smolenskim afgantsam vruchili medali," *Vesti.ru*, December 12, 2014.
50 Evgenii Gusev, "Festival' pamiati 'afgantsa'," *Literaturnaia Gazeta*, January 9, 2015.
51 P. A. Grishchuk, "Beseda s direktorom rossiiskogo gosudarstvennogo istoriko-kul' turnogo tsentra pri pravitel'stve rossiiskoi federatsii vitse-admiralom Iu. P. Kviatkovskim," *Voenno-istoricheskii arkhiv* 3:18 (2001), 8–11; V. I. Ostreiko, "Uchastie studentov mirza v geroiko-patrioticheskikh meropriiatiiakh," *Voenno-istoricheskii arkhiv* 9:97 (2007), 174–186.
52 The Russian General Staff, *The Soviet Afghan War: How a Superpower Fought and Lost*, trans. and ed. Lester W. Grau and Michael A Gress (Lawrence: University Press of Kansas, 2002), 1. The study was translated and published in the United States.
53 "Veterans Remember Afghan War as US Steps Up Fight," *St. Petersburg Times*, 1449, February 17, 2009.
54 Vasilii Kravtsov, "Kandagar byl i ostaetsia adom dlia chuzhikh i svoikh," *Nezavisimoie voennoe obozrenie*, September 23, 2011.
55 Alexander Bratersky, "Veterans from 1979 War Turn Detective, Bring Home Comrades," *St. Petersburg Times*, 1703:14, April 11, 2012, 10.
56 "Esli mne prikazhut streliat', ia prikaz vypolniu, no sebia prokliany," *Nezavisimoie voennoe obozrenie*, February 13, 2009.
57 Aleksandr Boiko, "My iz spetsbata!" *Krasnaia zvezda.ru*, December 25, 2014.
58 "V Penze proshel miting, posviashchennyi 35 godovshchine vvoda sovetskikh visk v Afganistan," *Vesti.ru*, December 29, 2014; Maria Zavodovskaia, "V Tiumeni veteran-afgantsy pochtili pamiat' odonopolchan na mitinge," *Vesti.ru*, December 26, 2014.
59 Boris Podoprigora, "S Rossiei na 'ty'," *Nezavisimoie voennoe obozrenie*, February 26, 2010.
60 David Nowak, "Jets, Guns but No Victory Day Tanks," *Moscow Times*, May 8, 2007.
61 Emil' Timashev, "Veterany boevykh deistvii v Chechne i Afganistane ne mogut poluchit' polozhennoe zhil'e," *Vesti.ru*, May 8, 2014.
62 "Gosdolgi 'Afgantsam'," *Nezavisimoie voennoe obozrenie*, February 13, 2009.
63 Emil' Timashev, "Veterany boevykh deistvii v Chechne i Afganistane ne mogut poluchit' polozhennoe zhil'e," *Vesti.ru*, May 8, 2014.
64 N. Burbyga, "Afghan Veterans Will Have Their Own Church," *Izvestiia*, 4, November 30, 1991, 4 in *CDSP*, vol. XLIII, no. 48 (1991), 25.
65 "V Samare okkryt pamiatnik voinam-internatsionalistam," *Samara segodnia*, re-posted on *Pravda.ru*, October 8, 2001; "'Afgantsy' obreli svoi pamiatnik v Moskve," *Pravda*, December 27, 2004.
66 "Po vsei Rossii pochtili pamiat' 'afgantsev'," *Pravda.ru*, February 15, 2007.
67 "Afghan Veterans Ask to Revise Negative Assessment of War," *Pravda*, February 11, 2014.
68 Bratersky, "Veterans from 1979 War Turn Detective, Bring Home Comrades," 10.
69 "Remains of Soviet Soldiers Who Died in Afghan Prisons to Be Returned to Russia," *Pravda.ru*, July 28, 2003.
70 Polina Sedova, "'Mne nuzhen ne geroi, a syn,' Vospominaniia materi pogibshego v Afganistane," *Argumenty i fakty*, February 15, 2014.
71 Inna Kireeva, "'Zhazhda stgrashnee puli.' Uchastniki Afgana o zhizni na voine," *Argumenty i fakty*, December 12, 2014. Vladimir Svartsevich, "'Prosti nas, Sasha, chto my zhivy... Vospominaniia o voine v Afganistane," *Argumenty i fakty*, 51, December 17, 2014; Sergei V. Podkuiko, "Krasnaia liniia generala Vasil'eva," *Nezavisimoie voennoe obozrenie*, February 21, 2014; Konstantin Rashchepkin, "Tovarishch komanduiushchii," *Nezavisimoie voennoe obozrenie*, September 6, 2013; Vladimir T. Roshchupkin, "Ochem peli tabla i dol'," *Nezavisimoie voennoe obozrenie*, February 28, 2014.

72 Vladimir Snegirev, "25 let nazad SSSR vybel voiska iz Afganistana. Izvlechen li urok iz etoi istorii?" *Rossiiskaia Gazeta*, February 14, 2014.
73 D. Garrison Golubock, "Divided by Borders, Afghan War Veterans Face Differing Challenges," *Moscow Times*, February 14, 2014.
74 Liubiov' Liu'ko, "Ne vvodit' voiska v Afganistan bylo nel'zia," *Pravda.ru*, February 15, 2014; "Russia Praises Veterans of War in Afghanistan," *Moscow Times*, February 17, 2014.

# 11

# THE PERSIAN GULF WAR IN AMERICAN POPULAR MEMORY

*Robert T. Jones*

Mr. Speaker ... members of Congress ... from the moment Operation Desert Storm commenced on January 16th, ... this nation has watched its sons and daughters with pride, watched over them with prayer. As Commander-in-Chief, I can report to you our armed forces fought with honor and valor. And as President, I can report to the nation aggression is defeated. The war is over.[1]

Thunderous applause greeted George H. W. Bush's remarks to a joint session of Congress one week after the cessation of hostilities in the Persian Gulf. The Persian Gulf War of 1991 was the American military's first major combat test since the close of the Vietnam War nearly two decades before. The rapid campaign, conducted with minimal casualties, appeared to be a decisive victory without historical precedent, and the successful outcome seemed to reverse a long period of perceived decline in the martial abilities and world leadership of the United States. Most American people felt a sense of euphoria and relief during the immediate aftermath of the conflict. The outcome of the war also marked a change in the public's perception and view of the armed forces. Some military and political leaders felt the professional and honorable conduct of the war had at last vanquished the negative feelings that had lingered long after the end of hostilities in Vietnam.

Yet, despite a surge in optimism and patriotic unity, within ten months President Bush was voted out of office and the positive feelings engendered by the Gulf War had begun to recede. A decade on, the victory in the Gulf War had diminished in significance, becoming a mere footnote in the pantheon of great American military victories. In retrospect, the apparently inept performance of the Iraqi military was no match for the overwhelming dominance of American military and technological prowess. Much of the change in perception can be traced to the Defense Department itself. Its carefully crafted images shaped the public's perception of modern war, and the Gulf War in particular, as a relatively bloodless endeavor.

Now, more than 25 years after the liberation of Kuwait, the public's memory and perception of the Persian Gulf War (sometimes referred to as the First Gulf War in light of subsequent US involvement in the region) has evolved yet again. America's long involvement in Iraq after the ouster of Saddam Hussein in the Second Gulf War was seen by many as an exercise in futility.[2] As the final legacy of this more recent conflict will not be determined for many years, the Persian Gulf War of 1991 is now viewed in yet another light—as an incomplete war.

American public memory and perception of the Persian Gulf War has changed over the past 25 years. Initially it was seen as a "just war" and an unequivocal success; however, within a few years the conflict had come to be viewed as a minor achievement against a second-rate opponent. This impression was further reinforced in 2003 as American forces executed a rapid and efficient campaign to occupy all of Iraq and topple the regime of Saddam Hussein. For some Americans, this second confrontation with Iraq was seen as unnecessary, as an operation that should have been completed 12 years before. In this context, and with the benefit of hindsight, the Persian Gulf War may be viewed as an incomplete war. As the period of America's involvement in Iraq stretched to nearly a decade, the perceived shortcomings of the earlier conflict seemed to come into sharper focus.[3]

The passage of a quarter-century allows us to view the Persian Gulf War in its context as America's last major conflict of the twentieth century, and also to see its place in American popular memory. This chapter will first examine the evolution of the public's perception of the war: from a just war with a decisive ending, to an insignificant conflict, to, finally, an incomplete foreign intervention with long-term consequences. Next, levels of public support before, during, and after the conflict are examined, as well as how those levels of support suggest a linkage to memories of the Vietnam War. Lastly, a brief discussion of physical monuments, both extant and planned, is presented along with a discussion of the war's legacy. To better understand the Gulf War's place in American memory, a brief summary of the conflict follows.

Iraq's invasion of Kuwait on August 2, 1990, provided the US military with the opportunity to overwrite the Vietnam War's legacy of failure. In a rapid campaign, the military of Saddam Hussein invaded Kuwait with 100,000 troops, completing its conquest in less than 48 hours. Saddam's grievances against Kuwait were both economic and political, and arguably not entirely without merit. Eight years of war with Iran from 1980 to 1988 had devastated the Iraqi economy and Kuwait's oil wealth was seen as a solution. From a political perspective, Saddam and many Iraqis had long contested the legitimacy of Kuwait, claiming it had been stolen from Iraq to suit the needs of Britain and other colonial powers.[4] With the invasion seen as a threat to the strategic interests of the United States, President Bush called for "the immediate and unconditional withdrawal of all Iraqi forces."[5] After a quick round of consultations with world leaders, including King Fahd of Saudi Arabia, the president ordered US troops to the Persian Gulf.

The Persian Gulf War ultimately consisted of two separate campaigns: a defensive phase, Operation Desert Shield; and the offensive phase, Operation Desert Storm.[6] Less than a week after the Iraqi invasion, American ground troops began arriving in the Gulf, backed by naval and air power. The initial objectives were to deter further Iraqi aggression in the region and to buy time to allow the buildup of forces for possible offensive operations. The United States eventually led a coalition of 37 nations and provided nearly 90 percent of the military forces.[7] By early November, sufficient forces had arrived in eastern Saudi Arabia to insure a successful defense. Concurrently, planning for potential offensive operations was conducted at all levels.

United Nations Security Council Resolution 660 established a deadline of January 15, 1991, for Iraq to withdraw from Kuwait. This extended timeframe allowed for diplomacy and economic sanctions to have an effect. When this deadline passed without Iraqi movement, Operation Desert Storm commenced with an air campaign on the night of January 16, 1991. For the next 38 days, coalition air forces struck Iraqi strategic and tactical targets at a rate averaging about 2,000 sorties per day.[8] During the final week of the air campaign, forces from two US corps repositioned up to 250 kilometers into the western Saudi desert to enable a massive single envelopment designed to strike the Iraqi defenses in Kuwait from an unexpected direction.[9] These two corps fielded a combined strength of approximately 262,800 men, 73,000 vehicles, and 1,500 aircraft.[10]

The coalition ground attack began on the morning of February 24, 1991. United States Marine Corps and Arab coalition forces conducted supporting attacks up the Kuwait coastal highway and from eastern Saudi Arabia directed towards Kuwait City. Progress was rapid as Iraqi defenders along the border surrendered in large numbers.[11] The coalition main attack consisted of the armored VII (US) Corps and the lighter but still powerful XVIII (US) Airborne Corps. This operation was launched ahead of schedule, about 15 hours earlier than planned.[12] These attacks quickly collapsed the western Iraqi defenses and cleared the way towards the campaign's operational objective: the destruction of the elite Republican Guard forces.

On February 26, coalition forces liberated Kuwait City and the VII Corps launched its main attack on a series of Republican Guard divisions. The VII Corps attack drove through the Iraqi units from west to east in the heaviest fighting of the campaign.[13] By the morning of February 27, the bulk of the Republican Guard, Saddam's strategic reserve in the Kuwaiti theater, had been destroyed. With the remnants of Iraqi forces fleeing deeper into Iraq and coalition objectives achieved, President Bush ordered a ceasefire after only 100 hours of ground combat. The coalition commanders, led by US Army General H. Norman Schwarzkopf, met Iraqi representatives at Safwan in Iraq, to arrange an armistice. Under Schwarzkopf's leadership, American and coalition forces had crushed the army of Saddam Hussein at minimal cost, committing no significant errors of strategy or tactics.[14] Military historian Robert Citino has stated that he considers Desert Storm to be the most successful campaign in US military history.[15]

The victorious American troops received an enthusiastic welcome upon their return home. Several major cities staged victory parades and military units were greeted by welcoming ceremonies at their home bases. As the senior American commander, Schwarzkopf was the subject of near universal public acclaim, perhaps the most popular military man since Dwight Eisenhower. In the months after his return from the Gulf, Schwarzkopf was honored at many public appearances, including at the Kentucky Derby and Indianapolis 500 and on Capitol Hill.[16] During this initial "honeymoon" period, with the American people flush with victory, public support for the war and its military and political leaders was at an all-time high. In total, three quarters of the American population believed the war had been worth fighting, and President Bush's approval rating stood at 88 percent, comparable to Harry Truman's at the end of World War II.[17] The military's popularity and the high levels of political support during this initial period were influenced to a large degree by the manner in which the media had reported on the conflict.

If Vietnam was the nation's first television war, then the Gulf War can be considered the first computer war.[18] During the two decades since the end of the Vietnam War, the US military had fundamentally transformed from a conscript force into an all-volunteer institution that was highly trained and well equipped.[19] Vast sums were spent on the most advanced weaponry available, including such high-tech wizardry as laser-guided weapons and cruise missiles. Computer-based command-and-control systems allowed effective control of forces arrayed throughout the expansive deserts of Kuwait and Iraq. Through the use of computers and television, the power of images shaped the public's view and subsequent memories of the conflict.

The American military's uneasy relationship with the media was a lingering after-effect from the Vietnam era. In covering the war in Vietnam, journalists essentially had free rein over the battlefield. On-scene coverage of the bloody fighting brought the war right into America's living rooms via the major television networks' evening news programs. In order to better script and control the flow of information to the public during the Gulf War, the military established press pools and presented daily press briefings to facilitate news coverage and reporting. More than 1,400 journalists covered the war from the Gulf, yet the use of press pools restricted their unfettered access to people and places.[20] At home, the Department of Defense (DoD) effectively used their Joint Information Bureau (JIB) to control media coverage and to orchestrate daily press briefings.[21] The daily briefings from CENTCOM headquarters and from the Pentagon were well attended and broadcast worldwide.[22]

One of the war's best remembered briefings occurred during the first week of hostilities. To illustrate precision targeting, Schwarzkopf presented a video clip showing an Iraqi vehicle crossing a bridge as viewed through the crosshairs of a guided bomb. The vehicle barely reached safety as the bridge exploded behind it. Schwarzkopf declared the driver to be "the luckiest person in Iraq."[23]

To meet the demands of a news-hungry public, the war was covered in depth by all the major networks, and especially by CNN. By CNN's estimate, coverage of the Gulf War was seen by more than one billion people in 108 countries.[24] During the months of military buildup and the six-week military campaign, war news dominated the press coverage, sometimes to the exclusion of other newsworthy events.

A Gallup poll from December 1990 revealed that 89 percent of the American public was following the news from the Persian Gulf "very closely" or "fairly closely."[25] With such a large audience and carefully controlled news and imagery emanating from the DoD, what were the initial popular impressions of the war?

Overwhelmingly, the conflict was seen as a pushbutton "techno war" that resulted in an easy, relatively bloodless victory. Powerful still and video imagery strongly reinforced these impressions. An excellent example of the media's presentation of the conflict as a techno war is seen in two video documentary collections: CBS's *Desert Triumph* and CNN's *Desert Storm: The Victory*.[26] Both were widely available and clearly presented the war as a triumph of US military technology. A common imagery technique used in both the documentaries and the daily press briefings was video clips taken from aircraft camera footage and even from the guidance cameras on the weapons themselves. Viewing the war through computer and video imagery enabled the public to see the war through the "eyes" of military technology.[27]

The combined effects of imagery and specialized military terminology furthered the popular impression of a clean and easy war. Terminology such as *smart weapons*, *cruise missiles*, and *precision strikes* implied that high-tech warfare enabled victory with minimal collateral damage to noncombatants and civilian infrastructure. The media's presentation of Operation Desert Storm was predominately that of a smart, high-tech, surgical, clean, and highly controlled war.[28] Yet, as any combat veteran can attest, war is an unpleasant, ugly, and often brutal endeavor. Reflecting on his own experiences, Gulf War veteran Alex Vernon found himself wishing that the war had been bloodier.[29] He goes on to say that he did not wish for additional American and Iraqi deaths, but only to "dispel the myth of a clean war."[30]

In retrospect, it is easy to see how the Gulf War could be described in such terms. America's involvements in Somalia and the Balkans just a few years later were anything but smart, surgical, and clean. Images have a powerful effect on the way a conflict is remembered, and perpetuate memories both good and bad. While media coverage and its associated images left strong impressions during and immediately after the Gulf War, such perceptions were not long-lived.

Popular support for the war effort and general euphoria over the quick victory lasted for some months after the president's speech to the nation declaring victory. In a selected survey, 67 percent of respondents considered the war to be successful.[31] In addition to celebratory parades and "welcome home" ceremonies, displays of military equipment were popular attractions at public gatherings such as parades, sporting events, and festivals. The US Army's 24th Infantry Division (Mechanized) established a "Victory Homecoming Team" to support public displays during the six months after the division's return from the Gulf. The team included up to 157 soldiers and key pieces of equipment such as the M1A1 Abrams main battle tank, the M2 Bradley infantry fighting vehicle, and other high-tech examples of military hardware.[32] As Gulf War veteran Dave Trybula remembers, "everywhere . . . we were met with an incredible amount of enthusiasm . . . people just wanted to thank us for the job we did in the Gulf."[33] While ordinary Americans celebrated the victory of their armed forces, some of America's leaders began to harbor doubts almost immediately.

One of the first indications of unease came from the president himself. At a White House press conference several days after his address to Congress, George Bush responded to a reporter's question concerning his somber mood:

> You know, to be very honest with you, I haven't yet felt this wonderfully euphoric feeling that many of the American people feel. And I'm beginning to. I feel much better about it today than I did yesterday. But I think it's that I want to see an end. You mentioned World War II—there was a definitive end to that conflict. And now we have Saddam Hussein still there—the man who wreaked this havoc upon his neighbors."[34]

Like many of the World War II generation to which he belonged, President Bush saw the world in terms of black and white. Certainly the president was reflecting on the lack of a clear-cut ending to the conflict. While the military objectives of the campaign had been accomplished, Saddam Hussein remained in power—the dictator not only remained in place, but indeed strengthened his hold on power during the immediate postwar period.[35] Saddam's strengthened position undoubtedly contributed to the feeling that the Gulf War was an unfinished conflict.

For the first few years after the Gulf War's termination, Americans continued to view the war as a successful, although perhaps incomplete, endeavor. The public's perception of the war as a successful application of high-tech weaponry persisted despite growing evidence to the contrary.[36] In addition, more than four years later, the United States was still involved in open-ended "police action," enforcing "no-fly zones" in both northern and southern Iraq.[37] Because of this, even military leaders began to sense a changing perception of the conflict. Senior leaders of the armed services became concerned with the portrayal of the war's legacy and their role in it. As commanding general of CENTCOM, Schwarzkopf had worked hard to shape the public's impression during the war. He now turned his attention to the postwar historical perspective. Schwarzkopf himself even advocated to a group of senior marine officers to "watch what you say . . . people are out writing their books."[38]

A decade after the end of the Persian Gulf War, the public's perception and mental imagery of the conflict had evolved to a noticeable degree. The passage of ten years allowed a certain measure of perspective that was not possible during the immediate postwar period. While writing a book about his own experiences in the war, Alex Vernon was informed by a colleague that the war was "historically insignificant."[39] Even as a participant, Vernon was himself unsure of its significance ten years later.

Historian and professor of international relations Andrew J. Bacevich has argued that by this time the Gulf War no longer appeared as it did in 1990 and 1991. It was no longer a colossal feat of arms or a decisive response to aggression—by 2001, such views had become obsolete.[40] Others argued that "the Persian Gulf War was already looking like a footnote to American history."[41]

Professor of cultural memory studies Marita Sturken maintains that a sense of collective amnesia surrounds the war. She attributes this amnesia to the war's lack of a final outcome, the government's scripting of the public discourse on the war, and the relatively empty spectacle of television images.[42] As much as images defined the narrative of the war, they also contributed to it quickly slipping from the public's consciousness. The impact of Gulf War images, while powerful at the time, did not endure. The nature of the images themselves contributed to their demise. Sturken asserts that television images are forgettable in their empty spectacle, that spectacle is about forgetting.[43] Writing 12 years after the conflict, Jeanne Colleran observed that there had been virtually no sustained interest in the war.[44]

The passage of time certainly affects human memories of even significant occurrences, especially for participants. Selective memory can obscure the true nature of events, and give rise to the temptation of revisionism. As Vernon recalled during his work on a collaborative memoir: "My memory stretches 10 years thin, and strains. The passage of time both helps and hinders perspective. Hindsight clouds. Events obtrude. Innocence beckons. Revisionism rears."[45] Bacevich and others have taken a postmodern revisionist tack that views the war from the perspective of television and computer simulated graphics.[46] The combined effects of American technology and the sub-par performance of the Iraqi military have led some to challenge the actual reality of the events themselves. It is certainly a matter open to interpretation and debate.

However, Vernon counters such perspectives with his observation that the Iraqi Army was the fourth largest in the world and possessed the ability to use chemical weapons. He went into a battle of indeterminate length and outcome, with his hand never far from the trigger.[47] Still, the massive viewership of the war has led some critics to refer to the conflict as "the Persian Gulf TV war," or as "infotainment."[48] Perhaps an argument can be made that technology has dissolved the distinction between the civilian spectator at home and the actual participant on the battlefield. In a sense, the use of televised and computer images allows the viewer to live vicariously through the projected images. Colleran noted the "nearly unassailable pull of live experience" while describing the minute-by-minute reporting that characterized the media's coverage of the war.[49] As much as imagery is a powerful component of memory, it is not the only factor. The human dimension and the interactive human experience contribute greatly to shared public memory.

The widespread popular support for America's involvement in the Persian Gulf may be attributed to three factors, all of which contribute to the collective memory of the conflict. First, the need to liberate Kuwait was presented as a "just war," as America would be coming to the aid of a peaceful people against the depredations of a bellicose neighbor. With Saddam Hussein villainized as a modern incarnation of Adolf Hitler, Americans easily accepted the premise of a good and just war. Second, as a just war, an appeal was made to innate American patriotism. Out of a sense of patriotism, in time of war many Americans tend to support their president and military forces, in what is known as the "rally effect." Finally, and perhaps most significantly, many Americans felt a deep-seated need to make amends for the nation's treatment of its Vietnam veterans. Public support for the troops during the

Gulf War was substantial, and included enthusiastic welcoming ceremonies which often involved Vietnam veterans as well. The congruence of these three factors is representative of the fact that war is an intensely human endeavor, for both the participants and those on the home front.

From the outset of the Persian Gulf crisis, there was an almost immediate effort to characterize America's intervention as a "just war." To some observers, Saddam's invasion of neighboring Kuwait seemed analogous to Germany's invasion of Poland in 1939. President Bush likely sought to draw parallels to World War II, the formative event of his generation. His immediate response was firm and uncompromising. In comments to reporters three days after the invasion, the president stated: "This will not stand, this aggression against Kuwait."[50] In presenting the Gulf crisis as a just war, Bush made several direct references to World War II: "as was the case in the 1930s, we see in Saddam Hussein an aggressive dictator threatening his neighbors" and "there's a parallel to what Hitler did to Poland and what Saddam Hussein has done to Kuwait."[51] The president's remarks frame the conflict as a classic battle of good versus evil.

Bush's approach proved to be very effective, as most Americans seemed to agree with him. In surveys assessing Americans' attitudes towards the war, 81 percent agreed with the Hitler analogy and 89 percent remembered World War II as a just war.[52] Historian Richard Lowery summarized this view in his military history of the conflict published in 2003: "America acted to protect a small nation that was overpowered by its neighbor. We fought fairly and did everything in our power to limit civilian casualties."[53] The idea of a just war played well with main-street America and appealed to the country's patriotism.

The Persian Gulf War of 1990–1991 is remembered as a time of great national unity. Historically, Americans unite behind their political and military leaders during times of national crisis. Political scientists describe this phenomenon as the "rally effect." Rally events, such as the Persian Gulf War, invoke feelings of allegiance toward national political institutions and policies.[54] Rallies around the flag occur when political leaders, regardless of party, unite behind the president to present a uniform picture to the public.[55]

Although there was Congressional debate in the months leading up to the actual commencement of combat operations, once hostilities began there was near unanimous support of the president's position. Even though there was some division of public opinion during the months prior to the war, President Bush successfully convinced the American public of the righteousness and justness of the military intervention. As measured by public opinion polls, and reinforced by still and video images that portrayed an unparalleled success, Bush's approval rating skyrocketed.[56] Political scientists see this as a classic example of the "rally around the flag" phenomenon.[57] In common with the media imagery that propelled them, the government's high approval numbers resulting from the rally effect were not long-lasting. Within a year, most polling numbers had returned to precrisis levels.[58] While polling data may be subject to interpretation, a more direct reflection of public unity became prominent: the yellow ribbon campaign.

The display of yellow ribbons, while not unique in American history, quickly became the most pervasive symbol of unity on the home front during the Gulf War.[59] The widespread use of ribbons to show support for the troops appeared in all strata of society and cut across most cultural barriers. The use of yellow ribbons in American culture to show solidarity with a loved one or support for a cause may be traced to nineteenth-century frontier army traditions. The practice continued sporadically throughout the early to mid-twentieth century in support of other causes.

While a discussion of the cultural nuances of the yellow ribbon campaign is beyond the scope of this work, it is worth noting the effect of the 1973 Tony Orlando song "Tie a Yellow Ribbon Round the Ole Oak Tree." The song brought the use of yellow ribbons to the forefront of public consciousness during times of crisis. The first large-scale use of ribbons came during the 444 days of the Iranian hostage crisis.[60] The duration and intensity of that event, coupled with its intense media coverage, made it inevitable that, the next time the nation went to war, yellow ribbons would be the emblem of home-front solidarity.[61]

During the Gulf War, the display of yellow ribbons was immensely popular and the sale of ribbons and related items grew enormously. America's leading ribbon manufacturer reported his sales grew from 5 to 50 million yards in one year, a tenfold increase.[62] Ribbons were widely displayed by businesses, churches, schools, private homes, and government buildings. The overwhelming presence of this symbol insured its use was subject to varying interpretations. For most, the yellow ribbon represented support for the troops, their families, or the justness of America's cause. However, support for the war was not unanimous, and therefore many ribbon users were careful to state that their ribbon supported the troops, but not necessarily the war.[63]

It is interesting to note that the same symbol could be appropriated by different constituencies to voice their support or opposition for the same issue. Regardless of the individual's stance on the war, the yellow ribbon served as a unifying force and as a tangible symbol to affirm America's respect for and support of the troops.[64] It is significant that the widespread support for the troops also served as a touchstone for another, more ambiguous and less popular conflict—the Vietnam War.

Any study of the political history or public memory of the Persian Gulf War reveals an overarching connection to the Vietnam War. As a watershed event for an earlier generation of Americans, the impact of Vietnam cast a long shadow over American political, military, and societal institutions. The war was a lasting memory for those who experienced it directly overseas or indirectly at home. A 1985 study of collective memories revealed that Vietnam and World War II were the two most frequently reported events in a survey of what Americans remembered as being "especially important."[65]

A connection between Vietnam and the Gulf War is seen in the treatment of the respective veterans and the way in which each conflict is remembered. The lack of a clear purpose, thousands of casualties, and ambiguous ending to Vietnam left an overwhelmingly negative impression in the minds of many Americans. Such negativity inevitably affected their view and treatment of the Vietnam veterans. Upon their return, the veterans were ignored and considered embarrassments by both the government and the general population.[66] Typical of the many thousands of returning veterans was Army Specialist Steven Slocum. The 18-year-old infantryman had seen a year of combat in Vietnam and had been severely wounded. His return to America was decidedly low-key. After a 17-hour military flight from Vietnam, he arrived at San Francisco International Airport to catch a commercial flight to his hometown in Florida. Still in uniform, he was neither welcomed nor hassled; he was simply ignored.[67]

One of the most important motivations for the yellow ribbon campaign was the need to make amends for neglecting the Vietnam veterans.[68] A commonly held belief is that returning servicemen were verbally abused or even spat upon, but actual evidence for such behaviors is rare. The more common experience was that of Specialist Slocum: No one paid any attention to him. Many in America felt a strong need to not only support the troops of Desert Storm, but also belatedly show their appreciation for an earlier generation of veterans. Yellow ribbons served as a tangible "measure of atonement . . . by a country that treated Vietnam veterans with unjustified contempt."[69]

From the perspective of the veterans themselves, there was some residual resentment over their treatment, but the majority embraced the yellow ribbon campaign. Most responded to the campaign as if it were the "welcome home" they had been denied for more than 15 years, and many organized and participated in events supporting the Gulf War troops.[70] Even the anti-war protesters of 1990 took a different context and tone in their approach to the Gulf War. Opponents of the war, including many Vietnam-era anti-war activists, accepted the need to express support for the troops.[71] The impact of the widespread and deeply rooted support for the Gulf War troops was felt at the highest levels of government.

The apparently decisive outcome of the Gulf War, combined with high levels of public support, was the likely inspiration for President Bush's proclamation "By God, we've kicked this Vietnam Syndrome forever!"[72] Sturken defines "Vietnam Syndrome" as "a mentality of overprotection, a weakness of resolve, and a fear of repeating a national mistake."[73] Even the Chairman of the Joint Chiefs of Staff, General Colin Powell—himself a veteran of Vietnam—expressed a similar sentiment. "We had given America a clear win at low casualties in a noble cause, and the American people fell in love again with their armed forces."[74]

While cultural historians might take issue with the veracity of the president's proclamation, the response of the American people was quite clear. On March 18, 1991, Brigade Command Sergeant Major Steven Slocum returned home from his second war.[75] He and his troops were warmly received as they landed at their home base in Fayetteville, North Carolina. A crowd of thousands greeted Slocum and his men with flags, banners, and cheers. Something more substantial than years had passed between the two homecomings. The manner in which the Gulf War troops were welcomed home had a marked difference to that of the Vietnam War returnees. The homecoming receptions and victory celebrations that followed the conflict are important elements in America's public memory of the Persian Gulf War.

Desert Storm troops began returning almost immediately after the end of the ground campaign, with the first return flights beginning in early March 1991. The sheer scale of the Desert Storm operation meant it would take several months for the majority of personnel to return home. As spring turned to summer, a number of American cities hosted Desert Storm Victory/Welcome Home parades. Chicago was the first city to host a major celebration on May 10, with General Colin Powell serving as the grand marshal.[76] Los Angeles followed on May 19.

By far the largest celebrations were held in the nation's capital on June 8 and in New York City on June 10. Millions turned out in what has been described as a "cathartic outpouring of national pride and appreciation."[77] The parades turned out to be a popular way of displaying pride in the nation's martial heroes and something of a competition emerged as to which city could host the largest and best celebration. In what was dubbed the "war between the cities," the mayor of New York City promised to host the "mother of all parades." More than four million New Yorkers viewed their parade, which featured 6,000 tons of ticker tape. It was Manhattan's largest parade since the end of World War II.[78]

The New York City parade may have been the largest celebration, but Washington, DC, hosted the most extravagant one. During the morning, President Bush presided over a memorial service for the fallen at Arlington National Cemetery. The parade that followed at noon was the latest in a long history of victorious military marches in the national capital. The procession that moved up Constitution Avenue was a modern military phalanx of 9,000 marching troops, combat vehicles, and military bands, with an overflight by more than 80 aircraft. More than 800,000 spectators cheered as the troops marched by.[79] But as the cheers faded away, how would the participants and events of the war be remembered and memorialized?

Public monuments and memorials reflect the way in which a nation remembers its past, sees itself in the present, and looks to the future. A quarter-century after its conclusion, the Persian Gulf War remains the largest American war of the twentieth century without a national memorial. The National Desert Storm War Memorial Association, with the support of veterans' groups and private citizens, is leading the effort to fund, design, and establish a memorial in the nation's capital.[80]

Over the years, many military units that participated in Desert Storm have established their own unit monuments and memorials to commemorate their participation in the war. Memorials may be found on military bases, in unit headquarters, and in various military museums around the country. They vary in size and design, from simple bronze plaques to more extravagant designs. However, all seek to preserve the memory of a victorious conflict and the sacrifices made by individuals and units.

One of the most notable and poignant of the Desert Storm memorials is the monument dedicated to the 14th Quartermaster Detachment, United States Army Reserve. Located at the unit's home armory in Greensburg, Pennsylvania, the monument commemorates the unit's tragic loss of life during Desert Storm.[81] On February 25, 1991, an Iraqi Scud missile struck a warehouse in Dhahran, Saudi Arabia, that housed the detachment and other military units. Out of a total strength of 69 personnel, the unit suffered 13 dead and 43 wounded, the highest casualty rate of any unit in the Gulf War.

No hometown in America was hit harder than Greensburg, a small town of 18,000 located southeast of Pittsburgh. As Army Reservists, the members of the 14th Quartermaster were part-time soldiers, continuing a long American military tradition of citizen soldiers that dates back to the colonial era. The monument to honor these fallen soldiers was dedicated on the one-year anniversary of the attack. A granite pylon flanked by two bronze plaques form the central structure of the monument. The pylon is topped by a bronze eagle. A trio of flagpoles flying the flags of the United States, Pennsylvania, and the army forms the backdrop. Life-size bronze statues of two soldiers and of a helmet, rifle, and boots (symbolizing a fallen soldier) complete the monument.

While monuments may provide tangible reminders of past events, what is the legacy of the Persian Gulf War and how will it be remembered?

The Gulf War's legacy remains a subject for historical debate. As the last major conventional war of the twentieth century, the conflict was reminiscent of World War II, but it also offered a potential glimpse of the future of warfare. Writing in 2001, Andrew Bacevich argued that while the war itself might be forgettable, the war's legacy would be important and enduring. Bacevich describes four elements that he considers essential to the legacy.[82] In his view, the war transformed America's view of the nature of war, namely by highlighting that industrial-age warfare was at an end and that a new era of information-age warfare was at hand. Next, the war redefined the relationship between military power and America's national identity. Bacevich argues that for better or worse, military power is now an integral part of the national identity. Subsequently, with respect to civil–military relations, he asserts that the boundaries between military and political spheres are more difficult to discern than ever. The final, and in Bacevich's view the most important, element of the legacy is the way in which Americans now view the immediate past and the immediate future. The successful conclusion of the Cold War and the Persian Gulf War marked the close of a century that was essentially a march of progress for the good of mankind. Bacevich acknowledges that this view is at odds with those of some postmodern intellectuals, but states that such grand ideals will fuel American's expectations in the new millennium.[83] Other analysts agree that the war's true legacy is its implications for the future, and its military and political lessons in particular.[84]

America's collective memory of the Persian Gulf War is multifaceted and has been slow to evolve. Marita Sturken believes the reason for this was the military's tight control of how the war was presented in terms of information and images.[85] Image and message control effectively shaped the public's perception during the conflict. After a quarter-century, the war continues to be remembered in terms of a high-tech, push-button, relatively bloodless conflict of good versus evil. The use and efficacy of high-technology weapons remains a central feature of Gulf War memories, even though postwar analysis revealed deficiencies in the performance of some highly touted weapons systems.

Alex Vernon argues that the true lasting legacy of the Gulf War is the myth that is was a clean war.[86] Perhaps the most glaring counterpoint to the "clean war" myth is the substantial numbers of veterans diagnosed with Gulf War Syndrome.[87] The prevalence of medically unexplained symptoms may be attributed to exposure to oil and chemical fires, and possibly to chemical weapons. The effects of Gulf War Syndrome continue to be studied to this day. Writing in 1997, Sturken asserted that the Gulf War legacy was that of a contested meaning and an emerging cultural memory.[88] With respect to Gulf War Syndrome and issues of cultural memory, her words continue to resonate.

The memory of the Gulf War as an unfinished war has also persisted. Critics of the war have repeatedly pointed out that not only did substantial Iraqi military forces escape to fight another day, but also Saddam Hussein remained in power. Coalition forces did, however, fulfill the UN mandate to remove the Iraqi Army from Kuwait and restore that nation's territorial sovereignty. Norman Schwarzkopf points out in his autobiographical account of the war that the coalition never even considered a major attack into Iraq or removing Hussein from power.[89] From America's perspective, there was no legal basis to do so. According to Michael Gordon and General Bernard Trainor, there was never a plan for terminating the war, and thus the war remained unfinished three years later.[90]

America's enforcement of postwar no-fly zones and the subsequent full-fledged invasion of Iraq in 2003 seem to support the view of many critics that the Persian Gulf War was indeed an unfinished war. In a remarkable bit of prescience, George Hilsman argued in his 1992 book *George Bush vs. Saddam Hussein* that Desert Storm (and by extension the entire Persian Gulf War) was only a battle in what may be a long and potentially costly war.[91] Given that the United States expended an enormous amount of blood and treasure in Iraq from 2003 until 2011, the memory of the Persian Gulf War as an unfinished war is likely to remain.

The Persian Gulf War holds a unique place in American military history and cultural memory. Militarily, the war displayed the destructiveness of a modern air campaign while featuring the last large-scale armored combat of the twentieth century. It was the first war in which high-technology weapons played a prominent and perhaps decisive role. Despite some shortcomings, such weapons demonstrated the potential to limit destructiveness and collateral damage in modern warfare.

From a cultural perspective, the conflict unified the American people behind their military to an extent not seen since World War II. Popular historian Rick Atkinson believes that the war "reaffirmed the bond between those in uniform and the larger republic, a delicate relationship that has waxed and waned for more than two centuries."[92] Of equal importance, the support for the troops exemplified by the yellow ribbon campaign enabled Americans to collectively heal their consciences concerning their treatment of Vietnam veterans. With the benefit of hindsight, perhaps the lasting legacy and memory of the Persian Gulf War is that of an unfinished war. A quarter-century after its end, the war remains subject to changing interpretations and debate. The passage of time will undoubtedly add new interpretations. Andrew Bacevich's perspective of the war, written on its tenth anniversary, remains relevant today: "As Desert Storm recedes into the distance, its splendor fades. But its true significance comes into view."[93]

## Notes

1. Miller Center of Public Affairs, University of Virginia. "George H.W. Bush Address Before a Joint Session of Congress on the End of the Gulf War (March 6, 1991)," http://millercenter.org/president/bush/speeches/speech-3430.
2. US military operations in Iraq are officially designated *Operation Iraqi Freedom* and *Operation New Dawn*.
3. American military forces conducted operations in Iraq from March 20, 2003 to December 18, 2011.
4. H.W. Brands, "George Bush and the Gulf War of 1991," *Presidential Studies Quarterly* 34:1 (March 2004), 114.
5. Ibid., 115.
6. There is no universally accepted term for this conflict. The US Army officially recognizes its involvement as "Southwest Asia Service" consisting of three separate campaigns: Defense of Saudi Arabia; Liberation and Defense of Kuwait; and Ceasefire. See Army Doctrine Publication 1, *The Army*. Popular historians have predominately used the terms "Gulf War" and "Persian Gulf War."
7. Lawrence Freedman and Efraim Karsh, "How Kuwait Was Won: Strategy in the Gulf War," *International Security* 16:2 (Fall 1991), 5–6.
8. Ibid., 25.
9. Stephen Biddle, "Victory Misunderstood: What the Gulf War Tells Us about the Future of Conflict," *International Security* 21:2 (Fall 1996), 145.
10. Robert H. Scales, Jr., *Certain Victory: The US Army in the Gulf War* (Washington, DC: Brassey's Inc., 1994), 148–149.
11. Ibid.
12. Rick Atkinson, *Crusade: The Untold Story of the Persian Gulf War* (New York: Houghton Mifflin Company, 1993), 392–394.
13. Biddle, "Victory Misunderstood," 146.
14. Atkinson, *Crusade*, 3.
15. Keith L. Shimko, *The Iraq Wars and America's Military Revolution* (New York: Cambridge University Press, 2010), 77.
16. Atkinson, *Crusade*, 493.
17. Ibid., 496.
18. Michelle Kendrick, "The Never Again Narratives: Political Promise and the Videos of Operation Desert Storm," *Cultural Critique* 28 (Autumn 1994), 145.
19. Scales, *Certain Victory*, 36.
20. Barbara Allen, Paula O'Loughlin, Amy Jasperson, and John L. Sullivan, "The Media and the Gulf War: Framing, Priming, and the Spiral of Silence," *Polity* 27:2 (Winter 1994), 270.
21. Ibid.
22. CENTCOM is the United States Central Command, the joint military command responsible for military operations in the Middle East.
23. Shimko, *The Iraq Wars*, 1.
24. Marita Sturken, *Tangled Memories: The Vietnam War, the Aids Epidemic, and the Politics of Remembering* (Berkeley: University of California Press, 1997), 137.
25. Howard Schuman and Cheryl Rieger, "Historical Analogies, Generational Effects, and Attitudes Towards War," *American Sociological Review* 57:3 (June 1992), 316.
26. Kendrick, "The Never Again Narratives," 131.
27. Ibid., 134.
28. Ginna Husting, "When a War Is Not a War: Abortion, Desert Storm, and Representations of Protest in American TV News," *The Sociological Quarterly* 40:1 (Winter 1999), 162.
29. Alex Vernon, "The Gulf War and Postmodern Memory," *The Wilson Quarterly* 25:1 (Winter 2001), 68.
30. Ibid., 77.
31. Barbara Norrander and Clyde Wilcox, "Rallying Around the Flag and Partisan Change: The Case of the Persian Gulf War," *Political Research Quarterly* 46:4 (December 1993), 766.

32 Alex Vernon, *The Eyes of Orion: Five Tank Lieutenants in the Persian Gulf War* (Kent, OH: The Kent State University Press, 1999), 266.
33 Ibid.
34 Michael R. Gordon and General Bernard E. Trainor, *The General's War: The Inside Story of the Conflict in the Gulf* (Boston: Little, Brown and Company, 1995), 443.
35 Saddam brutally suppressed rebellions by Iraqi Shiites and Kurdish minorities in the months after the ceasefire. See Gordon and Trainor, *General's War*, 448–449.
36 Kendrick, "The Never Again Narratives," 129–130.
37 Gordon and Trainor, *General's War*, xii.
38 Ibid., 463.
39 Vernon, "The Gulf War and Postmodern Memory," 72.
40 Andrew J. Bacevich, "A Less Than Splendid Little War," *The Wilson Quarterly* 25:1 (Winter 2001), 83–84.
41 Ibid., 83.
42 Sturken, *Tangled Memories*, 124.
43 Ibid., 136.
44 Jeanne Colleran, "Disposable Wars, Disappearing Acts: Theatrical Responses to the 1991 Gulf War," *Theater Journal* 55:4 (December 2003), 622.
45 Vernon, "The Gulf War and Postmodern Memory," 79.
46 The postmodern French philosopher Jean Baudrillard (1929–2007) published a series of controversial essays in which he argued that the Gulf War was conducted and presented as a media spectacle. The intentionally provocative title reflected his interpretation of the conflict as a simulation of reality, where spectacle replaced harsh realities. Like Vernon, Baudrillard wished to refute the notion of a clean war. See Jean Baudrillard, *The Gulf War Did Not Take Place* (Bloomington: Indiana University Press, 1995).
47 Vernon, "The Gulf War and Postmodern Memory," 82.
48 Ibid., 73.
49 Colleran, "Disposable Wars," 618.
50 Shimko, *The Iraq Wars*, 54.
51 Alberto Bin, Richard Hill, and Archer Jones, *Desert Storm: A Forgotten War* (Westport: Praeger Publishers, 1998), 32.
52 Schuman and Rieger, "Historical Analogies," 316, 318.
53 Richard S. Lowery, *The Gulf War Chronicles: A Military History of the First War with Iraq* (New York: iUniverse Star, 2003), 220.
54 Suzanne L. Parker, "Toward an Understanding of Rally Effects: Public Opinion in the Persian Gulf War," *The Public Opinion Quarterly* 59:4 (Winter 1995), 526.
55 Norrander and Wilcox, "Rallying Around the Flag and Partisan Change," 761.
56 Ibid.
57 Allen, "Media and the Gulf War," 260.
58 Parker, "Rally Effects," 541.
59 Lotte Larsen, "The Yellow Ribboning of America: A Gulf War Phenomenon," *Journal of American Culture* 17:1 (March 1994), 11.
60 The Iranian hostage crisis involved the seizure of the American Embassy in Tehran by militant Iranian students as part of the Iranian revolution against the Shah of Iran. In total, 52 American diplomats and citizens were held hostage for 444 days (November 4, 1979–January 20, 1981).
61 Tad Tuleja, "Closing the Circle: Yellow Ribbons and the Redemption of the Past," *Journal of American Culture* 17:1 (March 1994), 25.
62 Larsen, "Yellow Ribboning," 12.
63 Ibid., 16.
64 Ibid., 21.
65 Schuman and Rieger, "Historical Analogies," 316.
66 John Carlos Rowe, "The Vietnam Effect in the Persian Gulf War," *Cultural Critique* 19 (Autumn 1991), 122.
67 Scales, *Certain Victory*, 355.

68 Tuleja, "Closing the Circle," 27.
69 Larsen, "Yellow Ribboning," 20.
70 Rowe, "The Vietnam Effect," 126.
71 Thomas D. Beamish, Harvey Molotch, and Richard Flacks, "Who Supports the Troops? Vietnam, the Gulf War, and the Making of Collective Memory," *Social Problems* 42:3 (August 1995), 345.
72 Kendrick, "The Never Again Narratives," 129.
73 Sturken, *Tangled Memories*, 143.
74 Colin Powell with Joseph E. Persico, *Colin Powell: My American Journey* (New York: Random House, 1995), 532.
75 Scales, *Certain Victory*, 355–356.
76 Stephen A. Borque, *Jayhawk! The VII Corps in the Persian Gulf War* (Washington, DC: Department of the Army, 2002), 448.
77 Scales, *Certain Victory*, 340.
78 Alice L. Henry, "Desert Storm—the Parades: Overkill," *Off Our Backs* 21:7 (July 1991), 8.
79 Atkinson, *Crusade*, 488.
80 See National Desert Storm War Memorial website, http://www.ndswm.org/.
81 See US Army Quartermaster Corps, http://www.quartermaster.army.mil/oqmg/professional_bulletin/units/14th_QM_Det.htm.
82 Bacevich, "A Less than Splendid Little War," 87–94.
83 Ibid., 94.
84 Gordon and Trainor, *General's War*, 468.
85 Sturken, *Tangled Memories*, 124–125.
86 Vernon, "The Gulf War and Postmodern Memory," 76.
87 The Veteran's Administration defines Gulf War Syndrome as a cluster of medically unexplained chronic symptoms, or "chronic multisymptom illness." The VA does not use the term "Gulf War Syndrome." See Veteran's Administration website: http://www.publichealth.va.gov/exposures/gulfwar/medically-unexplained-illness.asp (accessed 25 June 2016).
88 Sturken, *Tangled Memories*, 144.
89 H. Norman Schwarzkopf with Peter Petre, *It Doesn't Take a Hero* (New York: Bantam Books, 1992), 497.
90 Gordon and Trainor, *General's War*, 461.
91 Earl H. Tilford, Jr., "The Meaning of Victory in Operation Desert Storm: A Review Essay," *Political Science Quarterly* 108:2 (Summer 1993), 330. See also Roger Hilsman, *George Bush vs. Saddam Hussein: Military Success! Political Failure?* (New York: Presidio Press, 1992).
92 Atkinson, *Crusade*, 495.
93 Bacevich, "A Less than Splendid Little War," 94.

# CONCLUSION

*Derek R. Mallett*

The essays in this volume illustrate several key themes about the evolution of public memory. That monuments say more about their builders than they do about the event or individual being memorialized is almost a truism in memory studies. The four nations' monuments considered in these chapters support this contention as well. Yet they also reveal that honoring individual identity on a memorial can sometimes transform that monument into something sacred, and that even the most contentious of wars can be memorialized in a way that creates a hallowed space for those who come to commemorate and to grieve. This volume also illustrates the extent to which the public often negotiates memory based on very practical present concerns. Financial support for infrastructure, military and diplomatic support for national survival, and profits from a thriving tourism industry all rank as concerns worthy of renegotiating a public's portrayal of the past. Historical accuracy and popular narrative sometimes diverge where national survival begins. Finally, the continual need for a nation to take pride in its past—perhaps its past wars, in particular—also leads to the evolution and re-evaluation of public memory. Pride buoys a nation in the midst of a devastating war. It can reshape a nation's aspirations and its role in international affairs. And wars seemingly fought with one goal in mind can be repurposed by later generations in search of pride in their past.

Uri Rosenheck defines a monument as a "man-made artifact that commemorates a human deed for eternity by its mere existence." The chapters in the first section of this volume, entitled "Monumental Conflicts: The Sacred and the Political," analyze four nations' war monuments. These essays deal with physical representations of the past, or tangible sites of memory, as opposed to intangible historical representations. Yet these sites contribute to public memory just as any portrayal of the past in a book, movie, or work of art might. And, as William Allison notes, public monuments and memorials are "without exception political."

So, what do these monuments and the collective memories they contribute say about society? Two main themes emerge from these four chapters. First, whether

British, American, Brazilian, or German, all these monuments speak to the values and perspectives of the period in which they were constructed. As the historian Patrick Hagopian states, all commemorations "are as much—sometimes more—about those who remember as they are about the objects of remembrance."[1] These examples provide no exception.

A second important theme arises from these chapters as well. They point to the difference between monuments that generate mainly political responses and those that create personal connections with the public. Hanna Smyth provides a compelling description of the IWGC's creation of "secular sacred spaces" at World War I memorials by including individual names on many of the monuments. Rules prohibiting any name being listed more than once honored individual identity and thereby created a physical "touchstone" for each missing individual in the same manner that a headstone in a cemetery does for the deceased whose body is buried beneath it. Visitors to these memorials to the missing naturally treat them as "sacred places," according to Smyth, where the dead are "guaranteed respect and admiration by virtually all segments of society."

William Allison's discussion of war monuments on the US National Mall in Washington, DC, illustrates a similar sacralization of a public space in at least one instance. The Vietnam Veterans Memorial remains, arguably, the most compelling monument on the mall. Part of the reason for its poignancy has to do, of course, with the highly politicized nature of the war itself. Yet what is also striking is the extent to which the monument succeeded in creating the same kind of "secular sacred space" in America that Hanna Smyth describes in IWGC World War I memorials. Because the Vietnam Veterans Memorial lists the individual names of all of the dead and missing from the war, it too creates a nexus between those who lost their lives in the war and those left behind. As Smyth also noted concerning IWGC memorials, traveling to see the Vietnam Veterans Memorial constitutes a "pilgrimage," whereas visiting the imposing World War II Memorial nearby smacks more of American nationalistic tourism.

Uri Rosenheck observes a similar personal connection with some of Brazil's World War II monuments. Rosenheck argues that numerous small, rural Brazilian communities continue to exhibit strong ties to their local World War II monuments because of the more personal nature of the war for these communities. Those in smaller communities were much more likely to know or even be related to one of the veterans from that community who served in the war, thus personalizing the memorial to some degree. Additionally, because the monuments emphasize the community's contributions to the war effort, as opposed to honoring a specific individual or military unit, they still resonate with local patrons as sources of community pride.

These four essays also raise other fascinating questions. Societies typically view military desertion as criminal. Yet, as Steven Welch demonstrates, some German monument-builders reasoned that, since the World War II German military—the *Wehrmacht*—had engaged in a "criminal war of annihilation," the act of deserting from the *Wehrmacht* was legitimate, indeed honorable. In other words, desertion from a military engaged in illegal or immoral activity is worthy of respect and commemoration. This contention has broad implications. What about deserters from other militaries that conducted "illegal" or "immoral" wars? Should we draw a distinction between those who simply deserted and then sat out the rest of the war and those who subsequently fought against the forces they had abandoned? And just how grossly illegal or immoral does a war have to be in order to justify desertion from the military waging it? Where are the lines to be drawn?

The idea that desertion from a military waging an immoral war is honorable appears to be gaining some traction in the United States as well. In 2016, STX Entertainment released a film entitled *Free State of Jones*. The film, based on actual events, chronicles a band of southern Unionists in the American Civil War. These men, largely deserters from the Confederate army, fight an insurgency against the Confederate government from their base in Jones County, Mississippi. The film portrays the group's leader, Newton Knight—played by Matthew McConaughey—as a hero for his opposition to the wealthy Southern planter class and the Confederate government that fought to maintain the institution of slavery. The implication, of course, is that the Confederacy had championed an immoral cause, making Knight's and his comrades' desertion worthy of commemoration.[2]

In the American Civil War, the Confederate military indeed represented a slaveholding power. Yet they did not commit the genocide and horrific atrocities that the *Wehrmacht* carried out in World War II. In regard to legitimizing military desertion, should we consider the difference between *jus ad bellum*—was the war waged for just reasons—and *jus in bello*—was the war conducted in a just manner? The *Wehrmacht* fails to meet either criterion. It waged an unjust war in horrendous fashion. But, while there is considerable debate about the causes of the American Civil War, there are few accusations that the Confederate military as a whole fought in an unjust fashion, except in the case of its treatment of black Union soldiers in the later years of the war. Does this make deserters from the Confederate army such as Newton Knight less worthy of commemoration than those from the World War II German military?

Commemorating desertion from militaries engaged in unjust wars, even if those militaries are conducting themselves in a just fashion, opens still further considerations. In the US war with Mexico in the mid-1840s, a group of recent Irish immigrants deserted from the US Army. They defected and formed a new unit called the San Patricio (St. Patrick's) Battalion, which fought for Mexico until the US Army captured them at the Battle of Churubusco in 1847. Following two separate courts-martial, the US Army hanged two thirds of the San Patricios for their desertion. Following the war, the Mexican government erected a memorial plaque in the battalion's honor on the grounds where some of the executions took place. Many historians might now consider the US war against Mexico to have been an unjust war of territorial conquest. So, how should the American public remember the San Patricios?

Any potential reconsideration of the San Patricios' desertion would seem to be a thornier proposition than the case of deserters from the *Wehrmacht*. First, the

American war in Mexico and the resulting territorial acquisition is clearly not of the same type as the genocidal war of annihilation waged by the Nazis in World War II. So, perhaps like the Confederacy in the Civil War, the causes of the US war with Mexico are debatable, but the US Army's conduct of it was largely just. Again, then, how unjust, immoral, or illegal does a war have to be in order to justify desertion from the military waging it? And is it appropriate for individual soldiers to make that determination? Moreover, like Newton Knight in the Civil War, the San Patricios actually defected; that is, they not only deserted, but in fact switched sides and fought against their former comrades in arms. Should this shape how we view their desertion, even if we could agree that the US Army was waging an unjust war at the time?

What about the most controversial of all American wars, the war in Vietnam? Would Americans ever consider honoring deserters or draft-dodgers from this conflict in the way that Germans commemorate deserters from the *Wehrmacht* in World War II? Clearly, the question becomes thornier still. While many view the American war in Vietnam as a mistake, the relative justness of the causes of the war remains debatable. Furthermore, what atrocities may have been committed by American troops in Vietnam pales by comparison to those committed by German forces in World War II. So, again, does this make desertion from the US military in Vietnam less honorable? What criteria should be used to make that determination?

Finally, Welch also notes that some German monument-builders simply honored the principle of desertion. This may be the thorniest proposition of all. Should it matter whether the desertion occurred prior to combat or in the midst of the fight? Are conscripted soldiers who desert more honorable than those who volunteered to serve and then deserted? What does one soldier's desertion mean for their fellow soldiers who rely on the deserter's expertise, protection, support, or medical service? Should we view conscientious objectors—those who refused military service on principle—in a different light than deserters who abandoned their posts after the fighting began? Clearly, the effects of desertion can extend far beyond simple opposition to killing. How can we determine when that is honorable?

The second section of essays in this collection examines negotiated public memories. Local populations adjust their conceptions of past wars for political and economic reasons. Public memory of wars waged by colonial or imperial powers evolves as the local need to attract investment or appease political demands from these powers continues. Consequently, current circumstances require negotiating remembrance of the past, and often distort it in fascinating ways.

The chapters by Brendan Wright and Christina Schwenkel point to the influence of the "industry of memory," as described by Viet Thanh Nguyen, over the ways in which the Korean War and the Vietnam War are portrayed and commemorated within these countries. In South Korea, the state has long viewed US military and financial aid as vital to its survival. Thus, as Wright demonstrates, the war was commemorated, portrayed, and taught to children in a manner that suited American tastes, best ensuring the continuance of that support. And with both the "Korean War" and the "Vietnam War"—the American labels for these conflicts—who has a greater ability to shape our images of that war than the American film industry? Nguyen notes that Vietnamese films about the American war in Vietnam are little known outside Vietnam, whereas Hollywood distributes its films all around the world.[3] The same could be said of the Korean films examined by Wright in this volume. Consequently, what most of the world sees in stark images is the American story of these wars, not the Korean or Vietnamese versions.

All three of the chapters in this section reveal that those nations with the greatest resources have the greatest influence on public memory. Would Palauans remember the Battle for Peleliu, the Koreans the Korean War, or the Vietnamese the Vietnam War as they do without the need for Japanese or American resources? And would public memory feature the Japanese and American perspectives so strongly if these two nations' financial resources were not so extensive? "The memories of the wealthy and the powerful exert more influence because they own the means of production," Nguyen observes. "So, too, are their feelings and memories the most powerful, made, packaged, distributed, and exported in ways that overshadow the feelings and memories of the weak."[4]

Stephen Murray's chapter also presents a timely comparison between the struggle of conflicting Japanese interests to control the memory of the Battle for Peleliu—and ultimately the Japanese role in World War II—and the current American reconsideration of its own Civil War past. Specifically, there seems to be a "war of monuments" occurring in the United States similar to that which Murray describes in Peleliu. One key difference, however, is that the Japanese groups in Peleliu built competing monuments, while the conflict in the US is more a struggle to decide whether to remove existing ones.

Much of the ongoing American controversy was sparked by the murder of a number of African Americans at a church in Charleston, South Carolina, in June 2015. Less than a year after the national uproar over the death of Michael Brown in Ferguson, Missouri, avowed white supremacist Dylann Roof unrepentantly shot and killed nine black parishioners. Roof's social media glorification of the Confederacy, its iconic battle flag in particular, surfaced after the murders. This prompted a visceral reaction from various government and private interests across the country.

Little more than a week after the murders, the US National Park Service requested that all of its vendors remove Confederate flag items from their gift shops. More significantly, after decades of flying the Confederate battle flag on capitol grounds, South Carolina state officials chose to remove it, largely as a public relations response to Roof's heinous act. The move garnered applause from those who see the flag as a divisive symbol of racism and white supremacy. Those who defend public display of the flag and the presence of Confederate monuments argue that these symbols simply represent Southern heritage; regardless, the tide seemed to have turned. In August 2015, the University of Texas removed its long-present statue of Confederate President Jefferson Davis. Two months later, the University of Mississippi announced it would no longer fly the Mississippi state flag because it features an inset of the Confederate battle flag. In 2016, Vanderbilt University removed a Confederate inscription from one of its halls, and the University of Louisville removed its statue honoring Confederate soldiers from Kentucky.

As of April 2017, Dylann Roof's mass murder had prompted the removal or renaming of "at least 60 such publicly funded symbols of the Confederacy."[5] In the same year, the groundswell for removal of Confederate relics only increased. Civil leaders in Charlottesville, Virginia, voted to remove a statue of Confederate General Robert E. Lee, although, at the time of this writing, the measure was still being contested in court. In May 2017, the city of New Orleans, Louisiana, followed suit removing all of its remaining Confederate monuments, including statues of Robert E. Lee, Jefferson Davis, and two others. Less than a month later, St. Louis, Missouri, began taking steps to remove a Confederate monument from a prominent city park. Ironically, the monument was so nondescript that few St. Louis residents even realized what it commemorated until the drive to remove it began.[6]

All of this demonstrates the evolution and contested nature of public memory. This debate also illustrates, once again, that monuments say more about those who build them—or tear them down—than they do about the events the monuments purport to commemorate. Have the events of the past few years reshaped collective memory of the "Lost Cause," or is the removal of Confederate monuments and battle flags simply a fleeting, knee-jerk reaction to a heinous crime? As with the Japanese "war of monuments" on Peleliu, would building monuments to more leaders of the civil rights movement in the United States, or perhaps even slaves who fought for their freedom, shape public memory in more enduring ways?

Consider Nat Turner. Turner was born into slavery in Southampton County, Virginia, at the turn of the nineteenth century. In the early hours of August 22, 1831, Turner and a handful of confidants broke into the home of Turner's owner and murdered him and his family in their sleep. Thus began a killing spree where the escaped slaves struck plantation after plantation, killing slave-owners and their families. Turner and his fellow slaves eventually murdered between 55 and 60 whites in the two-day spree. Is Nat Turner the kind of person a society should commemorate? After all, he professed to have visions and saw natural phenomena such as solar eclipses as signs from God. More importantly, he murdered dozens of men, women, and children in their beds. Is breaking the law ever justified, particularly if an unjust government established that law? Was Turner's illegal activity justified because it was perpetuated against a slaveholding society? To what lengths would any of us be justified in going to win our freedom and that of our loved ones? Confederate sympathizers suggest that Robert E. Lee and thousands of other Southerners were justified, even honorable, in fighting and killing in an attempt to obtain their "states' rights." Is a man who had been born into slavery and forced to endure slavery his entire life justified in killing for his freedom? Is Turner worthy of commemoration?

The chapters in the third section overwhelmingly reflect national pride. Pride in a war or a particular aspect of a war distracts the public from distasteful circumstances. Pride in a "just cause" elevates public memories of a past war. Additionally, modern society seems to have entered an era in which public support for soldiers themselves remains high despite any criticism, even condemnation, of the respective wars in which these soldiers fought.

Guillaume de Syon's essay about the myths of World War I aviation reveals a potential connection to modern popular film. Movie enthusiasts still seem drawn to films about fighter pilots, or "knights of the air," as de Syon refers to them. Does the attraction to films such as *Top Gun* (1986), *Iron Eagle* (1986), *Independence Day* (1996), *Pearl Harbor* (2001), and *Flyboys* (2006) stem from our earlier fascination with aviation in World War I?

The chapters by Davide Borsani and Robert Jones underscore an instructive difference in the use of the term "syndrome." Borsani refers to "Falklands Syndrome" to mean British confidence in using the military to address international issues—a confidence generated by their earlier victory in the Falklands War. Meanwhile, Robert Jones uses the term "Gulf War Syndrome." This refers to "medically unexplained chronic symptoms" among Gulf War veterans, including "fatigue, headaches, joint pain, indigestion, insomnia, dizziness, respiratory disorders, and memory problems."[7] Clearly, these two writers employ the term "syndrome" to mean very different things in relation to the respective wars they examine. Yet the different usages may represent a peculiar similarity: an unexpected result from each war. Borsani chronicles the manner in which victory in the Falklands restored British confidence in the international arena, an enduring phenomenon that Thatcher did not anticipate when she first ordered British troops to the South Atlantic. Similarly, Jones insinuates that the surprising frequency of Gulf War Syndrome reflects the contested nature of the Persian Gulf War, with its reputation as a clean, high-tech war at odds with the fact that thousands of its veterans suffer a mysterious malady.[8]

The chapters in this final section also speak to pride. What is striking, however, is the degree to which pride can emerge decades after the conclusion of wars that were highly controversial at the time they were waged. Society's continual re-evaluation of its past surely contributes to this process. Nevertheless, it also seems to be part of a general late twentieth- and early twenty-first-century public appreciation for the sacrifices made by soldiers. Robert Jones illustrates that, by the time of the Persian Gulf War in 1991, the American public felt compelled to make amends for its earlier neglect of veterans from the Vietnam War. Indeed, Jones argues that righting this earlier wrong against Vietnam veterans provided part of the motivation for the popular yellow ribbon campaign that emerged during the Gulf War. For the most part, the Vietnam vets welcomed the reception and participated in the ceremonies for the returning Gulf War veterans. Moreover, according to Jones, even opponents of the Gulf War protested in a manner that differentiated between the troops, for whom they showed support, and the war itself, which they opposed. It is noteworthy that Americans wished to show belated appreciation for soldiers who had fought two decades earlier in the most divisive war in American history. Curiously, Roger Reese demonstrates a similar evolution in Russia with veterans from the Soviet–Afghan War. Roughly 25 years later, the Russian public appreciates the service and sacrifices of their veterans from a war that was barely reported at the time and looked on with shame in the 1990s. Much like Americans, the Russian public came to distinguish between the respectable role the soldiers played and the controversial war that their government waged.

This ability to differentiate soldiers from the wars in which they fought seems to continue in the United States. William Allison notes the already developing plans for a memorial to veterans from the Global War on Terror. These veterans have long enjoyed enormous respect and appreciation from the American public, even though few Americans appreciate how involved the US military still is in both Iraq and Afghanistan. Curiously, Jones and Reese also illustrate how the Global War on Terror sparked an American re-evaluation of the Persian Gulf War and a Russian re-evaluation of the Soviet–Afghan War, yet with seemingly opposite results. Where Russians began to see their war more positively because of the struggling American military endeavor in Afghanistan more than a decade later, Americans became more skeptical of the Persian Gulf War because of the subsequent US invasion of Iraq in 2003. One wonders how the Global War on Terror will be remembered a generation from now. If Iraq is a functioning democracy and Afghanistan is no longer a haven for terrorists, will the US military be commemorated as a champion of republican ideals and the vanguard against violent extremism? Or will it be remembered as the tool of an American empire in the Middle East? And will the public still differentiate between the role played by military service members and the relative justness of the wars in which they served?

Jones' discussion of American memory of the Persian Gulf War also provides one more example of the power of the American industry of memory. Nguyen contends: "The blast radius of memory, like the blast radius of weaponry, is determined by industrial power, even if individual will shapes the act of memory itself."[9] Consequently, while the American military continues to display superior technology and overwhelming force, it also displays the overwhelming ability to shape the memory of its wars for succeeding generations of Americans and others around the world. Similarly, Hanna Smyth notes that the Imperial War Graves Commission's ability to commemorate the lost and missing from World War I emerged from the still vast resources of the early twentieth-century British Empire and its victory in the war. Likewise, William Allison's description of the American "War Mall" weighs the extent to which even American monuments influence international memory of these wars. As Nguyen laments, "countries with massive war machines not only inflict more damage on weaker countries, they also justify that damage to the world. How America remembers this war and memory is to some extent how the world remembers it."[10]

Regarding war memorials, Patrick Hagopian writes that "In themselves they are inert objects and they become meaningful only as they prompt or provoke human responses."[11] And, as Uri Rosenheck adds, "Observers must constantly assign the monument meaning." The same should be said of intangible forms of public memory as well. Each generation must see itself reflected in the popular narrative of a war for it to resonate with the public. Hence, each generation must assign its own meaning to the past. This explains a great deal about how public memory evolves and why.

What does public memory say about society? It says that present concerns—politics, survival, and pride—shape our view of the past. Of course, as one "present" gives way to the next, so too do the concerns of the time change. Each "present" needs to negotiate its memory of the past in a manner that meets its own needs. Thus, memory evolves alongside and in much the same way that societies do.

## Notes

1 Patrick Hagopian, *The Vietnam War in American Memory: Veterans, Memorials, and the Politics of Healing* (Amherst: University of Massachusetts Press, 2009), 5.
2 Matthew E. Stanley, film review of *Free State of Jones*. Gary Ross, director, screenplay writer, and producer; Jon Kilik and Scott Stuber, producers. STX Entertainment, 2016. 140 minutes. *The Public Historian* 39:2 (May 2017), 95–99.
3 Viet Thanh Nguyen, *Nothing Ever Dies: Vietnam and the Memory of War* (Cambridge, MA: Harvard University Press, 2016), 156–172.
4 Ibid., 107.
5 "Weekend Read: The State of the Confederacy in 2017," Southern Poverty Law Center, April 28, 2017. https://www.splcenter.org/news/2017/04/28/weekend-read-state-confederacy-2017 (accessed 15 June 2017).
6 Julie Bosman, "Few in St. Louis Knew Confederate Memorial Existed. Now, Many Want It Gone," *New York Times*, May 26, 2017.
7 "Gulf War Veterans' Medically Unexplained Illnesses," *Public Health*, US Department of Veterans Affairs. https://www.publichealth.va.gov/exposures/gulfwar/medically-unexplained-illness.asp.
8 The author wishes to thank memory scholar Bradley Keefer for helping to shape his thoughts on some of the themes raised in this chapter, the connection between World War I aviation and modern fighter-pilot films, and the use of the term "syndrome" in particular.
9 Nguyen, *Nothing Ever Dies*, 108.
10 Ibid.
11 Hagopian, *The Vietnam War in American Memory*, 20.

# INDEX

14th Division (Japanese) 93
14th Quartermaster Detachment United States Army Reserve 211–12
16th Royal Sussex Regiment 21
24th Infantry Division (Mechanized) (US) 205
29th Division 25
51st (Highland) Division 25
*60 Minutes* 48
76th Infantry Division (German) 81
81st Infantry Division (United States) 100
82nd Infantry Regiment (German) 78
9/11 terrorist attacks on the United States 171, 179, 190, 192
*A força expedicionária brasileira* (FEB) 57, 59, 60, 61–5
Abel, Jules 151–2
Accrington Pals memorial 21
Acheson, Dean 166
Adorno, Theodore 124
Afghan people 182, 183
Afghan Syndrome 172, 190
Afghanistan veterans' organizations 190
Afghanistan 171
*Afghantsy* 185, 186, 188, 190, 191, 193, 194, 195, 196
Afghanvet (St. Petersburg's association of)
Agent Orange 143
Ahwaz 23
AK-47 135
Aksoy, Mehmet 76, 77
Albright College 8
Algeria 194

*All Quiet on the Western Front* 79, 155
Allison, William Thomas 5–6, 217, 218, 224
All-Russia Public Movement of Veterans of Local Wars and Military Conflicts 188
All-Union Center for the Study of Public Opinion (VTsIOM) 193
Almog, Oz 57
Al-Qaeda 173, 190–1
Amazon 56, 61
American air siege of Babeldoab 92–5, 105
American amphibious landing vehicle 98
American Battle Monuments Commission 42, 49, 50, 51
American Civil War 41, 42, 219–20, 221, 222
American Comic Code Authority 160
American exhumation of bodies from Peleliu 97
American Revolutionary War 42
American Signal Corps 158
"American War" 131, 132, 135
Amiden, Jamil 62
Amiens 21, 24
Amin, Hafizullah 180–1, 193
Amnesty International 123
*An den Schießständen* 75
Andersch, Alfred 70, 78
Andropov, Iuri 181
Angaur Island 93, 96, 97, 100
Angaur, battle of 99, 100, 103
Anglo-American "special relationship" 171

Anglo-American invasion of Iraq (2003) 171
anti-communism 111–13, 117, 119, 121
anti-Nazi resistance 85
Antwerp (Belgium) 156
Apotheosis of Washington 43
April Revolution of 1978 (Afghanistan) 181, 182, 184, 187
Arab coalition forces 203
Araneta, Gemma Cruz 140, 143
Architect of the Capitol 44
Argentina 167, 168, 169, 172, 173, 174
*Argumenty i fakty* 195
Arlington National Cemetery 211
Arlington National Cemetery 44, 45
Ash Woods 49
Asquith, Herbert 15
Association of Southeast Asian Nations (ASEAN) 132
Atkinson, Rick 213
Axis 56, 60

Babeldoab Island 93, 95, 97, 102
Bacevich, Andrew J. 206, 212, 213
"backpacker" economy 131, 134, 135
Baden-Württemberg 70
Baez, Joan 139–40, 141, 142, 143
Baker, Herbert 15, 28
Bali 139
Balkans 78, 205
Barbusse, Henri 154
Barnett, Anthony 171
Basmachi tribe 181, 182, 187
battle exploit memorials 20
Baumann, Ludwig 77
Bavarian Parliament 73
*British Broadcasting Corporation (BBC)* 168
Beaumont-Hamel in the Somme, Newfoundland memorial 20, 24–5
Beaumont-Hamel 18, 26, 30
Bellenger, Georges 150
Bền Đình (Vietnam) 134
Bền Du'ọ'c (Vietnam) 134
Bền Hải River 136
Bereaved Family Associations (*yukjokhoe*) 117–18, 119, 121
Berlin Wall 75, 111
Berlin, battle of 193
Berthelot, Henri 150
Bible 16
Bible, King James 17
Bix, Herbert 100
Black Revolutionary War Patriots Memorial 39
Blair, Tony 175
Blériot (aircraft) 152

Blériot, Louis 149
Blomfield, Reginald 15
Bloody Nose Ridge 99, 101
Boelcke, Oswald 154
Böll, Heinrich 70
Boniface, Susie 174
Bonn (Germany) 75, 78
Borovik, Artem 186
Borsani, Davide 8, 223
Braunschweig (Germany) 84
Bremen (Germany) 72, 73, 74, 83
Brezhnev regime 188
British Armed Forces 175
Brodin, Roger M. 47
Brown, J. Carter 51
Buenos Aires (Argentina) 167
*Bundesbahn* (Germany Railway) 80
Bundestag 85
*Bundeswehr* 73
Bush, George H. W. 201, 204, 205, 206, 208, 210, 211

California-Riverside, University of 7
Cameron, David 172, 173, 175
Camp Carroll 137
Canadian War Museum 162
Capitol Hill 204
Capps, Chris 77
Carleton University (Canada) 7
carriers of memory 180
Castor and Pollux 26
Castro, Alicia 173
CBS News 45
CENTCOM 204, 206
Central America 71
Central Asia 181
Central Museum of the Great Patriotic War 195
Ch'oe In-hun 116
Chaplin, Charlie 139
Charleston, South Carolina 221
*Charley's War* 160
Charlottesville, Virginia 222
Chechens 190
Chechnya 194
Cheju 4.3 Peace Park 120
Cheju incident 117
Cheju Island 111, 115–16, 117
Cheju Province (Korea) 117
Chevalier, Gabriel 155
Chicago, Illinois 211
China 182
chivalry 159
Cho Chŏng-nae 119, 122
Chŏlla Province (Korea) 117

# 228 Index

Chŏng Chi-yŏng 122
Christian Democratic Union 70
Christians 111, 112, 121
Christie, Denis H. 21
Christie, Richard F. 21
Christmas bombing (1972) 133, 139, 141
Christmas Truce of 1914: 159
Chun Doo-hwan 118
Churilov, Dmitrii 191
Churubusco, battle of 219
Cimino, Michael 45
Cincinnatus 42
Citino, Robert 203
City Beautiful Movement 43
Clark Air Base, Philippines 135
Clinton, Bill 142
Cloud, David 96
CNN 204
Cold War 44–5, 49, 50, 60, 118, 165, 168, 171, 182, 189, 212
Colleran, Jeanne 207
Commission of Fine Arts 43, 45, 47, 49, 50, 51
Commonwealth War Graves Commission 14
Communist Afghan army 189
Communist Afghan government 190
Communist Party 183, 184
Communists 111–14, 115, 116, 118, 121, 122, 131
Confederate flag 221
Confederate military 219, 222
Confederate States of America 219–20
Congress of People's Deputies 187
conscientious objection 71
conscientious objectors 73
Conservative Party 169, 170, 175
Constitution Avenue (Washington, DC) 45
Constitution Gardens 5, 45, 51
Cooper-Lecky 50
Corbie communal cemetery 21
Corn, Joe 158
counter-revolutionaries 181, 182
Cowpens, battle of 42
Cross of Sacrifice 16, 18
Cruise missiles 205
Cù Chi Army Airfield 136
Cù Chi District (Vietnam) 134, 136
Cù Chi Tunnel Historical Remains 134
Cù Chi tunnels 130, 132, 133–5, 136, 138, 141, 142
Cuba 194
cultural memory 2

D'annnzio, Gabriele 158
Daddow, Oliver 175

*Daily Mail* 167
*Daily Mirror* 167–8, 173
DaMatta, Roberto 64
Dammtor railway station (Hamburg) 81
Dân Chù 139
Davis, Jefferson 221, 222
Day of Memory and Sorrow (22 June) 193
Day of Remembrance of Russians who Served Abroad 194–5
Day of the Internationalist Warrior 194
de Syon, Guillaume 8, 223
Debauche, Leslie Midkiff 158
Defenders of the Fatherland Day (23 February) 193
Defence White Paper (1981) 166
Delville Wood, South African national memorial 15, 23, 26
Demilitarized Zone (DMZ) (17th parallel, Vietnam) 132, 136, 141
Demilitarized Zone 111–12
Democratic Republic of Afghanistan (DRA) 180
*dép lốp (tire sandals)* 134
*Der Rote Kampfflieger* 155
*Desert Storm: The Victory* (CNN) 205
*Desert Triumph* (CBS) 205
deserter-monument movement 69–85
DeWeldon, Felix 44
Dhahran (Saudia Arabia) 211
Dix, Otto 156
DMZ Hotel 137
DMZ tour 136
Dolski, Michael R. 4
Dorgelès, Roland 150–1
Doss, Erika 3, 40, 48–49
Dower, John 106
*Dushmany* 181, 182, 187

Eastwood, Clint 1–2
*Ecclesiasticus* 44:14, 17
Edkins, Jenny 40
Egypt 194
Egyptians 41, 42
Eich, Günter 80
Eighth Conference of American Armies 60
*eirei* 99–100
Eisenhower, Dwight 204
Emperor Akihito of Japan 91, 93, 95, 96, 98, 100, 102, 104, 105, 106
Emperor Hirohito of Japan 91, 96, 100
Empress Michiko of Japan 91
Enola Gay 162
Erfurt (Germany) 79–80, 83
*Estado Novo* (New State) 56

Evans, Diane Carlson 47
*Evening Glow (Noŭl)* 116

Falkland Islands 166–76
"Falklands consensus" 173, 175
"Falklands Factor" 169, 170, 171, 172, 175
"Falklands syndrome" 171, 223
fascism 61, 157–58
Faulkner, William 155–6
*Febianos* 57, 62, 64
Federal Association of Victims of Nazi Military Justice 73, 77
Federal House of Representatives (Câmara Federal) (Brazil) 62
Female Mourner sculpture 30
Ferguson, Missouri 221
fern symbol (New Zealand) 21
Ferraz, Francisco Alves 60
Filbinger affair 70
Filbinger, Hans 70
First Gulf War 171, 202–13
*Flyboys* 223
Fonck, René 151, 156
Fonda, Jane 139, 142, 143
Foot, Michael 168
Foster, Jeremy 19
France 182
*Frankfurter Rundschau* 73
Franklin D. Roosevelt Memorial 39, 49
Franklin D. Roosevelt 52
*Free State of Jones* 219
frog bunkers 142
Fussell, Paul 162

Gallup 205
Galtieri, Leopoldo 167, 173
Gardiner, Nile 174
Garros, Roland 150, 152
Gaskarth, Jamie 175
Gebessler, Renate 77
general secretary of the Communist Party 183
Geneva (Switzerland) 184
*George Bush vs. Saddam Hussein* 213
German Democratic Republic 75, 79
German Resistance Memorial Centre (Berlin) 85
German reunification 79
German union movement 79
"Germany 1944" 82
Germany's invasion of Poland in 1939 208
Gettysburg Address 40
Gettysburg 42
Gibbon, Floyd P. 155
*glasnost* 179, 182, 183, 186

global war on terror 190, 224
Gönner, Ivo 75
Goodacre, Glenna 48
Gorbachev, Mikhail 171, 179, 183, 184, 187
Gordon, Michael 213
Göttingen (Germany) 78–9, 83
Gough, Paul 26
Grave of the Unknown Soldier (Brazil) 60, 62
Great Patriotic War 185, 186, 191, 192, 193, 194
Greatest Generation 50, 52
Greece 41
Greeks 41
Green Party 70, 71, 72, 73, 75, 79, 80
Greensburg, Pennsylvania 211–12
Grenada 1
Gromov, Boris 188
Guanabara Theatre 62
guerilla food 135
*Guernica* 157
"Gulf War syndrome" 213, 223
Guynemer, Georges 149, 152, 154, 160

Hagopian, Patrick 218, 224
Hamburg (Germany) 80, 82, 83
"Hamburger Hill" 137, 143
Hammond, Philip 172
Hanoi (Vietnam) 133, 138–42
*Hanoi Diary* 140
Hart, Frederick 47
Hass, Kristin Ann 40
Hastings, Max 172
Hausmann, Brigitte 75
Hayden, Tom 139
*Heartbreak Ridge* 1–2
Heißenbüttel, Helmut 82
*Hell's Angels* 158
Henderson, Nicholas 165, 167
Hero of the Soviet Union 188
Hess, Elizabeth 47
Hideki, Tōjō 103, 104
Hiền Lu'o'ng Bridge 136
Highway 1 (Vietnam) 136
Highway 9 (Vietnam) 136, 137
Hilsman, George 213
*Hindenburg* 157
Hindu soldiers 17, 23
Hinduism 17, 22
Hiroshi, Funasaka 96–7, 99, 100, 103
Hiroshima stone 101, 106
Hitler, Adolf 69, 73, 75, 83, 173, 207
Hitler's Army 83, 84
HMS *Endurance* 167, 170

HMS *Invincible* 166, 167, 170
Ho Chi Minh City (Vietnam) 133, 134, 135
Hobsbawm, Eric 170
Hohenzollerns 76
Hollywood 135, 158
homosexuals 84
Hooge Crater cemetery 22
House of Commons 168, 169, 175
Hrdlicka, Alfred 81
Huế (Vietnam) 136
Hunt, Nigel 2
Hussein, Saddam 202, 206, 207, 208, 213
Hwang Sok-yong 121, 124
Hwang Sun-wŏn 115–16
Hyŏn Ki-yŏng 117

Im Kwŏn-taek 122
Immelmann turn 153
Immelmann, Max 153–4
Imperial Japanese Army (IJA) 92, 93, 95, 96, 99, 105
Imperial Japanese Navy (IJN) 92
Imperial War Graves Commission 5, 13–33, 218, 224
*Independence Day* 223
India Office 27
Indian soldiers 22, 28
Indianapolis 500 204
industry of memory 1, 3–4
International Committee for Afghan War Veterans' Affairs 195
internationalist duty 183, 185
Iran 182
Iranian hostage crisis 209
Iraq War 77
Iraq 78
Iraq/Afghanistan Wars 52, 53
Iraqi Army 213
Iraqi invasion of Kuwait 202
Iraqi Republican Guard 203
"Iraqi syndrome" 172
Ireidan ("Association for consoling souls") 97, 102, 103
Irish Republican Army (IRA) 173
*Iron Eagle* 223
Islam 182
Islamic State (ISIS) 191
Italian fascism 158

Japan Teachers' Union 96
Japanese colonial migrants in Palau 91–5
Japanese constitution 96, 101
Jeanjean, Marcel 151
Jefferson Memorial 38, 42, 43, 44
Joint Information Bureau (JIB) 204

Joint Investigation Headquarters 117
Jones, Robert T. 8–9, 223
*Journal of Contemporary History* 6
June Democratic Uprising 118
"June 25" narrative (*yugio*) 112, 118, 119, 120
July 1 (1916) 25
Jünger, Ernst 154
*jus ad bellum* 219
*jus in bello* 219

Karlsruhe (Germany) 71
Karmal, Babrak 181
Kassel (Germany) 70–1, 72, 73, 74, 83
Keegan, John 17
Kennedy, Laurel B. 133
Kentucky Derby 204
Kentucky 222
Kernbach, Nikolaus 77
Keynesian reforms 165
KGB 181
Khalq faction 181
Khe Sanh Combat Base 137–8
Khe Sanh Museum 138
Kim Chae-kyu 118
Kim Dae-jung 119
Kim Dong-choon 120
Kim Il-sung 113
Kim Jong-un 123
Kim Wŏn-il 116
Kim Young-sam 119
King Fahd of Saudi Arabia 202
King George III 41
Kipling, John ("Jack") 16, 17
Kipling, Rudyard 16, 17
Kirchner, Cristina Fernández de 172
Kirchner, Néstor Carlos 172
Knight, Newton 219, 220
Kŏch'ang Incident Memorial Park 120
*Kokutai* 96
Komsomol (the Young Communist League) 186
*Komsomolskaia Pravda* 183
Korean armistice 111
Korean CIA 118
Korean importation of American values 118–19
Korean reconciliation 121–2, 124
Korean War Memorial Advisory Board 49, 50
Korean War Veterans Memorial 38, 40, 49–50, 52
Korean War 44, 49, 50, 52, 111–24, 220–1
Koror (Palau) 93, 102

Koror Island 92
Kosovo 171
Kovalev, Alexander 189
*Krasnaia, zvezda* 186, 193
Kunio, Nakagawa 96, 99
Kuwait City (Kuwait) 203
Kuwait 202, 204, 207, 208, 213
Kwangju (South Korea) 118
Kyŏngsang Province (Korea) 117

L'Enfant, Pierre Charles 41, 42, 43
*L'Humanite* 184
Labour Party 168, 169
Lang, Volker 81
Laos 137, 194
Lawrence, D. H. 157
Lebed, Alexander 188
Lee Myung-bak 123
Lee, Robert E. 222
*Lens Being Bombed* 156
*Les Croix de bois* 151
Lewis, Michael F. 44
Liakhovskii, Aleksandr 189
Liberal Democratic Party (LDP) (Japanese) 104, 106
Lin, Maya 5, 45, 46, 51, 52
Lincoln Memorial 5, 38, 42, 43, 45, 49, 51, 52
Lindbergh, Charles 159
"Lingering Legacies of War" 130, 143
*Literaturnaia gazeta* 185
Little Big Horn, battle of 42
*Living Memory* initiative, CWGC 32
London (UK) 156, 166
Longworth, Philip 17
*Los Angeles Times* 96
loss of Peleliu's main power-generation plant 104
"Lost Cause" 222
Louis Vuitton 139
Louis, Sherard Cooper-Coles 166
Lowery, Richard 208
Lucas, William 30
Luytens, Edwin 15, 30, 46

M1A1 Abrams main battle tank 205
M2 Bradley infantry fighting vehicle 205
McConaughey, Matthew 219
McMillan Plan 43
McMillan, James 43
Macmillan, Maurice Harold 166, 169
Major, John 172
maple leaf symbol (Canada) 21
Marburg (Germany) 84
Mark, Bernard 152

Martin Luther King, Jr., Memorial 39, 49
*Marxism Today* 170
Mayo, James 59
Mecklenburg, Norbert 84
Medvedev, Dmitry 194
Meighen, Arthur 14, 18
Melbourne, University of 6
"Memorial mania" 3, 48–9
Memorial Site for Deserters and Other Victims of Nazi Military Justice 81
memorial to the missing 15
memorials to the dead and missing 20
memory industries 3
Menin Gate memorial 16, 19, 24, 30, 31
Messerschmidt, Manfred 78, 84
Metropole Hotel (Hanoi, Vietnam) 132, 133, 138–42
Mexico City, American cemetery 42
Micronesia 91, 96
Middle East 78, 172, 224
Midleton Committee (National Battlefields Memorial Committee) 20
Minas Gerais 62
Ministry of Health, Welfare, and Labor (HW&L) (Japanese) 97, 100
Minjung ideology 118–19, 121
Minsk (Belorus) 186
modern Korean history 118–19
Moon Jae-in 123
Morgenthau, Hans J. 171
MORI 167, 169
Morrow, John 153
Mortane, Jacques 151
Morvan, Jean 152
Moscow Province 188
Moscow regional association of Afghan veterans 189
Moscow, battle of 193
Mosse, George 149, 155
Mother Canada 28, 29
Moulinais, Brindejonc des 152
Mount Suribachi 44
Mujahideen 187, 190
Munich (Germany) 84
Murray, Stephen C. 7, 101, 221

Nakamura, Steven 101
*Nambugun* 122
Nan'yo Jinja (Koror) 100, 102
Nan'yō Kōryū Kyōkai (NKK) (Japan-Nan'yō Cultural Exchange Association) 101
Nan'yo 92, 93, 95, 97, 105
National Air and Space Museum (Smithsonian Institution) 161

National Capital Memorial Advisory Commission (NCMAC) 43
National Capital Park Commission 43
National Capital Planning Commission 43, 51
National Coalition to Save Our Mall 51
National Desert Storm War Memorial Association 211
national exploit memorials 20
National French Air and Space Museum 162
National Holocaust Memorial and Museum 39
National Iraq War Memorial Council 53
National Japanese American Memorial to Patriotism during World War II 39
National Liberation Front 131, 133
National Mall, Washington, DC 5, 38–52
National Monument for the World War II Dead (Brazil) 60, 61, 62
National Park Service 44, 48, 51
National Sculpture Society 44
National Security Law (South Korea) 119
National Socialist (Nazi) Germany 69, 70, 73, 75, 78, 79, 80, 81, 82, 85
National Unity Day (November 7) 193
National World War I Memorial (at Pershing Park in Washington, DC) 39, 40, 53
National World War II Memorial (US) 6, 38, 40, 45, 51–3, 218
Nazi flag 78
Nazi war aims 85
Nekouz (Russia) 191
Neoclassical architectural style 42
Neuve Chapelle 15, 17, 23
Neuve Chapelle, Indian national memorial 17, 26, 27
New Orleans, Louisiana 222
*New York Times* 130, 132
New York, New York 211
New Zealand's Boer War monuments 58
Newfoundland 25
Ngerchol (Palau) 99
Ngermeskang (Palau) 95
Ngirablai, Saburo 98
Nguyen, Viet Thanh 1, 3–4, 220, 224
Nicolai, Thomas 80
Nihon Izokukai (Japan Association of War-Bereaved Families) 95–6, 97
No Gŏn-ri Incident 119–20
No Gŏn-ri Peace Park 120
no-fly zone 206
North Atlantic Treaty Organization (NATO) 71, 72, 182, 189, 191

North Korean regime 113, 115, 123
North Korean soldiers 120
North Vietnamese Army (NVA) 132
*Northerners, Southerners* 120

O Chŏng-hŭi 120–1
Obama, Barack 142, 143
October Revolution 181
*Ogonëk* 186
Okinawa 92
Old Rhinebeck Aerodrome 161
Oldenburg, Claes 46
Olick, Jeffrey 40
Oliveira, Dennison 60
Olmsted, Frederick Law 43
Operation Desert Shield 202
Operation Desert Storm 201, 202, 203, 205, 213
Operation Urgent Fury 1
Orlando, Tony 209
*Otechestvo* 188
Ottoman Empire 165
Owen, David 168
Oxford, University of 5

Pacific Rim 124
Pacific War 93, 107
*Pain* 186
Pakistan 182, 184
Palau Historic Preservation Office 103, 107
Palau 91, 94
Palbari 115–16
Palen, Cole 161
Paraná 62
Parcham (Afghan communist faction) 181
Paris (France) 150, 156
Park Chung-hee 114, 118
Park Chung-i 118
Park Guen-hye 123
Park Wan-suh 114–15, 117
Parsons, Tony 173
Party of Democratic Socialism (PDS) 80
*Password-"Revolution"* 186
Path of History: Bomb Shelter Tour 132, 138–42
Peace Park Memorial (Peleliu) 100, 101, 106
*Peanuts* 159–60
*Pearl Harbor* 223
Pearl Harbor, Hawai'i 135
Peleliu Island 91, 95, 96, 97, 98, 100, 101, 102, 104
Peleliu 7, 222
Peleliu, battle of 98, 99, 221
Penn State University 50

Pentagon 204
People's Army 113
People's Democratic Party of Afghanistan 181
Persian Gulf War 201–13, 223
Petit, Edmond 151
Petrópolis 59
Petrópolitan Expedicionario Song 59
philately 61
Philippines 92
Picasso, Pablo 157
Piehler, Kurt 44
*Pietà* 48
Pisano, Dominic 159
*Placid Civic Moment* 46
Platz der Einheit (Unity Square) (Potsdam) 75–6
Plumer, General 19
Poklonnaia Gora (Moscow) 194, 195
Politburo 181
Pope, John Russell 44
Post-Traumatic Stress Disorder (PTSD) 53
Potomac River 41, 43
Potsdam (Germany) 75–6, 77, 83
Powell, Colin 210, 211
*Pracinhas* 60
Prado, Rosane 64
*Pravda* 182, 184, 195
precision strikes 205
prisoners of war 96, 120, 122
Prussia 76
Puritanism 41
Putin, Vladimir 193, 194, 196

Quảng Trị Province (Vietnam) 136, 138, 142

rally effect 208
Rambo 135, 143
Rangers, US Army 1
Rape of Nanjing 96
Reagan Administration 1
Reagan, Ronald 171
re-Americanization of Vietnam 136
Red Army 181, 182, 188, 194
Red Baron 155
Red guerrillas 117
Redan Ridge Cemetery No. 2 16
Reese, Roger 8–9, 223
Reflecting Pool 45, 49, 51
Remarque, Erich Maria 79, 155
remembrance 2, 4, 52
Remengesau, Jr., Tommy 91, 104, 105
Renoir, Jean 159
Republic of Korea 113, 122, 123

Republic of Palau (ROP) 91, 104
Republic of Vietnam 131, 133, 143
Restat, Ulrich 70
Reunification Palace 130
Reynolds, David 169, 171
Rhee, Syngman 111, 113–14, 116, 117
Rhode Island School of Design 51
Richthofen, Manfred von 155, 161
Rio de Janeiro 59, 61, 62, 64
Rio Grande do Sul 62
"Rockpile" 137
*Rodina* 189–90
Roh Moo-hyun 119
Roh Tae-woo 119
Roma 85
Romans 41
Rome 41
Roof, Dylann 221
Rosenheck, Uri 6, 217, 218, 224
Rosenthal, Joe 44
Rousso, Henry 180
Royal Air Force (RAF) 155
Royal Institute of British Architects (RIBA) 15
Royal Newfoundland Regiment 20, 25
Russian Army General Staff 192
Russian Army 191, 192
Russian Minister of Defense 192, 196
Rutskoi, Alexander 188

Sadae, Inoue 95
St. Florian, Friedrich 51
St. Louis, Missouri 222
St. Mary's ADS Cemetery 16
Saipan 91
Sân bay Tà Co'n 137–8
San Francisco International Airport 210
San Patricio (St. Patrick's) Battalion 219
São Paulo 62, 63, 64
*Sartoris* 156
Sassoon, Siegfried 154
*Saudade* 59
Saudi Arabia 182
Saunders, John Monk 158
Savage, Kirk 40, 41, 42, 52
"Scar literature" 120–1
Schreiber, Jürgen 73
Schulz, Charles M. 159–60
Schwarzkopf, H. Norman 203–4, 206, 213
Schwenkel, Christina 7–8, 220
*Scientific American* 158
Scruggs, Jan 45
sealed caves on Peleliu 98, 103, 104, 105, 106, 107

Second Gulf War 202
Second Republic 117
Second World War 173
"secular sacred space" 19
Seibt, Rudi 71, 74, 84
Seiryusha ("Clear stream organization") 100–1, 102, 106
Senate Park Commission 43
Senie, Harriet 42, 48
Seoul (South Korea) 115
Serra, Richard 46
Serre Road Cemetery No. 2 17
shared Korean bloodline 116
Shiites 182
Shingo, Iitaka 101
*Shinryaku* 101
*Shinsyutsu* 101
Shinto 96, 100, 106
Shinzō, Abe 104, 106
Shmull, Temmy 104–5
Sierra Leone 171
Sinch'ŏn Massacre 121
Sinti 84
sites of memory 5, 14
Slocum, Steven 210
smart weapons 205
Smolensk provincial government 191
Smyth, Hanna 5, 218, 224
Snoopy 159–60
Social Democratic Party 168
Social Democrats 80
Socialist Republic of Vietnam 131
Sofitel 138
*Soldados da borracha* (Rubber Soldiers) 56
Somalia 205
Sontag, Susan 140
Sopwith Camel (aircraft) 155, 159
South African Union 26
South China Sea 143
South Hwanghae Province (North Korea) 121
South Korean Army 122
South Korean partisans 122
South Korean Workers Party 113
Southampton County, Virginia 222
Soviet Army 181, 182, 184, 186, 187, 189, 191, 192, 193, 194
Soviet Central Asia 181
Soviet civilians 183, 185, 192
Soviet Communist Party 171
Soviet forces 181
Soviet Minister of Defense 185
Soviet soldiers 179, 180, 182, 183, 184, 187
Soviet state 182, 183, 184
Soviet Union 113, 171, 179, 180, 181
Soviet youth 183
Soviet-Afghan War 71, 179–96, 223, 224
Spanish Civil War 157
*Spätverweigerer* 71
Special Act on the Fact-Finding Investigation into the April 3 Cheju Incident Victims and the Restoration of their Honor 119
Special Measures Act on the Restoration of the Honor of Those People Involved in the Kŏch'ang Incident 119, 123
Speer, Albert 51
*Spetnaz* (Soviet special forces) 180, 193
"Spirit on the Wind" 120–1
Springs, Elliott White 155–6
SS 69
Stalingrad, battle of 193
*Star over the City of Kabul* 186
*Stars of Courageous Fighters in the land of Afghanistan* 186
State Duma 189, 192, 194
Stedeler, Eckart 79
*Stein des Anstoßes* 74–5
*Stepped Elevation* 46
Stone of Remembrance 15, 17
Strachan, Hew 171, 172
strategic bombing 156–7
Sturken, Marita 2, 207, 210, 212
Stuttgart (Germany) 77–8, 83
Stütz–Mentzel, Hannah 74, 75
Subic Bay, Philippines 135
Suez 166
"Sunshine Policy" 123
Supreme Soviet 196
"swinging door" 135

*T'aegŭkki Hwinallimyŏ* 122–3
*Taebaek Mountain Range* 119, 122
Taft, William Howard 43
Taliban 190
Tel Aviv University 6
Texas A&M University 8
thankful villages 21
Thatcher, Margaret 165, 166, 168, 169, 171, 172, 173, 174, 175
Thatcherism 166, 170
Thatcherites 175
*The Battle over Peleliu: Islander, Japanese, and American Memories of War* 7
*The Cherries of Freedom* 78
*The Dawn Patrol* 158, 159
*The Deer Hunter* 45
*The Descendants of Cain* 115
*The Economist* 165, 169, 176

*The Grand Illusion* 159
*The Guardian* 167, 170, 173, 174
*The Guest* 121
*The Naked Tree* 114–15
*The Square (Kwangjang)* 116
*The Stone Carvers* 19
*The Sun* 168, 173
*The Times* 167
*The War in Afghanistan* 186
*The Winged Gospel* 158
Thélus cemetery 18
Thiepval, Memorial to the Missing of the Somme 15, 18, 30–1, 46
Third Reich 75, 81
Thống Nhất (Unification Hotel) 139
Three Servicemen 39, 47, 48
*Tia Belau* 91
"Tie a Yellow Ribbon Round the Ole Oak Tree" 209
Tiumen Province (Russia) 191
Tokyo (Japan) 91, 96, 97, 105
*Top Gun* 223
Toribiong, Joel 102, 105
*Tragediia i doblest' Afghana* 189
Trainor, Bernard 213
trench warfare 150
Truman, Harry 204
Trump, Donald 123
Trust Territory of the Pacific 96
Truth and Reconciliation Commission of South Korea 119, 120, 123
Trybula, Dave 205
Tsukane, Nakagawa 98, 104
Tucholsky, Kurt 75, 77
Turner, Alfred 26
Turner, Michael J. 175
Turner, Nat 222
Tyne Cot 24

Ulm (Germany) 74, 75, 76, 77, 78, 83
UN soldiers 114
unburied Japanese remains and bone collecting 91–2, 96–8, 100, 103–7
*Uncle Suni (Sun-I Samch'on)* 117
Union Army 42
Union Jack 167
United Nations Day 113
United Nations Educational, Scientific and Cultural Organization (UNESCO) 143
United Nations Security Council Resolution 660 203
United Nations 113, 114, 213
Union of Afghan War Veterans 196
United States Army 77, 100, 120, 219, 220

United States Holocaust Memorial Museum 49
United States Marine Corps 99, 100, 101, 106, 203
United States Navy 100
University of Louisville 222
University of Mississippi 221
University of Texas 221
unknown deserter 71
Urquhart, Jane 19
US Army Command and General Staff College 9
US bombs 135
US Capitol 41, 42
US Command 111
US Congress 41, 43, 53, 201
US Department of Defense (DoD) 201, 204, 205
US Executive Mansion 41
US invasion of Afghanistan 179, 190
US Marine Corps Memorial (Iwo Jima Memorial) 44
US military 202–5
US National Park Service 221
US Occupation of Japan 96, 100
US soldiers 135
US veterans 136, 137, 138
US War with Mexico 42, 219
US War with Spain 42
USS *Arizona* 44
USSR Ministry of Defense 184, 186
USSR 181, 182, 183, 187, 188, 189, 194, 196

Vanderbilt University 221–2
Vargas, Getúlio 56, 60
*Verfremdung* 81
Vergnet, Paul 152
Vernon, Alex 205, 206, 207, 212–13
Veterans Affairs Canada workshop 30
Vice-Chairman to the High Commissioner for New Zealand, IWGC 28
Victory Day (May 9) 193
Viet Cong (VC) 131, 132, 133, 134, 135, 143
Vietnam Veterans Memorial Collection 48
Vietnam Veterans Memorial Fund 45, 47
Vietnam Veterans Memorial 5, 38, 40, 45–9, 51, 52, 218
Vietnam Veterans Week 45
Vietnam veterans 207–8, 209–10, 213
Vietnam War 44, 45–6, 50, 52, 71, 130–43, 160, 184, 201, 202, 204, 209, 220–1, 223
Vietnam Women's Memorial 48

Vietnam Women's Memorial Project 47–8
Vietnam 194
Vietnamese guerrillas 133–4
Vietnamese quagmire 172
VII (US) Corps 203
Villers-Bretonneaux, Australian memorial 15, 23–4, 30
Vimy Charter for the Conservation of Battlefield Terrain (2000) 30
Vimy Memorial 18, 19, 20, 23, 25, 28, 29, 30
Vimy Ridge 20
Vimy, battle for 30
Vịnh Mốc tunnels 136
Virilio, Paul 130
Vis-en-Artois memorial 21
Voisin (aircraft) 150, 152
*Voprosy istorii* 188

war ace 153, 155
*War Birds: Diary of an Unknown Aviator* 156
war dead 15
*War Fliers on the Western Front* 158
*War in the Air* 156–7
war tourism 130–43
Ware, Fabian 13, 31
Washington Monument 5, 38, 41, 42, 45, 51
Washington, DC 211
Washington, George 41, 42
*Wehrmacht* 6, 69, 70, 72, 73, 77, 80, 84, 85, 218–20
Weimar (Germany) 80
Welch, Steven R. 6, 218–19
Wells, H. G. 156–7
West German Association of German Soldiers 73
Western Allies 85

Wette, Wolfram 84
"Where Are You Now My Son?" 139–40
White House 53, 206
White, Geoff 135
Williams, Mary Rose 133
*Wings* 158, 159
Winter, Jay 2, 4, 52
Wohl, Robert 152
Women in Military Service for America Memorial (at Arlington National Cemetery) 39
Workers' Party of Korea 122
Works Progress Administration 52
World War I Centennial Commission 53
World War II veterans' organizations 191
World War II 51, 56–7, 60, 61, 70, 71, 74, 75, 77, 80, 83, 85, 96, 99, 100, 101, 105, 106, 185, 186, 193, 194, 204, 206, 208, 209, 212, 213, 220
Wright, Brendan 7–8, 220–1

XVIII (US) Airborne Corps 203

Yale University 46
*Yangban* 115
yellow ribbon campaign 208–10, 213
Yeltsin, Boris 179, 187, 188, 190, 191, 194
Yi Ho-ch'ŏl 120
Yoji, Kurata 103
YouGov Institute 173
Young, James 56, 83
Ypres 30, 31
Yuji, Namekawa 100, 103
Yūko, Tōjō 103, 104

Zeppelin airships 156–7, 162
Zeppelinitis 157
Zuev, Alexei 195
Zwerenz, Gerhard 73